Forgotten Victorian Generals

Studies in the Exercise of Command and Control in the British Army 1837-1901

Edited by Christopher Brice

Helion & Company

Helion & Company Limited
Unit 8 Amherst Business Centre
Budbrooke Road
Warwick
CV34 5WE
England
Tel. 01926 499 619
Email: info@helion.co.uk
Website: www.helion.co.uk
Twitter: @helionbooks
Visit our blog at blog.helion.co.uk

Published by Helion & Company 2021
Designed and typeset by Mary Woolley (www.battlefield-design.co.uk)
Cover designed by Paul Hewitt, Battlefield Design (www.battlefield-design.co.uk)

Text © Christopher Brice and individual contributors as credited 2021
Images as individually credited
Maps 1-3 drawn by and © Susie Langley 2021, maps 4-6 drawn by George Anderson © Helion & Company 2021

Every reasonable effort has been made to trace copyright holders and to obtain their permission for the use of copyright material. The author and publisher apologize for any errors or omissions in this work, and would be grateful if notified of any corrections that should be incorporated in future reprints or editions of this book.

ISBN 978-1-910777-20-6

British Library Cataloguing-in-Publication Data.
A catalogue record for this book is available from the British Library.

All rights reserved. No part of this publication may be reproduced, stored in a retrieval system, or transmitted, in any form, or by any means, electronic, mechanical, photocopying, recording or otherwise, without the express written consent of Helion & Company Limited.

For details of other military history titles published by Helion & Company Limited contact the above address or visit our website: http://www.helion.co.uk.

We always welcome receiving book proposals from prospective authors.

Contents

List of Plates		iv
List of Maps		v
Introduction		vi
List of Contributors		viii
1	Field Marshal Sir George White (1835-1912) *Rodney Atwood*	10
2	General Sir William Lockhart (1841-1900) *Ian F. W. Beckett*	42
3	Field Marshal Sir Robert Cornelis Napier, 1st Baron Napier of Magdala (1810-90) *Christopher Brice*	71
4	Major-General Sir John Charles Ardagh (1840-1907) *Edward Gosling*	111
5	Sir Arthur Cunynghame General Officer Commanding Her Majesty's Forces at the Cape of Good Hope (1873-78) *John Laband*	154
6	Field Marshal Sir William Nicholson, 1st Baron Nicholson (1845-1918) *Paul M. Ramsey*	199
7	A Victorian Hero: Lord Wantage VC (1832-1901) *Roger T. Stearn*	237
Bibliography		265
Index		281

List of Plates

Field Marshal Sir George White.	12
View of the Takht-l-Suliman	25
Sir William Lockhart.	43
Field Marshal Robert Napier.	72
Major-General Sir John Ardagh.	112
General Sir Arthur Cunynghame.	156
Field Marshal William Nicholson.	204
Lord Wantage VC.	239

List of Maps

Map 1: Afghanistan and North-West Frontier	14
Map 2: Burma	20
Map 3: Natal	33
Map 4: Tirah Campaign, September 1897-April 1898.	55
Map 5: South Africa, 1877.	178
Map 6: Ninth Cape Frontier War, 1877.	185

Introduction

In his book *The Victorians at War* Professor Ian Beckett tells the story of a London public house named after the Victorian British Army General, Garnet Wolseley.[1] When it came time to repaint the pub sign, the artist mistakenly presented the owner with a portrait of Cardinal Wolsey, the Tudor Archbishop and stateman. Indeed, type the name Wolseley into an image search engine and you will have to trawl through numerous images of motorcars before you get to the man who was once described as 'our only General'. Though the latter reference, like his portrayal as 'the very model of a modern Major-General', was as much satire as it was factual comment, it does illustrate how well known and significant he was. You do not satirise someone who is unlikely to be instantly known.

If Wolseley is no longer recognisable to the general public, or even to a large number of military historians, there is little chance for the 'lesser mortals' of the Victorian British Army. Yet their careers should be full of interest for the historian and now, more than ever, it is important that we try to better understand men such as the subjects of this volume. Whilst their motivations and beliefs are ones that appear alien to us in the early 21st century, we should seek to truly understand them, rather than simply dismiss out of hand.

Perhaps this points to a general malaise about the past in the wider population, and a lack of education and understanding in this regard. It is also part of an increasing reaction against 'Empire' and a general desire to forget the part played by the British Army. In consequence its 'Generals' are also forgotten.

Study of the Victorian British Army is not a particularly 'trendy' path for historians to travel. Yet it is important for so many reasons. To the student of military history this should prove and interesting study of, as the subtitle puts it, the exercise of command and control during the Victorian Era. To the modern British Army this study of officers exercising command with limited manpower resources, particularly when compared to the numerous global responsibilities of Empire, has much to teach us. Whilst the principles, beliefs, and circumstances are a long way from what the modern Army faces, the challenges are in many ways similar.

The officers described in this book had varied careers. Yet at one time each of them played a significant role in public affairs, whether for good or ill. Each were very different in their exercise of 'command and control', and through their careers we encompass the whole Victorian era British Army. Some of the men featured in this book were prominent in Africa and India, the two great sources of colonial campaigns during the Victorian era, whilst other excelled in the War Office, or in the more political and civil-military relations side of the Army. In short,

---

1   Ian F.W. Beckett, *The Victorians at War* (London: Hambledon and London, 2003), p. xiv.

the officers featured in this book are a good eclectic mix of types, styles, career, outlook, and experience of military life during the Victorian epoch. Their careers also encompass the majority of Queen Victoria's reign.

My thanks are due to the contributors to this publication. Firstly, for their talent and expertise in preparing their chapters, and secondly, for their encouragement and support to myself as editor, and thirdly, for their patience and endurance during what has, for one reason and another, been a very long gestation period. Despite the long wait I hope that this book will help to fill in some of the background on these aforementioned forgotten Victorian Generals. Thanks, are also due to those at Helion who have assisted in making this book a reality, in particular my colleague Dr Michael LoCicero, and also due to George Anderson and Paul Hewitt.

Dr Christopher Brice

List of Contributors

Dr Rodney Atwood read history at McMaster University, Hamilton, Ontario and Churchill College, Cambridge. Between these two degrees he served in the Royal Tank Regiment. He is the biographer of Field Marshal Lord Roberts and General Lord Rawlinson and the author of an article on the Kipling Society website, 'Rudyard Kipling and the Great War'.

Professor Ian Beckett retired as Professor of Military History at the University of Kent in 2015. A Fellow of the Royal Historical Society, he has held chairs in both the UK and US and was Chairman of the Army Records Society from 2000-14. His most recent publications are *A British Profession of Arms: The Politics of Command in the Late Victorian Army* (Oklahoma University Press, 2018), and *Rorke's Drift and Isandlwana* (Oxford University Press, 2019).

Dr Christopher Brice read history and politics at undergraduate level before completing a PhD, which was initially part of a joint research agreement between De Montfort University and the Royal Military Academy, Sandhurst. He is the author of *The Thinking Man's General*, a biography of general Sir Henry Brackenbury and *Brave As a Lion*, a biography of Field Marshal Hugh Gough, 1st Viscount Gough. He is currently a Series and Commissioning editor for Helion & Co Ltd, and runs their 19th century series entitled *From Musket to Maxim, 1815-1914*. He is also a member of the council of the Victorian Military Society.

Dr Edward Gosling specialises in the history of the British Army and civil-military relations since 1850. His doctoral research examined the political and cultural transformation of the ordinary soldier in late Victorian society. Since completing his PhD Edward has taught history at the University of Plymouth and the University of Exeter and continues to research and publish on the history of the military in Britain and the Empire.

Professor John Laband is a Professor Emeritus of History, Wilfrid Laurier University, Canada, and a Research Associate in the Department of History, Stellenbosch University, South Africa. He is also a Life Member of Clare Hall, University of Cambridge, England, and a Fellow of the University of KwaZulu-Natal, South Africa. He specialises in war and society in colonial Africa, and among his recent books are *The Battle of Majuba Hill: The Transvaal Campaign 1880–1881* (2017); *The Eight Zulu Kings* (2018), and *The Land Wars: The Dispossession of the Khoisan and the AmaXhosa in the Cape Colony* (2020).

Paul M. Ramsey is a doctoral candidate in the Department of History at the University of Calgary. He was the Edward S. Miller Research Fellow in Naval History at United States Naval

War College. His research focuses on the career of the historian Spenser Wilkinson and the development of British strategy before and during the First World War

Dr Roger Stearn F.R.Hist.S. read modern history at Merton College, Oxford, and gained his Ph.D from the Department of War Studies, King's College London. He has contributed to learned journals and edited volumes. His last pre-retirement employment was research editor at the Oxford Dictionary of National Biography.

1

Field Marshal Sir George White[1]
(1835-1912)

Rodney Atwood

March, 1879 – Afghanistan. Soldiers of the British and Indian Armies had just defeated Afghan forces. The column of Major-General Sir Frederick Roberts was ordered to advance towards Kabul. The 92nd Highlanders, the Gordons, marched as reinforcements to join Roberts. With them went Major George White, a reserved, athletic, service-hardened veteran, who had been twenty-six years with the colours and was yet to distinguish himself. The Gordons advanced through a very wild country, narrow valleys commanded on both sides by high rocky hills, houses being towers built as little fortifications. The people were 'robbers and cut-throats', White wrote, only kept in awe 'by their great fear of reprisals'. His rough judgement was qualified when the 92nd halted at Ali Khel, and he enjoyed a hot bath and admired the cultivation of fruit trees clothed in bright blossom and the beauty of the local ladies. On 21 March he dined with Roberts, an old friend, who particularly enquired after White's wife and his daughter, 'the White rose'. As a former East India Company officer White, found it 'so odd' to be asked by 'swells like Brab' [Major John Brabazon on Roberts's staff] whether he would like whisky or rum after his soup.[2]

The 2nd Afghan War would transform White's career, and his association with Roberts would bring him to the highest rank in India. He would himself become one of the 'swells',

---

[1] Dr T.A. Heathcote, Dr Peter Boyden and Dr Keith Surridge kindly read and commented on this chapter in draft.
[2] India Office Library, Mss European F108 [henceforth 'White']/97(a), P2/54a, White to sister, 29 Mar, 1879; Mortimer Durand, *The Life of Field-Marshal Sir George White* (2 vols. Edinburgh & London: Blackwell & Sons, 1915), Vol I, pp. 163-5. This is the standard life with a good selection of letters and personal vignettes. Henceforth 'Durand'. To coincide with the siege of Ladysmith, two lesser biographies appeared: R.J. Bremner Smith, *Sir George Stewart* [sic] *White* (London, 1900), sixteen pages, vol 3 of the 'Soldiers of the Queen Library' and Thomas F.G. Coates, *Sir George White V.C. The Hero of Ladysmith* (London: Grant Richards, 1900). The *Oxford Dictionary of National Biography* (60 vols. Oxford: OUP, 2004) entry is by James Lunt, amending the earlier account by Frederick Maurice.

first as secretary to a Viceroy[3] and later as Commander-in-Chief India. White's career would shine in Afghanistan, in Burma, and in Balochistan. He would initiate the furthest advances of the 'forward' policy, a policy with which he had long disagreed,[4] and would preside over the unification of the separate Indian Armies, Bengal, Bombay, Madras, recommended by a committee during this very Afghan War.

If White's patron Lord Roberts served *Forty-One Years in India*' (the title of his famous autobiography), White outdid him by two years (1855 to 1898). They had met in White's early Indian days when Roberts was on the staff, and there was ostensibly nothing to mark White out from other regimental officers; Roberts, however, remembered faces and names and in White's case the recollection was to be well repaid.[5] White made his reputation in that 'English barrack in the Oriental Seas', as Lord Salisbury called India. It was the British Army's second home, or perhaps for a time its first, strengthening regimental identity, introducing words like khaki, cummerbund, puttees, into the argot of the British soldier.[6] White's fighting spirit was nurtured, like that of his friend Ian Hamilton, in that magnificent Scots battalion, the old 92nd, the Gordon Highlanders, 'the finest regiment in the world' as Winston Churchill called them.[7] At Whitehall and in South Africa, he would find himself a fish out of water, and although a hero to the public for his defence of Ladysmith, he earned the brickbats of historians.

George Stuart White was an Ulsterman of English and Scots descent. He was born on 6 July, 1835 at Rock Castle on the sea coast near Port Stewart, County Antrim, where his family was spending the summer, the second of three boys. One ancestor commanded militia during the Great Irish Rebellion of 1798; an uncle was the Whites' first regular soldier, serving in the Napoleonic Wars; but there was little family tradition of military service, his father being called to the bar. The wish to be a soldier seems to have come from White himself, 'the stupid one of the family' (his words).[8] He was strong and active, enjoying swimming. In thus qualifying for future soldiering, he is by no means unique.

He attended Bromsgrove School in Worcestershire, where he was unhappy, and King William's College on the Isle of Man, where things were better and he was known as 'Duck White'. A schoolfellow remembered him as very fair, blue-eyed, animated, and good looking.[9] On 9 July, 1850, at the age of fifteen, he entered Sandhurst. At school he had not distinguished himself in his studies. The Royal Military College, founded by Colonel John Le Marchant in 1802, was languishing under the indifferent regime of Sir George Scovell, governor from 1837 to 1857. There were barely 200 cadets, bullying was endemic and rioting in the local Yorktown customary.[10] White's Sandhurst record showed that he passed the various steps in

---

3   Dr T A Heathcote points out that the honorific 'Viceroy' did not have parliamentary sanction and was used properly only when the Governor-General acted as head of state rather than head of government.
4   White 98(a), P3/57, White to brother, 15 Nov, 1879.
5   Durand, I, pp. 89-90; Sir George Younghusband, *A Soldier's Memories in Peace and War* (London: Herbert Jenkins Ltd, 1917), pp. 228-230 for R's memory for faces.
6   T.A. Heathcote, *The Military in British India: the development of British Land Forces in South Asia, 1600-1947* (Manchester & New York: Manchester University Press, 1995), pp. 126-8.
7   After their attack at Doornkop outside Pretoria; W.S. Churchill, *Ian Hamilton's March* (London: Longmans, Green & Co., 1900), pp. 251-6.
8   Durand, I, pp. 10 and 15.
9   Durand, I, pp. 10-15.
10 Hugh Thomas, *The Story of Sandhurst* (London: Hutchison, 1961).

Field Marshal Sir George White.

the compulsory subjects, mathematics, French, fortification and military drawing, although it is doubtful that much importance can be attached to these. He also secured 'three decorations of merit'. For White the study of English grammar might have been more useful: his letters show little knowledge of punctuation or sentences. Later, he acquired a 'fine, bold hand' and his correspondence shows shrewdness, power of observation and humour. He told his children that he educated himself during his army service, and there seems no reason to doubt this.[11]

In 1853 he left Sandhurst and on 4 November was gazetted an ensign in the 27th Inniskillings.[12] In 1854 the regiment sailed for India, White embarking on the ship *Charlotte*. The *Charlotte* was wrecked near Algoa Bay, South Africa, and by his own account White, a strong swimmer, 'succeeded in saving several both women and men'.[13] The *Maidstone* took White and his detachment on to Calcutta, which he reached after a journey of six months, and they made their way to the Punjab. For a young officer wanting to see action, service in the 27th was a misfortune in the 1850s. They missed the Crimea and during the Mutiny remained in the Punjab. Suppressing Mutiny in the Punjab was vital to eventual British victory, for it was the base for the counter-offensive against Delhi.[14] White, who was then attempting to grow a moustache, does not seem to have appreciated the Punjab's strategic importance, although he praised the Sikhs who 'have stuck by us most manfully' and told his brother: 'We have disarmed every sepoy in the Peshawar valley and hundreds of them (who have been caught in treasonable correspondence or who have otherwise committed themselves) are working here on roads in chains…'[15]

---

11 Durand, I, p. 18;' White's Sandhurst Record, downloaded from the College website.
12 *Hart's Army List 1898* (London, 1898), p. 339.
13 Durand, I, p. 28 quoting White's letter 5 Oct, 1854.
14 Field Marshal Lord Roberts, *Forty-One Years in India* (New York: Methuen, 1897); Saul David, *The Indian Mutiny, 1857* (London: Viking Penguin, 2002), pp. 139-146, 271, 277; Durand, I, p. 76.
15 Durand, I, pp. 72 and 73. Not all Sikhs were loyal. See S.L. Menezes, *Fidelity and Honour: the Indian Army from the Seventeenth to the Twenty-First Century* (New Delhi: OUP, 1993), pp. 173 and 185.

In 1858 while the Mutiny was being stamped out in Oudh and Central India, the Inniskillings marched to Amballa for further inactivity. White's letter of 9 August, 1858 shows his keen interest in the French army and an admiration for Charles Napier as 'the prophet of the Indian Mutinies'.[16] Napier the conqueror of Sind was known for unorthodox views and clashes of personality; White admired Napier but did not emulate him; in his future commands he enjoyed good relations with political authorities, perhaps too good, so as to suppress independence of judgement.

The changes following the Mutiny – the abolition of East India Company rule and transference of its army to the control of the Crown – are omitted from his surviving correspondence, but as a member of a British regiment he was not directly involved. He attended a course at musketry school and obtained a first-class certificate of qualification as an instructor. He also gained a qualification in Persian and Hindustani, he was DAQMG at Allahabad in 1860, in 1863 he was at the Depot in Cork, gained command of a company and transferred into the 92nd.[17] With this regiment he was henceforth associated. In 1868, nearly thirty-three years old and a captain, he began anew his Indian service, and after another session of leave achieved his majority in January, 1874. On 31 October at Simla aged thirty-nine he married Amy Baley, only daughter of the Archdeacon of Calcutta. 'Tall and spare, almost gaunt, with strongly-cut features, he was in his Highland uniform a striking figure.'[18] Amy White, a keen horsewoman, was of a temperament to suit her husband, and at Multan they both took a prominent part in hunting and in paper-chases. Both paper-chases and steeplechases at high speed involved jumps, and as eighty to ninety people took part these jumps were narrow and dangerous. In paper-chases, both Whites showed courageous, indeed some might say reckless, horsemanship.[19] The marriage was a happy one, as White's extensive and confiding correspondence to his Amy shows; there were four daughters and a son.

In the absence of his seniors, White commanded the Gordons at the Imperial Assemblage (the great 'Durbar') outside Delhi to proclaim Victoria Empress of India. Lord Lytton, the Viceroy, had been sent to India by Disraeli not just to arrange the Durbar and proclamation, but to take a more active policy towards Afghanistan and possible Russian encroachment. The Eastern Crisis of 1878 brought Russia to the gates of Constantinople and the Russian General Stolietov to Kabul in July, 1878. When Lytton's demand that the Afghan Amir Sher Ali accept a British embassy was refused, war began with British successes in the Khyber and Kurram Passes and the occupation of Kandahar. George White was on leave in Ulster and feared he would miss the action again. He was skating at Broughshane in County Antrim when a telegram arrived ordering him to return to his regiment, about to be attached to Major-General Roberts's column in the Kurram Valley.[20] His years of success were about to begin.

In March, 1879, White and the 92nd joined Roberts's column, the Highlanders wearing the newfangled 'khaki'. He told his wife he looked more as if he were on a shooting excursion than a campaign.[21] The war seemed to have ended in British victory: Sher Ali fled to Russian

16 Durand, I, p. 82; on Napier, A.T. Embree in ODNB.
17 Durand, I, pp. 87, 90, 100, 101, 102.
18 Durand, I, p. 138.
19 Durand, I, p. 423, letter to friend about later paper chases.
20 Durand, I, p. 159.
21 White101(a), P6/9, 13 Mar, 1879.

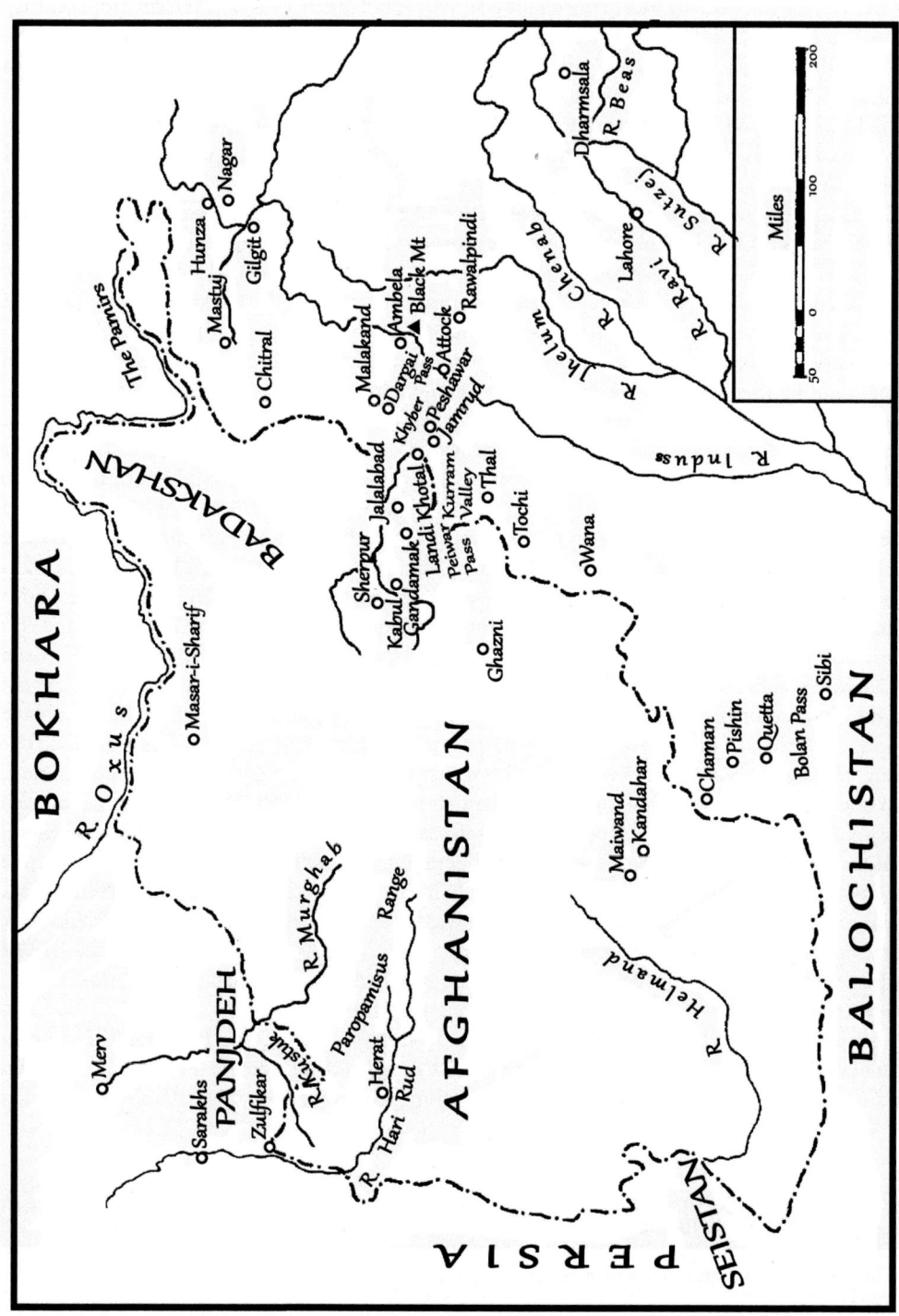

territory, his son Yakub negotiated the treaty of Gandamak accepting a British envoy at Kabul, and Major Louis Cavagnari with an escort from the elite Corps of Guides took up residence there. In September the shocking news reached Simla of the massacre of Cavagnari and his escort after several hours of heroic fighting against overwhelming odds. Roberts's column with White and the 92nd was ordered to advance to Kabul, eighty miles distant, and punish those responsible for Cavagnari's death. From Simla, White joined a rush of officers making for the front. Roberts had only 7500 men and twenty-two guns, including service-hardened infantry, Gurkhas and Highlanders, but inadequate transport. Only half the force could move at a time.

To his fighting duties White added the role of correspondent for *The Times* of London, no bad job for a future field marshal, but one he found a burden. He was angry that a Captain Norman, cashiered from the Punjab Frontier Force for forgery, was using a detailed gazetteer and White's letters to give the impression of first-hand knowledge.[22]

Before the war Sher Ali had reformed the Afghan army, the British supplying him with weapons and allowing former Indian Army NCOs to drill his men in European methods; Afghan artillery was thought to be particularly good, and British officers suspected the Afghans enjoyed an unlimited supply of pilfered ammunition from the arsenal at Dum-Dum.[23] Despite this, the British had won the first round of fighting in late 1878, and the widely held view was that the Afghans would not contest Roberts's march.

That this estimate was wrong became clear at dawn on 6 October when the rising sun showed to the watchers in Roberts's column masses of regular troops with artillery deploying on a crescent-shaped range of defensible hills blocking the advance. This position above a group of villages known as Charasia ran three miles roughly east-west at a height between 700 and 1500 feet above the plain. The Afghan commander, Sirdar Nek Mohammed, deployed eighteen guns, several regular regiments and a mass of irregulars, and expected an attack on the obvious Sang-I-Nawishta defile on his left. Roberts decided to attack, although nearly half his force encumbered with convoys of stores and ammunition was still to come up. Towards Sang-I-Nawishta he sent White initially with two companies to draw Afghan attention (and fire) while Brigadier Thomas Durand Baker advanced against the Afghan right with 2000 men. Roberts's confidence in his friend White, as yet untried in battle, was justified by results. White had spotted with binoculars that the steep slope enabled his men to advance in dead ground, and he took advantage of this to lure the superior enemy numbers from their breastwork and then rout them in close fighting.

Major Hammond of the 5th Punjab Cavalry described the action:

> Major White led in a most gallant & splendid way. They were met by a very determined fire from the enemy but advanced most steadily to a line of rocks halfway up the hill where they stopped a few minutes to take breath. After a very short time Major White came out leading his small party & when they had climbed a little higher I

---

22 White 101(a), P6/40, 23 Nov, 1879. Also with the column and writing for *The Times* was Major-General Luther Vaughan. See General Sir J. Luther Vaughan, *My Service in the Indian Army – and After* (London: Constable, 1904).

23 Major-Gen L N Soboleff, *The Anglo-Afghan Struggle*, transl by Major Gowan (Calcutta: the Government of India, 1885); Lt-Gen Sir M.G. Gerard, *Leaves from the Diary of a Soldier and Sportsman 1865-1885* (London: John Murray, 1903), pp. 229-230 and 310-311.

saw the enemy swarm out of their breast works in numbers which seemed enough to overwhelm the little body of Highlanders. They came on in numbers within a few yards of Major White who went steadily on followed by his men who were not to be denied. It was a very great relief when a sort of ducking movement was apparent to the more rearward of the enemy which continued like a ripple towards the leaders who stopped for a moment & then turned. Major White & his men were charging them the next moment & followed them closely over their breastwork & the hill was won. I never saw or heard of a more dashing brilliant thing.[24]

White then advanced to assist Baker, and the Afghan right and centre broke and fled. Outflanked by the British and enfiladed by their fire, the Afghans abandoned the position and retired in haste. The cavalry pursuit by Brigadier 'Redan' Massy was feeble.[25]

Both Roberts and Baker recommended White for the Victoria Cross, while White recommended Lieutenant Dick-Cunyngham. Dick-Cunyngham received his award long before White, later commanded the Gordons and was killed at Ladysmith. White, it seemed, was 'only doing his duty'.[26]

On the morning after the battle, Roberts advanced to the village of Beni Hissar three miles further on and sent Massy with the cavalry to reconnoitre Afghan battalions on the Asmai Hills and Baker to attack them, but it was dark before the latter was ready. Action was postponed and then had to be cancelled. White whose prediction that the Afghans would get away proved right was furious and told his wife that Roberts would have done better: "The enemy broke up into small parties & made off. Great recriminations between Baker & Redan Massy who commands the Cavalry & who is as arrant an imposter as ever drew a sword. Self-indulgent, timid good for nothing fellow."[27]

Despite Massy's sloth, the Afghan army had been dispersed and Roberts occupied Kabul. He established his forces in an extended camp, Sherpur, to the north of the city. He set up two commissions, one to investigate the massacre of Cavagnari and his escort, and one to try those held responsible. On viewing the Bala Hissar, scene of the last stand of Cavagnari and the Guides, smoke-blackened walls, bullet holes, bloodstains, even a heap of bones, White wrote that he would have made it much hotter for the people of Kabul, that the city should be razed "… instead of sprinkling rose water about as we are doing".[28] The two commissions officially finished on 18 November, and the report to Simla stated eighty-nine Afghans had been tried and forty-nine executed, but Brigadier MacGregor, Roberts's chief of staff who was

---

24   White 1, copy in mss of letter from Major F. Hammond, 5th Punjab Cavalry, Kabul, 3 Dec, 1879; also White's scribbled note to Roberts reproduced Durand, I, p. 197, if anything understating his achievement; H. Hanna, *The Second Afghan War* (3 vols. London Constable & Co., 1899-1910), III, pp. 68-75.
25   White 98(a), White to brother, 15 Nov, 1879; for Charasia, India Office Library, L/MIL/5/681, nos 7959 & 7961 encl Roberts's despatch 20 and 22 Nov, 1879; Brian Robson, *The Road to Kabul: the 2nd Afghan War 1878-1881* (Staplehurst: Spellmount, 1986), pp. 127-131; Soboleff, *Anglo-Afghan Struggle*, p. 58 on Massy.
26   Lt-Cols C.G. & A.G. Gardyne, *The Life of a Regiment: the History of the Gordon Highlanders from 1816-1898* (London: The Medici Society, 1929); Durand, I, p. 247.
27   White 101(a), P6/36, 15-17 Oct, 1879.
28   White 101(a), P6/36, 15-17 Oct, 1879; Howard Hensman, *The Afghan War* (London, 1881), pp. 51-6.

present throughout, recorded 163 and eighty-seven respectively in the *Official History*. Feeling for revenge was strong at the time, but White's sense of justice led him to change his mind. "We are thoroughly hated and not enough feared", he told his brother, describing how former sepoys found in villages were hanged.[29] Roberts wrote to defend his actions and his letter was read in the Lords, with good effect: of this, White told his brother the following April: "Sir F[red]. R[obert]'s part in the atrocities here deserves to be forgotten from the bravery with which he had lied about them."[30]

Although Roberts managed, in part at least, to assuage the press storm, at Kabul the hangings had enraged local feelings, already aroused by the abdication of the Amir Yakub and the apparent assumption of authority by Roberts. His requisitioning of food, forage and fuel from villages and the surrounding countryside for his troops further provoked Afghan resistance. News came to the British of the assembly of large bands of armed men inspired by the cry of *Jehad*. Roberts's intelligence told him that three Afghan armies were advancing from north, west and south, and he resolved to strike against these forces before they could combine. In fighting in both hills and valleys on 11, 13 and 14 December, the Gordons played a leading part, White as usual to the front, but Afghan numbers were too great. Roberts withdrew his troops into the cantonment. The ensuing siege lasted until about half an hour before first light on 23 December, when a signal fire on the Asmai heights above the camp unleashed, in White's words, "…the full tide of the Jehad…against the followers of the Christian's God". White was far from well: "I was wrapped in a poshteen [sheepskin jacket], with a worsted nightcap on my head, very actively sick at intervals of five minutes, and wishing to goodness that the children of Mahomet would go away and call another day". Under fire he felt better, especially when his orderly sent him a cup of hot tea. The shooting of Roberts's regiments and guns and the Afghan lack of artillery to breach the walls were decisive. The attack was beaten, and the remnants of the great host of besiegers dispersed.[31]

The Kabul garrison passed the winter in snowball fights, tobogganing, a pantomime for which Roberts's ADC Neville Chamberlain wrote the topical songs, and further reprisals against Afghan villages. When the roads became passable, Lieutenant-General Sir Donald Stewart marched from Kandahar to Kabul, and White was in a skirmish near Charasia where his horse was shot in the head. The spring election in Britain brought a Liberal government under Gladstone to power and a new viceroy for India, Lord Ripon, critic of Disraeli and Lytton's 'forward' policy. On 6 May White was astonished to receive a telegram from the new Viceroy offering him the Military Secretaryship.[32] For a man of action this was a change indeed: the Military Secretary was the controlling head of the Viceroy's household, supervising ADCs, managing entertainments, journeys and ceremonials. The post was comparatively new, being created by Lytton for George Colley, his chief military advisor in launching the war. Ripon's choosing White, a fighting soldier, for this position, suggests he shared his predecessor Lytton's view that the Indian Army establishment was hidebound and set in its ways. This is

29   White 98(a), P3/57, 15 Nov, 1879. For number of hangings see India Office, L/MIL/17/14/29, Major-Gen. Sir C.M. MacGregor, *The Second Afghan War* (6 vols. Simla & Calcutta, 1885-6), III, Appendix A.
30   White 98(a), P3/64, 13 April, 1880; contemporary attack on Roberts by the radical Frederic Harrison, *Martial Law in Kabul* (London: Chapman & Hall, 1880, reprinted from the *Fortnightly Review*).
31   White 101(a), P6/43, Dec, 1879.
32   Durand, I, p. 243.

supported by Durand's assertion that the Military Secretary would bring before the viceroy knotty problems associated with the work of the Military Department which, independent of the commander-in-chief, was responsible for supply, finance and much of the administration of the army in India. If true, it shows Ripon was bypassing his official advisors, notably his Military Member Edwin Johnston, unwell and unable to supervise his department properly.[33] At first, White told his brother that the work did not suit him in the least and he would rather be fighting Afghans.[34]

Fortunately, White much liked the Viceroy, a liking and respect which strengthened when Ripon allowed him to leave his post for further active service. The British had negotiated with a former pensioner of the Russians, Abdur Rahman, as their choice for Amir. His rival was Ayub Khan, a son of Sher Ali. At Maiwand near Kandahar Ayub decisively defeated a vastly outnumbered brigade of British and Indian troops, one of the most serious imperial setbacks of the nineteenth century. Ripon promptly arranged that an elite force of 10,000 should march under Roberts from Kabul to Kandahar and restore British fortunes.[35] Guessing that the Gordons would go with Roberts, White asked to be allowed to join them. Ripon replied at once, "Go. I took you because you were a good soldier, & I don't want to spoil you". His only condition was that White returned.[36]

Roberts's march, covering 313 miles in twenty-three days, and subsequent victory outside Kandahar, among the most celebrated of Victorian military triumphs, made his reputation and future career.[37] White was also celebrated for his part, henceforth hitched his career to the bright tail of Roberts's star, and advanced rapidly.

He took ninety-eight hours to reach Kabul, and soon found himself in the midst of the march "…with the finest force I have ever served with in India; I think I might safely say the finest Anglo-Indian force that ever marched". The troops were eager for the work of wiping out defeat.[38] Nonetheless, despite the help of previously hostile Afghans, assigned by Abdur Rahman to help the column with the obvious aim of knocking out his rival Ayub, it was an ordeal in heat and choking dust, especially for the camp followers. White, too, although mounted and without the 'fatigues' or working parties for ordinary soldiers and followers, was exhausted at the end of each day.[39] As they neared Kandahar, they heard that Ayub had raised the siege and retired behind a line of hills; his Herati regiments, fanatical Ghazis (equivalent of modern *Jehadis*) and artillery made him formidable. "All reports made us think we had a foeman worthy of our steel", White

---

33   Durand, I, pp. 244-6. Dr T.A. Heathcote, who points out that although Durand worked with White he served later Viceroys and may have included later practice in his description. For Edwin Johnson see my *Life of Field Marshal Lord Roberts* (London: Bloomsbury, 2014), p. 115.
34   White101(b), P6/67, White to wife, 6 July, 1880.
35   White 2, 18 Oct, 1880
36   Letter to brother quoted Durand, I, p. 255.
37   No account of the march and battle would neglect the documents subsequently published by the Viceroy's orders, *Kandahar correspondence: Sirdar Ayub Khan's Invasion of Southern Afghanistan, Defeat of General Burrows' Brigade, and Military Operations in consequence* (India Office Library, Miscellaneous Public documents, 2 vols, 1880-1) and its supplement, *Correspondence with Members of the Viceroy's Staff attached to the Forces for the Relief of Kandahar. Commencing from 10th August 1880*. Henceforth 'Correspondence'.
38   Correspondence, No 2, pp. 2-3, White to Viceroy, 10 Aug, 1880.
39   Correspondence, No 5, pp. 7-11, White to Viceroy, 3 Sept, 1880.

told his wife, "and that our work was cut out for us & would be no child's play".⁴⁰ On 31 August they arrived below the walls of Kandahar, and after they breakfasted, Roberts sent a reconnaissance in force to report on the enemy position. His favoured flanking movement would be around Ayub's right, the southern end of the Baba Wali hills, where the enemy position was strong by virtue of fortified villages, loopholed walls and strongpoints.

White led the 92nd in the battle; they and the 2nd Gurkhas headed Roberts's first brigade. British, Sikhs and Gurkhas advanced rapidly against stubborn resistance, White using fire tactics first and then shock and "…went at them with the bayonet whenever they made a stand", never giving them a chance to rally. As the Afghans abandoned their first positions, Roberts ordered up the third brigade for a final effort. White played a leading role in the battle's climax; "I rode up & down our line once or twice & explained to the men that their position was a dangerous one, pointed out the guns, and worked them up to the proper pitch for a last charge".⁴¹ This they executed in fine style, the last surge carrying them into Ayub's abandoned camp. The enemy were now in full flight, but unfortunately Roberts's cavalry brigade on the wrong side of the Argandab River could not cut them off, although the Bombay horsemen from the Kandahar garrison made better execution.⁴²

An officer who arrived three days after the battle found White, sunburnt and red, looking thin after his endeavours and not altogether strong. "They all say he led his men through everything and worked splendidly. The Highlanders and Gurkhas must have behaved gloriously rushing everything".⁴³ With pardonable exaggeration, White called Roberts's achievement "…the greatest military movement made by a British army in our day". The victory ushered in forty years of peace between British India and Afghanistan, although not until Abdur had personally defeated his rival in a year's time. The Russians accepted that the 2nd Afghan War had reduced Afghanistan 'to a tributary of the British Empire'.⁴⁴

White had undergone sufficient adventures for a volume by G.A. Henty: at Charasia a young soldier warning him just in the nick of time not to be shot, and at Kandahar his mare carrying him too far in front of his men and made him jump into a ditch as a last resort. White wrote to his wife, "I had a bad minute or two looking down rifle barrels but they were on the run & in a hurry to fire & be off & they missed me."⁴⁵

"Nothing could have been warmer" than Ripon's reception of his Military Secretary, and all round Simla he was received with the greatest warmth.⁴⁶ Once again recommended for the Victoria Cross, he at last received the award, along with the C.B. (Companionship of the Bath) and a brevet Lieutenant-Colonelcy.⁴⁷

There followed a fallow time. He was recouping his health. Part of the 92nd had gone to South Africa and shared there in Major-General Sir George Colley's humiliation at Majuba; White

---

40 White101(b) and (c), P6/73, 6 Sept, 1880.
41 White 101 (b) and (c), P6/73 and Correspondence p. 9.
42 Correspondence, no 594, pp. 212-212a for detailed account.
43 Correspondence, p. 13, Captain Muir to Ripon, 5 Sepot, 1880.
44 W.C. Fuller, *Strategy and Power in Russia 1600-1914* (New York: Free Press,1992), pp. 332-5.
45 White 101 (b) and (c), P6/73, 6 Sept, 1880.
46 White101(b) and (c), P6/74, White to his wife, 21 Sept, 1880.
47 *Hart's Army List* 1898, p. 339.

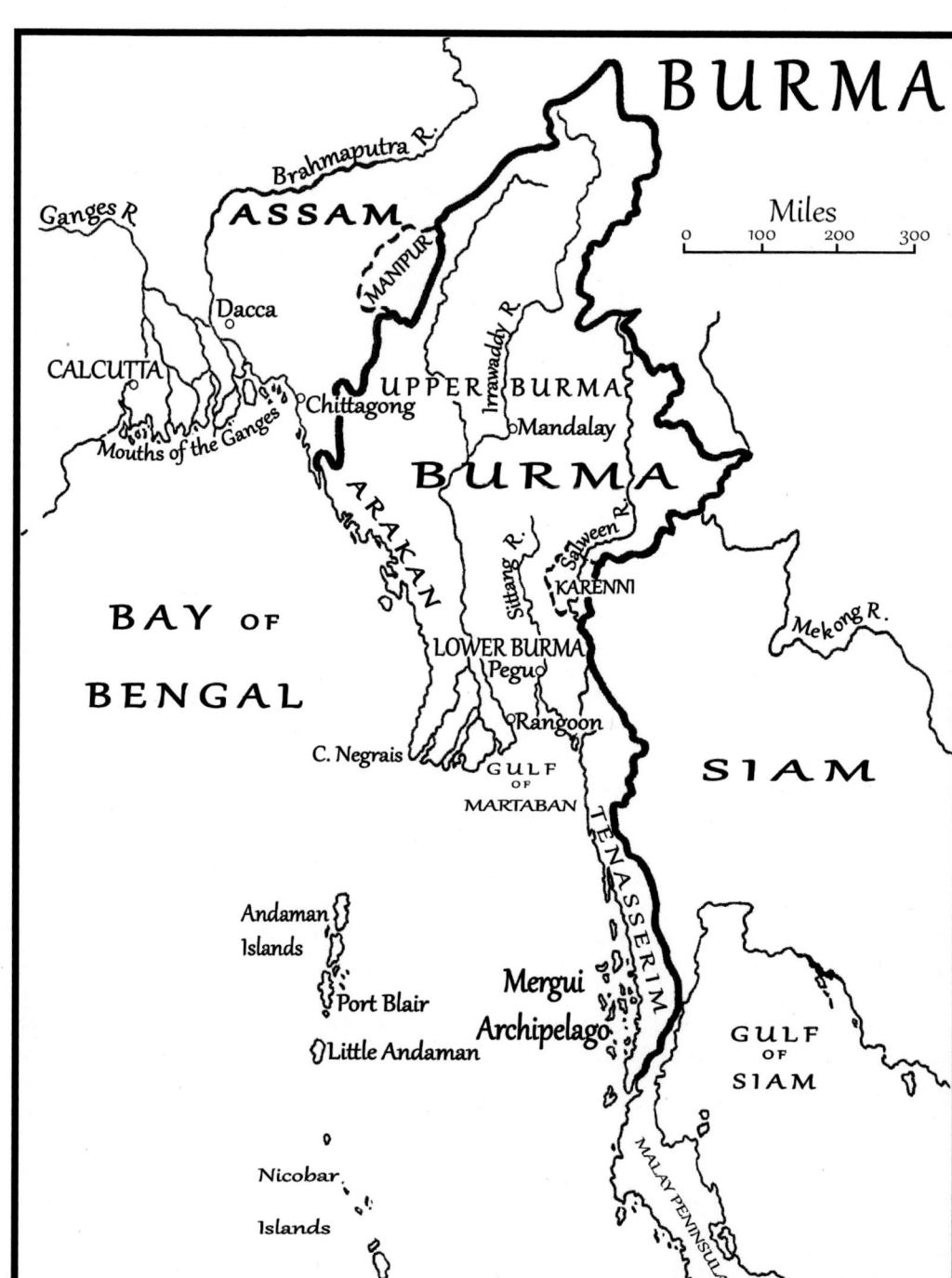

had tried to join them, and Ripon was willing, but the Duke of Cambridge refused.⁴⁸ After commanding the regiment at home for three years, he considered retiring from the service.⁴⁹ He served briefly in the Sudan in Wolseley's Gordon Relief Expedition. In September he returned to India to command a brigade at Kampti, and in November embarked at Madras with the 2nd Brigade of an Expeditionary Force to invade Burma.⁵⁰

Earlier in the nineteenth century Burmese rulers twice made the mistake of starting wars with the British in India, being beaten and losing Assam and Arakan in 1826 and lower Burma in 1852. The 3rd Burmese War followed deteriorating relations, allegations by the Burmese against the Bombay-Burmah Trading Corporation and British fear of growing French influence. When the Burmese refused a demand for arbitration over the dispute with the Corporation, the British issued an ultimatum on 22 October 1885; a reply unsatisfactory to the British led to a declaration of war. The Burma Field Force consisted of about 10,000 men in three infantry brigades, one from Bengal, two from Madras, George White commanding one of the latter. In overall command was fifty-one-year-old Sir Harry Prendergast, a Royal Engineer serving with the Madras Army. His instructions from the viceroy, Lord Dufferin, were to take the capital and dethrone King Thibaw 'rather by the display than the use of force'.

Prendergast had to overcome modern blockhouses guarding the Irrawaddy and reach Mandalay before the Burmese could obstruct the river. The river approach to Mandalay was defended by two formidable clusters of forts, the first at Minha. Fierce fighting there (17 November) showed the Burmese outmatched in everything but courage. One fort was easily captured, one proved very difficult. Despite good arrangements for the care of sick and wounded in hospital ships, cholera appeared, and the heaviest casualties were from disease. White was to lead the attack on Ava, the last and strongest fort before Mandalay. The Burmese surrendered before the assault, on 27 November, Mandalay was occupied on the 29th and the Burmese royal family deported that night. King Thibaw and his queens came on foot from the palace down to the river where they gave themselves up to the British, "… the most remarkable day of my life", thought White.⁵¹

White remained in command at Mandalay while Prendergast went up to Bhamo. White's position was precarious and isolated, the districts around the city covered with jungle and few roads. He sent a long telegram pointing out how much military action was still required. When Burma was annexed on 1 January, 1886, as a New Year's present to the Queen, Prendergast was showered with congratulations, but the annexation provoked an extensive insurgence. With a 9000-man force, without cavalry, mules or reinforcements, Prendergast was expected to conquer a kingdom the size of France. His fate was decided, however, by press sensationalism. E.K. Moylan, the Rangoon Correspondent of *The Times* had published an interview with Thibaw and an exaggerated account of disorder and looting in the city to show a picture of military

---

48 See White's judgement of Colley: White 101(b) and (c), P)6/93, 2 Feb, 1881: 'I wonder if I wrote to you that I thought Geo Colley had a weakness as a soldier & that it was want of judgement as to what soldiers can do & what they cannot do.'
49 Durand, I, p. 284, letter 4 Feb, 1883 to wife.
50 A.T.Q. Stewart, *The Pagoda War: Lord Dufferin and the fall of the Kingdom of Ava 1885-6* (London: Faber, 1972) supplemented by Martin Jones, 'The War of Lost Footsteps: a Re-assessment of the third Burmese War,' *Bulletin of the Military Historical Society*, vol xxxx, no 157 (August, 1989), pp. 36-40.
51 Durand, I, p. 318, quoting letter to wife, 7 Dec, 1885.

incompetence. Prendergast deported him for transgressing press regulations. Buckle, the editor of the *Times,* pulled strings, as a friend of Randolph Churchill, Secretary of State for India, to get Moylan back to Mandalay. White wrote that Moylan returned "...full of triumph and vindictiveness" and embarked on a bitter vendetta first against Prendergast and the soldiers, then against civilians. His story of the Provost Marshal's threats to extract testimony from a Burman about to be shot hit the press like a bombshell. Churchill wired to Dufferin that he thought that Prendergast was unfitted for command. There were questions in Parliament, and the Indian Secretary of State ensured that Prendergast's career was ended, despite long service including a Victoria Cross.[52]

Before Prendergast's departure, White had organised the formal state entry of the Viceroy Dufferin. White wrote: "The viceroy's State entry went off to perfection. It was left entirely to me, and I did all I could to make it a success ... It went off without a hitch, and Lord Dufferin sent for me and thanked me most warmly. I replied that if His Excellency thought the arrangements good, I was amply repaid for any trouble I had had on them. He repeated in his slow, rather forced manner, 'Good! They were more than good, they were ideal – they were dramatic.'"[53]

After dinner Dufferin went over to White and had another talk with him about the military situation. White told him frankly that there were not enough troops in the country to protect those who had a right to look for protection. Dufferin was upset and angry, but later acknowledged that White's frankness had been of great help. Years afterwards he used to relate that one day he was walking with White in Mandalay and asked how far British power in Burma extended. White pointed to a sentry pacing up and down the rampart and replied, "Up to that man and no further". After Prendergast's departure, White took command. He was delighted, but sorry for Prendergast's sake. "He is such a nice man, everybody likes him".[54]

By January, 1886, White was writing to his brother of a widespread insurrection by the former soldiers, who had been disbanded, losing their livelihood, and had become 'dacoits' (Bandits), enjoying some sympathy amongst the people who had been loyal to the ruling family. It was harrowing, White wrote, to hear of poor villages being burnt by these bandits.[55] He faced immense problems. Upper Burma was a vast area of mountain, plain and jungle, intersected by broad and often impassable rivers, and devoid of roads and telegraph lines. Outside Mandalay, the military situation deteriorated. He increased ten military stations to twenty-five, and planned to progress along the two great rivers, the Irrawaddy and the Chindwin, establishing military posts close enough to one another to obtain control of the whole area. The dacoits continued to loot and burn villages. At the end of April there was a disastrous fire which destroyed a large area of Mandalay. In the middle of August the bund (the dike protecting Mandalay against the Irrawaddy) burst. This led to flooding and misery in the city, but only twelve lives were lost. The British made rations of rice and half an anna per day available to those who needed relief. General Sir Herbert Macpherson from Madras was sent as commander-in-chief in Burma. He and White had served together at Kabul and Kandahar and got on well, but

---

52 Stewart, *Pagoda War*, pp. 118-130, 154-7; Colonel Henry M. Vibart, *The Life of Sir Harry N.D. Prendergast* (London: Eveleigh Nash, 1914) defends the subject of the biography, Vibart's friend.
53 Stewart, *Pagoda War*, p. 133.
54 Stewart, *Pagoda War*, p. 139.
55 White 98(b), P3/94, White to brother, 10 Jan, 1886.

in October Macpherson died suddenly from fever.[56] To reassure public opinion in Britain and India, Roberts was sent, arriving in November. A.T.Q. Stewart writes in his history of the war: 'The sending of Roberts had a calming effect on opinion in England, but he was under no illusion about the nature of his task or the length of time it would take. He was careful to pay generous tribute to the "two able officers at the head of affairs," White and Bernard, and to draw public attention to what they had achieved.'[57]

It took five years and the employment of 32,000 troops and 8,500 military police to re-establish peace and order in Burma. It was the longest of Queen Victoria's little wars and devoid of glamour.[58] The strategy -- large forces divided into small units, numerous garrisons and carefully co-ordinated flying columns, with Mounted Infantry organized by Colonel Penn Symons being the key – had been worked out before White took command, but he implemented it very ably. In 1887-88, when White's measures, protecting villages, collecting tax revenues and harrying the Dacoits became effective, he suddenly found himself in a series of hill wars with the minority peoples. They too were overcome by the small columns of roughly 120 men each commanded by subalterns. In the course of the campaign, over 600 British and over 1100 Indians had to be sent away to recover their health. Of two able Colonels who served under him, William Lockhart was also broken down by illness, while William Penn Symons earned his praise for organizing Mounted Infantry.[59] In November, 1887 White received news of his promotion to major-general.[60]

By early 1888 both Roberts and Dufferin thought White was ready for a change, and after leave in Britain in April, a brief return to Mandalay confirmed success: civil officers were now in control, the railway to Mandalay and roads were being extended, and a province the size of France had been added to the British Empire. He had proved himself as both a general and an administrator, working with senior civil servants such as Charles Bernard and Charles Crosthwaite, successive Chief Commissioners, and won praise from the Viceroy Dufferin as well as Roberts. On 1 May, White took command of a division at Quetta in Balochistan, a frontier post suited to his temperament.

Balochistan was a thinly populated, largely arid land of deserts and mountains. Quetta stood at 5000 feet in a beautiful valley surrounded by mountains. Its nominal ruler was the Khan of Kalat, its mixed population including Baloch and Pashtuns turbulent and not easily amenable to the Khan's control. During Lord Lytton's viceroyalty, Robert Sandeman had become British agent and re-established British influence there. He secured the lease of districts around Quetta including the strategic Bolan Pass to southern Afghanistan. Sandeman's admirers, known to his critics as 'Sandemaniacs', depicted him as, "...one of the most remarkable men who ever served on the Indian frontier", and that 'the Sandeman system' sent British frontier officers to

---

56 White 101(d), P6/169, White to wife, 24 Oct, 1886.
57 Stewart, *Pagoda War*, p. 178.
58 In addition to the sources in note 50 supra, see also Sir Charles Crosthwaite, *The Pacification of Burma* (London: Edward Arnold, 1912).
59 Durand, I, pp. 347 and 369.
60 White 101(e), P6/209, White to wife, 21 Nov, 1887. The story of the Duke of Cambridge's persistent opposition to White's promotion is best followed in his correspondence in the Royal Archives at Windsor.

the tribal people to bring them under British influence.[61] More accurately, Sandeman's officers paid the tribal chiefs, who after taking their cut compensated the tribesmen for the loss of booty from their raids. Only the districts around Quetta were under direct British control; others were ruled 'indirectly' by local warlords. 'British Balochistan' included Sibi and Pishin, ceded by the Afghans in the 2nd Afghan War; other frontier districts bordering Afghanistan and Iran were leased from Kalat and administered from Quetta.[62] White's letters show that he found Sandeman a difficult and demanding colleague, but he made every effort to work with him.[63]

The Zhob Valley expedition was White's main achievement during his time at Quetta. One clan had held aloof from Sandeman's arrangements, the Khiddarzai section of the Shirani tribe, who had long made their almost inaccessible mountain home a base for raids into British territory. Another centre of trouble lay to the west of the British post of Fort Sandeman, where some 250 dissidents ('outlaws and malcontents' in Durand's phrase) from all parts were gathered under the leadership of one Dost Muhammad. They preferred the old system of raids to Sandeman's pay-outs. White was dispatched with a force comprising two squadrons of Bengal Lancers, a mountain battery, a battalion of the King's Own Yorkshire Light Infantry, Bombay infantry and sappers; he concentrated his men at the start of October, 1890. A letter to the Afghan Amir warned him of the expedition's aim. Initially White marched on Dost Muhammad's stronghold in three columns and seized the place without a fight on 11 October. Dost Muhammad made his escape to Afghanistan, although hotly pursued by a detachment of Bengal Lancers.

White continued to advance through comparatively unknown territory with two lightly equipped columns down parallel valleys, the local tribesmen offering virtually no resistance, their attitude encouraged by the profitable trade in sheep and goats they made with the invaders. On 29 October White reached Fort Sandeman, where he planned the second phase of the campaign against the Shirani Khiddarzais.

These tribesmen with their flocks and herds felt secure on the spurs and pastures below the heights of the Takht-I-Suliman ('Throne of Solomon', 3375 metres), so White determined to outmatch them at their own game. He sent a column under Colonel Ross, 1st Sikh Infantry, to prevent the rest of the Khiddarzais interfering, and another under Colonel Nicholson, 30th Bombay Infantry, to clear a difficult pass which had been closed for some years by landslips and large boulders blocking it at its narrowest points.[64] White meanwhile took a small, lightly equipped column up into the Sulaimans and was able to look down on the Khiddarzais and impress them with heliograph signaling, showing they were cut off from assistance. Resistance ceased. White's column of 130 men of the King's Own Yorkshire Light Infantry and 170 of the Bombay Infantry (2nd Baluch Battalion) had climbed a final 1700 feet and then descended steeply 3600 feet into the Khiddarzais home. The night of the ascent was intensely cold, with a high wind and '20 degrees of frost'. White might have been fortunate that his *chowkidar* brought

---

61   Durand, I, pp. 381-2 adopting a 'Sandemaniac' position. It can be argued that Sandeman's interference from the Punjab had previously lost British influence in Balochistan.
62   Durand, I, pp. 381-3 describes. Both he and William Broad on Sandeman in the *ODNB* present a roseate view; corrected by Dr T A Heathcote. See his *Balochistan, the British and the Great Game: the Struggle for the Bolan Pass, Gateway to India* (London: Hurst & Co., 2015).
63   White 101(h), P6/269 to wife, 14 Oct, 1890.
64   White's report quoted in Captain H. L. Nevill, *Campaigns on the North-West Frontier* (Uckfield: The Naval & Military Press, 2005 reprint), p. 116.

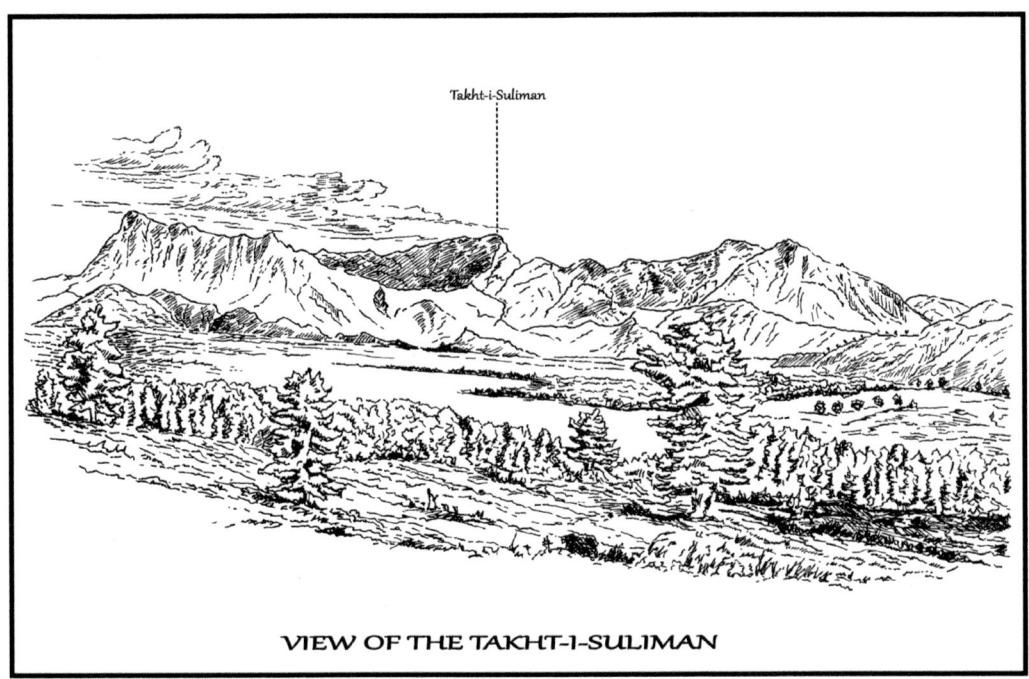

VIEW OF THE TAKHT-I-SULIMAN

him sheepskin boots and jacket and a blanket, but he hardly slept from cold and from worry over a soldier who had earlier been hurt by a falling mule.[65]

White's report emphasized that it was a campaign against nature rather than man, "…with the studied object of making friends and not conquering enemies…"[66] Operations were well planned and executed, despite rugged country preventing the use of transport animals and the men having to carry, besides rifles and ammunition, their bedding, rations and cooking utensils. Altogether the columns of the Zhob Field Force traversed 1800 miles, 828 over new routes.

Sadly, Sandeman did not live long to enjoy the success. He died in January, 1892 from pneumonia contracted on a tour made to try and re-establish British influence on the border with Persia.[67] So peaceful did White believe that Balochistan had become that he later quoted it as evidence that the warlike Afridis' and Mohmands' territories should be annexed.[68] He conducted his campaign (and his mountaineering) with skill, but it must be questioned whether the pacification of Balochistan was a 'lasting achievement' of the 'forward' school. 'British Balochistan' was South Waziristan, inhabited in part by Pashtuns, and has remained turbulent to this day.[69]

---

65 Letter to wife, 16 Nov, 1890, quoted Durand, I, p. 396.
66 Durand, I, p. 128.
67 Information from Dr T A Heathcote.
68 White 41, Printed memorandum on frontier situation, 22 Oct, 1897.
69 Dr T A Heathcote pointed this out. In late 2014 Waziristan, the North more than the South, was a base for Taleban insurgents.

Nonetheless, White's conduct of the campaign following that in Burma added to his reputation. In late 1892 there was considerable speculation as to Roberts's successor as Commander-in-Chief India. Liberal ministers in London, Campbell-Bannerman at the War Office and Kimberley at the India Office, wanted Redvers Buller, the Adjutant-General. The Duke of Cambridge also favoured Buller, but he refused the post, although pressed. White, despite his long service, was comparatively junior, but he had powerful backers: Lansdowne, the viceroy, Brackenbury, the Military Member of Lansdowne's council, and of course Roberts. When White went from Burma to Balochistan, Ian Hamilton had written to Amy White predicting her husband would be the next Indian commander-in-chief. Perhaps Hamilton knew of Roberts's intentions to push White's career? His crystal ball could not have told him of Lansdowne and Brackenbury's support, or of Buller's decision to refuse the position. Brackenbury when asked his view said: "I know of only one officer in either the British or the Indian Army of at all sufficient standing, who possesses all the qualities required in Lord Roberts's successor. That officer is Major-General Sir George White."[70]

White had doubts about succeeding a figure like 'Bobs', and had almost reconciled himself to Buller, telling Roberts there was no better successor.[71] It was a difficult time to take command, for the falling value of the rupee squeezed government revenues. To his brother White wrote:

> Altogether [Roberts] has left me as difficult a heritage as it is possible to imagine. Many of the measure he takes credit for having introduced have been kept over for me and I have stopped several of them which I thought ill-judged. His aim has been to get his name associated with endless measures. Through the agency of the press he has them cried up as 'One more great reform for Lord R'.[72]

With this in mind, most of White's measures were modest: increased pay for the Native Infantry, new clothing regulations for British soldiers, lobbying on behalf of the Indian Staff Corps for promotion to match that of officers in the British Army, better plans for mobilization. He continued Roberts's policies of encouraging good shooting and temperance. The *Times of India* in listing these noted that White's administration was, "…marked by sound, clear-headed commonsense, and by the practical application of the intimate knowledge gained during his long experience as a regimental officer."[73]

Lieutenant-General Menezes, historian of the Indian Army, is undoubtedly right in considering White a supporter of 'martial race' theory.[74] Roberts and others believed that the sepoys of the south had lost the fighting spirit of Clive's day, and it now resided in the Gurkhas, Sikhs, Punjabis, Dogras and other northerners. This owed something to Social Darwinism, something to peace in southern and central India, which meant the Bengal soldiers were the ones to see most action and ambitious British officers sought postings accordingly, and a good

---

70 Quoted Christopher Brice, *The Thinking Man's Soldier: The Life and Career of General Sir Henry Brackenbury 1837-1914* (Solihull: Helion & Co., 2012), p. 210. For the politics of the appointment see ibid., pp. 209-210 and 225-7 and the present author's *The Life of Field Marshal Lord Roberts*, pp. 171-2.
71 Durand, I, p. 408.
72 White 98(b), P3/110, 25 April, 1893.
73 *Times of India*, 18 Mar, 1898, p. 4
74 Menezes, *Fidelity and Honour: the Indian Army*, p. 290.

deal to Roberts's influence. In his autobiography he wrote of the garrison at Kandahar when his column arrived in summer, 1880: "They seemed to consider themselves hopelessly defeated and were utterly despondent; they never even hoisted the Union Jack until the relieving force was close at hand."[75] White was not alone in repeating this story,[76] yet in Burma he had praised the sepoys whom he commanded. He believed his Madras sepoys had regained confidence in themselves during the campaign, previously having lacked experience of active service.[77] Despite this observation, White as commander-in-chief followed the prevailing 'martial race' dogma. He and Roberts both recommended forming homogeneous 'class regiments' each of the same race, and the government of India accepted their views. Kitchener, Indian commander-in-chief 1902-1909, thought 'class regiments' produced 'a better and happier fighting machine', but made it more likely a whole unit would desert, being susceptible to influence of political or religious agitators. He reformed units on a class company basis.[78]

The most important measure, culminating a process which began with the Eden Commission enquiring into Indian army reform in 1879, was the abolition of the separate Bengal, Bombay and Madras Armies and their replacement with four army corps. Successive viceroys pressed for it, but strong opposition centered on the Duke of Cambridge and 'old India hands' on the India Council in London, who remembered that in 1857 when the Bengal Army mutinied those of Madras and Bombay remained largely loyal. As early as February, 1881, White had written to his brother: "Some startling changes proposed. I approve of them but as they are state secrets so far don't talk about them. The principal are the abolition of the Commanders in Chief in Bombay & Madras & the division of the whole army into 4 Army Corps ... There will be any amount of opposition at home. It will drive H.R.H. [the Duke] of Cambridge mad..."[79] The combined influence of Roberts and Brackenbury, who had been Lytton's Private Secretary in succession to Sir George Colley, brought a renewal of these plans. Logistical and administrative separation had already been eliminated, and Cambridge withdrew his opposition. Sir Donald Stewart who joined the India Council in 1893 gave enthusiastic support. Thus White's command coincided with the long-matured fulfillment of this plan with which he was in sympathy. The Madras and Bombay Armies Act of 1893 legislated for the transformation, but with the continued fall in the rupee's value there were unfortunately no savings.[80]

The Indian cavalryman George Barrow depicted White favouring Scots regiments (perhaps supported by White's own words)[81] but also as a thoughtful, well read and kindly leader, never letting kindliness override a sense of duty. Barrow noted the difficulty in following Roberts:

---

75   Roberts, *Forty-One Years*, p. 484.
76   Correspondence, no 5, p. 10, White to Ripon, 3 Sept, 1880; Gerard, *Leaves from the Diary of a Soldier and Sportsman*, p. 302.
77   The discussion can be followed in my *Life of Field Marshal Lord Roberts*, pp. 144-5.
78   India Office L/MIL/17/5/1617, *Record of Lord Kitchener's Administration of the Army in India 1902-1909* (Simla: the Government of India, 1909), pp. 303-5. Menezes, *Fidelity and Honour: the Indian Army*, chapter 10 exposes fallacies of the 'martial race dogma' but unfortunately says almost nothing about White.
79   White 98 (b), 21 Feb, 1881.
80   Heathcote, *The Military in British India*, pp. 140-157; Brice, *Brackenbury*, pp. 221-2; India Office L/MIL/17/5/1616, Summary of the Measures during the Viceroyalty of the Earl of Elgin and Kincardine 1894-1898.
81   Durand, I, p. 435 quoting a letter to his wife.

"Bigger in physical, but much smaller in mental, stature than Lord Roberts, his work in chief command was solid and he left it with credit."[82] Shortly after Roberts's departure the Indian Government purchased his Simla home, Snowdon, as the commander-in-chief India's official residence. A new double-storeyed building was constructed to provide rooms for personal staff, and an imposing gateway with large pillars was added to Snowdon's public entrance. During the five years that the Whites lived there, Lady White established a well-deserved reputation as a hostess, her dances and theatricals being as numerous as they were successful.[83]

The fulfilment of the Eden Commission reforms was matched by events on the North-West Frontier: White's term of command saw the greatest development of the 'forward' school. By pressing for Buller, Campbell-Bannerman and Kimberley had hoped to avoid fighting on the frontier, but instead there prevailed the continued influence of Roberts and of Brackenbury, who although disagreeing with Roberts on some aspects of Indian defence, shared his fear of Russian designs.[84] The Pendjeh incident of 1885, a Russo-Afghan clash which brought the British and Romanov Empires to the brink of war, and continued Russian advance in the Pamirs kept alive British fears for their north-western frontier.[85] By 1894 White's civilian chief was no longer his friend Lansdowne, but Elgin whose viceroyalty was marked by 'famine, plague and frontier wars'.[86] Kimberley and Fowler, secretaries of state in the Rosebery government, warned the Viceroy against pushing forward. Both Elgin and White believed that unless Russia were checked, the frontier would be ablaze. Elgin's view brought him into disagreement with Liberal colleagues at home. Already in January and February, 1891, before White assumed command, William Lockhart had led a column through Orakzai territory.

In 1893 Mortimer Durand had travelled to Kabul to negotiate with Abdur Rahman: the Amir received a much increased subsidy from the British in return for agreeing a northern frontier with neighbouring Russian territory and withdrawal of his claims to suzerainty over frontier tribes from Chitral to the Persian border. This 'Durand Line' still forms the Afghan-Pakistan border, but running through the territory of the border Pashtuns it was bound to be a source of friction.[87] The hill state of Chitral lay in the British sphere of influence; the ruler was assassinated, there was a revolution and the British agent Dr George Robertson was besieged.

There followed the 1895 Chitral campaign.[88] White directed a force under General Sir Robert Low to march by the direct route to relieve Robertson and the garrison, while from the eastward Colonel Kelly advanced from Gilgit through 220 miles of barren and hostile territory, in high passes waist-deep in snow. Kelly arrived first, and the siege of forty-six days was brought to a close. Low's leading brigades meanwhile inflicted heavy losses on resisting tribesmen at the Malakand Pass. In September White paid a flying visit to the force, was mostly pleased by what he saw, but contrary to the advice of his staff reduced the planned number of garrisons,

---

82   Gen. Sir George de S. Barrow, *The Fire of Life* (London: Hutchinson, 1942), p. 25.
83   E.J. Buck, *Simla Past and Present* (2nd edition. Bombay: Thacker, Spink & Co.,1925), pp. 80-1.
84   Brice, *Brackenbury*, p. 215.
85   Peter Hopkirk, *The Great Game* (Oxford: OUP, 1991), pp. 418ff.
86   P.E. Roberts, *History of British India* (Delhi: OUP, 1977), p. 501.
87   Percy Sykes, *Sir Mortimer Durand* (London: Cassell & Co., 1926), pp. 210-8 for negotiations and 218-222 for details of the line. Sykes's praise of Durand is not echoed by Captain Nevill, *Campaigns on the North-West Frontier*, p. 209, or by most modern historians.
88   It was preceded by a small expedition against the Abor people on the NE Frontier.

thus keeping men in the fighting line.[89] The Liberal government fell from power, and Salisbury's Unionists gave sanction to the 'forward school' by agreeing Chitral should be held by a strong garrison to be connected by a military road to the British frontier.[90] Lord George Hamilton, eight years at the India Office, stated the case for the 'forward school': leaving 'the other side' alone was unrealistic, the tribes were used to raiding, Britain's friends like the ruler of Chitral could not be abandoned, peace on the frontier depended upon vigilance and where necessary punitive incursions.[91]

Chitral was the curtain-raiser to 'the most formidable outbreak' on the Frontier. Rumours abounded in the bazaar at Malakand that the Mullahs were calling for a great rising in which 'the English would be swept away'. Over 200,000 men took arms, mobilized not only by 'religious fanaticism' but by fear that British encroachments into tribal territory were a prelude to permanent occupation; and by belief that Abdur Rahman would support the anti-British *Jehad*.[92] The first stage in the Tochi Valley was an anti-climax. Major-General Corrie Bird's two-brigade force met little opposition save sniping in building a bridge across the swollen Indus and destroying towers and hamlets. More serious was the rising in the Swat Valley and the attack upon Malakand Fort and Chakdara. There followed the revolt of the Afridis and Orakzais who burnt British posts in the Khyber Pass. The force that was mobilised, equivalent to two army corps (59,000 regulars), was commanded by General Sir William Lockhart, who was recalled from Germany where he had been taking the cure in an attempt to recoup his health. Lockhart had rendered good service in Burma and Waziristan and had been nominated as White's successor.[93] White and his staff were responsible for overall planning. The *Times of India* praised his foresight in preparing troops for prompt and successful action in relieving Malakand and Chakdara. Generals Blood and Elles were provided with well-equipped forces which duly inflicted chastisement on Swat and Bajour and on the Mohmands. When the British and Indians advanced, the tribesmen withdrew speedily into the hills; when the invaders fell back, tribesmen advanced to cut off small parties and attack rearguards. A cavalry subaltern with strong views thought the losses after a skirmish at Inayat Kila were proportionately "… greater than in any action of the British Army in India for many years".[94] He had forgotten Maiwand. Lockhart warned his men in November, 1897 that they were, "…opposed to perhaps the best skirmishers and best natural rifle-shots in the world, and that the country they inhabit is probably the most difficult on the face of the globe".[95] Conversely midnight sniping at one

---

89 Durand, I, p. 438 quoting letter to brother.
90 Nevill, *Campaigns on the North-West Frontier*, pp. 167-208; Hopkirk, *Great Game*, pp. 486-500;
91 Lord George Hamilton, *Parliamentary Reminiscences and Reflections* (2 vols. London: Murray, 1922), II, pp. 263-4.
92 Winston Churchill, *Frontiers and Wars* (London: Penguin Books, 1972), p. 29 (containing an abbreviated version of Churchill's *The Malakand Field Force*); Rob Johnson, *The Afghan Way of War: Culture and Pragmatism: a Critical History* (London: Hurst & Co., 2011), p. 149. Abdur had issued a treatise on *Jehad* but in the event stayed out.
93 White and Lockhart might qualify for the ludicrous, 'They were only playing leapfrog' in *Oh! What a Lovely War*. White was promoted major-general (July, 1887) before Lockhart (Sept 1891), but Lockhart got his step to lieutenant general before White (April, 1894 to April, 1895) and to general (Nov, 1896) while White had only local rank. *Hart's Army List 1898*, pp. 4 and 339.
94 Churchill, *Frontiers and Wars*, p. 103.
95 White 38, the Tirah Expedition, 11/37, circular instructions, 18 Nov, 1897.

British camp, fifty rounds falling closely into 100 square yards, had the sole result of hitting a single mule in the tail.[96] For the British the climax was the magnificent charge of White's old regiment, the Gordons, at Dargai into the teeth of heavy fire. British casualties of 36 killed and 159 wounded could have been avoided, according to Lockhart, if local commanders had followed his instructions to strike at the enemy's line of retreat.[97]

The *Times of India* had questioned whether White and Lockhart were right to keep their divisions massed and suggested several dispersed columns might have been more effective, although running the risk of being overwhelmed by the Pashtuns' superior numbers. The newspaper concluded, however, that the operations' success was shown by the submission of the various tribes and especially "... the Afridis, after receiving a punishment of extreme severity and paying in their fine in money and rifles". This was "...the clearest testimony to the ability and foresight with which all the operations necessary to this end have been conceived and organised by Sir George White".[98]

Although White had been a late convert to the 'forward policy', by the end of his term he was advocating it in the strongest possible terms: in a memorandum of October, 1897 he argued for the conquest of the Afridis and Orakzais and the absorption of their territory into India; only such measures would prevent 'the continuation of murderous raids'.[99] In a farewell speech at Simla, he made the same bold proposals. Newspaper opinion was divided, but *The Star* was horrified, claiming that the government and soldiers of India had squandered vast sums of money in immoral and useless adventures beyond India's borders.[100]

White had directed and Lockhart had conducted the operations with all possible skill, but they can be described at best as a short-term success. In 1901 George Curzon arrived as Viceroy, very conscious of the Russian threat and the security of India. He firmly modified frontier policy, creating the new North-West Frontier Province, bringing back some 11,000 troops from frontier garrisons and reducing manoeuvres there to avoid provocation. Malakand and Dargai were retained and fortified, but tribal levies such as the Afridis of the Khyber Rifles replaced regular troops.[101] This was not abandonment of the 'forward' policy of which Curzon was an advocate, but a major change based on experience.

White finished his command with a foolish accident. He had always maintained his fitness, but he loved paper-chases despite his wife's protesting as he was now in his sixties. He rode once too often: his horse came down at the last wall, and he sustained a badly fractured leg. While still on the ground he scribbled a note to Amy: "I have decided not to do any more paper-chasing!"[102]

---

96   Churchill, *Frontiers and Wars*, p. 130.
97   *The Times*, 20 March, 1900, Lockhart's obit.
98   *Times of India*, 18 Mar, 1898, p. 4. Account of expedition in Nevill, *Campaigns on the North-West Frontier*, pp. 209-324; General Sir Aylmer Haldane, *A Soldier's Saga* (Edinburgh & London: William Blackwood & Sons, 1948), pp. 81ff; and sympathetic to the tribesmen, Johnson, *Afghan Way of War*, pp. 149-173.
99   White 41, Memorandum 22 Oct, 1897.
100 White 48 contains a selection of newspaper views. *The Star* rather undermined its position by saying that this policy was against the advice of men like Roberts and Donald Stewart.
101 David Gilmour, *Curzon* (London, 1994), pp. 195-7; Roberts, *History of British India*, pp. 516-7.
102 Field-Marshal Lord Birdwood, *Khaki and Gown* (London & Melbourne: Ward Lock, 1941), p. 107.

In April, 1898, he landed in England, but hardly as a returning hero. His broken leg was in a plaster of Paris cast and he had to be carried about.[103] In his biographer's words, "Now, he was to exchange the large open life of India for a house in London, which he had always detested, and the command of three hundred thousand men for an office chair."[104] In India the Quartermaster General's department dealt with the active work of administration, operations and Intelligence. In London White as QMG gave his energies to providing food, forage, fuel and light, with quarters, stores and equipment, administering the Army Service Corps and the Pay Department and "…dealing with the sanitary questions relating to the Army". George Barrow tells us that White came to admire Wolseley, calling on Barrow when the latter was at Staff College and saying, "I used to be prejudiced against Wolseley, but I must admit, Barrow, that since I have been working with him I have come to admire him immensely. I have met no soldier, not omitting Bobs, the equal to him in breadth of military outlook, knowledge and versatility". White praised Wolseley for his battle for reform against vested and court interests.[105] Wolseley as commander-in-chief, however, resented his subordinates having access to the Secretary of State, the soldiers chafed under civilian control and were at odds with one another, according to Clinton Dawkins, Financial Secretary at the War Office: "[T]he real vice is not systems but persons; the greater part of the leading soldiers is devoted to "putting each other in the cast". It is a story which would be tiresome, if not serious of Wolseley, Buller, White and Wood all trying to knife each other."[106]

Burdened with work unsuitable for a man of action, White also disliked the round of London society, resenting having to spend his time at lunches and dinners with people who were not, as a rule, individually congenial to him. He remained at home as much as possible.[107]

A biographer seeks in this period some explanation of White's performance in the ensuing South African War, much less assured and decisive than Afghanistan, Burma, Zhob and the Indian command. Did his immobility dull his confident outlook? His leg broken in seven places had to be repaired. In a speech to Irish doctors he quoted a distinguished surgeon as calling it 'a bag of bones' and described the bones being attached 'with screws that long' and later having them removed.[108] In October, 1898, he explained, "I can now walk short distances at my own pace, which is a slow one…I shall always have a limp, but I hope to have a useful leg." He was no longer the athletic White scaling heights on the Zhob expedition.

Wolseley had already offered White the Gibraltar command, but his last campaign intervened. British soldiers believed war in South Africa imminent as tension increased between the two Boer republics and the British Empire, but Salisbury's cabinet did not expect hostilities, as Kruger had backed down previously over the Drifts Crisis. In September, however, they suddenly found war staring them in the face.[109] On the 6th Wolseley told White that he 'must be prepared

---

103 Durand, II, p. 1.
104 Durand, II, p. 2.
105 Barrow, *Fire of Life*, p. 26.
106 E.M. Spiers, *The Late Victorian Army 1868-1902* (Manchester & New York: Manchester University Press, 1992), pp. 50-3.
107 Durand, II, p. 5.
108 Durand, II, p. 4.
109 Iain Smith, *The Origins of the South African War 1899-1902* (London & New York: Longman, 1996), pp. 337 & 371.

to start almost immediately for Natal'.[110] His task was to hold Natal while in England an Army Corps some 48,000 strong under General Sir Redvers Buller was mobilised. To Wolseley's inevitable question about his leg's fitness for active service, White replied, "My leg is good enough for anything except running away."[111] On 16 September he sailed from Southampton.

His lengthy fighting experience had been against non-Europeans, often resourceful and courageous, especially on the North-West Frontier and Afghanistan, but usually inferior in weaponry and training to the British. Kruger had armed his forces with Krupp and Creusot artillery and Mauser rifles. The mounted commandos of the Transvaal (South African Republic) and Orange Free State made up "…the largest modern army yet seen in South Africa; the burghers were masters of fieldcraft, shooting and mobile warfare".[112] Despite its unparalleled experience of 'small wars', the British Army was about to receive a shock.

After reaching the Cape on 3 October and conferring with General Forestier-Walker commanding in Cape Province and the British High Commissioner Sir Alfred Milner, White proceeded to Durban which he reached on the 7th. He was fortunate that troops had been despatched promptly from India.[113] He thought he was fortunate in finding, as well as the Governor of Natal, Sir Walter Hely Hutchinson, Major-General Sir William Penn Symons, veteran of Burma and the North-West Frontier. In the Tirah campaign, Lockhart had written of Symons: *"No one* could have done better throughout this business than he has done…"[114] White also had with him Major-General Sir Archibald Hunter, due to join Buller as his chief of staff but who stayed with White, Major-General Sir John French in command of the cavalry, and Colonel Ian Hamilton whom he knew well from India.

One third of White's force was at Glencoe, a mining town in the northern wedge of Natal between the two Boer republics. White would have preferred withdrawal and concentration on Ladysmith forty miles south. Hely-Hutchinson, who feared a Zulu and Natal Afrikaner uprising, and Symons, who was confident he could hold Glencoe, persuaded him otherwise. Symons went to Glencoe and White to Ladysmith, arriving there on 11 October when the Boer ultimatum expired and hostilities began.[115]

In retrospect White would have been wiser to follow his inclination, as two telegrams to Symons on 18 October and a letter to his wife showed he belatedly realized.[116] On the morning of 20 October, Symons's garrison found Lukas Meyer's burghers with six guns atop Talana hill overlooking their camp, Boer artillery outranging the British. Symons' infantry pushed forward and after more than five hours' fighting took the summit, only to be shelled by their own guns. Symons, gallantly 'encouraging all about him by his words and example', had been

---

110 Durand, II, p. 6.
111 Durand, II, p. 7.
112 Bill Nasson, *The South African War, 1899-1902* (London: Hodder Education, 1999), p. 68.
113 J.A.S. Grenville, *Lord Salisbury and Foreign Policy: the Close of the Nineteenth Century* (London: Athlone Press, 1970) p. 246 writes, "But for the splendid efficiency of the British army in India, Natal would almost certainly have been lost during the first month of the war, and with it perhaps South Africa." CAB 37/50/69, marginal note 'decided at cabinet 8 Sept suggests the cabinet authorized the dispatch of troops.
114 White 38, 11/35, Lockhart to White, 2 Nov, 1897, apologising for his earlier traducing Symons.
115 Winston Churchill, *From London to Ladysmith via Pretoria* (London: Longmans, Green & Co., 1900), pp. 483-4 on Symons' courage and forceful character.
116 Telegrams quoted Durand, II, pp. 40-1; letter in White 101 (i), P6/310, 23 Oct, 1899..

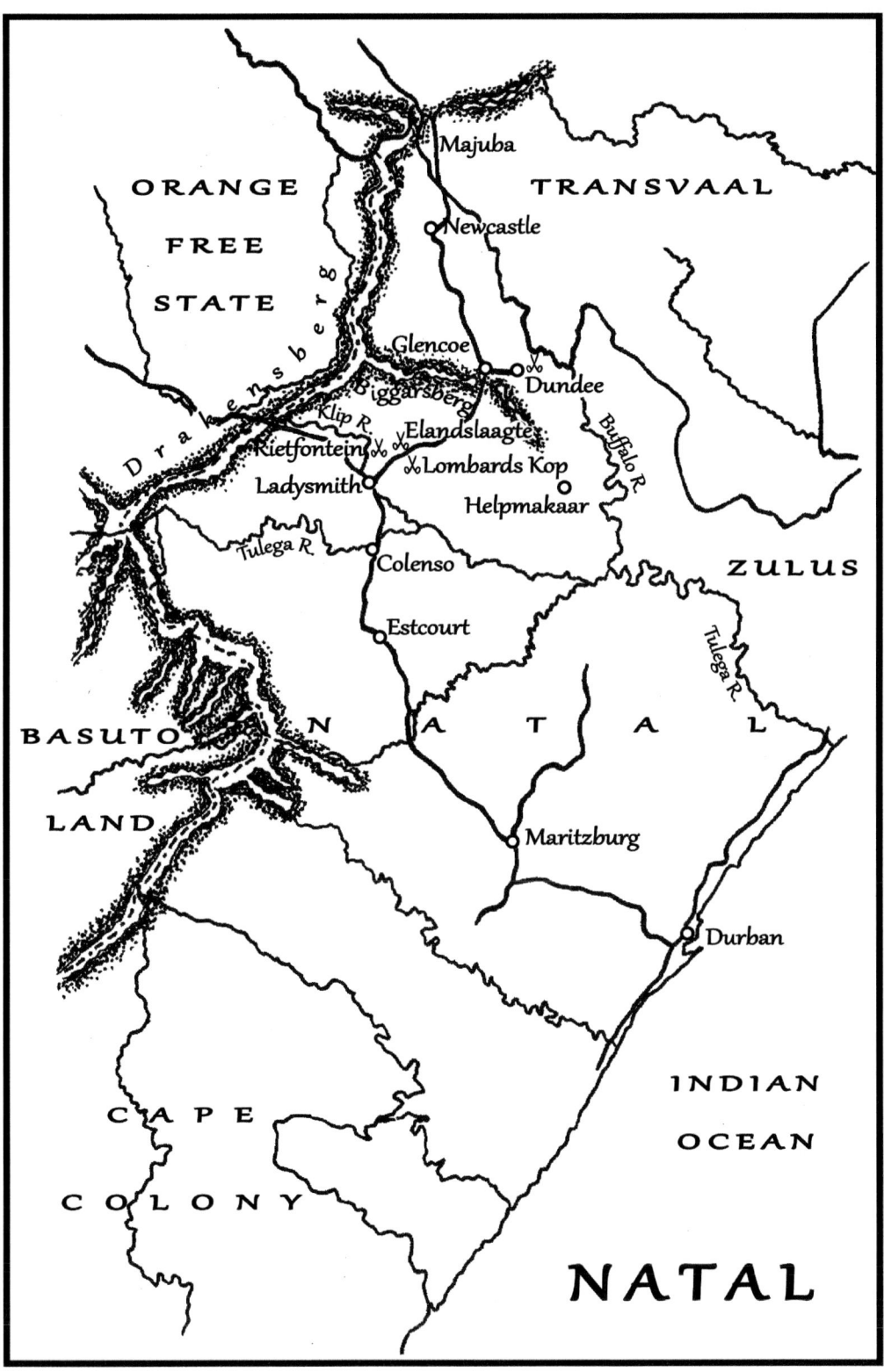

NATAL

fatally wounded in the stomach. Colonel Moeller with the cavalry, instead of falling upon the retreating Boers, ignored the advice of two experienced majors, divided his force and with 200 men was surrounded and forced to surrender.[117]

The following day battle was joined at nearby Elandslaagte. White was present, leaving Hunter in command in Ladysmith, but the conduct of the battle was in the hands of Sir John French and Ian Hamilton. Hamilton's infantry attacked in extended order, worked around the enemy flank, putting them to flight. A cavalry charge inflicted the *coup de grace*. White's confidence in both French and Hamilton had been repaid.[118]

Neither success, the limited one at Talana, the more substantial at Elandslaagte, produced lasting results. On reports that 10,000 Free Staters were advancing on Ladysmith, White withdrew thence. He instructed Brigadier Yule who had succeeded Symons: "You must try and fall back on Ladysmith. I will do what I may to help you when nearer."[119] Yule abandoned Dundee with its sick and wounded and covered by darkness of the night of 22 October began his withdrawal. The fourth night of the march was so murky the men linked hands as they floundered in torrential rain and knee-deep mud, the Boers pressing closer.[120] White moved out from Ladysmith with 5000 men to cover the retreat, and at Reitfontein on the 24th became involved in a more serious engagement than he intended, partly because of the rashness of Colonel Wilford of the Gloucesters, taking a company and the regimental Maxim Gun to close quarters.[121] This precipitate move caused a large proportion of White's loss of 114 killed and wounded including Wilford. Having achieved his objective, White withdrew and Yule's exhausted column reached Ladysmith.

Ladysmith was a tin-roofed township in one of the dips of Natal's vast rolling hills, shaded by a few green trees, with two parallel streets and detached villas. It was overlooked by surrounding heights, and thus it was logical for White to take the initiative to prevent the Boers closing. His decision led to a British disaster. He had sent up an observation balloon, and from it could be seen the semi-circle of hills with Pepworth at its centre on which the Boers were entrenching. White planned to attack Pepworth Hill with two brigades, a total of nine battalions, supported by six batteries of artillery and mounted troops. He would accompany Hamilton's brigade. To cover the attackers' left flank were two battalions commanded by Lieutenant-Colonel Carleton supported by a mountain battery; to cover the right was a cavalry brigade under Major-General French. Mishaps began with the preparatory night march, which suggests that White's cancellation of a previously planned night attack by Ian Hamilton was wise. His plan proved much less so, and his entire staff including Hamilton tried to persuade him to wait until the enemy was closer, unsuccessfully.[122] White's service so far had included leading company and battalion-sized forces in close combat, but with larger bodies only planning and administration.

---

117 Leo Amery, ed., *The Times History of the War in South Africa* (7 vols. London: Sampson, Lowe & Marton, 1900-09. Henceforth 'TH'), II, pp. 154-174; The Marquess of Anglesey, *A History of the British Cavalry, Vol. 4: 1899-1913* (London: Leo Cooper, 1986), pp. 44-5.
118 TH, II, pp. 175-195.
119 Quoted Durand, II, p. 69.
120 Rayne Kruger, *Good-bye Dolly Gray* (London, 1959), p. 89.
121 Frederick Maurice, *History of the War in South Africa* (3 vols. London: Hurst & Blackett, 1906-8. Henceforth 'OH'.), I, pp. 152-6.
122 Ian Hamilton, *The Happy Warrior: A Life of General Sir Ian Hamilton by his Nephew* (London: Cassell, 1966), pp. 136-7.

He was to be out of his depth commanding brigades; his subordinates' failures magnified his own.

Battalions of one of the brigades became separated and French's cavalry were nowhere to be seen. Boer mobility allowed them to outflank the British and move swiftly to reinforce threatened points. White decided to disengage and withdraw to Ladysmith. A hail of bullets followed the retirement. The British were saved from major disaster only by the excellent work of the artillery batteries including naval guns which arrived post-haste, thanks to Captain Henry Rawlinson's initiative, and deployed rapidly.[123] Boer superiority in open order, use of cover and volume and accuracy of fire was only too obvious.

Greater misfortune struck Carleton's flanking force at Nicholson's Nek, four miles beyond Pepworth. The mules carrying guns and ammunition stampeded and ran away during the night march, depriving them of their mountain battery. They were hard pressed by a Boer force, and a separated party under Captains Duncan and Fyffe raised a white flag. Boers rose to accept the surrender, thinking it was the whole force. Carleton, rather than repudiating it, called for a cease-fire. The Boers took over 900 prisoners, three-quarters of British losses. The Gloucesters' and the Royal Irish Fusiliers' surrender to the despised farmers was an imperial humiliation known as 'Mournful Monday'.[124]

White accepted full responsibility in his message of 30 October to the War Office. As his biographer points out, this chivalrous conduct went some way to disarm public criticism. Yet, as he admitted to his wife, he knew the opposition of most of his staff was vindicated. He could imagine "... the newspapers boys are now calling in London the terrible disaster", and the realization was a severe blow to his confidence.[125] The battle and surrender were auguries of Boer success: the commandos no longer followed half-hearted leaders Lukas Meyer and Erasmus, but Louis Botha and Christiaan de Wet.[126]

In early November French left the town by train on Buller's orders, and White lost one of his more enterprising commanders. The Boers soon cut the railway line.

Should White continue to hold Ladysmith, thus tying up 14,000 men, but also possibly an equivalent or larger number of armed Boers intent on penetrating Natal? In London the commander-in-chief doubted not that White had "...muddled the whole thing...when he found he could not hold Ladysmith, he should have retired to the Tugela – blown up his magazines, and destroyed his food...He is a gallant fellow, but no strategist."[127] Wolseley, however, may have been wrong: tying up the commandos in sieges made it impossible for 30-40,000 men to burst into Cape Colony; if that had happened, the war might have taken a different course.[128] Viscount Esher, who recorded Wolseley's views, changed his mind when he heard the testimony of both White and Roberts before the Royal Commission in 1903.[129]

---

123 In his closing despatch White gave Rawlinson credit; some would give it to Captain Hedworth Lambton or Percy Scott of the Royal Navy.
124 TH, II, pp. 245-260.
125 Durand, II, p. 94; White 101(i), P6/312, 30 O)ct, 1899..
126 Kruger, *Good-bye Dolly Gray*, pp. 93-5.
127 M.V. Brett, ed., *Journal and Letters of Reginald Viscount Esher* (4 vols. London: Ivor Nicholson & Watson, 1934-38), I, p. 245, 24 Oct, 1899.
128 Nasson, *South African War*, p. 111; TH, II, pp. 126-7.
129 Esher, *Journal and Letters*, I, p. 377.

On 31 October Buller arrived at Cape Town heralding the Army Corps' appearance in the theatre of war. Buller's most eminent defender, Thomas Pakenham, condemns White: staying at Ladysmith, he was 'a strategic liability' who knew of Buller's repeated warnings not to go north of the Tugela. But did he? Pakenham's evidence is Buller's letter from Aldershot to Lansdowne as Secretary of State for War, and one from South Africa dated 6 January, 1900, to the Queen's secretary, Sir Arthur Bigge.[130] Anything Buller wrote in January, following Colenso, would be defensive, and how would White have seen such a missive? As to the first, historians of the war are unanimous in agreeing that there was no strategic discussion or plan for the war, that until September Lansdowne and the cabinet believed Kruger would back down, and that both Buller and White were left to improvise. Pakenham is on stronger grounds in arguing that White was 'weak' both in allowing Symons to remain at Dundee and insisting on launching the Pepworth Hill operation against the advice of his staff.[131]

Moreover, if staying at Ladysmith was, "…the greatest strategic mistake of the whole war",[132] it was one Buller endorsed. On his arrival he telegraphed White to send him an 'accurate description of your views of the situation' and continued: "I doubt if Boers will ever attack you if entrenched. Hitherto you have gone out to attack them; can you not entrench and wait for events, if not at Ladysmith, then behind Tugela at Colenso?" White replied that his men needed rest, "… but I have the greatest confidence in holding Ladysmith for as long as necessary". Buller replied: "I agree that you do best to remain at Ladysmith, though Colenso and line of Tugela River look tempting.…" It would be 'at least three solid weeks' before he could attempt to reinforce or relieve him.[133]

White summarised his reasons for holding Ladysmith in his official dispatch of 23 March, 1900.[134] He argued that Ladysmith was a strategically important railway junction, that he should not abandon a mass of stores and a largely English population. Most important was Hely-Hutchinson's fear of Zulu and Natal Afrikaner uprising. Against withdrawing to the Tugela he wrote:

> The line of the Tugela from the Drakensberg to the Buffalo River is some 80 miles long … Against an enemy with more than double my numbers and three times my mobility, I could not help to maintain such a line with my small force, and any attempt to prevent their turning my flanks could only have resulted in such a weakening of my centre as would have led to its being pierced. Once my flank was turned on the line of the river the enemy would have been nearer Maritzburg than I should have been, and a rapid withdrawal by rail for the defence of the capital would have been inevitable. Even there it would have been impossible to make a prolonged defence without leaving it open to the enemy to occupy the important port of Durban …

---

130 Thomas Pakenham, *The Boer War* (London: Weidenfeld & Nicholson, 1979), p. 97 and notes 95 and 96.
131 Pakenham, *The Boer War*, pp. 150-2.
132 Ibid, p. 151.
133 Durand, I, pp. 100-3; the telegrams are in White 56 'Copies of telegrams'; Buller's is f. 56.
134 White 58, quoted in part Durand, II, pp. 104-5.

Holding out at Ladysmith, he could occupy the mass of the Boer armies.[135]

In any case it was now probably too late with Boer forces all about. These forces wasted their mobility in the sieges of Ladysmith, Kimberley and Mafeking, giving the British time to mobilize for two counter-offensives, the first Buller's (December, 1899), the second Roberts's (February, 1900).

The former ended in 'Black Week', for Buller in failure at Colenso, followed by confused, defeatist messages (heliogram to White, telegram to London):

> I tried Colenso yesterday but failed; the enemy is too strong for my force except with siege operations, & those will take one full month to prepare. Can you last so long? If not, how many days can you give me in which to take up defensive position? After which I suggest you firing away as much ammunition as you can and making best terms you can.

He repeated the message with an additional sentence: "Whatever happens recollect to burn your cipher, decipher and code books, and all deciphered messages." On 17 December he asked White's advice: "Can you suggest anything for me to do? I think in about three weeks from now I could take Colenso …"[136]

White was astonished and replied: "I can make food last for much longer than a month and will not think of making terms unless I am forced to … The loss of 12,000 men here would be a heavy blow to England. We must not yet think of it." And in a second message repeated this: "Abandonment of this garrison seems to me most disastrous alternative on public grounds." The Government took the same view, Lansdowne telegraphing: "The abandonment of White's force and its consequent surrender is regarded by the government as a national disaster of the greatest magnitude."[137]

Another message informed White of the appointment of Roberts with Kitchener as his chief of staff. Roberts's offensive led to the relief of Kimberley, the capture of Piet Cronje's force at Paardeberg and the occupation of Bloemfontein. Buller failed again to break through at Spion Kop and Vaal Krantz. It was to be more than 100 days before Ladysmith was relieved. Buller in his fourth attempt fought his way through the hills north of the Tugela. His CRA

---

135 White 58, 23 Mart, 1900. Among modern historians this finds support from Howard Bailes, 'Military Aspects of the War', in Peter Warwick, *The South African War: the Anglo-Boer War 1899-1902* (Harlow, Essex, 1980), p. 72.
136 The National Archives, WO108/399 Confidential telegrams, pp. 52-3, nr. 53D and 54 ; analysed by Julian Symons, *Buller's Campaign* (London: Cresset Press, 1963), p. 169; Pakenham, *Boer War*, pp. 239-240 defends this and his messages to London. 'If only Buller could have expressed himself more plainly…' Indeed! See Spiers, *Late Victorian Army*, pp. 312-5. Spiers notes Buller poorly understood the effect of new weapons in his tactical handbooks issued as Adjutant General.
137 WO108/399, p 55, nr 57; Symons, *Buller's Campaign*, pp. 169-170; Pakenham, *Boer War*, pp. 369-370, pleads that White's later testimony, that he thought the Boers had captured the British cipher and sent the message, was due to Ian Hamilton's hostile misinterpretation, but Rawlinson's diary cited selectively by Pakenham supports Symons' interpretation. National Army Museum, Rawlinson papers 5201-33-7-1, 16, 17 and 18 Dec, 1899; 5201-33-7-2, 9 and 10 March, 1900.

(Commander Royal Artillery) Colonel Lawrence Parsons's deployment of artillery was vital to success and prefigured creeping barrages on the Western Front.[138]

The siege meanwhile was waged against enemies without and sickness within. Chief scourges were enteric (typhoid) and dysentery. It was the height of the southern summer. The water supply from the Klip River had long been suspect; new filters had been ordered but failed to arrive. The isolated garrison tried to distill water by using a dismounted railway engine, and attempted to boil drinking water, but this was not possible for all troops. Enteric was endemic in South Africa, the Boers and besieged forces alike suffering.[139] A hospital was established outside the Ladysmith perimeter, nearly three miles to the south-east, at Intombi. Deaths from disease were 465; almost all were theoretically preventable with the knowledge of public health then available.[140] Correspondent Henry Nevinson records some corruption and theft of food at Intombi, but also that White sent Colonel Stoneman of the Army Service Corps to investigate; he paraded everyone, gave them separate tasks, insisted on beds and clean sheets for all and better distribution of food.[141]

Food not just for the sick, but for the whole garrison was a worry. Colonel Edward Ward in charge of supplies made remarkable efforts to supplement the un-tempting rations of beef and bread, improvising 'chevril' from the horses (which were slaughtered and so lost to service) and a sausage factory converting horse flesh into sausages. Dried meat or 'biltong' was also prepared. White praised Ward: "… the very best supply officer I have ever met, and to his resource, foresight and inventiveness the successful defence of Ladysmith for so long a period is very largely due."[142] Not knowing how soon Buller would break through, White had to cut the rations.

Long range fire from Boer guns was a menace. It killed and wounded garrison and civilians alike, except on Sunday when Boer gunners observed the Sabbath. On that day concerts and entertainments, cricket and football matches kept up morale, the Boer gunners on Bulwana looking on through their glasses and taking a sporting interest.[143]

Both Hunter and Henry Rawlinson urged sorties against the Boer artillery. On the night of 7 December Hunter led 500 men against Gun Hill; he achieved complete success, destroying a 6-inch Creusot and a 4.7 inch howitzer and capturing a Maxim. Three nights later a similar raid blew up a 4.5 inch howitzer. A party of Boers blocked the raiders' retreat, and they had to cut their way out with the bayonet; they believed they had killed thirty Boers and had lost nine dead and fifty-two wounded.[144] Ladysmith was surrounded by a cordon of hills fourteen miles

---

138 See my article 'How the Royal Artillery Saved Sir Redvers Buller', *New Perspectives on the Anglo-Boer War, 1899-1902* (Bloemfontein, 2013), pp. 11-36.
139 OH, II, pp. 68-9; for endemic nature of typhoid, see report of Dr H.H. Tooth, physician specialist attached to Lord Roberts's forces published in a paper read to the Clinical society in London, 8 March, 1901 (Vol XXXIV of the Clinical Society's Transactions). The Boers at Ladysmith and Paardeberg suffered from both dysentery and typhoid.
140 Philip Curtin, *Disease and Empire: the Health of European Troops in the Conquest of Africa* (Cambridge: CUP, 1998), pp. 209-211, using Robert Simpson's *Medical History of the War in South Africa*.
141 Henry Nevinson, *The Diary of a Siege* (London: Methuen, 1900), pp. 197-200.
142 OH, II, pp. 578-9; White 58, Despatch after relief…, pp. 14-15.
143 Archie Hunter, *Kitchener's Sword Arm: the Life and Career of General Sir Archibald Hunter* (Staplehurst: Spellmount, 1986), p. 147; White 58, despatch 23 Mar, 1900, p. 14 for 'chevril'.
144 Pakenham, *Boer War*, pp. 270-1; OH, II, pp. 548-9; TH, III, pp. 167-172.

long in a two-mile radius from the town, stone sangars, other fortified posts and artillery, linked by telephones. The most difficult sector to defend was 'Caesar's Camp' and 'Wagon Hill' in the south, the key to the position a defence line on the inner edge held by the Manchesters with 500-800 clear yards of fire. The rocky and boulder-strewn ground made trenches impossible: breastworks and sangars had to be built of stone.[145]

On 9 November the Boers had made an abortive attack in this sector. On 6 January at 3 a.m. they launched a much more serious assault around the eastern end of Caesar's Camp. White rushed reinforcements to the Manchesters to pin down the enemy. At 12:30 Boers led by Commandant J. De Villiers charged the position and put the defenders to flight. The British counter-attacked. In close-quarter fighting the rifle-pits changed hands. About 5 p.m. the Devonshires charged with fixed bayonets, the enemy fleeing. The Devonshires had won the day but lost all their company officers and a third of their men.[146] Rawlinson who visited the scene the next day wrote in his journal: "The Boers were bold and plucky to a degree which no one expected…They were only frustrated by the dash and gal[l]antry of Hamilton and some other officers who led the troops magnificently."[147]

The Boers made no further attacks, and the siege became one of endurance against sickness and shell fire. On 12 January Rawlinson recorded that White was "…thinking of a flying column or of attacking and marching towards Buller with whole garrison abandoning sick and wounded." Rawlinson thought it would be a great mistake; "…the garrison must stick it out." No such sortie was made. By late January White thought his position regarding provisions was becoming critical.[148] On 13 February a message from Roberts was relayed, that he had entered the Orange Free State with a large force, and the 27th he passed news of the surrender of Cronje's force at Paardeberg.[149] That same day Rawlinson wrote: "Buller has undoubtedly made a mess of it. If he does not succeed in relieving us before another ten days are out he will be a ruined man and we shall very likely find our way to Pretoria after all."[150] Buller did break through. On the evening of the 28th the first mounted men from his force rode into Ladysmith, the Boers fleeing. Cheering was heard across the town, the loudest and most heartfelt for White. The correspondent of the Melbourne *Argus*, Donald Macdonald, gave the best description of this occasion of joy and relief:

> The bowed back of the old fighter [White] straightened, his sunken cheeks flushed, and his eyes shone … More than once he tried to speak and failed…Finally he found his voice and beginning almost inaudibly thanked them for the loyal way they had, civilian and soldier alike, co-operated with him in the defence of the town. Then he struck the keynote that went straight to the hearts of all his people and roused them to an indescribable enthusiasm: 'Thank God we kept the flag flying'.

---

145 Hamilton, *Happy Warrior*, p. 139; for first part of siege, Liddell Hart Archives, King's College London, Hamilton papers 2/1/1, diary of siege of Ladysmith 26 Nov 1899 to 16 Jan 1900.
146 Hamilton, *Happy Warrior*, pp. 145-7; TH, III, pp. 176-205; National Army Museum, Rawlinson papers, 5201-33-7-1, 6 and 7 Jan, 1900.
147 National Army Museum, Rawlinson papers, 5201-33-7-1, 6 and 7 Jan, 1900.
148 White 101(i), letter of 28 Jan, 1900.
149 National Army Museum, Rawlinson 5201-33-7-1, 12 Jan, 1900; vol 2, 13 and 27 Feb, 1900.
150 Rawlinson 5201-33-7-2, 27 Feb, 1900.

"What a roar rose in the night air," wrote Macdonald. White's voice quavered as he went on: "It cut me to the heart to reduce your rations as I did." A smile came over his face and he saved the situation with a laughing, "I promise you, though, that I'll never do it again."[151] Another correspondent, Henry Nevinson of the *Daily Chronicle*, reported this day in more subdued tones, but later expressed his indignation at Buller's failure to order pursuit of the fleeing Boers. "Sir George White was made of different stuff [to Buller]", wrote Nevinson. "Mustering every man and horse that could crawl, he marched us out in column along the Newcastle Road in the hope of cutting off the Boers' retreat at their railhead by Modder Spruit." Nevinson terms the march 'pathetic' and 'heartrending'; along the whole route men were too weak to continue and fell down by the roadside. They saw the last Boer trains steaming away.[152]

That was on 1 March, and on the 3rd Buller led the relieving troops in a ceremonial march-past. "I never heard troops cheer like they did when they passed Sir George White today," wrote Rawlinson. "They waived [sic] their helmets in the air and simply yelled, such magnificent men too …"[153] White's heroic words and the successful defence of Ladysmith brought admiration from ordinary soldiers and civilians alike. Earlier complaints turned to respect. As Macdonald wrote: "So it is that in spite of the rigour of the time Sir George White is better loved and more admired by the people of Ladysmith today than at any period of the siege, and every taunt directed against him has recoiled upon those who made it. He has been cheered and feted …"[154]

White was a hero to the public, but his record in South Africa was mixed. He had put too much trust in Penn Symons's judgement. His accepting Hely-Hutchinson's fear that the Boers of Natal might rise has been supported by recent research; anticipation of Zulu rebellion was less justified. He realized himself that he had blundered in his plan for an assault on Pepworth. After Nicholson's Nek, he failed to send out the cavalry to escape and their horses perished. He appears for a time to have lost heart. Rawlinson wrote: "If Sir George White would go out a bit more and talk to the officers and men, he could do a lot to keep their spirits up."[155] His defence of Ladysmith was not as active as Hunter and Rawlinson wished, but nonetheless tied up large Boer forces, depriving them of early initiative. Belief in his passivity led to an unfortunate disagreement with his Ladysmith chief of staff, Archibald Hunter, over their respective roles on 6 January during the attack on Caesar's Camp and Wagon Hill. Hunter declared that he conducted the defence with White in bed; the claim was denied by White's staff and others. The tactless Hunter also said that schoolgirls could have shot as well as the Naval Brigade; for this he had to apologise.[156]

White's health broke down two days after the siege finished, and the relief of Ladysmith ended his active campaigning. His previous campaigns had been marked by courage and energy, and in Burma, Zhob and as Indian commander-in-chief organisational powers. He had studied

---

151 Donald Macdonald, *How We Kept the Flag Flying: the Story of the Siege of Ladysmith* (London: Ward, Lock & Co, 1900), pp. 281-2. Pakenham, *Boer War*, p. 366 largely lifts his description from Macdonald.
152 Henry Nevinson, *The Fire of Life* (London: James Nisbet & Co., 1935), pp. 102-3; cf. Nevinson, *Diary of a Siege*, p. 294. Also OH, II, pp. 583-4. In fact Colonel W.G. Knox led the sortie.
153 National Army Museum, Rawlinson papers, 5201-33-7-2, 3 Mar, 1900.
154 Macdonald, *How We Kept the Flag Flying*, p. 283
155 Byron Farwell, *The Great Boer War* (London: Allen Lane, 1977), p. 217 including Rawlinson quote.
156 White 6, BA4/1, Hunter to White, 29 Sept, 1903, giving his version; BA4/11, Lambton to White and Crichton to White, 22 Sept, 1903; BA4/24, Hamilton to White, 5 Nov, 1903, all other letters supporting White against Hunter.

his profession, and his talents impressed Lansdowne, Roberts and Brackenbury sufficiently that they supported him for the top post in India. At Ladysmith he lacked energy and spirit, and his strategy can be criticized, although Buller's defenders may have overstated their case. Nonetheless, Roberts, approving the "… manner in which Ladysmith was defended", thought it showed White had "… some of the old grit left in him"; he would have made him military governor of the Orange Free State, but he was too unfit.[157]

Now in his mid-sixties, White followed the career of the superannuated. He took up the Governorship of Gibraltar, enlivened only when he locked up a known anarchist armed with revolver and long knife who arrived during a royal visit by Edward VII.[158] On the same visit the King conferred on him the baton of a Field Marshal.[159] He enjoyed reading Kipling's masterpiece *Kim*, but thought "… the ramifications of the Indian Intelligence Department are the figments of Kipling's fine imagination rather than living portraits."[160] He served with Lord Roberts on the commission to adjudicate between Curzon as viceroy and Kitchener as Indian Army c-in-c on the position of the military member – Roberts and White both unsuccessfully opposed the government's taking Kitchener's side.[161] His last position was as Governor of Chelsea Hospital. He did not live to see his son Captain Jack White, DSO, veteran of South Africa, train the Irish Citizen Army of 1916 for its uprising.[162] He died in the Governor's quarters at Chelsea Hospital on 24 June 1912.[163]

If White's judgement and activity in Natal had equalled that of his earlier campaigns, he would stand high in the ranks of Victorian and Edwardian soldiers. As it is, he is not wholly forgotten. He may have given up paper-chases, but he still sits atop his bronze steed opposite number 47 Portland Place, London, onetime residence of Lord Roberts, his former commander and patron; he gazes resolutely south towards the BBC, Langham Place, whose view of his beloved Empire he must hold in disdain.

---

157 National Archives, WO108/399, Confidential telegrams, p. 150 nos. 202A and 202B, 11 and 12 Mar, 1900. Pakenham, *Boer War*, p. 370 incorrectly states that Roberts 'refused to employ him in any responsible position because of his strategic blunder'.
158 Esher, *Journal and Letters*, I, p. 1 398, Ponsonby letter, 12 April, 1903.
159 Weekly Irish Times, 18 April, 1903 proudly recorded 'Magnificent Reception – Field Marshal Sir George White'. The newspaper might have written 'dead men's shoes'.
160 Kings College London, Liddell Hart Archives, Ian Hamilton papers, 21/5, White to Miss Sellars, 26 Oct, 1901.
161 National Army Museum, Roberts papers 7101-23-90/147 and 148, White to Roberts, 5 Mar & 19 May, 1905.
162 'Citizen Army' was a grandiloquent term for 200 men. Donal Lowry, 'The Play of Forces World-Wide in their Scope and Revolutionary in their Operation: the South African War as an International Event', *South African Historical Journal*, vol. 41, issue 1 (1999), p. 102; F.S.L. Lyons, *Ireland Since the Famine* (London: Fontana, 1973), p. 285.
163 Durand, II, p. 314.

2

General Sir William Lockhart (1841-1900)

Ian F. W. Beckett

In January 1900 a hastily prepared third edition of Arthur Temple's *Our Living Generals* was able to add an account of Omdurman, fought in September 1898, to its final chapter on Major General Lord Kitchener. As the revised manuscript had been completed in October 1899, there was no reference to the war that had broken out that very month in South Africa. As the book had it, Kitchener was still in the Sudan, Field Marshal Viscount Wolseley still Commander-in-Chief at the War Office, Field Marshal Lord Roberts still in the Irish command, and General Sir Redvers Buller still in the Aldershot command but likely to be sent to the Cape in the event of hostilities. What is also striking about the Kitchener chapter is its opening statement that 'since the summer of 1897, the name of no British soldier, with the exception perhaps of Sir William Lockhart, has been more frequently mentioned by the "man in the street".'[1] Kitchener still has significant public recognition in modern Britain, primarily from Alfred Leete's famous Great War recruiting image that one millennium survey chose as the most powerful advertising image of the twentieth century.[2] But who now remembers Lockhart?

Within just three months of the publication of Temple's hagiographical study of 12 of Victoria's generals - Lockhart was not otherwise mentioned than in the one brief sentence - Lockhart himself was dead, having been actively Commander-in-Chief in India only since October 1898. Lockhart, who had made the public reputation to which Temple alluded primarily from his conduct of the 1897-98 Tirah campaign on the North West Frontier of India, had no contemporary biographer. He appears in a single page entry in Charles Robinson's well-known *Celebrities of the Army*, published in 1900, and shares a short chapter with Field Marshal Sir Donald Stewart in George Forrest's *Sepoy Generals*, published in 1901, but that is all.[3] Colonel Robert

---

1   Temple, Arthur, *Our Living Generals* (London: Andrew Melrose, 1900), p. 182.
2   On Kitchener's reputation, see Surridge, Keith, 'More than a Great Poster: Lord Kitchener and the Image of the Military Hero', *Historical Research* 74 (2001), pp. 298-313.
3   Robinson, Charles N., *Celebrities of the Army* (London: George Newness Ltd, 1900), p. 67; Forrest, George W., *Sepoy Generals: Wellington to Roberts* (Edinburgh and London: William Blackwood and Sons, 1901), pp. 292-318.

H. Vetch contributed an account of Lockhart's life to the Dictionary of National Biography in 1901 that drew mainly on Lockhart's obituary in The Times.[4] Nor did Lockhart leave any body of personal papers and it was only in 2011 that a short, privately published biography by a local family historian and genealogist appeared.[5] It seems appropriate, therefore, to restore Lockhart to his proper place in the Victorian military pantheon.

Lockhart's early career was a steady progression. Born at Inchinnan, Renfrewshire, rather than as usually stated at the family home at Milton Lockhart in Lanarkshire, on 2 September 1841, William Stephen Alexander Lockhart was the fourth son of the Rev. Lawrence Lockhart and his wife, Louisa. One of his elder brothers was to become Major General David Blair Lockhart and another, Laurence Maxwell Lockhart, a novelist. Lockhart received an ensigncy in the Indian army on 4 October 1858 and went out on the P&O steamer, Pera, to Alexandria, and then on the Candia from Port Suez to Calcutta. A lifelong friend, C.S. Noble, who went out with Lockhart described him at this time as powerful and erect figure with blue eyes and fair hair, with a "courtly, gentle, attractive voice and manner".[6] Curiously, perhaps there are not many other descriptions of Lockhart at any point in his career. Captain (later General Sir) George Barrow, who served as Lockhart's Assistant Adjutant General (AAG) in the Tirah campaign, wrote in 1897 that Lockhart's "commanding stature and handsome

Sir William Lockhart.

---

4   Vetch, R. H., 'Lockhart, Sir William Stephen Alexander', rev. T. R. Moreman, *Oxford Dictionary of National Biography* (Oxford: Oxford University Press, 2004) at http//www.oxforddng.com/view/article/16910, accessed 30 Dec. 2014
5   Smith, Martin, *General Sir William Stephen Alexander Lockhart: Soldier of the Queen Empress* (Hunstanton: Privately published, 2011). There are no footnotes and Smith apparently used few primary sources. It is most useful for genealogical information on Lockhart's family.
6   Smith, *Lockhart*, p. 11.

presence, his genial smile, and frank cordial manners all marked him out as a leader of men, and inspired their confidence and admiration". Interestingly, however, Barrow also remarked of a speech Lockhart made to the men of the Northamptonshire and Dorset Regiments during the campaign, "His speech was rather bald and abrupt and he missed the opportunity of saying a few words of encouragement. It is a pity Sir William is not a better speaker."[7]

Rather similarly, Captain (later General Sir) Aylmer Haldane, Lockhart's Deputy Assistant Adjutant General (DAAG) in the Tirah suggested that he was "a strikingly handsome man - tall, somewhat stout, and with keen blue eyes that seemed to look you through and which were rather close together". Managing to get appointed as an orderly on Lockhart's staff in the Tirah in March 1898, the young Winston Churchill found Lockhart "a charming man - vy amiable and intelligent".[8] When some criticism was directed at the conduct of the Tirah, Lockhart's chief of staff, Colonel William (later Field Marshal Lord) Nicholson, suggested that Lockhart's "nature is a very sensitive one, and he is very much distressed at the false rumours about him". Reporting on Lockhart in 1895, the Commander-in-Chief in India, Sir George White, considered him as ambitious, enterprising and, somewhat mysteriously, "thoroughly high caste".[9]

Lockhart joined the 44th Bengal Native Infantry, one of those regiments that had been affected by mutiny. He served in Oudh during the latter stages of the Indian Mutiny, attached to the 5th Northumberland Fusiliers and to the 7th Dragoon Guards, and was promoted to Lieutenant on 19 June 1859. He had subsequent attachments to the 26th Punjab Infantry and to the 10th Bengal Cavalry between 1861 and 1863. On 14 September 1864 he married Caroline, the daughter of Major General Edward Lascelles-Dennys, with whom he had two daughters and three sons. Lockhart's best man was the future Major General Sir Charles MacGregor, who was to become a noted specialist on the defence of India. Lockhart was then adjutant of the 14th Bengal Lancers in the Bhutan campaign from 1864 to 1866, in which he received recognition for a reconnaissance to Chirung. Lockhart was Aide de Camp (ADC) to Colonel William Merewether on the Abyssinian expedition of 1867-68. The Government of India's Resident Agent at Aden, Merewether headed the first party to land at Zula in advance of the arrival of the main expedition under Sir Robert (later Field Marshal Lord) Napier. Merewether was then given command of the cavalry brigade for the advance on the stronghold of Emperor Theodorus at Magdala. Lockhart, who took part in the action at Arogee on 10 April 1868 and in the capture of Mahdala on 13 April, was promoted Captain on 16 December 1868.[10] Interestingly, apart from Lockhart, three other future Commanders-in-Chief in India served on the expedition, Napier (C-in-C, 1870-76), being its commander; Donald Stewart (C-in-C,

---

7   British Library (hereafter BL), Asia, Pacific and Africa Collection (hereafter APAC), Barrow Mss, Mss Eur E420/27, Diary, 17 November 1897, and added comment circa 1920.
8   Haldane, Sir Aylmer, *A Soldier's Saga: The Autobiography* (Edinburgh and London: William Blackwood & Sons, 1948), p. 71; Churchill, Randolph S., *Winston S Churchill Volume I Companion Part 2, 1896-1900* (London: Heinemann, 1967), p. 886.
9   National Army Museum (hereafter NAM), Roberts Mss, 7101-23-052, Nicholson to Roberts, 14 March 1898; BL, APAC, IOR/L/MIL/7/17039, Bengal Annual Confidential Reports, 15 March 1895
10 For Abyssinia generally, see Chandler, David G., 'The Expedition to Abyssinia, 1867-68', in Brian Bond (ed), *Victorian Military Campaigns* (London: Hutchinson, 1967), pp. 105-60; Bates, Darrell, *The Abyssinian Difficulty: The Emperor Theodorus and the Magdala Campaign, 1867-68* (Oxford: Oxford University Press, 1979).

1881-85) commanding the Bengal Brigade; and Roberts (C-in-C, 1885-91) being Stewart's Assistant Quartermaster General (AQMG).

Lockhart was mentioned in despatches for his services as Deputy Assistant Quartermaster General (DAQMG) to the Hazara Field Force to the Black Mountain in 1868, having carried out "most nobly and resolutely" a reconnaissance of the village of Belean.[11] With another officer, he was awarded the bronze medal of the Royal Humane Society for rescuing two women from drowning in Morar Lake, Gwalior on 26 December 1869. Staff service followed as DAQMG in Bengal. One of his tasks was to assist his old friend, MacGregor, in 1870-71 in the preparation of a Gazetteer of Central Asia, Lockhart being responsible for the section on Khiva, not so easy a task when it was not until 1875 that Lieutenant Colonel Fred Burnaby famously penetrated this remote area of Central Asia.[12] Unusually, Lockhart also served in Aceh on Sumatra in the Dutch East Indies in both 1875 and 1877. On the first occasion, Lockhart visited Aceh out of interest while on leave to observe Dutch operations but on the second occasion he was British military attaché to the Dutch army and took part in the capture of Lambadde. He was not permitted to accept the Dutch Order of William but was allowed to wear the Dutch campaign medal. It is while in Sumatra in 1875 that he contracted malaria, which was the beginning of persistent health problems thereafter. Lockhart came close to death but insisted on being carried aboard a steamer bound for Singapore.

More significant recognition was to come from his service in the second phase of the Second Afghan War. Promoted to Major on 9 June 1877 and to Lieutenant Colonel on 6 April 1879, Lockhart was made road commandant of the Khyber Pass in September 1879 to keep it open during the advance of Roberts's Kabul Field Force. Roberts's despatch to Kabul followed the massacre of the head of British political mission in Kabul, Louis Cavagnari, and his escort. The establishment of Cavagnari's mission had been part of the treaty negotiated with the Afghan Amir, Yakub Khan, at Gandamak in May 1879 following the initial British operations in Afghanistan that had commenced in November 1878 to compel the Afghans to accept a British mission to displace Russian influence at Kabul.[13] In November 1879 he was appointed AQMG at Kabul, apparently on the recommendation of MacGregor, who was Roberts's chief of staff.[14] He took part in the actions fought by Roberts around the city in December 1879, Roberts's force being temporarily besieged in Kabul. Working in close proximity with Lockhart, the acerbic MacGregor began to find Lockhart "flabby and uninteresting" but MacGregor did not want Edward Chapman to get the post of DAQMG to Stewart, who had taken command at Kabul in May 1880, as he saw this as a threat to his own position and he detested Chapman. MacGregor therefore advised Lockhart to protest if Chapman were preferred to him.[15] There is no surviving paper trail surviving beyond MacGregor's diary but Lockhart did secure the post of DAQMG, returning with Stewart's force to India in August 1880. Mentioned in despatches,

---

11   Forrest, *Sepoy Generals*, p. 308.
12   MacGregor, Lady, *The Life and Opinions of Major General Sir Charles Metcalfe MacGregor* 2 vols. (Edinburgh and London: William Blackwood and Sons, 1888), I, p. 327.
13   For the Second Afghan War generally, see Robson, Brian, *The Road to Kabul: The Second Afghan War, 1878-81* (London: Arms and Armour Press, 1986).
14   MacGregor, *Life and Opinions*, II, p. 99; Trousdale, William (ed), *War in Afghanistan, 1879-80: The Personal Diary of Major General Sir Charles Metcalfe MacGregor* (Detroit: Wayne State University Press, 1985), pp. 75, 131, 145.
15   Trousdale (ed), *War in Afghanistan*, pp. 168, 184.

Lockhart was appointed to the Companionship of the Bath (CB). MacGregor seems to have wanted to try and get Lockhart a regimental command since, in the expectation that he would become Quartermaster General (QMG) in India - he was so appointed in 1881 – MacGregor felt Lockhart would not be "so good an office man" as to be his deputy.[16]

Lockhart himself joined the Intelligence Branch at army headquarters as Deputy Quartermaster General (DQMG), remaining there until 1885 apart from a brief mission back to Aceh to rescue the crew of the Nisero, this being a British-owned ship that had run aground in November 1883 and its crew taken captive by a local rajah. The Dutch had failed to secure their release and a joint military operation was contemplated but it would appear that a ransom was eventually paid, Lockhart securing the survivors in September 1884.[17]

Given a brevet colonelcy on 6 April 1883, he left the Intelligence Branch to take command of the 24th Punjab Infantry in May 1885.[18] Lockhart was then appointed to lead a political and reconnaissance mission to Gilgit, Chitral and Kafiristan in 1885 to establish relations with the Chitral ruler or Mehtar, Aman ul Mulk, and to survey the territory and assess potential northern invasion routes into India. Lockhart's mission was one of a number of similar enterprises in the wake of the Penjdeh incident of March 1885, in which Russian and Afghan troops had clashed south of Merv. Starting from Kashmir on 25 June 1885, Lockhart's party consisted of a surgeon and two other officers beside himself, escorted by a Sikh company, and with a few servants and some 200 porters. The party crossed the Kamri Pas some 13,100 feet above sea level. Lockhart halted at Gilgit on 29 July due to swollen mountain rivers. Resuming on 8 August, the party crossed the Shandur Pass at 12,100 feet, eventually reaching Chitral on 11 September. Lockhart concluded an agreement of sorts with the Mehtar and his party observed the Dorah and Zedek Passes, both over 14,800 feet. It also penetrated into Kafiristan, probably to forestall its exploration by a civilian traveller, Ney Elias, who was also active in the region. After returning to Gilgit for the winter, the Wakhugrins Pass at over 16,200 feet was visited in the following May as Lockhart moved towards Hunza. Lockhart's party, however, crossed the Kilik Pass into Afghan territory, causing considerable difficulties for a furious Lieutenant Colonel R. K. Ridgway VC, who was the principal British representative on the Anglo-Russian Afghan Boundary Commission established to delineate Afghanistan's northern frontier in the wake of Penjdeh. Apart from the survey work covering some 12,000 sq. miles, the mission also collected flora and fauna. Having seen all the main routes from the north, Lockhart assessed that the Pamirs could be crossed in summer but not on a large scale – although even a small Russian force could cause a great deal of political mischief – and that the Chitralis could hold the passes long enough for British troops to assist them. He proposed a permanent military presence at Gilgit.[19] Lockhart was recalled in July 1886 to act as QMG at army headquarters in

---

16 Ibid., p. 213
17 Smith, *Lockhart*, pp. 79-82.
18 BL, APAC, IOR/L/MIL/7/7717, Baker to Johnson, 13 May 1885.
19 The report by Lockhart and his surveyor, Colonel Robert Woodthorpe, is to be found in BL, APAC, IOR/L/P&S/20/B57, but there was also a published version; Lockhart, William, and Woodthorpe, Robert, *The Gilgit Mission, 1885-86* (London: Eyre & Spottiswode, 1889). Forrest, *Sepoy Generals*, pp. 310-14, briefly covers the mission, as does Ewans, Martin, *Securing the Indian Frontier in Central Asia: Confrontation and Negotiation, 1865-95* (Abingdon: Routledge, 2010), pp. 117-20. There is a popular treatment in Keay, John, *The Gilgit Mission: The Explorers of the Western Himalayas* (London: John Murray, 1977). The best analysis, however, is to be found in Johnson, Robert, 'The Penjdeh Crisis and

the absence of Major General Edward Chapman, his mission leaving the following month to return to Kashmir.

Now C-in-C in India, Lord Roberts, however, had no wish to keep Lockhart away from brigade command.[20] Thus, Lockhart next commanded a brigade in Burma from September 1886 to March 1887, for which he received another mention in despatches, and was advanced to Knight Commander of the Bath (KCB) and appointed Companion in the Order of the Star of India (CSI). Upper Burma was annexed in November 1885 but so-called dacoits waged a bitter guerrilla campaign against British occupation. When the designated commander for the pacification effort, Lieutenant General Sir Herbert Macpherson, died in October 1886, Roberts himself took command. Roberts was determined to get Lockhart to Burma although there were more senior officers available and Lockhart received command of the 3rd Brigade in the Burma Field Force, the whole commanded by Major General Sir George White.[21] Lockhart's sector was the Ningyan and Yementhin districts, some eight punitive expeditions being launched by him between October and November 1886. There was some dispute on brigade boundaries between Lockhart and Brigadier General Charles East.[22] Lockhart also proved somewhat impatient of the restrictions placed on him by the Chief Commissioner, Sir Charles Bernard. White cautioned Lockhart that Bernard was obliged to carry out the orders of the Government of India and that Lockhart should take more account both of the public opinion in Britain that was critical of burning villages, and also of the need to protect the villagers against the dacoits who were intimidating them.[23] It foreshadowed some of Lockhart's complaints about political interference in later frontier campaigns.

Lockhart became ill, leading to particular concern on the part of Roberts, who thought his services indispensable.[24] On his return to India, Lockhart briefly commanded a second-class district in Bengal, the new system of first and second-class districts replacing the older divisional and brigade structure. Roberts had considered him initially for a brigade on the eastern frontier but felt Lockhart would prefer to remain closer to the North West Frontier and suggested Lockhart perhaps take the appointment of Colonel on the Staff at Sialkot pending something better. Subsequently, Roberts also considered him as a permanent replacement for Chapman, whose health forced him to resign as QMG in February 1889.[25] In the event, another severe attack of malaria forced Lockhart to go back to Britain to recuperate. Prolonged separation had led to the Lockharts divorcing in 1883 and, on 19 May 1888, Lockhart remarried, his new bride being Mary, the daughter of the late Captain William Eccles. For six months he was employed preparing an account of his diplomatic mission for the India Office and was then appointed Assistant Military Secretary (AMS) for Indian affairs at the Horse Guards in April

---

    Its Impact on the Great Game and the Defence of India, 1885-97', Unpublished PhD, University of Exeter, 1999), pp. 134-39, 147-50.
20 NAM, Roberts Mss, 7101-23-100-1, Roberts to Cambridge, 27 August 1886; ibid., 7101-23-100-4, Roberts to White, 4 July 1886.
21 NAM, Roberts Mss, 7101-23-100-2, Roberts to Harman, 26 July 1889.
22 BL, APAC, White Mss, Eur Mss F108/3, White to Roberts, 11 May 1887.
23 Durand, Sir Mortimer, *The Life of Field Marshal Sir George White* 2 vols. (Edinburgh and London: William Blackwood and Sons, 1915), I, pp. 352-54.
24 NAM, Roberts Mss, 7101-23-100-4, Roberts to Lockhart, 2 February 1887, and 2 May 1887.
25 NAM, Roberts Mss, 7101-23-100-2, Roberts to Lockhart, 29 October 1888; ibid., 7101-23-100-2, Roberts to Cambridge, 1 February 1889; ibid., 7101-23-100-6, Roberts to Chapman, 1 February 1889.

1889, the post entailing advice to the military authorities at Horse Guards on Indian military appointments.

There were three other candidates in Edward Chapman and in Colonels Adam Hogg and Montagu Gerard. Chapman had never performed regimental duty with native troops, Gerard was of no real distinction and it was felt Hogg would attempt to magnify the office so Lockhart seemed the best choice.[26] Neither Roberts nor Lockhart's predecessor as AMS, Sir Charles Brownlow, had expected Lockhart to be interested in the post. Brownlow found Lockhart intelligent and "not likely to go on the rampage to help and advertise himself, which is the fashion of the day." Brownlow, indeed, believed Lockhart was "not an ambitious busy body". Lockhart's manners and appearance would be much in his favour and "when he has seen a good tailor he will do credit to India in those important respects!"[27]

While Roberts would have preferred Lockhart back in India, he believed it was essential that he had someone like Brownlow at Horse Guards with whom he could communicate freely and, through him, to submit his ideas to the Duke of Cambridge without them being seen by his rival, Wolseley, who was now Adjutant General at home, and Sir Henry Brackenbury, head of the War Office Intelligence Department.[28] To his horror, however, Roberts discovered that a memorandum outlining Wolseley and Brackenbury's strategic ideas had swayed Lockhart. This envisaged that any future war against Russia would be waged on the peripheries in the Baltic or the Balkans rather than from India, and that Persia and Ottoman Turkey should be enlisted as allies to facilitate amphibious operations. Roberts professed that Lockhart's apparent conversion made him feel; "rather sick", writing to the Government of India's Foreign Secretary, Sir Mortimer Durand, "I cannot help [being] disappointed in Lockhart being so easily convinced by arguments from the opposition."[29] The memorandum in question was that prepared in August 1889 by Brackenbury and the Military Member on the Indian Home Council, Major General Edward Newmarch. By contrast, Indocentrists such as Roberts and Lockhart's erstwhile best man, MacGregor, who died in 1887, believed that India rendered Britain a great power, that the threat to India was the greatest priority for the British empire, and that it would be in Afghanistan that the decisive battle would be fought against Russia.[30] Lockhart was a fighting soldier first and foremost and there is no particular evidence of deep strategic insights.

Brownlow reported in March 1890, that the Commander-in-Chief, the Duke of Cambridge had only seen Lockhart half a dozen times since he had taken up the post.[31] While this might

---

26   BL, APAC, IOR/L/MIL/7/3723, Memorandum by Allan Johnson, n. d.
27   NAM, Roberts Mss, 7101-23-100-2, Roberts to Brownlow, 6 December 1888; ibid., 7101-23-12, Brownlow to Roberts, 1 February 1889, 1 March 1889, and 29 March 1889.
28   NAM, Roberts Mss, 7101-23-100-2, Roberts to Lockhart, 25 March and 19 July 1889.
29   NAM, Roberts Mss, 7101-23-100-2, Roberts to Lockhart, 30 August 1889; ibid., 7101-23-100-6, Roberts to Durand, 27 August 1889.
30   For the strategic debate generally, see Preston, Adrian, 'Sir Charles MacGregor and the Defence of India, 1857-77', *Historical Journal* 12 (1969), pp. 58-77; idem, 'Frustrated Great Gamesmanship: Sir Garnet Wolseley's Plans for War against Russia, 1873-80', *International History Review* 2 (1980), 239-65; Johnson, Robert 'Russians at the Gates of India? Planning the Defence of India, 1885-1900', *Journal of Military History* 67 (2003), pp. 697-744; Beckett, Ian F. W, 'The Stanhope Memorandum of 1888: A Re-interpretation', *Bulletin of the Institute of Historical Research* 57 (1984), pp. 240-47.
31   NAM, Roberts Mss, 7101-23-12, Brownlow to Roberts, 15 March 1890.

suggest that Lockhart had little impact, he did raise one fundamental issue while AMS that gained Cambridge's support. This related to the continuing problem of the Indian Staff Corps, the abolition of which had been recommended by the Eden Commission in 1879. Introduced in 1861, the system had established separate staff corps for each of the presidential armies, to which all officers serving in staff appointments were transferred in order to create a reserve of qualified staff officers. It had resulted, however, in some officers spending their entire careers in staff rather than regimental duties while others were reluctant to enter directly into the Staff Corps. In 1869 British officers were encouraged to gain language qualifications in order to enter the Staff Corps and, from 1878, the requirement for a candidate for the Staff Corps to have served with a British regiment in India was also abandoned. From 1875 candidates for Indian army commissions had to pass through the Royal Military College, Sandhurst. The Indian army, however, remained under strength in regimental and staff officers, and there was a particular reluctance on the part of British officers to enter the Bombay or Madras Staff Corps. Moreover, in the event of a major war in Europe or outside of India, the flow of British recruits into the Staff Corps would almost certainly cease, as the British army would need all its own officers. Lockhart proposed that officers be recruited directly to the Indian army from Britain not just from Sandhurst but also from the universities, public schools and militia. Cambridge endorsed Lockhart's memorandum, as he believed too many British officers were trying to enter the Bengal Staff Corps at the earliest opportunity, while others destined for the Indian army were trying to stay with British regiments beyond their probationary periods in India. Lockhart's suggestion of recruiting from the militia was accepted and, in 1891, the establishment at Sandhurst was increased so that 20 cadets in every intake would be committed to the Indian army for their whole careers. A consolidated Indian Staff Corps was created in 1892.[32]

Lockhart next received the prestigious command of the Punjab Frontier Force in November 1890, for which he had been strongly recommended by Roberts's successor as Commander-in-Chief, Sir George White, and the Military Member of the Viceroy's Council, who was none other than Sir Henry Brackenbury.[33] Promoted to Major General on 1 September 1891, Lockhart conducted a series of punitive military expeditions, becoming recognised in the process as the army's foremost frontier expert. He led the Miranzai Field Force in January and February 1891, a brigade in the Hazara Field Force under Sir William Elles in March and April 1891, and then led the Miranzai Field Force again from April to June 1891. Lockhart's operations, however, were not without criticism at the highest levels.

The 'forward policy' practised on the frontier between 1876 and 1881, had been revived when the Russians reached Merv in February 1884. For its advocates such as Roberts, the security of British interests demanded extending British authority and control - what Malcolm Yapp has characterised as a 'zone of insulation' - well beyond the Indus in order to confront and defeat

---

32 BL, APAC, IOR/L/MIL/7/2511-2512, Lockhart memorandum, 15 June 1889; Heathcote, T. A., *The Military in British India: The Development of British Land Forces in South Asia, 1600-1947* (Manchester: Manchester University Press, 1995), pp. 173-77.
33 Royal Artillery Museum (hereafter RAM), Brackenbury Mss, MD 1085/1, Brackenbury to White, 31 July 1891 and Brackenbury to Roberts, 3 October 1891; Cambridge University Library, Cambridge Mss, Add 8782/31, Lockhart to Cambridge, 22 December 1891.

all external threats at source.³⁴ Limited 'butcher and bolt' retaliation across the frontier was no substitute for a more permanent military presence, particularly beyond the western approaches to key passes. Tribal violence in itself also suggested a lack of government control on the frontier that, in turn, might easily impact upon opinion in India where the British were dependent on majority acquiescence in British rule.³⁵ It seemed essential, therefore, to demonstrate British military power in tribal areas.

In 1888 Roberts had been incensed by the conduct of the Black Mountain expedition by Major General John McQueen. The Black Mountain tribes - the Hassanzais, Akazais, Parari Saids and Tikariwals - had failed to pay reparations for previous outrages against friendly villages in the British controlled Agror valley, affairs culminating in the deaths of two British officers on patrol in June 1888. McQueen appeared ready within just five days to withdraw and even prepared to inform the more distant tribes that their territory would not be entered by his troops. Roberts considered this, and any premature withdrawal, would have the worst possible effect on the tribes when McQueen had 8-10,000 men available to him. Indeed, continuation was necessary to "teach them such a lesson as will prevent their troubling us again for many years".³⁶ Ultimately, having been ordered to continue his operations, and at a cost of 86 casualties, McQueen effected an agreement on 14 November whereby the tribes paid 14,000 rupees in fines, and promised neither to raid British territory nor to prevent road construction. Roberts decided that McQueen should never again be entrusted with command of an expedition.³⁷

As Roberts had feared, the appearance of weakness in 1888 led to further troubles with the Black Mountain tribes when they opposed road construction in 1890. As a result, a new expedition was mounted in March 1891. It coincided with an expedition in April 1891 to punish the Orakzais of the Miranzai, whose raids across the frontier had increased, and also with the murder of the Chief Commissioner of Assam, his military commander, and three other officers in Manipur on the eastern frontier of India. Lockhart had led the earlier foray into the Miranzai in January 1891 with some 5,000 combatants divided into three columns. Fines had been imposed of the Orakzais, about 20 tribal towers demolished, three fortified posts established on the Samana ridge, and rifles surrendered.³⁸ But Roberts believed that Lockhart had come away prematurely when a more prolonged occupation should have been undertaken. The new Black Mountain expedition would be on a far large scale than that in 1888. In view

---

34 Yapp, Malcolm, 'British Perceptions of the Russian Threat to India', *Modern Asian Studies* 21 (1987), pp. 647-65, at p. 664.
35 Tripodi, Christian, *Edge of Empire: The British Political Officer and Tribal Administration on the North West Frontier, 1877-1947* (Farnham: Ashgate, 2011), pp. 1-20; Beattie, Hugh, 'Negotiations with the Tribes of Waziristan, 1849-1947: The British Experience', *Journal of Imperial and Commonwealth History* 39 (2011), pp. 571-87.
36 NAM, Roberts Mss, 7101-23-100-2, Roberts to Brownlow, 3 November 1888; ibid., 7101-23-100-6, Roberts to McQueen, 18 October 1888. NAM, Roberts Mss, 7101-23-100-6, Roberts to Lyall, 24 October; Roberts to McQueen, 10 and 29 October 1888.
37 NAM, Roberts Mss, 7101-23-98, Roberts to Dufferin, 4 November 1888; ibid., 7101-23-100-6, Adjutant General to McQueen, 1 November 1888; ibid., 7101-23-100-3, Roberts to McQueen, 25 July 1891.
38 Nevill, H. L., *Campaigns on the North West Frontier* (London: John Murray, 1912), pp. 124-26; Intelligence Branch, *Frontier and Overseas Expeditions from India* 6 vols. (Calcutta: Superintendent of Government Printing, 1907-13), *II: North-West Frontier Tribes Between the Kabul and Gumal Rivers* (1908), pp. 228-33.

of Lockhart's perceived failure on the first Miranzai expedition, Roberts decided not to give Lockhart the command of the Hazara Field Force in the Black Mountain expedition, "as I was afraid that, with the prospect of a larger command, he might be induced to hurry over the lesser one".[39] Command of the Black Mountain expedition was given to Major General William Elles, whom Roberts wished to afford an opportunity to demonstrate his military capabilities.[40]

Elles proved far from brilliant and was much criticised in the press but Roberts considered that he was doing his best within the limits of his political instructions, which confined operations to the Akazais and Hassanzais. Lockhart, however, was then despatched as Elles's second in command in March 1891, taking command of a brigade.[41] Elles complained that Lockhart was disputing his authority, to which Roberts responded that Lockhart would have failed in his duty if he did not offer his views:

> He merely suggested "with deference" a change in your plan, and though, of course, these words may have been, as you think they were, used ironically, I notice in his final telegram he says, "whatever you decide you may depend upon my brining up my two battalions to the point and at the time you may direct". As regards Lockhart's manner you can only judge, and I am sorry to hear you thought it "contemptuous". For this there can be no possible excuse. I am the more surprised to hear of it, as I know Lockhart to be a good soldier, and I have seen him behave, under very trying circumstances, with a marked appreciation of discipline.[42]

The second outbreak of the Orakzais, who attacked the outposts on the Samana Ridge in the belief that the establishment of the posts there would lead to annexation, necessitated detaching Lockhart's brigade to the Miranzai. He was instructed to ensure roads and posts were completed before he left Miranzai a second time. Using the reserve brigade from the Hazara Field Force, Lockhart had about 7,400 fighting men. As with the first Miranzai expedition, there was relatively little opposition - Lockhart suffered 28 killed and 73 wounded - and the tribe submitted on 9 May 1891.[43] Even then, however, it was suggested that Lockhart had still rushed Miranzai in order to get back to join the Black Mountain expedition. In the event, while the tribes promised to stop preventing road construction, to pay suitable fines, and to exclude named 'fanatics', within five months the terms had been violated. Lockhart, therefore, was sent to punish the tribes sufficiently heavily for no further expedition to be required. Lockhart's Isazai Field Force - two brigades with 6.250 fighting men - set out on 2 October 1892 and destroyed a number of villages before withdrawing on 11 October.[44]

Whatever Roberts's doubts about Lockhart's tendency to rush, it did not prevent him from intending to further his career. Roberts resolved that Lockhart, as well as Charles Nairne and

---

39   NAM, Roberts Mss, 7010-23-100-3, Roberts to Cambridge, 3 April 1891; ibid., Roberts to Lyall, 14 April 1891; ibid., 7101-23-100-7, Roberts to Lockhart, 8 January 1891.
40   NAM, Roberts Mss, 7101-23-100-7, Roberts to Lockhart, 8 January 1891; Cornwall Record Office, Pole-Carew Mss, CO/F9/4, Nicholson to Pole-Carew, 31 May 1891.
41   NAM, Roberts Mss, 7101-23-100-7, Roberts to Elles, 22 March 1891.
42   NAM, Roberts Mss, 7101-23-100-7, Roberts to Elles, 27 April 1891.
43   Nevill, *Campaigns*, pp. 126-29; *Frontier and Overseas Expeditions*, II, pp. 233-47.
44   Nevill, *Campaigns*, p. 124; *Frontier and Overseas Expeditions from India, Vol. I: Tribes North of the Kabul River* (1907), pp. 188-89.

Robert Low should receive the next three prominent commands that would become vacant. Roberts felt Lucknow might be an appropriate first class district for Lockhart although it would take him away from the frontier but Roberts intended that Lockhart would be made use of when any frontier operation was required. Roberts even contemplated making the Punjab Frontier Force command equivalent to a first class district so that Lockhart could stay at hand.[45]

Lockhart, meanwhile, conducted another expedition, this time into Waziristan against the Mahsuds following an attack in November 1894 on the camp of the commission delineating what became known as the Durand Line to fix the southern frontier of Afghanistan, and which inevitably ran through tribal territory. Lockhart, who had been promoted to Lieutenant General on 1 April 1894 divided his Waziristan Field Force into three brigade columns advancing from Wana, Jandola and Bannu towards respectively Kaniguram, Makin and Raznak. The troops suffered most from the winter weather as there was little real resistance. Indeed, the advance was not unduly delayed by the snow and frost while it prevented the Mahsuds from escaping into the mountains, compelling them to remain in the valleys where they were more vulnerable. The tribes came in to negotiate on 21 January 1895, agreeing to the construction of posts, the security of roads, paying fines, and surrendering weapons. The demarcation of the frontier through Mahsud territory was then successfully completed. Although barely opposed, the expedition was notable for the fact that the 2nd Battalion, The Border Regiment became the first unit to carry the new Lee Metford rifle on active service in India.[46]

It might be noted that some observers felt these 'butcher and bolt' operations largely worthless. Lieutenant General Sir George MacMunn, a prolific writer on the Indian army, who saw service on the frontier as a subaltern during the Tirah campaign suggested punitive expeditions were "by no means deserving of all that the name implies" for they were punitive "in the sense that they would not be undertaken had not the resources of civilisation been exhausted". In other words they were a last resort to counter incursions, murder, and kidnapping if "the invitation to 'Come, let us reason together' had been spurned". Even then, they were "far more humanising than punitive" with the payment of fines and withholding of tribal allowances the most likely outcome. General Sir O'Moore Creagh, who was to be Commander-in-Chief in India between 1911 and 1914, similarly wrote that, as the tribes invariably knew that an expedition was intended, everything of value was removed and all that could be done would be to "destroy the towers, villages, cultivation and fruit trees". However, the amount of money spent by the government paid for the fines levied and also provided ample compensation for damage. Indeed, blockade or exclusion from British territory was likely to be more effective.[47] Such conclusions also beg the question, given the temporary nature of the destruction wrought by punitive operations, as to how far the tribes shared the British perceptions of the value of penetrating tribal territory.

---

45 NAM, Roberts Mss, 7101-23-100-3, Roberts to Stewart, 18 August 1891; ibid,.., Roberts to Cambridge, 14 October 1891; ibid., 7101-23-100-7, Roberts to Brackenbury, 1 October 1891; ibid., Roberts to Lockhart, 5 October 1891; Roberts to Brackenbury, 17 January 1892.
46 Nevill, *Campaigns*, pp. 150-63; *Frontier and Overseas Expeditions*, II, pp. 414-30.
47 MacMunn, Sir George, *The Romance of the Indian Frontiers* (London: Jonathan Cape, 1931), pp. 166-67; Creagh, Sir O'Moore, *The Autobiography of General Sir O'Moore Creagh* (London: Hutchinson, 1924), pp. 143-44.

Lockhart's reward for the Waziristan expedition was elevation to Knight Commander in the Order of India (KCSI), it being felt that the War Office would not favour offering the Knight Grand Cross of the Order of the Bath (GCB).[48] Lockhart's second son by his first marriage, Dennys Blair Lockhart, had died of typhoid while commanding a Sikh detachment of Malay police in November 1891, and Lockhart's nephew, Lieutenant Douglas Lockhart, was accidentally shot dead during the Waziristan expedition in January 1895. Aylmer Haldane, who was Douglas Lockhart's cousin, replaced him as Lockhart's orderly officer.[49]

There had been some consideration given in January 1893 to Lockhart having the Bombay command but, at that point, he was considered too junior as a Major General and, in any case, White believed Lockhart too valuable on the frontier to be sent to Bombay. Roberts, too, felt Lockhart should be kept for the Punjab command, his knowledge of the frontier being constantly stressed. Just as importantly, the tribes respected Lockhart.[50] The Punjab command would be a new one since the long discussed abolition of the three presidential armies of Bengal, Bombay and Madras would be finally effected in 1895 to be replaced by a four corps system with the Punjab Command on an equal footing with the Bengal, Bombay and Madras Commands, each under a Lieutenant General.

Lockhart had to go home ill in May 1894,[51] but was sufficiently recovered to return in August 1894 and to be given the Punjab command from 1 April 1895 despite some fears that he was lacking in experience of dealing with financial matters and administration generally. Lockhart was promoted to General on 9 November 1896.[52]

One issue that was increasingly of significance was Lockhart's connection with Colonel William Nicholson, who was to be a divisive figure throughout his career culminating in his appointment of Chief of the Imperial General Staff from 1908 to 1912.[53] Having been military secretary to Roberts, Nicholson became DAG to Lockhart in the Punjab in July 1895. Nicholson was certainly distrustful of Sir George White, believing him under the influence of Brackenbury. Lockhart and Nicholson keenly felt the preferment of Sir Robert Low for command of the Chitral expedition in 1895. Interestingly, White himself had been prepared to accept Nicholson as Lockhart's DAG because he felt that Colonel St. John Fancourt Michell, who coveted the post, would have been an even more malign influence over Lockhart. The future Field Marshal Lord Methuen suggested in 1897 that Lockhart was "as simple minded

---

48 RAM, Brackenbury Mss, MD 1085/4, Brackenbury to White, 18 April 1895.
49 Haldane, *Soldier's Saga*, pp. 73, 76.
50 BL, Campbell-Bannerman Mss, Add Mss 41221, Kimberley to Campbell-Bannerman, 29 Jan. 1893; NAM, Roberts Mss, 7101-23-90, White to Roberts, 13 January 1893; ibid., 7101-23-100-3, Roberts to White, 21 February 1893; BL, APAC, White Mss, Eur Mss F108/17, White to Lockhart, 12 June 1893; ibid., IOR/L/MIL/7/17039, Bengal Annual Confidential Reports, 15 March 1893.
51 BL, APAC, White Mss, Eur Mss F108/17, White to Lockhart, 15 May and 10 August 1894.
52 Devon County Record Office, Buller Mss, 2065M/SS4/27, Brackenbury to Buller, 7 March 1894; BL, APAC, White Mss, Eur Mss F108/17, White to Buller, 28 February 1894, and White to Gipps, 28 February 1894.
53 See, for example, Beckett, Ian F. W., 'Selection by Disparagement: Lord Esher, the General Staff and the Politics of Command, 1904-14', in David French and Brian Holden Reid (eds), *The British General Staff: Reform and Innovation, 1890-1939* (London: Frank Cass, 2002), pp. 41-56.

as a child". It would appear that Methuen might have meant it in terms of Lockhart's naiveté, which suggests the possibility that he could be swayed by powerful characters like Nicholson.[54]

As White's retirement form the chief command in India came closer, Lockhart seemed the obvious choice as his successor. White had not been as strong an advocate of the forward policy as Roberts and there was not quite the same strategic controversy as in the past. Lockhart's lack of strategic vision, therefore, was not a drawback.[55] Lockhart was upset by press speculation that Sir Charles Mansfield Clarke might be preferred to him. White felt that any appointment of Mansfield Clarke would result in considerable resentment within the Indian army and also warned that Brackenbury might be a candidate, for all that the latter had suggested to Nicholson that it should be Lockhart.[56] Lockhart, however, was the only serious candidate and the Queen formally approved the selection on 30 September 1897.[57]

Lockhart went back home for what was intended as an eight months' furlough in February 1897 in order to take the waters at Bad Nauheim in Germany.[58] He was still there when the frontier erupted in June 1897. Trouble began in the Tochi valley on 10 June with an attack on a military party at Maizar escorting a political officer to collect an unpaid fine levied for a previous murder. The Tochi Field Force was duly dispatched under Major General Corrie Bird to exact suitable punishment, its operations lasting from July to November 1897. But there was then a large scale attack on the garrison of the Malakand on 26 July, necessitating the dispatch of the Malakand Field Force under Brigadier General Sir Bindon Blood, Blood then subsequently leading the Buner Field Force to punish the Bunerwals who had also risen. The Malakand Field Force operated from August to October 1897, and the Buner Field Force in January 1897. In August 1897, the Mohmands also rose, the Mohmand Field Force being entrusted to Brigadier General Edmond Elles and operating from August to September 1897. The Khyber garrison of tribal levies was also attacked on 23 August and overrun on 26 August, and posts were attacked in Kohat, the Kurram valley, and on the Samana Ridge. By far the most serious outbreak, however, was that of the powerful Afridi tribes of the Tirah, who now combined with the Orakzais in late August, the latter apparently largely taking advantage of opportunism.[59]

It is not entirely clear what triggered this unprecedented rising and the apparent combination of tribes usually hostile to each other. Some saw the rising as an inevitable consequence of the revived forward policy. There were also deep suspicions of the involvement of the Afghan

---

54 NAM, Roberts Mss, 7101-23-52, Nicholson to Roberts, 15 April 1895 and 29 April 1895; ibid., 7101-23-90, White to Roberts, 20 February 1895; Miller, Stephen, *Lord Methuen and the British Army: Failure and Redemption in South Africa* (London: Frank Cass, 1999), p. 57.
55 Durand, *Life of White*, I, p. 444; Beckett, Ian F. W., 'Soldiers, the Frontier and the Politics of Command in British India', *Small Wars and Insurgencies* 16 (2005), pp. 280-92.
56 NAM, Roberts Mss, 7101-23-90, White to Roberts, 24 November 1896; ibid., 7101-23-52, Nicholson to Roberts, 5 January 1897 and 16 March 1897.
57 BL, APAC, IOR/L/MIL/7/15516, Haliburton to Godley, 2 September 1897; Godley to Haliburton, 6 September 1897.
58 NAM, Spenser Wilkinson Mss, OTP 13/13, Nicholson to Wilkinson, 15 February 1897.
59 Nevill, *Campaigns*, pp. 209-324 chronicles the entire rising, as does Barthorp, Michael, *The Frontier Ablaze: The North West Frontier Rising, 1897-98* (London: Windrow & Greene, 1996). Two contemporary accounts of the Malakand are Fincastle, Viscount, and Eliott-Lockhart, P. C., *A Frontier Campaign: A Narrative of the Operations of the Malakand and Buner Field Forces, 1897-98* (London: Methuen & Co, 1898); and Churchill, Winston S., *The Story of the Malakand Field Force: An Episode of Frontier War* (London: Longmans & Co, 1898).

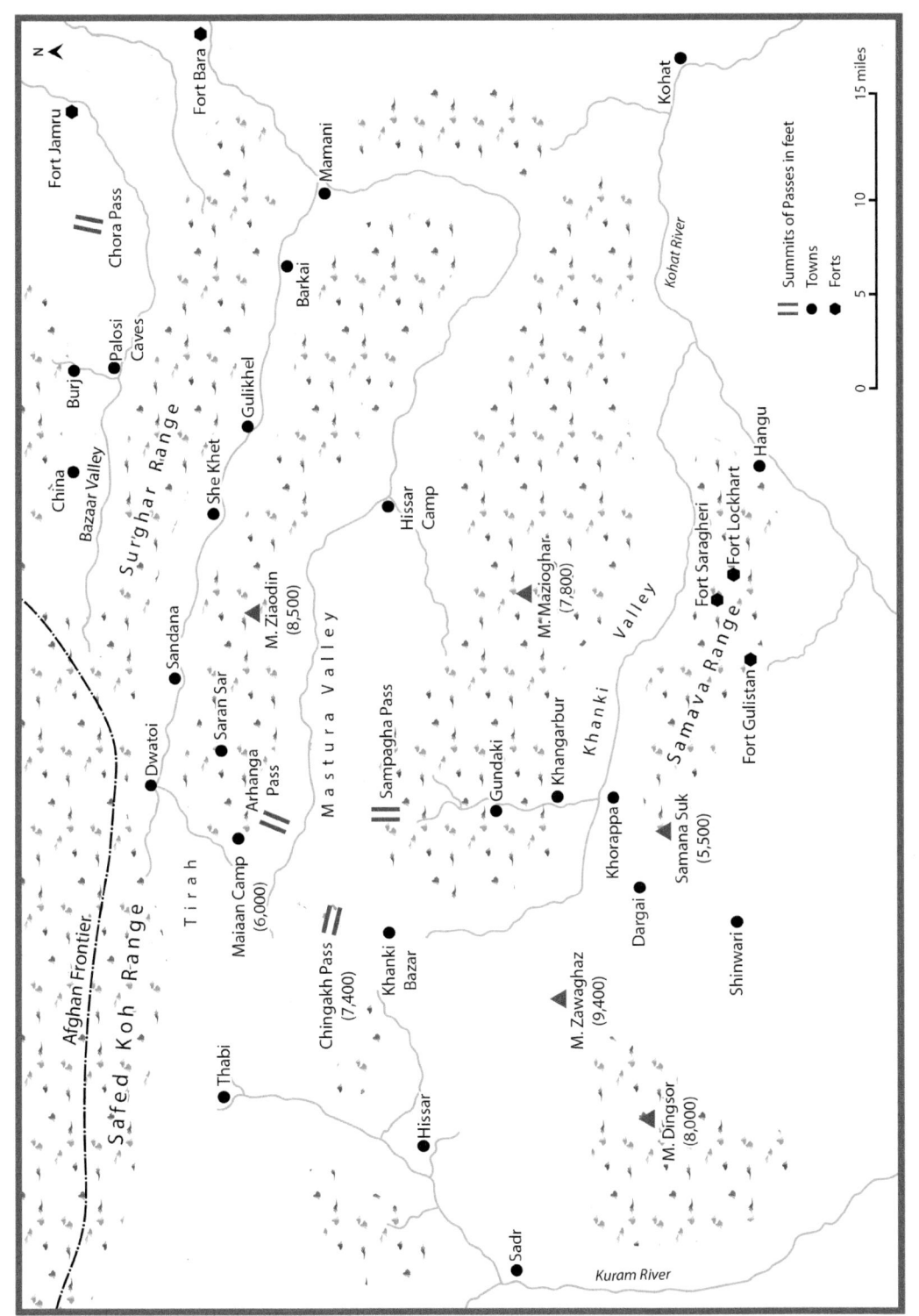

Map 4: Tirah Campaign, September 1897–April 1898.

Amir, Abdur Rahman, who had grown increasingly hostile, and was trying to increase his influence over the tribes although, in the event, he provided no material assistance to them. The apparent evidence of pan-Islamic connection to the rising was also worrying, with various mullahs making capital out of Ottoman successes in the brief Greco-Turkish War. The so-called Fakir of Swat proclaimed a jihad in the Malakand, predicting miraculous events that would sweep the British from tribal territory.[60]

The Tirah would clearly require the greatest effort in view of the potential of the Afridis and Orakzais to bring 40-50,000 men into the field. Apart from Lockhart, Lieutenant General Sir Arthur Power Palmer commanding the Punjab Frontier Force was also away from India.[61] White had little confidence in Lockhart's temporary successor in the Punjab Command, Lieutenant General Sir George Wolseley, the younger brother of Field Marshal Lord Wolseley. Still DAG in the Punjab, Nicholson, was only an ex officio Brigadier General and had no field command experience. Lockhart would take time to return even if he was fit and it would be better, White believed, to allow him to make a full recovery before assuming the chief command in India. Another possible candidate, Major General George Sanford, commanding at Meerut, was also not in the best of health and had applied for home leave from November. Indeed, Sanford turned down the chance to command. Accordingly, White proposed to the Viceroy, Lord Elgin, that he should take personal command in the Tirah.[62] This was rejected.

Lieutenant General Sir Charles Nairne, commanding at Bombay, also offered his services in the event that White was not allowed to go but he had recently badly damaged his arm in a carriage accident and recognised that it was right to recall Lockhart. Nairne commented, however, that Lockhart "is getting stout & easy going tho' he will harry any enemy he may get at". Even after White was refused permission to take the field, Nairne believed erroneously that he still resisted the appointment of Lockhart, and had then wished to appoint Sanford, which astonished him: Nairne had not realised that the offer to Sanford predated the recall of Lockhart.[63]

White wished to appoint Major General William Penn Symons to command the lines of communication but Lockhart did not want him. Colonel (later General Sir) Ian Hamilton, who accompanied Lockhart to India in the hope of participating in the campaign, wrote to his wife that Lockhart disliked Penn Symons.[64] According to Lockhart, however, there was nothing personal in his objection and his judgement rested on his assessment of Penn Symons's military abilities back when commanding a brigade in Waziristan in 1894-95. He recognised Penn Symons's physique, keenness, and devotion to duty but rated him below other district commanders in the Punjab "in the matter of cool judgement & common sense". Nicholson, too, reported that, while he personally recognised the value of both Bindon Blood and Penn

---

60 Surridge, Keith, 'The Ambiguous Amir: Britain, Afghanistan and the 1897 Northwest Frontier Uprising', *Journal of Imperial and Commonwealth History* 36 (2008), pp. 417-34; Tripodi, *Edge of Empire*, pp. 84-89; Johnson, Rob, *The Afghan Way of War: Culture and Pragmatism – A Critical History* (London: Hurst & Co., 2011), pp. 150-71.
61 BL, APAC, White Mss, Mss Eur F108/38, Cambridge to White, 24 September 1897.
62 BL, APAC, White Mss, Eur Mss F108/20, White to Elgin, 27 August and 1 September 1897.
63 BL, APAC, Sam Browne Mss, Mss Eur F486/13, Nairne to Browne, 9 September 1897; National Library of Wales (hereafter NLW), Hills-Johnes of Dolaucothi Mss, L12999, Nairne to Hills-Johnes, 15 October 1897; ibid., L13000, Nairne to Hills-Johnes, no date.
64 Hamilton, General Sir Ian, *Listening for the Drums* (London: Faber & Faber, 1944), p. 232

Symons, he felt they had been given previous service opportunities and other Major Generals commanding districts should have been appointed.[65]

Notwithstanding Lockhart's objections, White decided to appoint Penn Symons to command the 1st Division, and to request the services of Palmer for the lines of communication. Palmer had telegraphed from Hamburg that he was available and had set out before receiving the reply that, at that stage, he was not needed. Based on his services in Burma, and in commanding a brigade in the Tochi Field Force, White believed Penn Symons the most capable British officer available, and it was important that there should be British army representation in command. Consequently, White would not budge from his decision. As Brigadier General P. D. Jeffreys was required to remain in the Malakand, Brigadier General Francis Kempster was brought from Madras to command a brigade in the 2nd Division. Kempster had a good reputation from service with the Egyptian army between 1886 and 1892 and had recently been selected as second in command of the Ashanti expedition of 1895-96.[66] In the event, Lockhart was compelled to acknowledge Penn Symons's success, apologising to White, and saying that Penn Symons was as different as was possible from the man he had known in 1894-95, suggesting Penn Symons had then been suffering from a fall on his head.[67]

The appointment of Penn Symons was not the only clash of wills. As Commander-in-Chief, White reserved the right to select staff for the expedition. He suggested to the Secretary of State at the India Office, however, that he would bear Lockhart's likely preferences in mind in the context of choosing those best fitted. White telegraphed Lockhart - the message reached Lockhart at Port Said - to suggest that Ian Hamilton be appointed chief of staff with Nicholson taking a brigade command as a means of getting Lockhart "out of difficulty" although Nicholson professed not to know what this difficulty might be: it was, of course, Nicholson's perceived influence over Lockhart. Moreover, Hamilton lacked staff experience, and the positions were soon reversed with Hamilton taking the brigade and Nicholson as chief of staff. From Aden, however, Lockhart had telegraphed, in turn, his objection not only to Penn Symons but also to the appointment of AAG of the now Colonel J. K. Ridgway VC, whose boundary commission Lockhart had so disrupted back in 1886. Lockhart wanted Palmer for the division rather than Penn Symons and Michell, who was AAG in the Punjab, rather than Ridgway. If Palmer was not available then Lockhart suggested Sanford, not realising that White had offered Sanford the command of the expeditions as a whole.

As suggested by his earlier preference for even Nicholson over Michell as DAG in the Punjab, White believed Michell self-seeking and that he would make mischief in Lockhart's "ear". White took offence not only at Lockhart's presumption, calling it "disloyal", but also at the wish of the Secretary of State, Lord George Hamilton, that Lockhart get the staff he wanted. White was not prepared to allow Michell to go on the expedition even in the expectation that Nicholson would "sit on him". At least White felt that Captain and Brevet Lieutenant Colonel George Barrow, whom Lockhart suggested if Michell was not available, would be a

---

65 BL, APAC, White Mss, Mss Eur F108/38, Lockhart to White, 30 September 1897; NAM, Roberts Mss, 7101-23-52, Nicholson to Roberts, 14 September 1897.
66 BL, APAC, White Mss, Eur Mss F108/19, White to Lockhart, 27 September and 15 November 1897; ibid., F108/20, White to Elgin, 13 September 1897, and 20 December 1897.
67 BL, APAC, White Mss, Mss Eur F108/38, Lockhart to White, 2 November 1897; ibid., F108/20, White to Elgin, 16 November 1897.

safe pair of hands as AAG and Barrow was duly appointed. Ridgway was appointed AAG on the staff of 2nd Division. White was also anxious that there should not be too many Punjab Frontier Force officers in leading command positions given that Corrie Bird was in the Tochi; Brigadier General Charles Egerton had the 1st Brigade under Bird; and Lockhart, Brigadier General Alfred Gaselee and Brigadier General A. G. Hammond were all appointed to the Tirah expedition, Gaselee taking a brigade in the 1st Division and Hammond commanding the Peshawar Column.[68]

Rather like Bindon Blood, Lockhart usually distrusted political officers. In Waziristan in 1894, for example, in echoes of the situation in Burma, Lockhart had tried to remove Robert Bruce and assume political responsibility himself. The Viceroy, Elgin, had supported Bruce since he believed Lockhart was not prepared to countenance any good in the Mahsuds. By contrast, Lockhart felt Bruce had not pressed the Mahsuds hard enough in negotiations and he was supported by White, who insisted Lockhart have both military and political control. Lockhart also violently disliked the prominent political officer, Colonel Harold Deane, but fortunately he was attached to Blood's Malakand Field Force. White found Lockhart's wish to appoint Colonel Robert Warburton, who had recently retired from his political post in the Khyber, as his adviser in the Tirah as unwise. This was presumably because Warburton shared Lockhart's suspicions of the Afridis and because both Lockhart and Warburton opposed the policies of Sir Richard Udny, the Commissioner at Peshawar, whom they believed had failed to detect the coming trouble in the Khyber. Udny was then made chief political officer, but subordinated to Lockhart, whom Elgin for one felt was not a good judge of political officers' work.[69]

Hamilton and Gaselee were given the brigades in Penn Symons's division while the 2nd Division went to Major General Arthur Yeatman-Biggs, with its brigades under Brigadier General Kempster and Brigadier General Richard Westmacott, who had commanded a brigade in the Mohmand Field Force. A reserve brigade under Brigadier General C. R. Macgregor was assembled at Rawalpindi while separate columns were formed under Brigadier General Hammond at Peshawar and under Colonel W. Hill for the Kurram. In all, Lockhart would have command of some 34,506 combatants in the Tirah Field Force, of whom 11,892 would be British as opposed to Indian troops. There were 19,934 non-combatants, and 42,810 transport animals. It was the largest field force ever yet assembled for a frontier expedition, involving 36 infantry battalions, of which 12 were British.[70]

---

68   NAM, Roberts Mss, 7101-23-52, Nicholson to Roberts, 10 October 1897; Wiltshire and Swindon History Centre (hereafter WSHC), Methuen Mss, 1742/6335, Methuen diary, 27 October to 1 November 1897; BL, APAC, White Mss, Eur Mss F108/20, White to Elgin, 10 and 13 September 1897; ibid., Lockhart to White, 12 September 1897; ibid., F108/986, White to John White, 14 May 1897; Haldane, *Soldier's Saga*, p. 104.
69   Hogben, W. Murray, 'British Civil-Military Relations on the North West Frontier of India', in Adrian Preston and Peter Dennis (eds), *Swords and Covenants* (London: Croom Helm, 1976), pp. 123-46; BL, APAC, White Mss, Eur Mss F108/20, White to Elgin, 13 September 1897.
70   Apart from those general texts by Nevill and Barthorp already indicated, there is also the account in *Frontiers and Overseas Expeditions*, II, pp. 61-117. Contemporary accounts of the operations of the Tirah Field Force are Hutchinson, Colonel H. D., *The Campaign in Tirah, 1897-98: An Account of the Expedition against the Orakzais and Afridis under General Sir William Lockhart based on Letters Contributed to The Times* (London: Macmillan & Co., 1898); James, Lionel, *The Indian Frontier War: Being an Account of the Mohmund and Tirah Expeditions, 1897* (London: William Heinemann, 1898); Shadwell, Leonard, *Lockhart's Advance Through Tirah* (London: W. Thacker & Co, 1898); and Thomsett,

Lockhart left Brindisi for Aden on the steamer, *China*, on 3 September 1897. Ian Hamilton; Aylmer Haldane, who had joined him at Bad Nauheim; and Major General Lord Methuen, who had recently commanded the Home District and now hankered to see the campaign on the frontier, accompanied him. In the event, Lockhart was refused permission to employ Methuen when Lieutenant Colonel C. W. O'Bryen of the 31st Punjab Infantry was killed, because it would set too much of a precedent, and Methuen had to content himself with the role of press censor.[71] On receiving White'e telegram at Port Said, Lockhart consulted Hamilton, who had been White's military secretary, as to some of those White had suggested for brigade command. Aylmer Haldane then despatched the telegram from Aden with Lockhart's demands.[72]

Taking passage from Aden on the *Shannon*, Lockhart reached the concentration point for his force at Kohat on 6 October 1897. While Kohat was some 31 miles away from the nearest railhead at Khushulgarh, it was connected by road, and had the advantage over Peshawar of offering a better-known route into the Tirah. Unfortunately, it did require the collection of the very substantial animal transport. While camels, pack-bullocks and mules were used, many proved to be so-called pack ponies in poor condition and great loss was suffered from poor animal management. MacMunn, serving with the Kashmir Mountain Battery, described the transport as "the sourings of the countryside with dregs of the bazaars in charge".[73]

Lockhart's advance began on 11 October, his plan being for Yeatman-Biggs's 2nd Division to lead from Kohat to Shinawari and into the Khanki valley, over the Sampagha and Arhanga Passes, and through the Mastura valley to reach the strongholds of the Afridis at Bagh and Maidan. Initial progress was slower than Lockhart had hoped.[74] The 1st Division was lagging some 16 miles behind the 2nd Division. Hamilton broke his leg in a fall from his horse on 16 October and had to be replaced by Brigadier General Reginald Hart, VC. On 18 October a reconnaissance of the road to the Khanki valley over the Dargai Ridge was conducted by Westmacott's brigade, which secured it without great difficulty for the loss of just ten men killed and 53 wounded, its Orakzai defenders fleeing. With Yeatman-Biggs unwell, Palmer, who had come up from the lines of communication, had directed the assault. Palmer had accompanied Kempster's brigade, which had been undertaking an outflanking movement, and arrived some two hours later but it was then decided by Lockhart to withdraw to Shinawari some 5,000 feet below. It was reasoned that, with the 1st Division still not at hand, there were not enough troops both to hold Dargai and the lines of communication back to Shinawari; that there was no water available between the two positions; that the men committed to the assault had taken only one's days supplies with them; that the tribesmen would be misled as to the intended axis of advance if Dargai were abandoned; and that further preparation by the 2nd Division of the tracks would deter the tribesmen from re-occupying Dargai. Aylmer Haldane suggested that he had urged on both Lockhart and Nicholson the importance of retaining control of Dargai on 18 October

---

Richard, *With the Peshawar Column, Tirah Expeditionary Force* (London: Digby, Long & Co, 1899). Subsequently, there was the analysis of Callwell, Charles, *Tirah, 1897* (London: Constable & Co, 1911).

71 WSHC, Methuen Mss, 1742/6335, Methuen diary, 2 October 1897; Miller, *Lord Methuen*, p. 57.
72 Hamilton, *Listening for the Drums*, pp. 230-31; Haldane, *Soldier's Saga*, pp. 104-05.
73 MacMunn, *Romance of the Indian Frontiers*, p. 233. See also idem, *Vignettes from Indian Wars* (London: Sampson Low, Marston & Co., 1932), pp. 187-89, 193.
74 BL, APAC, White Mss, Mss Eur F108/38, Lockhart to White, 11 October 1897.

but had been ignored.⁷⁵ Westmacott also queried the order with Palmer but was told to leave Dargai. Dargai was duly re-occupied by Afridis.

To Nicholson, while popular with his men, Westmacott appeared "a regular type of the fossilised Bombay officer" although he performed well throughout the campaign. It became increasingly clear, however, that Yeatman-Biggs was far from well, taking regularly to his tent. Methuen found Yeatman-Biggs full of excitement and energy. He had certainly been looking forward to the campaign after a long period without active service but he had suffered from chronic diarrhoea for at least seven years. Captain (later Field Marshal Lord) William Birdwood, who was Yeatman-Biggs's orderly officer, believed that the complaint when back further to Yeatman-Biggs's service during the Taiping rebellion in China in 1862. By the end of the campaign, Yeatman-Biggs was so weak, Birdwood had to help him into the saddle. White and Lockhart directed Yeatman-Biggs to undergo a medical but the medical officer passed him fit and, therefore, they could not justifiably remove him.⁷⁶

Yeatman-Biggs resumed his command on 19 October. Lockhart, who was back at the post known as Fort Lockhart on the Samana Ridge because it seemed healthier than Shinawari, now wanted Yeatman-Biggs to advance over the Chagru Kotal to Karappa. Yeatman-Biggs replied that to avoid any threat from Dargai he would advance on Karappa by way of another track through Gulistan. Lockhart considered that route was not viable and directed Yeatman-Biggs to conform to the original intended axis of advance. He understood that Yeatman-Biggs would now need to mask Dargai just 1,500 yards from his route but assumed this would be done with artillery. Yeatman-Biggs, however, resolved that he must seize Dargai once more.

Arriving at Yeatman-Biggs's headquarters in the late afternoon of 19 October, George Barrow, Lockhart's AAG, went to see Yeatman-Biggs to point out that Lockhart did not want a frontal assault on Dargai, and to urge that he contact Lockhart. Barrow was then summoned to see Yeatman-Biggs at about 0100 on 20 October and was told that an attack would proceed. Barrow urged Yeatman-Biggs to at least mask the attack with artillery. Yeatman-Biggs acknowledged Barrow's right to state Lockhart's views but was intent on attack. Barrow tried once more, unsuccessfully, to dissuade Yeatman-Biggs at 0400 and did not see him again until 21 October. Major G. H. W. O'Sullivan, the AQMG, later said that Yeatman-Biggs had the spent the day of the attack lying down and was "so seriously ill as to be quite unfitted to command a force in action". By 11 December Methuen was describing Yeatman-Biggs as looking like a corpse.⁷⁷

Kempster's brigade began its assault about 0430 on 20 October but was repulsed from the heights. Yeatman-Biggs ordered another attempt at 1200 and this time the ridge was carried by the 1st Battalion, The Gordon Highlanders. Piper George Findlater famously continued to play the pipes despite being wounded in the neck. In all, 36 men were killed and 159 wounded,

---

75   National Library of Scotland (hereafter NLS), Haldane Mss, MS 20247, Haldane diary, 20 December 1897; ibid., MS 20255, Haldane to his mother, 23 October 1897.
76   NAM, Roberts Mss, 7101-23-52, Nicholson to Roberts, 21 November 1897 and 9 December 1897; WSHC, Methuen Mss, 1742/6335, Methuen diary, 9 October 1897 and 27 October 1897; BL, Hutton Mss, Add Mss 50095, Yeatman-Biggs to Hutton, 26 September 1897; BL, APAC, White Mss, Eur Mss F108/19, White to Wood, 15 February 1898; Birdwood, Field Marshal Lord, *Khaki and Gown: An Autobiography* (London: Ward, Lock & Co, 1941), pp. 82-83
77   BL, APAC, Barrow Mss, Mss Eur E420/27, Barrow to Nicholson, 17 February 1898; ibid., IOR/L/MIL/7/15521, Wood to Wolseley, 4 August 1898; ibid., Barrow Mss, E420/27, O'Sullivan to Barrow, 17 February 1898; WSHC, Methuen Mss, 1742/6335, Methuen diary, 11 December 1897.

an unprecedented loss for frontier warfare.[78] Findlater won the VC, as did an officer of the Sherwood Foresters, a private of the Dorsets, and a private of the Gordons. By the time the heights had been cleared it was too late to continue the advance into the Khanki valley and the troops bivouacked where they were. Further mismanagement then became evident with the track back to Chagru Kotal entirely blocked by baggage animals that had been loaded up in the morning and left there laden all day without forage or water. Consequently, large numbers perished, requiring delays while fresh animals and supplies were brought up.[79]

Following Dargai, White and Lockhart again demanded that Yeatman-Biggs undergo a medical but, once more, the medical officer pronounced him fit, arguing that if Yeatman-Biggs was to be regarded as unfit then so, too, were Lockhart and Palmer. While Palmer was suffering from gout, Lockhart had gone down with fever from a bladder infection. It appeared this had been brought on by the sudden change in temperature. Lockhart had not been sleeping well and had a particularly severe attack of fever on 1 November, and another on 15 December. Some claimed Lockhart confined himself to his tented headquarters enclosure. Drinking only barley water and weak claret, however, Lockhart was always able to ride and, contrary to some reports, was never carried in a dhooli. It was even rumoured falsely that he had been under the influence of quinine.[80]

On 21 October Westmacott's brigade entered the Khanki valley, reconnoitring the Sampagha Pass, and waiting for the 1st Division to close up. Once Lockhart had joined the force for the advance over Sampagha, Yeatman-Biggs lapsed into inactivity, not even making arrangements to prevent sniping of the camp at night.[81] The 1st Division led the assault on the Sampagha Pas on 28 October covered by the largest concentration of mountain artillery ever employed on the frontier. Lockhart also had a rocket battery but it was so erratic that he had it returned to base.[82]

Both divisions then entered the Mastura valley, which had never before been penetrated by Europeans. Hart's brigade remained in the valley while the rest of the force marched over the Arhanga Pass into the Tirah proper on 31 October. The Afridis had not seriously contested the advance since Dargai, dispersing into the hills and side valleys so as to frustrate any British attempt to force a decisive engagement. Ambush of foraging parties and sniping became the main activities against which the troops had to guard. There were over 50 casualties, for example, back at Karappa on 25 October, Penn Symons having neglected to crown the surrounding heights, necessitating hasty improvisation of shelter trenches and walls inside the camp.[83] Maidan was occupied and a reconnaissance made to Bagh, Lockhart's force also collecting much needed supplies. Lockhart avoided wholesale destruction beyond village towers, sending out summonses to tribal leaders to offer terms. On 9 November a reconnaissance was made to the Saran Sar peak in the territory of the Zakka Khel clan of the Afridis, during which the 1st

---

78 Moreman, Tim, *The Army in India and the Development of Frontier Warfare, 1849-1947* (Basingstoke; Palgrave, 1996), p. 59.
79 MacMunn, *Vignettes*, p. 193; Birdwood, *Khaki and Gown*, p. 84.
80 NAM, Roberts Mss, 7101-23-52, Nicholson to Roberts, 20 February 1898; ibid., 7101-23-78, Stewart to Roberts, 18 February 1898; BL, APAC, White Mss, Mss Eur F108/38, Lockhart to White, 2 November 1897; WSHC, Methuen Mss, 1742/6335, Methuen diary, 24 October 1897; NLS, Haldane Mss, MS 20247, Haldane diary, 8 October, 2 November, 15 and 19 December 1897.
81 NLS, Haldane Mss, MS 20247, Haldane diary, 7 November 1897.
82 Moreman, *Army in India*, pp. 60, 80-81.
83 Ibid., pp. 59-60.

Battalion, The Northamptonshire Regiment suffered 22 dead and 30 wounded. The Orakzais signalled their submission to terms on 12 October but the Afridis showed little sign of doing so.

Another foray by Kempster into the Waran valley resulted in a further hard fought rearguard action on 16 November. Two days later Lockhart moved his force to Bagh and reconnoitred the Bara valley, which led back to Peshawar. Lockhart had now authorised wider destruction and, with winter approaching, the evacuation of the Tirah began on 7 December, 1st Division retiring through the Mastura and Waran valleys, and 2nd Division down the Bara. The retreat of the 2nd Division in increasingly bad weather was fiercely contested, much of the burden of rearguard action falling to Westmacott's brigade, which suffered 111 out of the 164 casualties during the retirement.

Kempster, contemptuously referred to by Nicholson as "this Egyptian hero" was far from popular in his brigade, tending to blame his subordinates for his own mistakes.[84] On 11 December Kempster's brigade was to act as rearguard to 2nd Division. Rather than staying out with his rearguard, however, Kempster returned to camp early with his advance guard, suggesting at the very least a lax attitude to his responsibilities to his brigade when 11 companies of the rearguard were still engaged. The difficulties of the rearguard were increased by the premature withdrawal of route picquets that then had to be replaced under fire. Yeatman-Biggs had given Kempster discretion to join Westmacott's brigade or stay where he was as dark fell. Birdwood, sent out with the instructions, suggested to Kempster he should stay where he was but Kempster decided to press on to camp. Kempster was ordered back out the following morning with two battalions to extricate his troops, some 350 of whom - a mixture of Gordons, Dorsets, Punjabis and Ghurkhas - under Major Gordon Downman had been cut off. In all, there were 41 casualties among the troops and over 100 among the camp followers. Lockhart complained to White's military secretary on 15 December that both Yeatman-Biggs and Kempster "seem to think that their responsibility ceases as soon as they have given an order and fail to satisfy themselves that the order is understood and complied with". Reporting officially to the Adjutant General, Gerald Morton, on 1 January 1898, Lockhart concluded that, with 134 baggage animals also lost, Kempster was "seriously to blame for neglecting to regulate the movement of his transport animals and to keep up communication with his rear guard". Kempster claimed that his proper place was with his main body; his brigade was marching as a separate force with its own rearguard; that it was not strongly pressed; and that he had had full confidence in Lieutenant Colonel Mathias of the Gordons who was commanding it. Kempster was not believed and, accordingly, was sent back to Madras. The affair dragged on until March 1898 when Morton indicated that White had rejected Kempster's final appeal.[85]

Lockhart believed that he also needed to visit any remaining Afridi villages, sending the 2nd Division back into the Bara valley on 22 December 1897 and pushing the 1st Division and Peshawar Column through the Khyber to Landi Kotal. White had earlier objected to Lockhart moving the Peshawar column along the Bara valley as it exposed Peshawar when the reserve

---

84 NAM, Roberts Mss, 7101-23-52, Nicholson to Roberts, 10 January 1898, and 20 February 1898; WSHC, Methuen Mss, 1742/6335, Methuen diary, 11 December 1897.
85 NLS, Haldane Mss, MS 20247, Haldane diary, 16 November and 11 December 1897; BL, APAC, White Mss, Eur Mss F108/19, White to Wolseley, 20 January 1898; Birdwood, *Khaki and Gown*, pp. 87-88; NAM, Kempster Mss, 1976-07-37. Official correspondence on the events of 11 December is to be found in BL, APAC, IOR/MIL/7/15892.

brigade was intended for Tochi and the Malakand.[86] It was during the operations in the Khyber that Lieutenant Colonel John Haughton, who had distinguished himself in the rearguard action on 16 November, was killed in another similar action at the Shinkamar Pass on 29 January 1898 when a piquet was mistakenly withdrawn prematurely. In all, Lockhart's campaign had cost 1,150 British and Indian casualties of whom 297 were killed or missing. It had been particularly costly in officer casualties, 27 being killed and 72 wounded, the tribesmen seeking to pick them off.

Given that Yeatman-Biggs was dying - he died on 4 January 1898 - Lockhart's final despatch was diplomatically expressed, merely remarking of Dargai, "I think it necessary to point out that the advance was not conducted in the manner which I had intended and, as I thought, had already indicated."[87] Palmer moved to take command of Yeatman-Biggs's division with Hamilton, now recovered from his broken leg, taking command of the lines of communication. Originally, Hamilton had been slated to replace Westmacott, who had gone down ill but recovered. Then Bindon Blood asked for Hamilton on his lines of communication, only for it to be decided that Hamilton should replace Edmond Elles at Peshawar. Elles would then replace Palmer, who would take over command of the expedition from Lockhart. Lockhart had suggested that Major General Charles Moorsom replace Yeatman-Biggs but Moorsom had not actually seen any field service since the Crimean War when he was an 18-year-old subaltern. Thus, White suggested that Elles be sent since Palmer might be required to take over from Lockhart if he was incapacitated or wished to leave the field early. Lockhart then decided to remain until the very end, so Hamilton replaced Kempster.[88] Effectively, however, the campaign had ended at Shinkamar, although it was a further two months before the Zakka Khel became the last of the Afridis to submit. The overall terms for settlement were a fine of 50,000 rupees and the surrender of 500 breechloaders.

The Tirah campaign was the first occasion on which the British encountered opponents armed with modern rifles, plenty of smokeless ammunition being captured when the Khyber forts were overrun. These were not just Martini Henrys but even Lee Metfords acquired by theft, capture, or illicit trade: by 1898-99 it was calculated that the tribes had access of 49,000 firearms, of which 7,700 were breechloaders. Subsequently, during the campaign, the tribesmen also captured Dum Dum rounds, adding even more to their effectiveness. Moreover, many tribesmen had served previously in the Indian army and were able to instruct others in British tactics and to convey the importance of picking off officers whom they could readily identify.[89] Compared to the experienced force Lockhart had commanded in Waziristan in 1894-95, many of the British regiments allocated to the Tirah campaign lacked frontier experience. Lockhart suggested, for example, that the senior officers in the Northamptonshire Regiment did not understand their work.[90] But then the Northamptons and the 1st Battalion, The Dorset

---

86 WSHC, Methuen Mss, 1742/6335, Methuen diary, 16 October 1897.
87 BL, APAC, L/MIL/7/15521, Lockhart despatch, 21 September1898.
88 Hamilton, *Listening for The Drums*, pp. 234-36; BL, APAC, White Mss, Eur Mss 108/20, White to Elgin, 20 December 1897.
89 Moreman, *Army in India*, pp. 70-71, 79-80; idem, 'The Arms Trade and the North West Frontier Pathan Tribes, 1890-1914', *Journal of Imperial and Commonwealth History* 22 (1994), pp. 187-216
90 Haldane, *Soldier's Saga*, pp. 107-09; BL, APAC, White Mss, Mss Eur F108/38, Lockhart to White, 16 November 1897.

Regiment had never previously served on the North West Frontier. The 2nd Battalion, The Sherwood Foresters (Derbyshire Regiment) had been in India for 15 years but only one or two of its officers had ever crossed the Indus although it had been on the eastern frontier. Lockhart, therefore, did issue some brief notes of guidance on skirmishing in the expedition standing orders on 9 October.

After the mauling of the Dorsets during Kempster's rearguard action on 16 November following on that of 9 November, Lockhart noted that it was "the second occasion on which a British regiment has shown its inexperience of hill warfare, the first during the retirement from the first reconnaissance of the Saran Sar heights, when a proportion of the 1st Battalion, Northamptonshire Regiment, allowed itself to become isolated, entered a deep ravine, and lost heavily in consequence". The enquiry into the earlier action concluded that the troops lacked sufficient training in hill warfare, while both Westmacott and the battalion commanding officer, Lieutenant Colonel Robert Chaytor, had made basic errors. Lockhart recognised that his British units were "at a serious disadvantage when opposed to Afridis, who are experts in guerrilla warfare".[91] It was at this point that Lockhart addressed both battalions and, on 18 November, issued a memorandum of guidance to his troops through Nicholson. Lockhart reminded his men of the skills and local knowledge of their tribal opponents and warned against small parties being cut off. Primarily, Lockhart wished to convey rules for withdrawal. Retirement should be conducted by successive lines and no troops should return to camp without direct orders lest other troops become unsupported. Extended formations should always be used, and artillery employed to cover rearguards withdrawing to their supporting lines.[92]

Generally, it was appreciated that frontal assaults and quarter column advances without cover were not advisable; that more tactical dispersion was required; that marksmanship must be improved; that there must be more consideration of the evacuation of casualties under fire; and that a large weight of fire had to be brought to bear both to cover advances and to stop tribal rushes. It has been suggested that the memorandum had relatively little impact and that it was simply increasing experience that counted most in the improvement of skills towards the end of the campaign. The campaign as a whole, however, revitalised generally the study of hill warfare and training in appropriate tactics. An operational and tactical training manual, *Frontier Warfare* was issued in India for the first time in 1901.[93]

Lockhart certainly appreciated that, on this occasion, there should be no withdrawal from the Tirah until the tribes were subdued and controlled, or they could paralyse any future operations in Afghanistan. He initially opposed burning villages but resorted to this as it appeared the only means available to punish the tribes sufficiently. So many modern rifles were now in the hands of the tribes that any further operations would be even more difficult in the future. It was, however, "the accuracy of the fire, not the number of rifles, that has caused my recent losses".[94]

91 Moreman, *Army in India*, p. 64.
92 *Frontier and Overseas Expeditions*, II, pp. 126-27; BL, APAC, White Mss, Mss Eur F108/38, Nicholson memorandum, 18 November 1897, and Lockhart memorandum, 20 November 1897.
93 Johnson, *Afghan Way of War*, pp. 155-56; Moreman, *Army in India*, p. 65; idem, 'The British and Indian Armies and North-West Frontier Warfare, 1849-1914', *Journal of Imperial and Commonwealth History* 20 (1992), pp. 35-64.
94 BL, APAC, White Mss, Mss Eur F108/38, Lockhart to White, 2 November 1897 and 165 November 1897; ibid., Elgin Mss, Mss Eur F84/71, Lockhart to Elgin, 16 December 1897.

On reflection, Lockhart felt that improved communications were required to prevent further trouble, suggesting the extension of the Indian strategic railway system to Kohat and Bannu in the west and to Landi Kotal and Dargai in the north. He also believed that it would be a mistake to disband the Khyber Rifles or to reduce tribal subsidies. It was not government policy, however, to remain permanently within Afridi territory, Lockhart's idea of a 'cantonment' in tribal territory being too readily equated with annexation.[95]

The great theorist of Victorian small wars, Charles Callwell clearly believed that the campaign had achieved its objective:

> ... to overrun these valleys, and to prove to the formidable tribesmen that whatever might have been their experience in the past, they had now to do with a foe capable of bursting thorough the great mountain barriers in which they put their trust, and of violating the integrity of territory which they believe to be incapable of access by organised troops.....For the enemy had learned that an Anglo-Indian army could force its way into these fastnesses, could seize their crops, destroy their defences, burnt their villages, and could, after making its presence felt in very ravine and nook, get out again; and that settled the matter.[96]

But then Callwell laid great stress on the moral effect of force, having written in 1885, "It is the moral effect of the spectacle of a trained and organised army thrusting itself forward, slowly but surely, into their territory that brings about the downfall of a barbarous or semi-civilised people."[97]

Lockhart himself suggested that no more difficult campaign had been encountered than that of the Tirah:

> Its operations have been carried out in a country destitute of roads, the physical configuration of which is such as to present the maximum of difficulty to the movement of regular troops. The enemy were for the most part skilled marksmen, exceptionally active and well-armed and expert in guerrilla tactics. Whilst avoiding serious resistance to the advance of the troops they have lost no opportunity of harassing both on the march a in bivouac, a system of fighting admirably suited to the nature of the country, and which has necessarily occasioned us considerable loss, not only in action, but also from toil and expense.[98]

But he considered that while the difficulties were formidable, "in none has the punishment inflicted been more exemplary, or the submission more complete." The Afridis even came to see

---

95 BL, APAC, White Mss, Mss Eur F108/42, Memorandum by Lockhart to Cunningham, February 1898, and Lockhart Memorandum, 11 March 1898; ibid., Lansdowne Mss, L(5)47, Roberts to Lansdowne 29 November 1897, and Lansdowne to Roberts, 5 December 1897.
96 Callwell, Charles, *Small Wars: Their Principles and Practice* 3rd edn. (London: HMSO, 1906), p. 39.
97 Callwell, Charles, 'Notes on the Strategy of Our Small Wars', *Minutes of the Proceedings of the Royal Artillery Institution* 12 (1884), pp. 531-52, at p. 420.
98 BL, APAC, IOR/L/MIL/7/15887, Morton to Newmarch, 24 February 1898.

Lockhart off at Peshawar at the end of the campaign in admiration for his fighting qualities, trying to hoist him on their shoulders and to drag his carriage to the station.[99]

From the tribal perspective, while there had been physical destruction of habitation, crops and livestock, they could be restored. They had suffered heavy casualties but, in turn, they had been able to inflict losses on the British and almost certainly regarded the affair as at least an honourable draw. Indeed, many more Pathans now wanted to serve in the Indian army, and this may well explain their warm send off for Lockhart.[100] Arguably, however, the expeditions had the required impact in at least some cases. There was only one other punitive expedition into the Tirah area between 1898 and 1930, this being one against the Zakka Khel Afridis in 1908, although this had a knock on effect in stirring further trouble amongst the Mohmands, against whom another expedition also had to be mounted. There were to be no further expeditions into the Malakand at all. Nonetheless, it was clear that such mobilisation of military effort and expenditure could not be easily countenanced, and that what had been an unprecedented combination of tribes raised significant issues, not least the religious aspect of the rising, and the re-opening of older civil-military divisions in the British response. Accordingly, it resulted in what has been characterised as a 'modified close border' policy in 1901, by which influence was maintained through political officers distributing subsidies and directing tribal levies. Lord Curzon, who became Viceroy in 1899 noted at the end of his tenure in 1905 that his administration had spent only £248,000 on frontier operations compared to the £4.5 million spent between 1894 and 1899, of which the Tirah accounted for £2.4 million.[101]

Terminating his command on 4 April 1898, Lockhart received the thanks of the government and was elevated to GCB. Controversy, however, continued to dog the campaign. Lockhart himself complained that his remark at a volunteer dinner when back in Britain that the Afridis had believed he could take an army into the sky, having forced his way up the Tirah, had been misrepresented as saying it would have been as possible to take Dargai as the sky.[102]

One ground of criticism was that little had been achieved when so many troops had been available. Nicholson pointed out privately to the defence journalist, Henry Spenser Wilkinson, that there were only some 30,000 men rather than the 50,000 the press claimed, and that once troops had been deployed to secure the lines of communication, only 12,000 were actually available for active operations. There had been many rearguard actions but they had caused the enemy great loss. Nicholson also refuted the claims of poor staff work, pointing out that a total of 45 officers in staff roles was not excessive. Moreover, 19 of them had passed the Staff College and 23 more had staff experience: only three staff officers had no war experience and two of them were Staff College graduates. Nor could allowance have been made for Haughton misinterpreting his orders at Shinkamar on 29 January but Lockhart did not feel disposed to

---

99   Hutchinson, *Campaign*, pp. 221, 223; Haldane, *Soldier's Saga*, p. 121; Churchill, *Winston S Churchill*, p. 911; BL, APAC, Barrow Mss, Eur Mss E420/27, Barrow diary, added comment, circa 1920.
100 Johnson, *Afghan Way of War*, p. 171.
101 Beattie, Hugh, *Imperial Frontier: Tribe and State in Waziristan* (Richmond: Curzon, 2002), pp. 190-91; Tripodi, *Edge of Empire*, p. 89; Johnson, *Afghan Way of War*, p. 172.
102 King's College, London (hereafter KCL), Liddell Hart Centre for Military Archives (hereafter LHCMA), Hamilton Mss, 1/2/24, Lockhart to Hamilton, 16 May 1898.

cast aspersions on a dead man. Ironically, just before his death, Haughton had written that things would have gone better generally if Lockhart had been in good health.[103]

The criticism and the evidence of Lockhart's ill-health raises the question of command generally. Clearly, the Tirah was at the upper end of the scale of late Victorian small wars. The largest force put into the field outside of India between the end of the Crimean War and the beginning of the South African War was the 31,394 officers and men despatched to Egypt in 1882, 16,416 being sent from Britain, 7,552 from Mediterranean and garrisons, and 7,426 from the India with an additional 7,315 followers for the Indian contingent.[104] All such campaigns invariably involved overcoming difficulties imposed by climate and terrain, with supply problems a constant, and the need to adapt to the particular enemies encountered. Given the distances involved from centres of authority, field commanders had to be capable of exercising both military and political judgement at a time of increasing domestic media coverage. Irrespective of the interplay of internal politics within the military profession, there were also the complications arising from highly personalised command styles in the absence of an evolving and still improperly understood staff system when so much depended upon the man in command. In the last analysis, improvisation was no substitute for an adequate general staff structure.[105]

Sir Charles Nairne, now acting as Commander-in-Chief between White's departure and Lockhart's arrival, echoed older criticism in suggesting Lockhart had hurried the end of the campaign. The tribesmen may well have carried Lockhart on their shoulders but Nairne felt the tribes had obtained the rifles they surrendered from tribal allies and had paid the fines with money lent them by Afridis in British service. So far as he was concerned, Lockhart had made no arrangements for the repayment for the loss of government and private property and it was clear that not all rifles taken from British and Indian forces had been returned. He put this down to Lockhart being "ill a great part of the time" although he was quite well by the end of the campaign.[106] Nairne also noted that Lockhart's failure to praise any unit involved at Dargai other than the Gordon Highlanders had caused offence. There was also the "unusual friction" that Nairne attributed to Nicholson's influence: "There was too much Nicholson & not enough Lockhart & men in Yeatman-Biggs & Symons' position could not stand it & kept away after the earlier stages & Nicholson made many enemies among the Brigadiers." Nairne felt that since Lockhart's health had been impaired, it left Nicholson to "irritate" the senior generals, and the "independent dash & go of his former expeditions were not apparent in this".[107]

William Birdwood also commented in his later memoir that Nicholson not only lacked actual experience of frontier warfare but also "any faculty for mixing with the fighting men or keeping a finger on the pulse of the troops". Thus, there was little real contact between the headquarters

---

103 NAM, Spenser Wilkinson Mss, OTP 13/13, Nicholson to Wilkinson, 2 March 1898; Yate, A. C., *Lieutenant Colonel John Haughton: A Hero of Tirah - A Memoir* (London: John Murray, 1900), pp. 195, 224.
104 Maurice, J. F., *The Campaign of 1882 in Egypt* (London: HMSO, 1887), pp. 108-11; *Frontier and Overseas Expeditions: Vol. VI Expeditions Overseas* (1911), p. 46.
105 Beckett, Ian F. W., 'Command in the Late Victorian Army', in Gary Sheffield (ed), *Leadership and Command: The Anglo-American Military Experience since 1861* (London: Brasseys, 1997), pp. 37-56.
106 BL, APAC, San Browne Mss, Mss Eur F486/13, Nairne to Browne, 12 May 1898.
107 NAM, Roberts Mss, 7101-23-48, Nairne to Roberts, 29 January 1898; NLW, Hills-Johnes Mss, L13001, Nairne to Hills-Johnes, 9 February 1898.

staff and the troops in the field with correspondence the rule even when units were actually close enough to permit discussion. Birdwood felt that, with Lockhart ill, "there was a notable absence of that confident and happy sprit which is always so important in military operations". He determined that he would never make the same mistake himself, putting this into practice when chief of staff on the Mohmand expedition in 1908.[108] Methuen, who found Nicholson clever but sarcastic, also suggested that Nicholson had effectively been in command when Lockhart was indisposed although this had not resulted in as much anger as supposed for Nicholson had not been quite as rude to Lockhart's subordinate commanders as reported. Methuen felt the real problem had been Nicholson acting both as chief of staff and military secretary.[109]

Nairne also appeared to openly criticise Lockhart. Nairne had attended a lecture at the United Service Institution of India and made comments seemingly in support of Yeatman-Biggs. Both the Commander-in-Chief at the War Office, now Wolseley, and the Adjutant General, Sir Evelyn Wood, felt that Nairne had committed a serious breach of discipline and should be dismissed. Nairne expressed his deep regret, suggesting that he was unaware that Yeatman-Biggs had attacked Dargai against Lockhart's orders and that his comments had related to the method of frontal assault adopted and had not been intended as a reflection on Lockhart. The Secretary of State for War, Lord Lansdowne, recognised that Nairne had breached discipline but agreed with the Secretary of State for India, Lord George Hamilton, that Nairne should only be reprimanded with the comments expunged from the records of the occasion.[110]

Technically, Lockhart was supposed to return to the Punjab command before then assuming the chief command in India. He had taken 90 days' privilege leave, which expired in July 1898, and wanted to prolong his stay in Britain until October. There was also the question of his passage back to India. Normally, this would have been free for a man going out as commander-in-chief but the authorities were not disposed to pay twice, having paid for Lockhart's return in September 1897. Understandably, Lockhart pointed out that he had gone home immediately after the campaign because of ill health "which would in all probability not have been the case had I been able to complete the course of German baths I was undergoing last September instead of giving up a considerable portion of my leave early in that month to command the Tirah Expedition". Somewhat reluctantly, it was agreed that Lockhart had a strong claim and he was given special dispensation on both additional leave and passage allowances.[111] Lockhart was also able to vary the usual arrangements for personal staff. Normally, three ADCs would be taken but, ominously, alongside Captains Aylmer Haldane and C. G. K. Agnew, Lockhart was allowed to take his personal physician, Surgeon Captain William Beyts of the Royal Army Medical Corps.[112] Haldane really wished to get out to the Sudan for Kitchener's campaign and Lockhart seemed willing to do what he could. Lady Lockhart, whom Haldane believed had

---

108 Birdwood, *Khaki and Gown*, pp. 83, 190.
109 WSHC, Methuen Mss, 1742/6335, Methuen diary, 24 September 1897, 2 November 1897, and 21 November 1897.
110 BL, APAC, IOR/L/MIL/7/15521, Wood to Wolseley, 4 August 1898, Wolseley to Haliburton, 4 August 1898, Godley to Haliburton, 5 August 1898, Wood to Nairne, 9 September 18987, and Nairne to Haliburton, 3 November 1898; ibid., Lansdowne Mss, L(5)37, Lansdowne to Wolseley, 22 August 1898; ibid., L(5)28, Lansdowne to Lord George Hamilton, 24 August 1898.
111 BL, APAC, IOR/L/MIL/7/15516, Lockhart to Newmarch, 16 June 1898; ibid., Onslow to Lockhart, 14 July 1898.
112 Ibid., Lockhart to India Office, 8 August 1898.

great influence over her husband, objected and remained disagreeable for some time. Haldane believed this to stem both from his refusal to regard escorting Lady Lockhart's highly capable maid from Wimbledon to Tilbury as part of his duties, and also because Lady Lockhart felt him "rather indispensable" as an ADC.[113]

Having met the Queen prior to his departure, Lockhart finally sailed for India on 12 October 1898, formally taking over command on 4 November 1898. Already before reaching India, he had been consulted on appointments becoming vacant such as the Bombay command. There were three possible candidates in Lieutenant Generals Sir Robert Low and George Sanford, and Major General George Corrie Bird. Lockhart considered Sanford the best choice although this would mean three Royal Engineers in prominent positions, namely Sanford at Bombay, Bindon Blood at Meerut, and Nicholson as Adjutant General. The Secretary of State for War, Lansdowne, initially thought that Nicholson was an officer of the Indian army and that a British officer should be appointed when the Commander-in-Chief was of the Indian army. Lockhart quickly put Lansdowne right on Nicholson's status but he was well aware of the continuing talk about Nicholson's influence over him "but I don't think it matters what people say so long as the best man is selected for such posts or at any rate the man whose selection seems to be the most desirable one".[114] In the event, Lord George Hamilton, preferred Low for the post. Lockhart did get his way, however, in having Major General Gerald Morton removed as Adjutant General and replaced by Nicholson in February 1899. Nairne for one believed Morton badly treated and also felt that Lockhart was inclined to do less and less work himself.[115] As soon as he took over command in South Africa, however, Roberts requested and obtained Nicholson's services as his military secretary.[116] Lockhart also wanted Hamilton for QMG but Hamilton was simultaneously offered the post of Commandant of the School of Musketry at Hythe and opted for that instead even though the salary was considerably less. Lockhart bore no ill will, believing the army would benefit from Hamilton's particular expertise in musketry.[117]

Lockhart had little time to make his mark, falling ill in February 1900. Lockhart took a short sea voyage to try and recover in early March. He then discussed resignation with the Viceroy, Lord Curzon, on 16 March but Curzon decided he should not do so for the present and it was decided that Lockhart should take ship home on 21 March to aid his recovery. In the event, Lockhart died on 18 March 1900 and was buried in the Fort William's military cemetery. Death was certified as from malaria complicating gout. He left a modest £2,737.8s.3d. Subsequently, a monument to Lockhart was erected in Rawalpindi in 1903, and another in St Giles Cathedral, Edinburgh in 1909.

It is difficult to assess how successful a Commander-in-Chief Lockhart might have proven given a complete term and full fitness. One pressing problem since the establishment of the corps scheme in 1895 had been the tension from the increased centralisation inherent in the

---

113 NLS, Haldane Mss, MS 20247. Haldane diary, 20 May 1898, and 20 January 1899; ibid., MS 20257, Churchill to Haldane, 11 August 1898; Haldane, *Soldier's Saga*, pp. 122-23.
114 BL, Lansdowne Mss, L(5)28, Lansdowne to Lockhart, 11 May, and 12 May 1898; ibid., Lockhart to Lansdowne, 12 May 1898; ibid., APAC, IOR/L/MIL/7/15520, Lockhart to Newmarch, 15 July 1898.
115 NAM, Roberts Mss, 7101-23-48, Nairne to Roberts, 18 August 1898.
116 NAM, Roberts Mss, 7101-23-110-1, Roberts to Lockhart, 26 December 1899.
117 Hamilton, *Listening for the Drums*, pp. 240, 267. Lady Lockhart's Visitors Book while her husband was CinC is to be found in BL, APAC, Mss Eur D810.

abolition of the presidential armies. It had led to a growth in the responsibilities and power of the Military Department with the Military Member emerging as something of a rival to the Commander-on-Chief. Nairne had been aware of it but had felt powerless to act in the short period of his acting tenure. White had warned Lockhart of the need to act. Already bored by administration and increasingly ill, Lockhart did not have sufficient time to respond.[118] Originally nominated to officiate during Lockhart's illness, Arthur Power Palmer was never fully confirmed as his successor and continued to officiate for another three and a half years. It took, therefore, the arrival of Kitchener as Commander-in-Chief in November 1902 to fundamentally reform the Indian army's organisation by abolishing the Military Department, as well as to begin to prepare the army for modern war. In the process there was a considerable struggle between Kitchener and Curzon, who was effectively forced out of office. Lockhart had first met Curzon in 1894 and counted him as a personal friend so it is unlikely that there would have been quite such a controversy. On the other hand, it may be doubted whether Lockhart would have undertaken the sweeping reform Kitchener instituted.[119]

Lockhart's greatest campaign was overshadowed by illness as well as dogged by the inexperience of the British regiments involved, and the formidable opposition of tribesmen now equipped with modern breechloaders. It revealed some earlier aspects of Lockhart's character to his detriment in the tendency to clash with the political authorities, and to endeavour to rush results to some extent. It also suggested that, for all his own evident charisma, he did generally defer to stronger willed individuals like Nicholson in what remained a personalised command system. Lockhart, however, did grasp the nature of the changed conditions on the frontier and, doubtless, would have contributed to the renewed emphasis on training for hill warfare. Nonetheless, the Tirah campaign was a success in terms of the requirements by which contemporaries usually judged 'butcher and bolt' operations on the frontier. His all too brief term as Commander-in-Chief allows little real assessment of what might have been.

Despite Arthur Temple's indication of Lockhart's public profile in 1897-98 as a result of the Tirah campaign, and notwithstanding the contemporary adulation for Piper Findlater, Lockhart and the Tirah were soon eclipsed by Kitchener's re-conquest of the Sudan and by the altogether larger conflict in South Africa. But as Lockhart himself had written in the wake of the criticism of his conduct of the Tirah in some quarters, "We live so fast in these days that praise or blame or even ridicule cannot remain in the public memory for more than a few hours."[120]

118 BL, APAC, Sam Browne Mss, Eur Mss F486/13, Nairne to Browne, 12 May 1898; Durand, *Life of White*, I, p. 440; Cornwall Record Office, Pole-Carew Mss, CP/F9/4, Lockhart to Pole-Carew, 1 March 1899.
119 Smith-Dorrien, General Sir Horace, *Memories of Forty-Eight Years' Service* (London: John Murray, 1925), p. 297; Heathcote, *Military in British India*, pp. 180-97; Smith, *Lockhart*, pp. 109-10.
120 KCL, LHCMA, Hamilton Mss, 1/2/24, Lockhart to Hamilton, 16 May 1898.

3

Field Marshal Sir Robert Cornelis Napier, 1st Baron Napier of Magdala (1810-90)

Christopher Brice

Although largely forgotten today Robert Napier was at one time the most respected of British Generals. Before the emergence of Garnet Wolseley and Frederick Roberts, he was the 'go to man' for British politicians. This is seen by the fact that when in the late 1870s war with Russia seemed likely, Napier was temporarily removed from his position as Governor of Gibraltar to be on hand to lead any British expeditionary force deemed necessary. Indeed, part of the reason he had been offered the Governorship of Gibraltar was so that he would be strategically placed to answer any call upon his leadership in Europe, Africa, or India.

His qualifications for such an important campaign against Russia were numerous. He had great experience in military campaigning. Although largely in minor colonial wars, his service during the Mutiny in India in 1857 and his leadership during the Abyssinian Campaign made his name stand out amongst the other candidates. The latter campaign had highlighted his administrative skill, careful logistical preparation and planning, and command capability. The campaign was like so many of the era: the main danger was not the military capability of the enemy but the logistical problems of dealing with the logistical, climatic, and topographical conditions.

As a large part of any force employed against Russia might come from India, Napier's experience in India and as an Indian Army officer would be useful. Just as important as the above qualifications was the fact that he was liked and respected, not only by the politicians of the day, but just as importantly by the Commander-in-Chief of the British Army the Duke of Cambridge, cousin of Queen Victoria.

Although the name of Napier is well known throughout this period of British history, Robert Napier was not a direct relation of the better known members of the family. Charles James Napier the conqueror of the Scind, the historian General William Francis Patrick Napier, Lieutenant General George Thomas Napier, Admiral Sir Charles John Napier, the mathematician John Napier and many others famous were part of the Scottish family the Napier's of Merchiston.

There was certainly a belief that Robert Napier's ancestors had at one point been part of the Scottish family, but exactly where they fit in is unclear. Robert Napier's father was Major Charles Frederick Napier and his grandfather William Napier. William Napier was a Scottish

Field Marshal Robert Napier.

gentleman who claimed to be descended from the Napier's of Merchiston. William had three sons and for some unexplained reason two of them were Christened Charles Frederick Napier. The elder Charles Frederick Napier's was the father of Robert Napier. The confusion was added to when both joined the Royal Navy and served on the active list. At some point the elder brother left the Navy and after passing the examination at Woolwich was commissioned into the Royal Artillery. After service in various garrisons in the British Isles he was appointed to a company of artillery based at Colombo, Ceylon.[1]

In December 1803 he married Catherine Carrington, sister of Sir Edmund Carrington, Chief Justice of Ceylon. Catherine was well connected with high society in Colombo. Most notable amongst her friends was Fredrick North the Governor of Ceylon, later 5th Earl of Guilford and the son of the British Prime Minister Lord North. This connection meant that the Napier's were given use of Frederick North's cottage at Point de Galle. This became a family home before too long. Charles and Catherine already had one son, also called Charles, and two daughters, Angela and Emily, when on 6 December 1810 Catherine gave birth to Robert Napier.

Shortly after his son's birth Major Charles Napier was away campaigning on the Dutch held island of Java. The Dutch had been allies of Napoleon and in 1810 the Netherlands were annexed to the French Empire. As a consequence, a British force from India and Ceylon was readied to capture the economically important island of Java in the Dutch East Indies. A British force of around 12,000 engaged the forces of the island who were upward of 17,000 strong. On 20 April 1811 the British expedition had left Madras on route to Java, arriving in Batavia Bay on the 4 August 1811.

The city of Batavia surrendered four days later, and attention was turned to Wiltevreeden. Although this was taken, Fort Cornelis proved difficult to take and a more prepared assault was

---

1 Napier, H.D, *Field Marshal Lord Napier of Magdala: A Memoir by his son* (London: Edwin Arnold & Co, 1927), pp. 2-3.

required. Unsurprisingly artillery played an important role in the build up to the assault, and Napier was given command of all the artillery. After seven days of bombardment the Fort was attacked and taken.

The elder Napier received much praise for the handling of the artillery. It was in honour of this battle that his son Robert received the middle name of Cornelis.[2] The Christening of Robert Napier had been delayed by just over a year not only due to the absence of his father in Java but also due to a serious illness suffered by his mother. Whilst Mrs Napier recovered, Major Charles Napier also suffered ill-health. In 1812 his health forced him to apply to be invalided back to England. On the evening of the 26 February 1812 Charles Napier and his family embarked for a destination that the invalid Major would never see. On the 21 March 1812 he died on board ship and was buried at sea.[3]

Unsurprisingly the early loss of his father had a dramatic effect on the future of his youngest son. In later years Robert Napier would become extremely proud of his fathers' 'name' and career. Indeed, Robert Napier's son remarked that, '…no fame or honours that came to himself afforded him the same gratification which he felt in a few words of the old Java Despatches.'[4] The death of his father also had a more immediate effect upon his lifestyle. The family had never been wealthy but with the death of the main source of income Mrs Napier was left with few resources and four children to support. On their return to England they lived for a time in Buckinghamshire near to her own family at Missenden Abbey. The elder son Charles was soon to enrol at the Royal Military Academy, Woolwich and the family moved to London to prepare him for the entrance exam.

At this time Robert Napier was sent to stay with Lady Huntingdon and was educated by a Mr Pollard who had a 'school' in Cadogan Place. In effect he was a private tutor, and one can only believe that the money to pay for this came from Catherine's family. By 1819 Robert Napier was sharing a tutor in Woolwich with his brother. Of his schooling Napier would later say, 'I don't think I learnt anything at that school, unless perhaps a little Latin.' Napier would claim that the lessons were too mixed and that with one man trying to teach so much he actually taught very little.[5]

One interesting story from this period tells us something of his nature and points to his future. Napier was said to play 'truant' from school towards the end of the afternoon so that he could go and watch the artillery practice at the nearby barracks at Woolwich. He would stand at the end at which the firing was being aimed and follow the flight and direction of the shot and became able to estimate where the shot would land long before it reached the ground. This was in a sense a practical education in mathematics. It was perhaps at this moment that his career path became clear. In another way it possibly helped him to feel a little closer to the father he had never really known by understanding something of his profession.[6]

A more formal education was acquired for him thanks to the intervention and influence of his uncle Mr George Carrington. The latter obtained for him the promise of a cadetship in the East India Company and in preparation for his entry to the Company's training college at

2   Cornelis is simply the Dutch spelling of Cornelius.
3   Napier, *Napier of Magdala*, pp. 5-6.
4   Napier, *Napier of Magdala*, p. 6.
5   Napier, *Napier of Magdala*, pp. 6-7.
6   Napier, *Napier of Magdala*, p. 7.

Addiscombe, Napier was sent to Hall Place school in Bexley. This school had a reputation as a preparatory school for the military. Again Napier would claim he learnt little from the teachers. However, there was certainly a physical and character building education obtained by the young Napier. Military drill was part of the curriculum under the supervision of a Sergeant from Woolwich.

There was also a physical toughening up of Napier that went beyond drill. There is a story that relates to his dealing with a bully that gives us an early insight into his determination and strength of character. A noted bully, several years older and physically much bigger, had taken to targeting the young Napier. The latter's response had been to challenge him to a fight. In the semi-official bout that followed Napier held his own against the much bigger boy for several rounds, until the fight was stopped as an uneven contest by some of the older schoolboys. Napier gained much credit for his actions.[7]

Napier's reputation at school was as something of a loner, who would spend a great deal of time in private reading. He developed a love of military history particularly of the ancient world and developed a great interest in Julius Caesar. So, whilst he had learnt little from formal education he had developed his own interests and his own skills, all of which were leading to a military career.

On the 4 February 1825 at the age of just fourteen he entered Addiscombe and began his long association with the East India Company. The description of him by his contemporaries as, '...a gay, frank, engaging boy, full of spirit and ever ready for a frolic; with a high sense of honour and good abilities' does not fit with his reputation up to that point. It is likely that Napier had now found his 'home', both in terms of a profession but also in terms of fellowship and community. His own family life had been somewhat disjointed. This was not helped when around this time his mother moved to Belgium, partly for reasons of economy but also for the education of her daughters.[8]

After two years at Addiscombe Napier was ready to leave and he wished to join the Royal Artillery. However, his uncle George Carrington persuaded him to stay on for an extra term and take the exam for the Engineers. His motivation for this is unclear. It may be that Carrington was looking beyond a military career believing that a good engineer would be in high demand in India both for civil and military projects, a fact that Napier's career would bear out.

Carrington's argument won out and in December 1826 Napier took the engineers exam. During the winter holidays he spent much of his time with a private tutor developing his knowledge and understanding of mathematics. His engineering skills were then developed through a year of study at the Royal School of Military Engineering at Chatham, which he entered on the 7 June 1827 as a Gentleman Cadet with the temporary rank of Ensign.

Napier certainly benefited from this year at Chatham and learnt a great deal. The presence of a number of Peninsular War veterans amongst the teaching and instructing staff who had practical experience of military engineering was something that Napier found particularly helpful. He would always look back at his time at Chatham fondly and later remarked, 'I always feel a deep obligation to our old Chatham School, to (Lieutenant Colonel) Pasley and our senior officers who inculcated such a high standard of the duty of an engineer, whether official

---

7 Napier, *Napier of Magdala*, p. 8.
8 Napier, *Napier of Magdala*, pp. 10-11.

or private'.⁹ It is interesting to hear him speak so well of Lieutenant Colonel Pasley, who was generally not popular with cadets.¹⁰ This is an early indication that Napier was able to see past personal differences to respect and appreciate the talent of an individual.

If Napier was modelling himself on Palsey, then he had picked a good role model. A story is told which perhaps illustrates why Pasley was not fondly thought of by his students but also shows us that Napier learnt an important lesson early on. In his studies Napier was asked to prepare plans for an operation connected with a theoretical siege of Paris. Napier worked extremely hard and completed plans in great detail which were submitted to Pasley. They were returned to a surprised Napier who was informed that they needed correction. Napier double checked his calculations and could find no fault, and asked Pasley to explain where the error lay. Pasley replied that he had forgotten to mention the needle and thread necessary to secure the hose with powder to ignite the mines under the enemy's defensive works! Although this sounds a somewhat pedantic objection it speaks to the thoroughness of Pasley and the lesson was taken on board by Napier. Indeed, Napier would later use the phrase "It is all a question of the needle and thread" when talking about the importance of attention to detail.¹¹

Although he may have been a reluctant convert to engineering, Napier had soon found not only a liking but a great talent for it. As he would remark to his brother some years later:

> I do not think any position really higher than that of an engineer who, amid the unknown dangers of the dark night, or in the face of contending combatants by day, exercises a calm judgement and walks in the presence of death with a calm and steady courage under the consciousness that on his skill and judgement depend the fate of thousands, or the issue of a campaign.¹²

Whilst his skills could be put to good use for civilian purpose it is clear from Napier's comments that he clearly saw himself as a 'military' engineer. It is difficult to say definitively that he saw himself as a soldier first and an engineer second. His conduct in future operations would suggest this, particularly during the First Sikh War when there was little use for his skills as an engineer and he performed the duties of a staff officer. Yet this should not in any way be seen to belittle his skills as an engineer, as his future career would prove.

Following his year at Chatham he was commissioned into the Bengal Engineers (at this time still called the Bengal Sappers and Miners) with the rank of Lieutenant and departed for India towards the end of the year. It was on the 8 November 1828 that Napier landed in Calcutta and started a long and fruitful connection with India. After a few weeks in Calcutta, he moved up country to Aligarh to the headquarters of the Bengal Sappers and Miners. Even in these early days as he travelled up country, Napier was taken with India. This can be partly put down to the fact that he was a young man of almost eighteen who was visiting a new and exotic country for the first time. However, there was also a sense in which he already appreciated that this was

---

9   Napier, *Napier of Magdala*, p. 12.
10 Lieutenant Colonel, later General Sir, Charles William Pasley was a highly intelligent and accomplished engineer who had founded the School of Engineering at Chatham. He had seen considerable active service during the Napoleonic Wars and was a great writer on military engineering.
11 Napier, *Napier of Magdala*, p. 12.
12 Napier, *Napier of Magdala*, p. 13.

a land of opportunity. As he travelled along the rudimentary transport system of the country Napier could see that there was much to which his skills as an engineer could be put to good use.

In June 1829 Napier received his first command that of a company of the 1st Bengal Sappers then stationed at Delhi. Napier had already started to embrace the culture, history, heritage, architecture, and language of this new land. The latter point of language is particularly interesting as he was the only one of the new officers arrived from Calcutta who had troubled himself to learn any of the local languages. By speaking, at least in part, the local languages he was able to communicate better with the men under his command but also the local inhabitants. For many officers of this era this was something they had no intention of doing and the failure of officers to understand and communicate with their men would play an important role in the outbreak of the Great Mutiny of 1857. Napier had also been greatly impressed by the Mughal architecture he had seen on his journey through India. By speaking local languages, he was able to learn much about the construction and techniques of building that had been used successful in India in the past.

Napier set down to his work with a determination that was often lacking in the officers of the East India Company during this period. In the early months of his command, he smartened the men up, forbade irregular dress that had been allowed to creep in, had set aside one day each week for drill, and another for target practice. The fact that Napier had to reintroduce such practice points to the poor order in which he found the company. In the early days he met resistance from the men, which Napier countered with quite severe punishment. However, once his authority had been affirmed and the boundaries clearly marked, his men grew to respect and admire him. It was not just the men that were in a bad state, as Napier found that the company accounts and rolls were woefully out of date.[13]

In early 1830 Napier suffered an attack of pleurisy and had a bad fever. In April of that year he was able to obtain sick leave and visited the hills station at Mussoorie to recover. Even in his convalescence he continued to learn and explore his surroundings, becoming fascinated with the flora and fauna, which had particularly fascination being on the edge of the Himalayas. Once recovered Napier returned to Delhi and remained there until March 1831.

At this point he transferred to the Canal Department, a highly sort after appointment. Given the poor nature of the roads the canals were an important source of transportation. On his first journey to Delhi, Napier had formed a friendship with Lieutenant Proby Cautley, an artillery officer serving with the Canal Department.[14] The friendship was renewed, quite by chance, during Napier's period of recovery at Mussoorie. It was therefore no coincidence that when appointed to the Doab Canal, sometimes called the Eastern Yamuna canal, he was under the command of Lieutenant Cautley. In so doing he had taken a place also sought after by Henry Lawrence a man who was well connected and who would gain fame as an agent on the North West Frontier and die whilst leading the defence of Lucknow in 1857. Despite this Napier and Lawrence began a friendship that would last until the latter's death.

---

13 Napier, *Napier of Magdala*, p. 14.
14 Cautley, later Sir Proby Thomas Cautley, would play an important part in the reconstruction of the Doab Canal but is perhaps best remembered for his role in the construction of the Ganges canal. Although an officer in the East India Company he would spend most of his career attached to civil engineering and would build a substantial career in that direction after leaving the Company. His career was perhaps an example of what Napier's could have been had events turned out differently.

The Doab Canal of Mughal construction dates back to around 1657, although the use of the river for transportation goes back to antiquity. The canal had by the 1820s fallen in to disrepair and it was its reconstruction that Captain Robert Smith and Cautley had been tasked with completing. It was formally reopened in late 1830 after which Smith returned home and Cautley was promoted superintendent of the canal, now with Napier as his assistant. There was much to do as when the canal had been opened it became clear that the ferocity of the water had not been properly calculated and thus many of the bridges were either unstable or had been washed away completely.

There was a continual fight against the build-up of silt and the uneven nature of the canal bed. This was temporarily solved by raising the river bank, whilst attempts were made to level off the canal bed to a uniform level so as to overcome the problems. This intriguing and intricate work was an interesting practical test of Napier's engineering knowledge and skills. Only four months into his time as assistant Napier found himself in temporary charge during Cautley's leave of absence. It was during his temporary tenure of command that the Mas Kura dam was flooded and Napier found himself having to deal with the consequences of a flood surge along the Doab Canal.

His ingenuity was not found wanting as he invented a new means of fighting the flood waters that would become the standard defence for many years to come. This involved the use of large crates loaded with brunt bricks, exactly what made Napier think of this is unknown but it was proof of his skill and ingenuity as an engineer. Later in the year Napier was given the independent task of overseeing the building of mills at a point along the canal. Although completely without experience in this regard he performed admirably in his task so much so that many years later Cautley would write of these mills that, "The buildings are perfect, they were constructed under the immediate eye of Lieutenant Robert Napier, of the Engineers, in 1831-32, and are, in my opinion, amongst the best of the canal works".[15]

Napier spent five years working at the Doab Canal and he learnt much by working under such a talented officer as Cautley who helped to develop not only his professional skills but his interest in architecture, geology, botany, and even palaeontology. Napier developed affection for him and would in later years recall the important part he had played in his development in his profession by calling him "My Master". It was demanding and tiring work that had an effect upon Napier's general health. During the five years he took no leave and despite his religious convictions was known to often work Sundays. Despite this Napier also found time to improve his Hindustani and even acquire a little of the Persian language.

His time on the Doab Canal came to an end in 1835 due to illness. In April and May, two of the hottest months of that year, he undertook some surveying work which had required him being exposed to the sun too much and as a consequence he became ill. This time sick leave at a hill station did not do the job and he was forced by the end 1835 to apply for three years furlough. It was in April 1836 that he started the long sea voyage back to England. The six month voyage aided his recovery. So much so that when the ship's purser died Napier volunteered to fill in, an offer which the ship's Captain gladly accepted. He even helped to nurse the ship's doctor when he fell ill with 'brain fever'. The doctor's illness required them to make a longer stay in Cape Town than was normal. During his short stay at the Cape, Napier was asked to act as a second

---

15 Napier, *Napier of Magdala*, p. 20.

for an artillery officer in a duel with an officer of one of the ships in the harbour. Napier did not name the officers in his account but told how he accepted the position of second determined to prevent the duel by forcing the two officers to meet and discuss the matter, with Napier acting as an impartial judge having no connection to either man. As a consequence, there was no duel.

After a short stay in England, he travelled to Belgium to visit his mother. He stayed in Belgium until the end of the year 1836, and developed friendships with many officers in the newly formed Belgium Army. In early 1837 he visited his brother who was stationed with the Rifle Brigade at Dover. During this period he made the acquaintance of both Isambard Kingdom Brunel and George Stephenson. By the summer he was back in Belgium where he took great interest in the canal system. He continued to learn, not simply of canal systems, but also architecture, history, military science including accounts of the recent siege of Antwerp, geology, chess, and even learnt to speak a little Italian.

Shortly before his return to India in 1838 Napier met a young lady called Anne Pearse, a friend of his sister Emily and the daughter of Dr George Pearse, Inspector General of Hospitals in Madras. Napier fell in love with her and after an eighteen month association wished to marry her. However, the match was not initially approved of by her parents. After a period of two months they approved, somewhat grudgingly, to the marriage. This was on condition that Napier obtained a suitable position in India from which he could support his new wife.

This he obtained through Captain Henry De Bude (sometimes spelt Debude) an officer in the Bengal Engineers whom Napier had briefly assisted in surveying the defences of Aligarh when he first arrived in India. De Bude, now Superintending Engineer in the Public Works office, helped Napier obtain the position of Acting Executive Engineer of the Barisal administrative division of Eastern Bengal, making Napier responsible for all the public buildings in the region. Despite the important nature of the post covering such a vast area with the important river of the Ganges flowing through much of it, Napier was unable to find out many details about the area or his responsibilities. Indeed, Napier later claimed that nobody in Calcutta could even tell him where the office for this area of responsibility actual was.

In late June of 1839 he received orders to go to Darjeeling to be assistant superintendent responsible for clearing a dense forest and to then build roads in preparation for a new settlement. His task was a difficult one. The new settlement was around 7,000 feet above the plains and Napier's task was to initiate communication between the two before laying out the new settlement. He had no staff to assist him and Napier, at his own expense, hired a group of locals who he gave basic tuition in measuring and who were also employed to carry his equipment. The leader of this group employed by Napier was not a native Hindustani speaker, neither were the others, but he knew enough to converse with Napier whose knowledge of the language had increased. The unit he raised to assist him during this period would later become the Sebundy Sappers and Miners and a regiment in the Bengal Army.

This period in rough conditions, relying on tea and sardines to sustain him, with little in the way of comfort was good training for the life of a soldier on campaign and stood him in good stead in the years to come. The cold at night was a particular problem, as were the strong winds. As Napier himself recalled, 'When you pitched your tent at night, you never knew but a tree would come down and make an end of you on the spot.'

In the late summer of 1840 he obtained his first leave. The strain had already taken its toll and on the journey to Calcutta he fell ill with what was described as 'jungle fever'. For over a month he was in a very serious state and considered close to death. A curious turn of fortune was to be credited with saving his life. The decision had been taken to transport him from Calcutta to Madras. On the journey the ship was becalmed, and it took thirty days to reach Madras. A doctor later told Napier that it was this sea voyage, with the notable change in temperature and near total rest that saved his life. The Doctor was convinced that had it not been for this that Napier would surely have died.

On the 3 September 1840 Napier was sufficiently recovered to finally marry his fiancée. After a brief honeymoon in Madras the newly married couple set out for Darjeeling so that Napier could resume his work. During his absence from Darjeeling a house had been constructed for him in anticipation of the married couple's arrival. In late November they arrived in Darjeeling and whilst Napier continued with his hard work his life certainly benefitted from wedded bliss. Although it might sound unkind to Mrs Napier, the added distraction of a wife was what Napier needed. Although he in no way neglected his work it gave him other responsibilities which meant that he took much needed breaks from his work.

On the 14 October 1841 Mrs Napier gave birth to their first child who was named Catherine after his mother. Around the same time Napier was appointed Executive Engineer of the Sirhind administrative division in the Punjab. However, the authorities in Calcutta had been so impressed with Napier's work and were reluctant to lose him during the completion of the new settlement at Darjeeling that they successfully appealed to the Government of India to defer Napier's transfer until the autumn of 1842. Upon his leaving an unnamed individual in the Calcutta government remarked, 'It has so frequently been my duty to report on the value of the services done by Captain Napier while he was employed here, that I have nothing now to add farther than that the completion of his roads especially, and of his other works generally, is very much to the credit of the zealous and able character he has held.'[16]

The journey to Umballa (modern day Ambala) was a long and difficult one. Without extensive roads or the advent of the railways the waterways were almost the only way to travel and thus the Napier's set sail in September 1842 on their journey to Umballa. During the journey they had to abandon their ship one night during a severe storm that threatened to sink them. Napier and his family managed to get ashore barefooted and still in their night attire. Although many other ships in the vicinity were sunk theirs survived and they were able to continue their journey.

Napier's task on arrival was to oversee the construction of new barracks and a complete cantonment designed largely for troops returning from the indecisive First Afghan War. Existing barracks were cramped and insanitary. Indeed, it was the high mortality rate amongst the troops in existing barracks that prompted the decision to build a new cantonment. Napier had no experience of such work but had rather sensibly, and on his own initiative, visited every cantonment and barracks he could find as he travelled along the route to Umballa. This convinced Napier that the main reason for the build-up of disease was the close proximity of barracks to one another and a lack of space for 'clean air' to move between the buildings.

On his arrival at Umballa he found a suitable site lying between two rivers some 4 miles from the town. The rivers were not close enough to present a problem in terms of flooding but provided fresh water and a cool breeze. Napier also selected a site that was some 25 square miles in size. The barracks were laid out in 'echelons'. Both factors helped to allow plenty of air and created a less crowded and oppressive atmosphere in the cantonment. In the words of the noted

---

16 Napier had been appointed Captain on the 25 January 1841,

soldier and writer General Sir George Chesney 'The wide roads and spacious gardens and the lofty barracks of Umballa constituted the beginning of a new epoch in the structure of Indian Cantonments.' So successful was the design that in future years the 'Napier System' became the standard layout. Considering that Napier had never worked on such a project before it is testament not only to his skill as an engineer but his thoughtful, considered, and intelligent approach to the task at hand.

In later years, as we shall see, Napier would return to this subject when economy threatened to overrule experience. Writing in 1890 Chesney would further remark that, '…while the Napier barrack for the British soldier was cited in those days as a patent example of the innate extravagance of the engineer. It is now (writing in 1890) recognised to be in reality of a most economical kind.'[17] This was because it allowed for greater efficiency, fewer invalid soldiers, and as a consequence saved a great deal of money elsewhere. Napier had made a significant contribution to the improvement of the lot of the private soldier but also the efficiency of the army. The free hand he was given is not only testament to his reputation as an engineer but a sign that he was starting to be appreciated further afield. After the completion of the cantonment, Lord Ellenborough, the Governor-General, visited the area to inspect the new construction. To Napier he expressed his approval and his appreciation of what he had achieved.

We know that at this point Napier was continuing to press himself hard. His wife recorded that during this period he looked, '…very thin and sunburnt.'[18] He would get up at first light and work until 2200hrs, only stopping for meals. In a climate that was not conducive to the health of 'Europeans' this would have been a great ordeal. He was again suffering with his eyes, no doubt due to the continual exposure to strong sunlight.

Although he had become successful Napier was frustrated that he was becoming largely a civil employee rather than a military one. This is why in 1843 he jumped at the opportunity for active service when disturbances in Khythul led to the despatch of a force of around 4,000 men. Napier played an important part, as an engineer, in securing the route. However, there was to be no fighting, which added to Napier's frustration. It is a constant problem for the civilian mind to understand the desire of the soldier to see action. Yet for the most part it is simply a desire to test themselves in their chosen profession. Occasionally there is a desire for danger and excitement but often it is simply the desire to do what they have been trained to do. In Napier's case it was also a desire to remind people that he was a soldier first and an engineer second.

It was also a good means to career advancement. Whilst successfully building settlements, roads, canals, and cantonments would gain him the appreciation of his superiors and further employment, it did not advance him in rank to anywhere near the extent that a 'good' campaign could. Napier knew this and despite the fact that he had a wife and now three children he wanted to take the field.

The opportunity for active service would come quite soon. In December 1845 war broke out between the Sikh Empire and British India. Napier had received the assurance of Major Patrick Grant Deputy Adjutant General of the Army that if the Sikhs crossed the Sutlej River, into territory that was under British protection, that Napier would be ordered to join the army. Such was Napier's frustration that he had decided that if the order did not come he would resign from

17   Napier, *Napier of Magdala*, p. 35.
18   Napier, *Napier of Magdala*, p. 36.

the army. Fortunately, the order did come and two days after the outbreak of war on the 14 December 1845 Napier set out on the 150 mile journey to join the Army under the command of General Sir Hugh Gough gathering at Mudki.

The details of British preparations are beyond the scope of our narrative; suffice it to say they had not been ideal. Sir Henry Hardinge, now Governor General, had wanted to avoid conflict with the Sikhs. As a consequence he had overruled Gough, the Commander-in-Chief, and prevented many of his preparations before the conflict. As a result heavy artillery, a field hospital, extra 'European' troops, and numerous supplies of food and ammunition had been stopped from moving forward before the conflict. Once war broke out much of this was immediately ordered to resume their journey, but precious time had been lost. It was therefore a rather hurried and ill-conceived advance that brought the army to Mudki. Whilst Hardinge's interference had hindered plans, they had not been helped by Gough. The latter was an incredibly brave and courageous soldier but lacked as an administrator and organiser. He was also poorly served by his staff.

It is also important to recognise that this was no ordinary 'native' army that they were facing. The Sikhs had become a 'warrior race' and had benefited greatly from the influence of 'European' officers in the development of their military machine. Indeed, in some circumstances Sikh equipment was superior to that of the British, most notably in their field artillery, and the quality of Sikh gunners often surpassed that of their British counterparts. Thus the Sikhs were to prove to be one of the hardest opponents that the British ever had to face during the colonial era.

Napier left us a very intriguing narrative of the conflict, which is seldom used.[19] In it he is very candid about the strengths and weaknesses of the various senior figures he came into contact with. Napier joined the army near Mudki on the 18 December 1845 on the eve of battle and offered his service to Major General Gilbert, a division commander who Napier technically fell under the command of due to his appointment at Umballa. Napier's offer of service to Gilbert was rather bluntly refused by his Adjutant with the words that, '…this was not the time when engineers were wanted.'[20] Whilst Napier could appreciate the accuracy of the statement it did not help him. However, Napier recalled that the exact words of his order were to report to Major Grant, the Deputy Adjutant General. Thus Napier reported to Grant who informed Gough, and Napier was appointed to the staff of the Commander in Chief.

With the Sikhs advancing battle was imminent and Gough decided to move to attack them rather than wait for their arrival. In what was to become known as the Battle of Mudki Gough was concerned that the left flank of his army was lagging behind the rest of his army by stating, '…someone desire them to take up more ground.' Napier responded to this and was given direct orders by Gough and instruction on where he wanted the left wing of his army to move. In attempting this Napier was attacked by enemy cavalry who opened fire on him killing his horse. Napier managed to make it to a nearby British battery but had to leave his horse saddle and

---

19 Robert Napier, *Personal Narrative written shortly after the Actions of Moodkee and Feroze-shuhur* (Hertford: Privately Printed, 1873). A copy of this very interesting source on the First Anglo-Sikh War can be found in the British Library.
20 Napier, *Personal Narrative*, p. 4.

many of his belonging behind him which were almost immediately plundered by the enemy cavalry.[21]

Napier attempted to continue his mission on foot. In so doing he was found by his servant, Shehab Khan, who had attempted to follow him. Khan insisted that Napier take his rather tired horse to continue his mission. By the time Napier arrived on the left, Major Grant had already arrived in person to attempt to bring order to the situation which had been exacerbated by the death of many senior officers to Sikh marksmen.

Seeing that Grant had the movement of the army under control Napier decided that he could be of more use helping the wounded officers to reach the rear, and it was in this task that he was occupied when they were attacked by Sikh horse artillery. Napier records that at first it was presumed that they were British, as the horses and uniforms of the men '…were so like our own.'[22] The volley fire from the 31st Regiment organised by Grant forced them to withdraw. However during the firing Grant was hit, as was his horse and Napier rode to his rescue. Grant collapsed and Napier arranged to have him carried to the rear. The regiments had now formed square to meet a reported movement of enemy cavalry in the area. Napier decided to attempt to find Gough, both to inform him of Grant's injury, and to see if he could be of assistance. However in the gathering gloom he found this impossible to do and realising that to attempt this further was both useless and dangerous he joined the 50th Regiment. From here he watched the remainder of the battle.

Later that evening the troops returned to camp. Napier having lost his kit was able to share with Captain Garvoch, and a Lieutenant Tritton who was on outpost duty and lent him his bed. At the same time Napier lent his horse, or more accurately his servants' horse, to assist in bringing the numerous wounded from the field. This had the consequence that the following day his horse was in no state to move and was on the point of dying from exhaustion. Napier managed to borrow a 'pony' from Captain Rawson and eventually re-joined Gough.

On the morning of the 19 November Napier watched with amazement '…a scene which I hope never again to witness. Orders were given by the C in C; counter orders by the Governor General. Troops were told to go to their lines to cook, then to stand fast, then to cook.'[23] The problem was differing reports as regard the movement of the Sikhs. The already difficult relationship between Gough and Hardinge was exacerbated by the issue of command. Hardinge was not only Governor General, and therefore had ultimately responsibility, but also a Lieutenant General in the British Army. Gough, the Commander-in-Chief in India, was also a Lieutenant General in the British Army but senior on the Army List to Hardinge, and also had the local rank of full General. Hardinge had placed Gough in a difficult position by offering to serve under him as second in command. Gough had felt compelled to accept, but expressed foreboding in a private letter to his son.[24] As has already been seen Hardinge had countermanded Gough orders before the war, he how did the same again and unfortunately it would not be the last time before the war was over.

---

21 Napier, *Personal Narrative*, pp. 4-5.
22 Napier, *Personal Narrative*, p. 5.
23 Napier, *Personal Narrative*, p. 6.
24 Christopher Brice, *Brave As a Lion: The Life and Times of Field Marshal Hugh Gough, 1st Viscount Gough* (Solihull: Helion & Co Ltd, 2017), pp. 308-309.

Napier spent much of the 19 and 20 of November resting. On the 21 November the army marched from Mudki to attack the Sikh army that had entrenched around the village of Ferozeshah. Gough had intended to attack immediately on arrival. Napier tells us that Major Broadfoot, the political agent of the Governor General on the Sikh frontier and considered an expert on the Sikhs, urged Gough against the attack stating that what lay ahead was only a detachment and that if he beat them today he would have to beat the main force tomorrow. Napier states that in this Broadfoot was incorrect, and in this he was only partly right.

Hardinge wanted to wait until Major General Littler's force from Ferozepore moved up to support them. Gough had planned to use Littler's force as a reserve as when it would eventually appear on the field it would cut off the retreat of the Sikhs thus, in Gough's mind, ensuring their defeat turned into a rout. Hadringe was reluctant to attack without Littler, and thus although militarily Gough subordinate used his political authority as Governor General to overrule his Commander in Chief. When Littler arrived battle was commenced. This had created serious delays and had wasted much of the daylight hours.

For the battle of Ferozeshah as it would become known Napier again acted on the staff and made himself busy around the battlefield. This close observation of a battlefield was a useful experience for his future career. The Anglo-Sikh Wars provided some of the fiercest fighting the British Army had ever seen. There were many Peninsular War veterans present during the campaign and many claimed never to have seen fiercer fighting than against the Sikhs. Ferozeshah was one of the hardest fought battles. It could also be said, perhaps slightly unfairly, that Napier received a good lesson in how not to fight a war. What he certainly learnt was that a commander-in-chief needed to be just that and have command over all the elements of the army and the campaign. His later insistence on having all under his command without subsidiary commanders or agencies determining the course of action he had initially agreed upon with the civil authorities was largely influence by his experiences at this time.

Whatever criticism there might be of Gough no one could doubt his courage, and he moved around the battlefield without care for his own safety. As a consequence many of the officers who followed him were either wounded or killed. On that morning Napier was fortunate that it was only his horse that was killed by the enemy artillery. Napier spent the rest of the day on foot joining the 45th Native Infantry. Napier was offered the command of a company due to the shortage of officers but as he recalled, '…that was not a situation in which I could well act.' As the infantry advanced towards the Sikh entrenchment, Napier spotted a loose horse and managed to catch it and thus re-joined Gough and his staff.

Napier gives us an account of the confusion when the British entered the Sikh entrenchments, and there were many casualties due to 'friendly fire'. Napier does not name any particular regiment, but it has been generally accepted that much of the damage was done by native infantry regiments who were badly handled and fired wildly. At this point both Hardinge and Broadfoot rode forward. Broadfoot was killed, quite possibly by a shot from his own side. Captain Saunders Abbott, Hardinge's a.d.c, and Napier stopped by Broadfoot's body and the former began to search his pockets for any valuables, letter, or documents. As they searched the body both men were hit. Napier was likely hit by a piece of artillery shell. Both men survived but Napier was in severe pain. He had been hit in the back and he records taking his hand to feel where he had been hit. On looking at his hand his glove was covered in blood.

The battle was over for the time being. Night had fallen and the men attempted to settle down as best they could. However, they had no food, little water, and no equipment except what they carried. For Napier, his wound was now causing him considerable pain. Napier paints a picture of disorder that night. He claims that many officers came to him asking for orders, as he was a staff officer, but he had none to give them. Even when order was attempted it had a rather confused nature. Lieutenant Colonel Barr was attempting to reform the troops however he had rather carelessly reformed then one in front of the other. As Napier stated, 'Had there been an alarm the confusion would have been terrible', with the obvious potential of formations unable to fire for fear of hitting friendly troops in front of them.[25]

Napier attempted to remedy the situation and approached Barr suggestion an alteration of the line with the added benefit of protecting the flanks against cavalry. Barr rather curtly responded to Napier's suggestion with the words, 'I do not know where you come from Sir.' Napier was not in the mood to be tactful, as he had approached in a polite manner and offered an observation. He was also in considerable pain, tired, thirsty and hungry and thus had limited patience. Napier annoyed response was 'very well' and started to walk away. However, he could not let it go and returned to Barr and said, 'I wish to make myself useful, as it seems there is a great want of officers to do so.' Barr responded apologetically that he was hard pressed and finding it difficult to bring any order and would appreciate any help that Napier could give.[26] Thus Napier proceeded to form up units where he could and issue orders to the waiting officers. Together they created some kind of order that meant that if another attack came it would not be total chaos and they would be able to put up some sort of fight.

After this Napier settled down to sleep. The morning of the 22 November brought the discovery that he had lost yet another horse. This time it had broken free as in his tired state Napier had not tied it up properly. Unable to find a horse Napier joined with the 31st Regiment. The regiment had suffered heavy losses and were grateful for all the help they could get.

In the movement through the Sikh camp Napier became detached from the 31st and could not find them again. Thus he joined with the 29th Foot. Napier wanted to find Gough, but without a horse and walking in some discomfort due to his wound was unable to do so. Thus when the final attack from the Sikhs came he was still with the 29th. For reasons that have never been fully explained, and for which we do not have the time to go into here, the Sikhs did not press home their attacked and instead withdrew from the field. Later that day Napier finally managed to re-join Gough, where he was able to get some food and settled down for the night.

On the morning of the 23 November Napier was shocked to find that it was rumoured that they were to abandon their position and march to Ferozepore. Napier himself summed up the situation; 'This seemed to me to be ruin. We could not carry the guns with us. The enemy was near enough to return, and we should have lost the victory, our trophies, and the enemy might have placed himself between us and our sick and wounded at Moodkee (Mudki), and our supplies and baggage.' Napier immediately sought out Gough to urge him to remain and outlined the above argument. According to Napier Gough response was, '…that he certainly agreed with me, that he should do all in his power to remain, but that if overruled by political considerations, he could not help it.'[27] Once again we see an insight into the difficult relationship between Commander-in-Chief and Governor General. Napier was convinced from this conversation that Hardinge wished to retire on Ferozepore.

25 Napier, *Personal Narrative*, p. 10.
26 Napier, *Personal Narrative*, p. 10.
27 Napier, *Personal Narrative*, p. 14.

Napier leaves us with an interesting insight into Gough command style. On the evening of the 23 Napier mentioned to Gough that he intended to sleep alongside the troops for fear of a night attack. Napier records the rest of the event as follows:

> I fear I somewhat offended the Commander in Chief, for, when I told him of my intention, he said, "Faith, I think I will sleep with the troops too, for if there is an alarm during the night, I'll never be able to get to the front amidst such confusion". I said: "If I may venture to make a suggestion, I would recommend the 29th Regiment. You will find Colonel Taylor and excellent clear-headed soldier". The Chief replied: "I want the hearts of the army, not their heads, Captain Napier". I am not politician enough to make any reply.[28]

Although this tells us much about Gough style of command it also points to the fact that Napier had other ideas. Gough was 'old school', a distinguished Peninsular War veteran, whereas Napier was of a new generation who were starting to appreciate that courage, or heart, was in and of itself not enough. A 'clear head', if not necessarily intellectual ability, was becoming increasingly important.

On the 24 the army moved forward to Sultan Khan Walla once it had been ascertained that the Sikhs had withdrawn. On the 26 Napier left the main army on an errand for Major Grant to bring forward the mortars that were at present at Ferozepore. Napier was asked to do this by the 29, in preparation for an attack that day. Although there was no attack, Napier had succeeded in bringing the mortars to the main army by the evening of the 27.

Up to this point Napier had been the senior engineer present, but in the aftermath of the battle of Ferozeshah reinforcements were brought up including Colonel Edward Smith who assumed the position of senior engineer. However, as a reward for his efforts to date Napier was appointed Brigade Major for the engineers, despite the fact that there were now two senior officers on the scene. We know very little of Napier's role in the battle of Sobraon that in effect ended the war. He was however mentioned in the despatch of Gough for that battle. Napier continued the advance with the army upon Lahore. At the end of the conflict Napier briefly returned to his duties at Umballa.

Napier had had a 'good' if not spectacular war. He was mentioned in despatches and given a brevet promotion to Major. It had been a good experience for the future and certainly proved that he was more than just an engineer. Napier's biographer states that unnamed friends felt he deserved more credit. However, Napier himself did not and gave the following reason:

> From the time I stood in the entrenchment at Sobraon after the battle, and saw hundreds of bodies of gallant soldiers, pile one above the other, men whose services could have no earthly reward, I felt ashamed of my passing discontent, and then and there resolved that come what might, I would make it a principle always to consider that I had had more rather than less than my due. From that resolve I think I have never since wavered.[29]

---

28   Napier, *Personal Narrative*, p. 15.
29   Napier, *Napier of Magdala*, p. 53-54.

This demonstrates a wisdom, maturity, and thoughtfulness to what he had experienced.

By March 1846 Napier was back to his work as an engineer. His projects included the development of the cantonments and 'hill stations' of Kasauli and Sabathu. In May 1846 he was appointed Chief Engineer to a force under the command of Brigadier General Hugh Wheeler. The fort of Kangra Kot had been ceded to the British as part of the treaty of Lahore that had ended the First Sikh War. The fort however remained in 'rebel' hands and it was felt necessary to take it. The fort at Kangra had been considered impregnable due to it being a mountain top fortress only accessible through rough and difficult country.

Napier's main task was to enable the movement of the artillery to a position where it could attack the fort. Given the difficult nature of the terrain the plan had been only to take light guns, but Napier determined that these would be quite inadequate for the task at hand. He sent through an urgent request for 18 pdrs. Napier's request was greeted with surprise and he was informed that it would be impossible to move them into position. To this he replied, 'There are few places where ingenuity and plenty of labour will not enable you to carry 18 pounders, and nothing else can be depended on against a wall of any strength.'[30] In short, Napier's engineering brain told him that it was possible. In this view he was opposed by virtually all the artillery officers of Wheeler's force. However, such was his growing reputation that trust was placed in him that he would be as good as his word.

The route took them over hills, often more like mountains, with fast running streams that crisscrossed and thus had to be crossed several times a day. Napier calculated that he rode over a hundred miles during this manoeuvre. He was ably assisted by the political department, most notably Major Henry Lawrence, who helped in the supplying of labour. Eventually Napier achieved his task, and the guns were brought before the fort, which surrendered without the need for them to be used. Napier held firmly that, '...nothing but the arrival of the 18 pounders had the effect of bringing the garrison to reason. I was glad that the loss of life, if even of a single man, was spared by the surrender, and doubly so, when I saw the number of women and children who were shut up in the fort.'[31] Further on in the same letter Napier gives us an insight into his tactical understanding. He believed that the mortars and lighter guns might have reduced the garrison, but 'If men see that you cannot get at them, they may endure a destructive bombardment, but if, in addition, they see the road being opened for the cold steel, it has a wonderful effect on the nerves.'[32]

His success was duly noted and he was favourably mentioned in despatches and received the thanks of the Government. He had ended the campaign under difficult circumstances. At the last minute he was once again replaced as Chief Engineer by Edward Smith, now a Brigadier. The tense relationship between the two continued and Napier paints a picture of Smith as being a burden rather than a help. Whereas Napier rode everywhere Smith insisted upon being carried in sedan chair. Smith later praised Napier although one senses a little reluctantly. 'Major Napier combined his usual talent with unremitting labour in promoting the operations generally.'[33] Brigadier General Wheeler on the other hand sent in a very positive report on Napier, and the

---

30   Napier, *Napier of Magdala*, p. 57.
31   Napier, *Napier of Magdala*, p. 58. This is taken from a letter by Robert Napier to Major, later General Sir, Edward Lugard.
32   Napier, *Napier of Magdala*, p. 59.
33   Napier, *Napier of Magdala*, p. 59.

latter believed that his receiving the thanks of the Government was due to the comments of Wheeler.

After the fall of Kangra Napier spent several weeks surveying the area for future development. His main task was to build a road through the area. The exertion of the past few months led to deterioration in his health and he contracted a fever. Once recovered, he returned to Umballa where a large backlog of work awaited him. He now learnt it was not only his health that had been bad in recent months. His wife and children had suffered ill-health and he received news from Europe that his mother was ill. All his added to his anxiety and whilst he had enjoyed his time at Umballa he was not upset when in December 1846 he received a new appointment.

Since the end of the First Anglo-Sikh War, British influence at Lahore had grown. Henry Lawrence, an acquaintance of Napier's, was British Resident in Lahore and exercised great influence over the Council of Regency that nominally ruled the area. Napier was offered the appointment of consulting engineer to the regency. The task would be to improve the infrastructure of the Punjab but also to build and develop British military positions in the area. His first task was the building of roads. Napier found much to do, and his engineering skills were put to good use. However, the desire for military service was never far away and in 1848 the opportunity presented itself during what would be known as the Second Anglo-Sikh War.

The second war was considered inevitable by many on the British side. The ending of the first war had left the Sikhs nominally independent but largely under British influence. The British did not exercise complete control, and the Sikhs did not have any real independence. It had not helped when in early 1848 the very able Henry Lawrence had been forced to return to England due to ill-health. His replacement, Sir Frederick Currie, whilst a very able man, had neither the knowledge, nor the tact, of his predecessor.

War broke out after an incident at Multan. This important position controlled by, Dewan Mulraj, had been allowed a degree of autonomy. Currie acted rather rashly and attempted to replace Mulraj with a 'loyal' Sikh named Khan Singh and sent with him two British officers Lieutenant Patrick Vans Agnew and Lieutenant William Anderson accompanied by a small escort of native troops. Having demanded that Dewan Mulraj stand down, they were attacked and wounded later in the day by men loyal to Mulraj. Although escaping the two British officers were deserted by their escort and brutally murdered the following day. This developed into a major Sikh revolt against British influence. Lieutenant Herbert Edwardes, a political agent, attempted to end it before it really started and with his own guard of Pathans and a supporting Sikh force he was able to defeat Dewan Mulraj and force him back to Multan. A British force was being prepared, once again under Gough's command, but again largely due to political interference of the Governor General, now Lord Dalhousie, the preparations were delayed and hampered.

The British started to gather a force to take Multan, under the command of Major General Whish, and Napier was appointed its Chief engineer. A military siege would be required and Napier started the preparations with his usual efficiency and drive. Napier favoured an attack as soon as possible. This was both a realisation of the problems of a prolonged siege but also an understanding of the desire to shatter the rebellion. He recommended a heavy artillery assault to open a breach before an attack by the whole force to storm the fortress.

However, he was alone in this view and at a council of war held on the 6 September 1848 it was decided to take a more cautious approach concentrating on the north east angle of the fort which was to be attack gradually and then taken by regular approaches. Whish bowed to the majority view but would perhaps have been better trusting to the opinion of the expert, namely the engineer.

Napier's view was vindicated as the chosen plan failed due to the scarcity of water and the difficulties of a prolonged siege. Then a plan was put forward by Lieutenant Lake, Edwardes engineer officer, which required an attack on two different sides at once. This proved impractical due to the lack of resources to undertake two separate attacks.

In the end they adopted Napier's original plan. However too much time had been wasted and the attacks stalled. On the attack on the 12 September Napier was to the fore. Although part of the suburbs was captured the main defensive position remained intact. Napier was badly wounded during this attack and suffered a leg wound from a cannon shot that would keep him out of action for several weeks. Whilst Napier was out of action a force of 10,000 Sikhs under Rajah Sher Singh went over to the enemy. As a consequence, another council of war was held, this time in Napier's tent for his convenience. The decision was taken to lift the siege, and withdraw a short distance, until reinforcements could arrive.

However, the Sikhs now prepared to take the offensive and a battery of guns was placed in range of the British position. Napier resumed duties in November and immediately urged action against the Sikh positon. This would result in the action of Suraj Kund on the 7 November 1848. The battle had seen the feint of a frontal attack whilst another brigade manoeuvred and attacked the enemy in the flank. The frontal attack was then developed into a full attack and the Sikhs were beaten back. Napier joined with Brigadier Markham's Brigade making the flanking movement. Markham remarked that, 'To Major Napier, Chief Engineer, who accompanied me throughput the day, I am indebted more than I can express.'[34]

This battle and the arrival of reinforcements allowed General Whish to recommence the siege of Multan. The reinforcements saw the arrival of Colonel Cheape who assumed responsibilities as Chief Engineer. Cheape now proposed exactly the same plan that Napier had presented several months ago. This time it was listened to. It took several days to create a breech as in the intervening period the Sikhs had thrown up considerable defensive earthworks. Although the attack had started on the 7 December it was not until January 22 that Multan fell, without the need for a final assault.

The ending of the siege allowed Whish to move the majority of his force to join Gough's main army. Gough had already fought the abortive action at Ramnagar and the drawn battle of Chillianwala. The latter had seen him sustain considerable casualties and thus the arrival of Whish's force was welcomed and allowed him to seek battle once more. This would occur on the 21 February 1849 at Gujrat. Napier was Chief Engineer for the right wing of the army under the command of Major General Sir Walter Gilbert. Whilst Napier advanced with this force perhaps his most important work had taken place before the battle when he had personally scouted both the ground over which the right wing would advance and the Sikh positions. After the battle he joined in the pursuit of the enemy to the Afghan border and would be present at the final surrender of the Sikhs.

For his service he was mentioned in despatches and promoted to brevet Lieutenant Colonel. In the aftermath of the war the Sikh state was officially annexed. A board on administration for the Punjab was set up and Napier was appointed to it as civil engineer. In this role he commenced a

---

34 Napier, *Napier of Magdala*, p. 62.

large programme of public works of epic scale. This included a 275 mile road between Peshawar and Lahore, a new Bari Doab canal system, irrigation projects, new public buildings for the British administration, and numerous other infrastructure projects such as minor roads and bridges. There were also military projects such as cantonments, forts, and frontier defences that he worked on. Napier thoroughly enjoyed such demanding and challenging work.

However, on the 30 December 1849 he was struck by personal tragedy when his wife died in child birth whilst bearing her third son, James Napier.[35] In the aftermath of the tragedy Napier sent his children back to Europe to be looked after by his mother. He felt the blow deeply and threw himself into his work even more than usual as, '…the best sedative and consolation left to him.'[36]

In late 1852 he had the opportunity for further active service during the Black Mountain expedition under Colonel Frederick Mackeson. This took place in the mountains of Hazara where two British customs officials had been murdered by what were referred to at the time as 'Hindustani Fanatics'. They had seized the fort at Kotla, which although not British was the possession of a British ally. Napier was given command of one of the three columns that advanced into this region.[37] Once again there was little fighting, and the main obstacle was the terrain. Thus, having an engineer in command of a column was a good idea.

The 'fanatics' fled at the advance of the British and the fort was easily reoccupied. Mackeson said of Napier that, 'My obligations to Colonel Napier are greater than I can express for the steady and skilful manner in which he brought his column through many difficulties of ground and determined opposition by the enemy.'[38] It was clear that the campaign had done Napier's reputation a great deal of good. He had for the first time been given a major command beyond that of his responsibility as an engineer.

In January 1853 Napier returned to his role in the Punjab. In late November he was again on campaign this time in the Bori Valley expedition under the command of Colonel S. B. Boileau. This was in response to raids against British territory and that of their allies by the Jowaki Afridis, one of the clans inhabiting the Kohat pass. The campaign largely consisted of an advance and then the burning of a few villages. John Lawrence, the Chief Commissioner for the Punjab, remarked that, '…the success of the expedition was mainly due to the exertions and ability of Lieut.-Colonel Napier, the Civil Engineer for the Punjab, and Major Edwardes.'[39]

Once again he returned to his position in the Punjab, with a new job title. With the abolition of the board of administration he became Chief Engineer to the Chief Commissioner, the aforementioned John Lawrence. It was clear that his efforts were appreciated further afield. Lord Dalhousie, still Governor General, wrote in 1854 of the work he had done that:

> Such results could not have been obtained without the presence of abilities and exertions such as call for the grateful recognition of the Government…to Colonel

---

35   Colonel James Pearse Napier of the 10th Royal Hussars, although the third son, would later succeed to his father's title as the 3rd Baron Napier. However this would not occur until 1921.
36   Napier, *Napier of Magdala*, p. 67.
37   One interesting thing to note is that under Napier's command was a battalion of Sikhs, newly raised under British command.
38   Napier, *Napier of Magdala*, p. 64.
39   Napier, *Napier of Magdala*, p. 64.

Napier himself, the Governor General in Council is anxious to render the honour that is due. For several years the Governor-General has been in close relations of business with Colonel Napier, and has seen and marked the deep devotion with which he has laboured in the discharge of the many and various duties of his important office... Whatever may be the credit due to those whose efforts have been directed to the physical improvement of the Punjab, a principal share of that credit is justly due to Lieut.-Colonel Napier, whose professional abilities, unwearied industry and judicious guidance have contributed so largely to the material result which has happily been attained.[40]

Particularly coming from a man like Dalhousie, who was not known for giving out praise lightly, this was a significant recognition of his talents.

In November 1854 Napier had been promoted to brevet Colonel in recognition of his work in the Punjab, both civil and military. In April 1856 he would also receive promotion in his regiment by becoming a Lieutenant Colonel in the Bengal Engineers. After seven years in the Punjab he relinquished his command and in the autumn of that year returned to England on leave.

In England, his time was spent in the furtherance of his professional knowledge. He visited railways and bridge builders, and even a brick and tile manufacturer who had new machinery he wished to see exported to India. He also took a great interest in the harbour improvements at Dover and spent several days examining them. He visited his mother and his children in Belgium, but even here he took the opportunity to visit a new Belgium railway which was on the then unheard of gradient of 1 in 40.

Soon it was time for him to return to India and in May 1857 he set sail. It was whilst he was still at sea that news of the Mutiny was heard. His arrival at Calcutta coincided with that of Lieutenant General Sir James Outram. Outram had been leading British and Indian forces during the Anglo Persian War of 1856-57. In the June of 1857 he had been recalled due to the deteriorating situation in India. On arrival he was placed in command of two divisions of the Bengal Army. Napier, being both respected and available, went with him as both Chief Engineer and Chief of Staff. Napier threw himself into his work but found time to write a very clear and concise letter to his mother that quite expertly sets out the position in India and the remedy to the present uprising.[41]

Throughout August 1857 Napier was largely occupied in the duties of a staff officer coordinating the forces in the area commanded by Outram. By September they had both reached Cawnpore where Outram waived his technical seniority to Henry Havelock so that the latter could continue with his plans for the relief of Lucknow.[42] With Outram serving as a volunteer assisting where he could this left Napier in a rather ambiguous positon. Napier took

---

40 Napier, *Napier of Magdala*, pp. 65-66.
41 Napier, *Napier of Magdala*, p. 72. The letter was undated but is believed to have been written in September 1857.
42 Henry Havelock had already attempted to relief Lucknow. Although successful on the field of battle he was compelled to withdraw. He simply did not have enough men to complete the task. Thus whilst his decision to withdraw is generally considered to be the most prudent course of action it did have the effect of increasing the revolt as many wavering Indians interpreted Havelock's withdrawal as a defeat.

the opportunity to assist where he could as a 'wandering' staff officer, similar to what he had done in the First Anglo-Sikh War. This meant that as they advanced towards Lucknow Napier was often to the fore during the fighting as Mangalwar, Alambagh, and Charbagh.

The force under Havelock's command was just over 3,000 strong consisting of six understrength British battalions and one Sikh battalion, three artillery batteries and around 150 volunteer cavalry. Havelock recommenced his advance on Lucknow on the 21 September and by the 26 September had relieved the town. However in so doing they had lost over 500 men, many during the final assault. The garrison was down to around 900 men. Outram, exercising his authority as Governor of the Oudh, took command. It had initially been hoped to withdraw the garrison, but with the numbers under his command Outram determined that this was infeasible, given the large number of sick and wounded that would need to be transported. Thus a second siege of Lucknow began within a few days. Napier found his engineering skills put to good use as he sought to improve the defences.[43]

Napier had played an important role, and this was not only confined to his general staff work. During the final advance the artillery, baggage train, and wounded, became separated. A force of 250 men was sent to find them and bring them into Lucknow. However they also became separated. Napier was sent with 100 men of the 78th Highlanders to bring in all the units. Under cover of darkness he moved and with the assistance of Mr Kavanagh a local resident who knew the land well he managed to find a way through the enemy lines and safely back into Lucknow.[44]

During the siege Napier was ever active not only in engineering works but also in counterattacks against the enemy as Outram determined to keep up an active defence. Every couple of days he felt it necessary to harry the enemy. A second relief force was on its way, commanded by General Sir Colin Campbell, around 4,500 strong. Lucknow was finally relieved on the 17 November 1857 after heavy fighting. On that same day Napier was wounded in the leg and was largely out of action for a month. Campbell decided against holding Lucknow considering the advantage not worth the cost in men or supplies. Thus with the evacuation the force moved towards Cawnpore where Campbell won a major victory against the mutineers. Napier spent his convalescence in Cawnpore and was characteristically far from idle as he assisted in improving the defences of that place.

It was not until January 1858 that Napier was able to take the field again. On the 12 January he joined Outram at Alambagh acting as Chief Engineer to his force of 4,000 men. Lucknow had been re-occupied by the mutineers and although Campbell wanted to delay operations in the Oudh during the campaigning season of 1858 the Governor General Lord Canning insisted that the Oudh be cleared of 'rebels'. Canning, no doubt based on the experience of Havelock's initial failure to break through to Lucknow, believe that if the Oudh was not taken yet more Indians would go over to the 'rebels'. Campbell now had reinforcements from Britain and newly raised 'loyal' native units, many being Gurkhas and Sikhs who felt they had more to fear from the 'rebels' than the British. His army was around 30,000 strong.

---

43   *Robert Napier, Report on the engineering operations at the siege of Lucknow in March 1858: by the chief engineer (now Brigadier General Sir R. Napier)* (Calcutta: Surveyor General's Office, 1859). This is Napier's own account of the siege of Lucknow.
44   Thomas Henry Kavanagh was at the time a member of the Bengal Civil Service. He is one of only five civilians ever to have been awarded the Victoria Cross.

Plans for the capture of Lucknow were drawn up for Campbell by Napier. It was only sensible that a man who had once organised the defensive improvements of Lucknow would be able to judge its weaknesses. Campbell had been so impressed with Napier that in his capacity as Commander-in-Chief in India he offered him the appointment of Quarter Master General. Napier somewhat reluctantly turned the offer down explaining that, '…the allowances are not better than my own, and I thought I should have a great deal of expense during the next two years while the country is getting settled, which my health might not bear, so, great as the honour was, I declined it.'[45] The financial aspect should not be overlooked as he was supporting his mother and his children back in Europe, and there are suggestions that he was also providing for certain nieces and nephews. Thus, he had to seriously consider the financial consequences of such an appointment and weigh them against the undoubted honour of such a high command.

Napier continued to play an active role in the siege of Lucknow until it finally fell on the 21 March 1858. Napier drew up plans for the permanent military occupation of Lucknow which were approved two months later. The ending of the siege was also the end of his association with Outram. The latter wrote of Napier 'Indelibly engraved on my heart are those traits of the brave soldier, the able and scientific officer, the upright man, and the warm friend which every day of our long and intimate intercourse furnished.'[46]

Outram and Campbell were not the only ones impressed by Napier and he appeared to be the rising star of the army during this period. Napier was made a C.B in March 1858 and then in June was selected to take command of the Central India Field Force. Although only a Colonel he was given the local rank of Brigadier General, replacing Major General Sir Hugh Rose who after a long campaign was to take sick leave. However, this plan was overtaken by events. Almost at the same time as Napier was appointed the 'Mutineers', under Tantia (or Tatya) Toipi captured Gwalior. Although almost incapacitated by sickness Rose immediately resumed command and ordered the army to march on Gwalior. Napier joined the force on the 16 June and took command of the 2nd Brigade. That same day he led the brigade during the attack on the Morcar cantonment.

Gwalior fell on the 20 June and Napier was sent in pursuit of Tantia Topi. Commanding a mobile force of 672 cavalry and horse artillery he attacked Tantia Topi's force of 12,000 at Jaora Alipur on the 22 June. He took them completely by surprise and routed the vastly superior force capturing all their 25 guns, ammunition, and baggage. Many of the enemy only escape by abandoning their arms and fleeing as fast as they could. Exact figures of enemy casualties are unknown, but few escaped the field of battle. Napier had once again proved his considerable fighting abilities. He had also proved himself as an all-round soldier. In this action he commanded cavalry in battle for the first time and did it with great ease, he also handled the horse artillery with great skill.

On June 29 he formally took command of the Gwalior Division when Rose finally departed India on sick leave. A month later, Napier was rewarded with a K.C.B in recognition of his service during the suppression of the mutiny. Whilst the major fighting was over there were still small parties of rebels at large and Napier became responsible for the pursuit of such groups. He organised a series of flying columns. In August Napier supported Brigadier-General Edward

---

45 Napier, *Napier of Magdala*, p. 96.
46 Napier, *Napier of Magdala*, p. 104.

Smith, of previous acquaintance, in an attack on the town of Pauri. Smith had attempted to take the town previous but had insufficient force, particularly in terms of artillery. Given the history between the two men Napier would have been forgiven for a wry smile when receiving the appeal for help from Smith. Yet if there was any feelings of bitterness towards Smith it did not show. Napier brought with him 600 cavalry, five 18 pdr guns and four mortars. The high angle fire of the latter was particularly effective against the defences of Pauri. At the same time as the mortars did their work Napier used his five guns to create a breech in preparation for the attack. After a twenty-four hour bombardment the 'fortress' was taken.[47]

Whilst the 'rebellion' was dying down, in the latter part of 1858 a new 'rebel' arrived on the scene namely Firoz Shah who had been inspired by the actions of Tantia Topi and was attempting to join him. Napier deployed three columns to attempt to intercept him as he made his way through Gwalior territory, eventually ambushing the enemy at Ranod, and then later on at Goona. Napier's engineering skill taught him the importance of preparation and logistics and thus his columns were always prepared and remarkably fast moving.

By early 1859 Napier had moved his military headquarters from Gwalior to Sironje. There were several villages still held by Rajah Man Singh. To enable the pursuit of the enemy Napier ordered the building of several roads. However, in early April the Rajah surrendered to the British on the 2 April 1859, and on the 7 April Tanti Topi was betrayed and arrested by the British. This was in effect the ending of the campaign in central India.

Napier had gained great experience from fighting the 'mutineers'. His reputation increased, he had been honoured by his country, and had risen in rank. Yet despite this Napier was somewhat bleak about his own future. With the ending of the rebellion the East India Company was disestablished, and the British Crown assumed responsibility for the governance of India. This presented a problem to Napier as he had always been a servant of the East India Company and always an officer in their army rather than the British Army.

In a letter to his mother dated 31 May 1859 Napier remarked that, '…we poor 'Company' Officers must hide our diminished heads now. We are reduced to Militia'. In January the following year he remarked to a friend that, 'I expect to be kept as a local general for show, but all real opportunities will be kept for the British (i.e. Queen's) Officers'.[48] This trepidation and fear regarding his future was the reasons he accepted an appointment to the expedition to China that was being planned.

The Second Anglo-China War had in effect been going on since the Arrow Incident of October 1856. The majority of the action up to that point had been in the form of 'gunboat diplomacy', although there had been some amphibious assaults during the period up to 1860. The 'Mutiny' in India had been far more important, and consequently there was little support for operations in China. The attack upon the Taku Forts at the mouth of Peiho River on 25 June 1859 had ended in failure. The British landing party had to be evacuated with the loss of 81 dead and 345 wounded.

---

47 Some reports give the total length of the bombardment as thirty-four hours.
48 Napier, *Napier of Magdala*, p. 124. Napier was as it turns out being pessimistic. As Rodney Atwood's research has indicated, many ex-Company officers thrived in post mutiny India, such as Napier, the future Lord Roberts, Donald Stewart, Edwin Johnson and the future Field Marshal Sir Henry Norman. Rodney Atwood, *The Life of Field Marshal Lord Roberts* (London: Bloomsbury, 2015), pp. 49-51.

With relative calm in India it was decided to undertake a major operation against China to resolve the war that had drifted on for several years. A force of two infantry divisions, a cavalry brigade, and a small siege train of heavy artillery was despatched. Each division had two infantry brigades made up of two British battalions and one Indian. Attached to each division were two batteries of artillery and a company of engineers. The 2nd Division which Napier would command consisted of the 3rd Brigade, consisting of the 3rd (the Buffs) Foot, 44th (East Essex) Foot, and the 8th Punjab Native Infantry, and the 4th Brigade consisting of 67th (South Hampshire) Foot, 99th (Lanarkshire Foot), and the 19th Punjab Native Infantry. As this was to be a combined operation with the French, the British were augmented by a French force of around 6-7,000 troops and a number of warships, under the overall command of General Charles Cousin-Montauban.

One senses reluctance on Napier's part to take the appointment, but a fear that if he did not his future might look bleak. After the arduous campaigning during the Mutiny he desired rest. Also, news from Europe was not good as his mother was said to be seriously ill, and her death would drastically alter all his domestic arrangements regarding his children. Such was his state of mind that on 9 February 1860 Napier wrote 'How much better for me it would have been had I remained quietly at Calcutta as Chief Engineer and been contented.'[49] This goes against Napier's previous desire to advance in the army both as an engineer and as a soldier and tells us much about his state of mind. He was depressed, and the exhaustion of recent campaigning and the worry regarding his domestic affairs cannot have helped his state of mind.

However, looking back one can see that in many ways the China expedition came at the right time for Napier both in terms of his career but also his own well-being as it meant that he had something else to occupy his mind other than family concerns and his own career prospects. On reaching Calcutta Napier was appointed to superintend the movement and embarkation of all the equipment and troops destined for China. Indeed, every detail of the planned expedition from food to ventilation, and sanitation, on the journey was to be Napier's responsibility. This arduous and difficult task was in many ways just what Napier needed to help him out of the malaise into which he had sunk.

We have not the space to fully examine here the magnitude of what he achieved.[50] Suffice it to say that he prepared over 10,000 men; both infantry, cavalry, and artillery, for transportation to China all of which was undertaken in relatively good order. His preparations for a journey of over 5,000 miles, against much opposition form vested interests in Calcutta, such as the Clothing Department and the Marine Department, was a great achievement. Napier was able to find ways around such objections backed as he was by Sir Henry Bartle Frere, an important member of the Governor-General (or Viceroy's) Council, and the Commander-in-Chief Colin Campbell, now ennobled as Lord Clyde.

The fact that Lord Clyde simply remarked that '...the operation appears to have been most admirably well done' speaks more of British understatement than it does any belittling of Napier's work.[51] Lord Clyde had been anxious to avoid the loss through disease and climatic

---

49 Napier, *Napier of Magdala*, p. 125.
50 *Robert Napier, Despatches of Major-General Sir R. Napier reporting the operations of the second division of the China force in the expedition of 1860* (Hertford: Privately Printed, 1873). This is Napier's own account of the expedition, printed privately. A copy can be found in the British Library.
51 Napier, *Napier of Magdala*, p. 128.

conditions that his long career of campaigning in India had given him an example of. Thus, the handing of the responsibility to Napier is testament to the confidence and faith in his ability that Lord Clyde held.

By the 25 March 1860 Napier had completed his task, and on that same day he sailed for China. After a short stop in Singapore, Napier reached Hong Kong on the 12 April. He was greeted with the news that the Chinese had rejected the Anglo-French ultimatum and military action was now assured. Napier was appointed to command the British camp at Kowloon as preparations continued. He continued in this command until the 11 June when Napier, commanding the 2nd Division of the British force, sailed with his staff for the rendezvous of British forces off Tahlien Bay (modern day Dalian Bay). On the 26 June the British force was landed on the slopes above Tahlien Bay, where the sea breeze helped to alleviate some of the problems caused by the extreme heat.

There was disagreement between the British and French commanders as to what the next action should be. It was decided that no decision would be made until the French force completed its arrival, not expected until the 25 July. On the 26 July the combined fleets, numbering roughly 330 vessels of various configurations, set sail and anchored two days later off Pehtang (modern day Beitang). On the 1 August the army started to land. The forts at Pehtang were abandoned by the Chinese and occupied by the British divisions. It was not until the 5 August that Napier was able to start disembarking his 2nd Division, as priority had been given to landing the 1st Division and the cavalry. By the time this occurred heavy rain had fallen, and troops were sometimes up to their knees in mud as the disembarkation continued. As a consequence, it took two days to land the 2nd Division.

The first priority was to move against the village of Sinho, which was reported to be held in strength by the Chinese. After disagreement between the allies a plan of attack was agreed that would see Napier commanding his 2nd Division and the British Cavalry Brigade attack from the North across the mud flats. The march against Sinho commenced at 0400hrs on 12 August. Once again the heavy rain and subsequent mud caused a problem and it took the Division six hours to move just four miles. By the time he arrived Napier could see the French and the British 1st Division approaching the causeway to the Sinho, in front of which the Chinese occupied an entrenchment.

Napier immediately ordered an attack, which had the effect of outflanking the Chinese position.[52] Chinese, or more accurately Tartar, cavalry moved out to attack Napier. However, with the deployment of his own cavalry and artillery they were forced back. The combined movements of the allies forced the Chinese to withdraw, abandoning Sinho which the allies quickly occupied. Beyond Sinho lay the large town of Tongkoo, separated from the former by a large causeway. The town was defended by a formidable looking rampart that mounted over fifty guns, and a ditch surrounding the town which the recent heavy rains had partly turned into a moat. Tongkoo occupied the ground midway, about six miles, between Sinho and the nearest of the Taku forts, the ultimate short-term objective of the allied force.

52 This attack saw the first shots fired in action by the new breech loading Armstrong guns that accompanied the expedition. The still experimental weapon was being trialled in this campaign, and although impressing, it was not taken into full service. This was partly due to cost, partly because it was still an emerging technology, and also had a great deal to do with the conservative nature of the British Army.

On the 13 August, whilst awaiting supplies and ammunition to be brought forward, Napier had the area ahead scouted. One of his A.D.C's, Major Greathed, discovered a dry section of ground along the salt marshes leading towards the town, thus negating the need for a frontal attack along the causeway. On the following day the attack was launched and Tongkoo taken with relative ease.

The target was now the Taku forts. The French favoured attacking the southern forts first, whereas the British, and in particular Napier, thought that success was more likely if the attack was confined to the northern forts. The compromise was reached that the forts would be attacked simultaneously. It was not ideal but it had its advantages, not least of all that it maintained the harmony of the respective allies.

From the 14 August to the 18 August the allies worked to build bridges over the canals, construct a wider boat bridge across the marsh land, to build a raised causeway, and to improve the roads so that the heavy artillery could be brought forward. In the latter point Napier played an important role, once again proving that it was possible to bring forward heavy guns over terrain that would usually have been thought impassable. Consequently the heavy guns were brought within 800 yards of the northern Taku Forts. Indeed such was the success of Napier's boat building and general engineering skill that the senior allied Commander Hope Grant decided that the concentration of the attack should be made on the northern front alone. The French objected strongly, with General Montauban going so far as to say the attack was '…completely useless', but Napier's hard work and engineering skill meant that Hope Grant could entirely justify such a course of action. However to make sure that the Chinese were also occupied elsewhere when the attack was made Admiral Sir James Hope fleet of ships would bombard the forts at the mouth of the river.[53]

By the 20 August all the preparations were in place and the decision was made to attack the following morning. The French still objected strongly with General Montauban lodging '…a strongly worded protest.'[54] Eventually he gave way, but whilst offering French troops for the assault he declined to take any responsibility for the subsequent results.[55]

At 0400hrs on the 21 August the allied batteries opened fire. The bombardment, which was answered by the many Chinese guns that lined the forts, continued for three hours. Although the Chinese had a large number of guns, including two British 32 pdrs salvaged from a sunken ship, they were outclassed by the allied bombardment. Two hours into the bombardment the British scored a lucky hit when an 8 inch mortar shell landed a direct hit on the magazine within the fort. After a further hour of firing the Chinese guns were all but silenced and Hope Grant committed his infantry to an assault on the forts.

The problem now facing Napier's men was that the pontoon bridge that had been carried forward by Royal Marines to enable his force to cross the many ditches that acted as a moat around the fort, had been an easy target for the Chinese and most of the marines had been killed. Improvising, Napier ordered scaling ladders to be used to get men across the ditches. At the same time, he brought forward some of his heavy guns, to within eighty yards of the ramparts and ordered them to fire over the heads of his men. This was partly to stop the firing

---

53 Napier, *Napier of Magdala*, pp. 142-143.
54 Napier, *Napier of Magdala*, p. 143.
55 Although Montauban promised 1,000 infantry and two field batteries it appears that his reluctance effected his subordinates who delayed so that only one battery and 400 men were ever committed.

from muskets and gingalls by the Chinese, but also to create a larger breech in the wall to which his men could stream through.

The small French force had partly managed to enter the fort but were unable to hold it. Napier was able to create a partial breech near the gate into which his troops could pour. The Chinese put up heroic resistance. As Napier put it, '…foot by foot the brave garrison disputed the ground.'[56] The reserves were called forward to support the attack and ultimately the fort was taken a little after 0830hrs. The Chinese had lost around 400 killed, out of a garrison of around 500. This points not only to the determined resistance of the Chinese, but also to the strength of the fortification that enabled only 500 men to hold off an army over twenty times its size for so long. The British had 201 casualties, but only seventeen of them were killed. The French casualties were 159, but again only seventeen were killed. Napier himself had been close to the action, having his field glasses shot out of his hands, his sword hilt broken by a shell fragment, and three bullet holes in his coat and one in his boot.

Preparations were made to attack the other forts but, as Hope Grant had thought likely, the other forts surrendered as their position had become untenable with the falling of the northern fort. By the early evening the allies were in possession of the forts, and with this the river route to Peking (Beijing) was open.

The following day naval forces were advanced thirty five miles along the river to Tientsin and over the next few days the land forces were advanced to join them. Napier and the 2nd Division were delayed in their advance as they were given responsibility for making sure the forts were secured before moving further up river. Hope Grant had hoped that he would not need to bring the 2nd Division forward. Indeed he had written to Napier after the battle for the Taku Forts congratulating him and saying, '… you took all the Takoo forts and, in fact, finished the war.'[57] Negotiations were taking place between the British and the Chinese, but the British became increasingly convinced that the Chinese were playing for time in the hope that they could stall them until the winter came and forced the British to at least partly withdraw. At the same time the Chinese were bringing up extra troops, artillery, and supplies.

Napier's division, save for the troops left to garrison the forts, reached Tientsin on 5 September. Negotiations were continuing but on the 11 September the Emperor had appointed two new envoys who were known to be hardliners opposed to further negotiations. At first negotiations continued, but the British became increasingly concerned about the increased number of extra Chinese troops brought to the area. On the 18 September negotiations broke down when the Chinese changed their minds on several points that had been conceded previously. The British delegation had decided that for the time being further negotiations were pointless, but on attempting to leave they were surrounded and captured.[58]

This breech of the laws of war, for they were negotiating under a flag of truce, incensed Hope Grant who sent forward a combined Anglo-French force of 3,500 men to attack the Chinese. Although much larger, the Chinese forces were driven from the field and some eighty guns were captured. The allies now continued the advance, and Hope Grant wanted to bring forward the

---

56 Napier, *Napier of Magdala*, p. 145.
57 Napier, *Napier of Magdala*, p. 146.
58 Many of the prisoners were held in the Board of Punishments and were subjected to horrific torture, during which many died. Of thirty nine British and French prisoners only nineteen survived to be released.

2nd Division to support him. Napier's division was weakened yet further as a detachment had to be left behind to garrison Tientsin. Remarkably Napier managed to march his force, including heavy artillery, seventy miles in just sixty hours.

By the time Napier reached army headquarters a further battle had been fought by Hope Grant on the 21 September at Palikao Bridge. The Chinese had launched a near suicidal frontal assault on the allied force and been cut to shreds. The defeat meant that there was nothing standing between the allies and Peking. At this point the Emperor fled and left his brother to negotiate peace with the British. The French, and to a lesser extent the British, sacked his summer palace and an enormous amount of 'loot' was taken.[59]

Negotiations dragged on and Hope Grant was forced to begin preparations for an assault on Peking, something he was against due to the prestigious nature of the walls around the city: said to be forty feet high and sixty feet thick. Even with his heavy artillery this would take some breeching. A date of the 13 October was set for all prisoners to be released and the city to be surrendered, if not the assault would begin, with Napier's division earmarked to attack the An-ting (Antung) gate. The prisoners were released between the 8 and 13 October and at the last minute on the 13 October the gates were opened and the city surrendered, thus avoiding what would have been a bloody battle for all concerned.

Negotiations were concluded on the 24 October with the Chinese finally ratifying the 1858 Treaty of Tientsin. British demands were met in full. Already, on 22 October, the heavy artillery and many of Napier's supplies had started their journey back to Tientsin. It was not until 7 November that Napier and his division left Peking, arriving in Tientsin five days later. On the 18 November Napier and his staff left Tientsin for Hong Kong, reaching the latter late on the 27 November. It was almost a month later on 22 December 1860 that Napier arrived back in India.

On his return he stayed for a time with the family of Major-General Edward Scott. According to Napier's son, Henry Dundas Napier, the chief attraction was Scott's eldest daughter Mary, an attractive eighteen year old recently returned from Ireland. Mary's feelings toward Napier were that of hero worship, again the words of Henry Napier.[60] Despite the age difference, for Napier was fifty and had two daughters around Mary's age, such were the feelings between the two that only a few months later, in April 1861, they were married. They would go on to have nine children together, six sons and three daughters.

The China expedition increased Napier's reputation as a soldier. He received the thanks of Parliament, the China medal and two clasps, and in February 1861 was promoted full Major-General. On his return to India he was appointed military member of the council of the Governor-General of India. This unique post combined the duties of a chief of staff with that of a war minister. In short the entire administration, logistical, and supplies needs of the army became his responsibility. Although junior in rank to the Commander-in-Chief in practice the military member wielded even greater 'power'.

Napier held the posting at a difficult time, coinciding with significant reform of the army and indeed the machinery of government in India. Local 'European' forces were to be disbanded and the native army was to be greatly reduced and reorganised. This was a difficult reorganisation and as a former East Indian Company officer Napier could appreciate the concerns of its former

---

59   This is not to suggest that the British were in anyway adverse to looting. The simple fact of the matter was the French got there first and therefore had greater opportunity.
60   Napier, *Napier of Magdala*, pp. 159-160.

officers and men. His good relations with many serving on the council, including Lord Canning the Governor-General, assisted him. It was largely at Napier's insistence that an Amalgamation Commission was appointed to report on the situation. This was opposed by many on the council who thought it unnecessary. However, its report helped to alleviate the worst of the outcry and proposed a compromise that would see a great reduction in the number of officers but see them fairly compensated.

Napier's time was also to see the improvement in the lot of the regular soldier. He was able to increase the size of living quarters, introduce married quarters for N.C.O's, build new two-storied barracks, and create the transport arrangements, both rail and road, to barracks and hill stations. This not only improved military efficiency but also helped to sooth many of the grievances of recent years. He also did much to improve the conditions of the penal colony on the Andaman Islands, and also the relations with the 'aboriginals', as this was technically a military post.

Perhaps in recognition of his work and his growing reputation Napier was, in early 1863 appointed president of the Council of the Governor-General of India. This increase in power and authority did have some unfortunate consequences with regards to his relationship with the Commander-in-Chief Hugh Rose. Rose was not the first, nor by any means the last, Commander-in-Chief to feel threatened by the Military member. There were also military differences between the two men, and it was thought at one stage that Rose was so incensed that he may resign. This led to the rumour that Napier would be appointed his successor, and the further rumour that Napier was actively opposing Rose in order to bring this about. The rumour appears to have little foundation in fact. Indeed Napier was unlikely to be appointed, because of his junior status and because the appointment would be made in London not Calcutta.

Between 21 November and 2 December 1863 Napier briefly acted as Governor-General of India, due to the death of Lord Elgin. This brief tenure was due to his position as President of the Council and lasted until Sir William Denison, Governor of Madras, arrived to become acting Governor-General until the arrival of Sir John Lawrence as permanent Governor-General. Napier did not particularly like John Lawrence, although he had been a great friend of his brother Henry. The reason seems to go back to their days in the Punjab when John Lawrence's constant demands for economy hindered Napier's work.

Napier was now actively looking for a new posting, and there was lobbying for him to be appointed Commander-in-Chief of the Bombay army. The Duke of Cambridge, Commander-in-Chief of the British Army, was initially reluctant to appoint him. Firstly because he was an 'engineer', and secondly because as an 'Indian' the Duke doubted whether Napier would be able to maintain discipline amongst the 'Queen's' (British Army) troops. Both stereotypes did not apply to Napier, and slowly the Duke was made to see that Napier was an experienced military commander who had commanded 'Queen's' troops on several occasions.

Napier had been advised to go home on leave and see the Duke of Cambridge personally. This he did but by the time he arrived home in early 1865 his appointment had already been confirmed. He did meet with the Duke and after a meeting lasting half an hour the latter's concerns were removed. Indeed a lifelong friendship and respect was commenced between the two men, assisted by Napier keeping the Duke apprised of all matters concerning the Indian Army.

Napier's appointment as Commander-in-Chief of the Bombay Army had been announced in January 1865. Before taking up his appointment Napier took several months of leave in

England, which proved a much needed rest. On returning to India he got to work immediately, attempting to fight some of the reductions in the size of the Bombay Army, that had already been agree to by his predecessor. In this he had some success. He once more turned to the matter of barrack accommodation. In this he was assisted by the Governor of Bombay, Sir Henry Bartle Frere. He had always enjoyed good relations with Frere, even though they had occasionally clashed over matters of economy.

They briefly clashed in their new positions over the appointments of divisional commanders, which in the Bengal and Madras armies was done by the nomination of the Commander-in-Chief of that army, but in Bombay was done by the Governor. Napier wanted the same authority as his counterparts. Initially refused, Napier's appeal to the Secretary of State for India was successful. However, for reasons that have never been explained Napier subsequently withdrew his demand.[61] It may simply be that he wanted to make a point rather than change the present system. At any rate he was now unlikely to face much opposition in his appointments from the civilian government.

In March 1867 Napier was appointed to the rank of Lieutenant General. This promotion, slightly earlier than would have been expected, spoke not only of his ability and reputation but also of the influence of the Duke of Cambridge. This influence was to be felt again later in the year when Napier was appointed to command a proposed expedition to Abyssinia.

The story of the lead up to the Abyssinian campaign is too long to be included in this short biographical work.[62] It involved the imprisonment of British subjects, including the British consul Captain Cameron, by the Emperor Theodore (Tewodros) of Abyssinia. The once dynamic and modernising Theodore had declined in both physical and mental health. He had done much to unite the country and had attempted to modernise it by reaching out to the European powers for expertise. Indeed, it was many of those engineers and technical advisers who were now being held as prisoners. His decline was hastened by the deaths of his wife, Walter Plowden the first British consul, and John Bell, another Briton who had been a close friend and ally of Theodore.

Theodore became paranoid, particularly about Egyptian and Ottoman influence in his country, and the fact that Cameron had arrived via Egyptian territory had not helped matters. Neither had the fact that due to a mistake in the Foreign Office Theodore's letter of friendship and good will towards Britain had never been answered. Theodore's suspicion and paranoia was growing and the imprisonment of all Europeans followed shortly afterwards.

If only for matters of prestige, never mind humanitarian concerns, a response was needed by the British. The leading world power could not be seen to be insulted and its subjects imprisoned, and perhaps worse, by an 'uncivilised' African monarch. An expedition to free the prisoners and restore pride had to be organised, if they could not be released any other way.

How, and from where, such a campaign would come was a difficult question. There were many difficult logistical problems. The first problem was who should organise the campaign. Within the British Cabinet it was decided that the task would best be handled from India.

---

61   Even his son could not through any light on the reason in his biography of his father. Napier, *Napier of Magdala*, pp. 195-197.

62   For a brief account of the campaign see Christopher Brice, 'The Expedition to Abyssinia, 1867-68', in Stephen. M. Miller (ed), Queen Victoria's Campaigns: British Military Campaigns, 1857-1902 (Cambridge: Cambridge University Press, 2021) and David. G. Chandler, The Expedition to Abyssinia, 1867-8, in Brian Bond (ed), Victorian Military Campaigns (London: Hutchinson & Co, 1967)

Thus the Secretary of State for India Sir Stafford Northcote contacted the Governor General, who in turn felt it would be best handled by the Bombay presidency. The Governor of Bombay, now Seymour Fitzgerald, passed it on to his Commander-in-Chief. As a consequence Napier, in conjunction with his Quartermaster General Colonel Phayre was tasked with planning the operation in Abyssinian. At this stage there was no suggestion that Napier should lead the expedition.

The problems faced in planning such an operation were so numerous as to make the exercise seem almost impossible. Indeed, no other nation on the face of the earth could have even considered such an operation let alone make it work. The first problem was simply where to land. Abyssinia had no coast line. The answer was found by persuading the Egyptians to allow use of their territory on the Red Sea Littoral. However even the landing site at Zula in Annersley Bay south of Massawa had no harbour. Moreover it was still over 380 miles from Theodore's capital at Magdala.[63]

To enable the force to land and then operate from Zula would be a major undertaking. It would mean building a harbour and stone piers where there was none, which was done so well that signs of it could still be seen in the 1970s. Lighthouses and warehouses were also built.[64] From the harbour a railway was built to take the supplies 20 miles in land to the first major forward depot. From here a road was built to take the army further in land. A telegraph was constructed to allow messages to be passed form the harbour inland. In short the British would build their own facilities and infrastructure where there had been nothing.

Yet these were just the preparations for the expeditionary force itself. The size of this force presented many other problems. The British Government had hoped that an expedition of a few thousand men, acting as a flying column, would be sufficient. Napier refused to accept this argument and resolutely declared that to ensure success a far larger force would be necessary. Napier's proposal called for a cavalry force made up of half a British regiment and four Indian cavalry regiments. Rather than acting as an independent brigade the cavalry was split between the two infantry brigades, the pioneer force, and the four garrisons that were to be maintained along the route from the coast. The infantry consisted of four British and ten Indian battalions. The artillery consisted of one battery of 9pdrs, two batteries of heavy mortars, and three batteries of mountain guns. There was also one company of British engineers, and seven native companies. This created a force around 14,000 strong.

Yet this was only a small part of the total manpower required. To enable the advance of this army a force of over 26,000 camp followers were required, not to mention large number of local labour. Added to this was the considerable number of animals that were required. 19,580 mules and transport horses, 2,538 horses for the staff and cavalry, 6,045 camels, 7,086 bullocks, 1,850 donkeys and 44 elephants.

To transport a force of this size a fleet of over 300 ships was required. The vast majority had to be especially chartered and this was to prove the largest expenditure of the campaign. Indeed, after the campaign the expense would be the cause of much criticism, although this should not be attached to Napier as he had to abide by the regulations of the authorities in India. Indeed

---

63 It has been suggested that the advancing army actually marched 420 miles, due to the topography of the area. Whilst quite feasible this is difficult to prove.
64 One of the lighthouses shone inland to illuminate the surrounding countryside as the belief was that the Abyssinians had a predilection for night attacks.

Napier had complained about the situation and circumstances of many of the charters. There was to be the need for many of them to remain on station, and therefore under charter, for much of the campaign.

Part of the reason for this takes us into the realm of the technological advantages that Napier attempted to exploit to the fullest extent. A major problem for a force of this size with so many men and animals was always going to be the enormous demands for fresh water. For example, the daily requirements of the animals of the force averaged at over 200,000 gallons of water per day. To help meet this demand a number of modern steam ships with water condensers were chartered and had to remain on station throughout.[65] The exact amount that such ships could provide varied according to how many were on station, but they averaged about 30-40, 0000 gallons a day, and throughout the campaign it was estimated that over 500,000 gallons was produced in such a way. Although extremely helpful it was only a small part of what was required. To help provide further water other technological advancements were used. Miles of iron piping was used to bring water from the mountain streams to the harbour. Also fifty highly advance Norton patented water boring and well sinking devices were purchase from the USA, and to aid the drawing of water fifty Basticr's chain pumps had been despatched from England.[66]

Yet water was only one resource that needed to be secured. Indeed the supply needs of the force were to be enormous. The original hope had been that such supplies could be provided and maintain by India. However this soon proved infeasible and a huge quantity of stores had to be sent from England. Much of this went to Bombay, to be sent forward as required. However some material was despatched directly to Zula, or via Aden or Alexandria.[67]

The demands for supplies was so varied, and a brief look at what was being sent helps to illustrate the meticulous attention to detail that Napier was providing to the expedition. Major items sent from England included 12,000 ships boats, 70, 000 lbs of pork and the same amount of beef, 15,000 lbs of 'preserved' potatoes and the same amount of 'compressed' vegetables, 30,000 waterproof sheets, and 34,000 lbs cocoa and 225 tons of biscuits. Whilst this might sound significant it is important to remember that this is only what despatched from England to supplement sources of supply in India.

One problem was that the expected climatic conditions meant there was a requirement for both summer and winter clothing. To this end 4,000 pairs of mittens and 4,000 pairs of gloves were transported from England. There was a requirement for tents both to guard against the cold and the sun. From England 323 bell tents, 667 single tents and 50 hospital marquees were despatched. Given the expected climatic conditions and the disease associated with it, medical precautions were taken extremely seriously. Three ships were chartered and fitted out as hospital ships with every modern scientific device aimed at preventing high mortality rates.

---

65 There were also some land based condensers but it is questionable when they arrived and how effective they proved.
66 Some accounts say there were 100 Norton devices. The fifty mentioned came from England, and it is possible that another fifty were despatched from India. However this is unclear.
67 This was of course in the days before the completion of the Suez Canal. However many shipping companies in effect kept two fleets of ships either side of the Sinai peninsula to enable transportation from Alexandria to be taken on further east.

When one looks at the list of material that was shipped to the Red Sea Coast the detail is immediately apparent. Smaller things, such as 500 bottles of Warbury's anti-fever drops, 2,800 lbs of axel grease, and 12,000 spare boat laces, help to demonstrate this. The sheer scale of the organisation that went into the planning and preparation for the campaign was immense but showed the importance that Napier attached to such matters and his realisation that such organisation was vital to the success of the campaign.

One other technological advantage that Napier called for was the rearming of his British troops with the new Snider-Enfield breech loading rifle. Although it had entered service in 1865 the replacement of traditional muzzle loading weapons had been slow.[68] To equip the British troops 4,114 Snider Rifles and 1,000 Snider Carbines were shipped from England. 2,500,000 rounds of Snider ammunition was sent to Bombay, and a further 2,420,000 rounds were sent to Alexandria as a reserve.

With preparations underway the matter of who should commander the expedition continued to be debated. Napier appeared the logical choice because he had both planned the operation and because much of the expedition came from the Bombay Army. Both Sir Stafford Northcote and the Duke of Cambridge championed Napier for command. In reality there were few alternatives due to the British Army's perennial problem of a lack of higher command leadership.

In October 1867 an advanced party had been landed in Annersley Bay to begin preparations and scout the route ahead.[69] Gradually the expeditionary force and all its supplies started to gather in the newly built facilities on the Red Sea Coast. Unsurprisingly it took considerable time to gather all the troops, supplies, and equipment being despatched from so many different points. Inevitably there were difficulties with the landing and organisation once ashore. Yet if it was 'chaos', as some sources suggest, then it was most certainly 'organised chaos'! It would be naïve in the extreme to expect that such a landing and such an undertaking could be done smoothly and without a hitch.

Despite the inevitable problems one has to marvel at what was achieved. Given that there had been no British presence on the cost before the end of October 1867 it is quite remarkable that by the 25 January 1868 the first part of the army was ready to advance. This speaks not only to the technological ability and resources of a 'superpower' but also to the organisational skills that Napier and his staff brought to the operation.

Progress along the 400 mile route to Magdala, the fortress of Theodore, was difficult. It took until 10 April before the advanced army reached the Magdala plateau. Despite urging from the political authorities to advance quickly Napier had determined that he would only march when ready and would not take undue risks with the health or safety of his Army. Yet despite his caution by the time the army reached the outskirts of Magdala it was suffering. The terrain was difficult, and despite the best efforts of all concerned, there was still sickness amongst animals and men. Supplies were slow in coming up and more than once Napier had to reduce the daily

---

68 This was partly due to the slow rate of production, caused by the need for economy, but also because in 1867 the rifle had been slightly altered by the adoption of Colonel Boxer's improved brass centre fire cartridge.
69 A number of excellent maps were produced during this period. Waterproofed and highly durable, some of the originals can be found in the National Archives. The National Archives (TNA) WO 107/8: Abyssinia Expedition, Quartermaster General, Bombay Army.

ration to his men. Soldiers who had been equipped from India suffered the worst as the inferior quality of Indian produced products, most notably socks and boots, was exposed.

One notably incident regarding discipline is worthy of comment, particularly for the way in which Napier responded. As the leading battalion the 33rd (Duke of Wellington's) Regiment of Foot had been particularly hard-pressed during the advance. As one of the first battalions to land they had been employed in manual labour at Zula to help prepare the base of operations. The movement from Lat to Dida proved the final straw for many of the men.[70] Dozens of men of the 33rd Foot sat down and refused to move, their own officers were ignored. The staff officers sent forward to urge them on were jeered and verbal abused. Colonel Dunn marched into camp with only a small part of his battalion, the rest following in dribs and drabs throughout the night.

In and of itself the incident was minor. No real harm had been done and the incident could be explained by the hard march and a number of other factors.[71] Yet Napier was not content to let the matter rest. Whilst to overreact might worsen the situation, not to react at all could be construed as condoning the action. Napier judged his reaction to perfection. The following morning he paraded the 33rd and 'tore them off a strip'. Given their attitude of the previous day this in and of itself was unlikely to have too much impact, even coming from the commander of the expedition, but Napier understood soldiers. Napier said their behaviour was a disgrace and that they were not fit to lead the advance. Again, this in and of itself might have had only marginal impact on their 'pride'. The genius of Napier's decision was to order forward the 4th (King's Own) Regiment of Foot to replace them in the advanced position. There was a certain 'honour' in leading the army forward and to give this to the 4th was a double blow. Firstly, the fact that the 33rd was a Yorkshire regiment, and the 4th were a Lancashire regiment meant there was a natural rivalry to begin with. Whilst the two battalions had served together in India, this had developed further. Napier's decision to replace them with their rivals was one that would hurt their 'honour' and 'reputation'. It was also likely to be something that the soldiers of the 4th Foot would not let them forget in a hurry.

This firm but intelligent handling of discipline was the hallmark of Napier's command style. He dealt with the matter firmly but intelligently and as a consequence brought the matter to an end. When later in the campaign Napier would call upon the 33rd Foot he found a battalion determined to prove their worth. Under the difficult circumstances in which the expedition was operating such an approach was vital. The combination in Napier of such intelligent handling of discipline and attention to logistical detail help to illustrate what an able commander in the field he was.

Least one should think that this was a perfect campaign and that Napier was infallible, it is worth noting that the major battle of the campaign at Arogi, on the 10 April, came about because Napier was caught off balance. The march towards Magdala saw some difficult terrain and Colonel Pharye decided that as the path ahead was very steep he would go ahead and establish a base, thus allowing the baggage and artillery to follow by the easier route. Phayre informed Napier of his decision and the latter could see no reason to disagree and immediately

---

70 The exact date is unclear, but it was likely either the 23 or 24 March.
71 It has been argued that Colonel Dunn had allowed discipline to deteriorate during the campaign. It was also stated that the large number of 'Irish' in the regiment helped to explain the ill-discipline. Both comments are rather harsh.

started off the baggage train and guns. However, Napier underestimated the amount of time it would take these men to move forward. As a consequence the baggage and artillery were moving largely undefended. On realising this Napier at once sent his A.D.C to bring forward the 4th Foot. The exhausted men of the regiment made their way forward and reached Phayre and Napier in the forward position just as the first shots were fired by the Abyssinians.

Theodore and his army of some 10,000 men and numerous guns had been watching. Theodore believed Napier had made a grave mistake seeing what he thought was an unarmed supply column, unaware of the nearby presence of the 4th Foot. He therefore despatched 5-6,000 of his best troops under the command of his 'favourite', Chief Gabi, to attack the column.[72] The baggage and perhaps more importantly the guns appeared exposed, and Theodore had seized the opportunity.

Whatever errors Napier may or may not have made leading up to the attack, his response was instant and decisive. He ordered forward the 23rd Punjab Pioneers and the mountain guns to secure the pass. The Naval Brigade with their 6pdr Hale's rockets were ordered to a spur overlooking Arogi, although this typically inaccurate fire did little damage to the enemy. It did however slightly delay the Abyssinian advance. This proved vital and gave the 4th Foot, two companies of the 27th Native infantry, and a company of Royal Engineers time to reach the field.

It was now that the new Snider service rifle that Napier had insisted on equipping his men with came to the fore. The 4th Foot opened a devastating and rapid fire upon the advancing Abyssinians. Just in time they had reached the field of battle and inflicted heavy losses on the enemy. A company of the 4th Foot, along with the 23rd Punjab Pioneers, defended the baggage and the guns, the latter making great use of the bayonet. Technology, drill, discipline, and decisive action had won the battle. The Abyssinian's had around 700 killed, including Chief Gabi, and over 1,200 wounded. The British casualties were only 20 wounded, two of whom would later die of their wounds. Theodore, who had hoped for an easy victory, withdrew to his fortress at Magdala with what remained of his army.

Napier remained where he was overnight, using the waggons of the baggage train as a makeshift defensive position. The following morning, the 11 April, the remainder of his supply column and the 2nd Brigade arrived in support. Although Theodore had seen the writing on the wall and was prepared to release his 'European' prisoners he was not prepared to meet Napier's other demand that he surrender unconditionally.[73] Napier continued to negotiate with Theodore, including returning the body of Chief Gabi for burial. By the afternoon of the 12 April all the 'European' hostages and their families had been released. This freed Napier's hands, as he had been reluctant to attack Magdala whilst the hostages remained at risk. Theodore and 2-300 loyal soldiers remained in Magdala, and Napier could not withdraw and leave them in

---

72　The exact nature of the armament of this force is unclear. Exactly how many guns Theodore brought to the field is unknown, although we know that he managed to bring into the field his pride and joy a 70 ton mortar manufactured by German craftsmen. This weapon however only fired one shot before exploding. Of the men that attacked at Arogi the majority of them carried firearms of one sort or another. There were a surprising number of modern rifled percussion cap shotguns found amongst the dead Abyssinian soldiers. Such weapons were theoretically superior to those carried by the Indian army contingent of Napier's force.

73　It is said that on the evening after Arogi Theodore attempted to commit suicide with a pistol, ironically a gift from Queen Victoria. The pistol misfired and Theodore survived.

place without risking his retreat, which would be difficult enough as it was. Napier now had to storm the mountain fortress, something he had been reluctant to do fearing high casualties.

At 0900hrs on the 13 April 1868 Napier began the advance on the fortress. The company of Royal Engineers and the 33rd Foot led the attack supported by a battery of mountain guns. The advance and the movement of the whole army into position to prevent Theodore breaking out and escaping took some time to accomplish. After considerable reconnaissance Napier decided to attack the Kokilbir, or lower gate, of the fortress that stood some 230 feet above the plain of Arogi. Napier had little choice but to order a frontal attack. To try and protect his advancing force, and increase their chances of success, he had brought up his heavy guns, many of them having to be manhandled into position.

Consequently, it was not until 1500hrs that the attack began with an artillery bombardment lasting an hour before Napier committed his infantry. The advance went well until they reached the gate, here an element of farce entered the proceedings as it was discovered that the engineers had forgotten, or lost on route, their powder bags and fuses with which to blow the gate. The men of the 33rd Foot, perhaps feeling they had a point to prove to Napier, managed to find ways through and over the defences. The actions of Private Bergin and Drummer Magner in climbing the wall and laying down covering fire whilst helping their comrades over the wall would see them both awarded the Victoria Cross. Eventually the 33rd Foot entered the fortress and were able to fight their way to the gate and open it for the rest of the force to enter. Despite the difficult nature of the assault total casualties were only 15 wounded.

With the fall of Magdala the fighting was over. Theodore killed himself, and for a short time the British flag, in the form of the colours of the 33rd Foot flow over Magdala. However, this was not a campaign about territorial aggrandisement and there was no desire, nor practical purpose, in continuing an occupation. Napier evacuated Magdala and had the fortress destroyed. Thus on the 15 April preparations started for the long march back towards Zula. The march proved far more difficult than the advance. The weather had turned, and severe storms hampered the return journey. Morale was also falling. Yet the army made it back to the coast and slowly but surely the army began to evacuate. By the 18 June 1868, the last of the British force had left Abyssinia.

Napier had left on the 10 June but rather than returning to India he had been ordered to England. On his arrival he was feted as a national hero and received numerous honours. He was raised to the peerage as Lord Napier of Magdala and Caryngton, appointed G.C.B and G.C.S.I, given a pension of £2,000 a year for himself and his next surviving male heir, and had the freedom of the cities of London and Edinburgh conferred upon him. Although criticism of the campaign was made at the time, and continues to be made to this day, Napier deserves great credit for his leadership during the campaign. Although the campaign highlighted the 'reach', power, and technological advancement of the British Empire, this could all have counted for naught had it not been for the leadership and skill of Napier.

Napier spent little time in England and was anxious to return to command of the Bombay Army. He returned to India in late 1868 but returned to England again in the summer of 1869. Whilst in England he was sounded out about becoming Commander-in-Chief in India, an appointment he was to take up in January 1870.[74] Once again he tried very hard to improve the living conditions of soldiers in India, both British and Indian. He continued his previous efforts at improving barrack facilities and also introduced a weekly holiday on each Thursday for the men. With typical military humour the holidays were dubbed 'St Napier's day'. As well as attempting to improve the lot of the soldiers he also attempted to improve them as a fighting force, overseeing improvements in tactics, training, and drill.

In the six years that Napier was Commander-in-Chief there was no major call upon the Indian army but there were numerous minor campaigns that required his attention, most notably in the Tochi Valley, the Lushai campaign, and the Duffla Expedition. All were minor and easily dealt with, but it did strengthen Napier's hand somewhat when fighting demands for economy and reduction in the size of the Indian Army. So did the fact that he could point to his recent campaign in Abyssinia which had relied heavily on the Indian Army and the Army in India. At the same time there were increasing concerns about Russia's advance towards the frontiers of India, and particularly possible interventions in Afghanistan and Persia. Napier had at first been rather cool to this threat, but towards the end of his time in office he increasingly held the viewpoint of the 'forward school' and was inclined to venture into Afghanistan to meet the Russian threat there.

Yet there were continual demands by the political powers in India, and the home government, to make reductions in the expenditure of the army, often by reducing the size of the native army. Napier opposed such demands strongly and was often, but not always, successful. Another example of attempts to reduce costs was seen in the strong opposition to Napier's increase in the number of camps of instruction (training and manoeuvres) that were held. The importance Napier attached to this can be gleaned from his correspondence: '…I believe I have given a good stimulus and direction to Field Exercise, leading Commanding Officers not to be glued to their parade grounds, but to shake out their regiments in the open country and make use of the intellects of their officers.'[75] This illustrates that Napier appreciated the need to keep the army ready for possible action: as battles would be fought in 'open country' not on parade grounds. It also speaks to his desire to encourage the initiative of junior officers, something few of his contemporaries would have held with.

In late 1874, with Napier's five year term almost at an end, there was pressure brought to bear by the India Office, who wished Napier to stay on for a further two years. Although an honour, it was not particularly agreeable to Napier. As his son wrote, '… he had begun to feel the burden of forty-six years in India.'[76] However faced with the request from the Duke of Cambridge, Lord Salisbury and Lord Northbrook to continue for two more years, Napier felt compelled to stay on.

In October 1875 Napier was involved in arranging the military aspects of the Prince of Wales tour of India, which took place the following December and January. Napier was present at the great review of the India army that took place in Delhi. Napier rode throughout the review and the whole spectacle was greatly appreciated by all concerned. However that is not the full story. A few days before the review, Napier had fallen from his horse and broken his collar bone.

---

74   Although the appointment was date January 1870 Napier did not arrive back in India until early April 1870.
75   Napier, *Napier of Magdala*, p. 265.
76   Napier, *Napier of Magdala*, p. 289.

Although he was told that he should not even think of riding, such was his determination that he mounted his horse and rode throughout the parade which lasted for several hours. The story perfectly illustrates the determination, devotion to duty, and tenacity of Napier.

In 1876 Napier finally ended his association with India after forty-eight years. On the 10 April 1876 he left India for the last time. The *Civil and Military Gazette* said of his leadership of the Indian Army that he had brought 'Firmness and justice tempered with mercy.'[77] He had led the army through a difficult period and there is no doubt that he left it in a far better condition than the one he had inherited. He had also done a great deal to improve the lot of the soldier in India, both British and native, and had led a determined and often successful resistance to the worst demands for economy that could have had dire effects and consequences for British India. Perhaps the greatest honour to Napier would have been as the *Bombay Times* of India put it, 'He bears with him the regard of the entire command, native and European'.[78] Simple words, but ones which would have meant a lot to Napier.

Before leaving India he had been sounded out about becoming Governor and Commander-in-Chief of Gibraltar. Although on the face of it this would appear a great come down for a man who had been Commander-in-Chief India, there were many motives behind the appointment. The late 1870s and early 1880s were a turbulent time in European affairs, and there appeared to be a very real possibility of war. There were many in government who realised that Napier was now the leading general of the British army and were therefore keen to have him close at hand. Also, if the manpower strength of India should be required who better to combine this with British arms than Napier. His appointment was also strongly supported by the Duke of Cambridge, partly for the same reason, but also because the Duke greatly respected Napier's advice and was keen that he should be near enough to provide this speedily when required.

The appointment was also something of an honour in that it combined both civil and military responsibilities. That Napier was suited to the role was proved by the improvements to life in the colony that Napier brought about. Using his engineering skills, he did much to improve the facilities and amenities on the 'Rock'. His first action was to turn to the military facilities concerned as he was about the naval defence and storage of the magazines. At his behest two new 100 ton guns were placed in defensive positions in Gibraltar. The first named Victoria was installed in 1879 and the second installed in 1883 was named the Napier of Magdala battery.[79] Napier also did much to improve relations with Spain.

In February 1878 things looked bleak and Napier was recalled to London to consult about possible British actions in the event of a European war. Napier was appointed to command the expeditionary force with Garnet Wolseley as second in command. Although theoretically the combination of Napier and Wolseley was an exciting prospect, it was perhaps just as well that they were never required as the two men had a poor relationship. Indeed, in a letter to the Duke of Cambridge, that was no doubt warmly received given the readers own antipathy towards

---

77 Napier, *Napier of Magdala*, p. 295.
78 Anon, *Lord Napier of Magdala* (Bombay: Times of India, 1876), p. 17. This was a special booklet or pamphlet published by *The Times* of India to mark the departure of Napier from India.
79 Although the Victoria battery is long since gone, Napier of Magdala battery can still be seen in the British Overseas Territory of Gibraltar to this day.

Wolseley, Napier was deeply critical of Wolseley and questioned what he had actually achieved as a commander.[80]

In 1883 Napier left Gibraltar and was promoted to the rank of Field Marshal in January of that year. Although retained on the active list, Napier held no active military command until his death. Napier's opinion was still sought on numerous occasions and his advice was still appreciated in the higher levels of government. At the age of seventy-three it was not inconceivable he would be given active command in the future, but it was unlikely. In a sense a new era had dawned and with it new commanders such as Wolseley and Roberts. Although an effective leader, commander, and administrator, Napier was 'old-school' and 'conservative' in many ways.

Indeed there are many paradoxes when looking at Napier's career. He preferred the 'old order'. He was a great friend and support of the Duke of Cambridge, sometimes called an 'arch-conservative'. Indeed, through examination of the correspondence between Napier and Cambridge we see a very different picture of the Commander in Chief. Cambridge's intelligence and understanding is illustrated in a way that rather goes against the perceive image of the man. Napier disliked Wolseley and many of the 'ring' who supported him. He had little time for their 'self-laudation' and 'reformist' ideals. He saw Wolseley as an intriguer who was advancing himself on a platform of reform that was more to do with the benefits to Wolseley and his gang than the improvement of the Army. He had a great many doubts about the other 'modern' commander Lord Roberts, although in his case Napier was prepared to make exceptions and certainly held him in higher esteem than Wolseley.

Yet whilst not wishing to see vast change and reform in the army, Napier is proof that it is wrong to identify 'conservatives' in the army with 'incompetence' or a neglect of modern techniques. In Abyssinian Napier had made the best use possibly of modern technology, which had made the campaign practical. The inclusion of a photographic team for the first time on campaign was at Napier's insistence. Whilst this gave little assistance from the point of view of fighting the campaign, it gave a lasting record of events that have proved interesting to future generations of historians. There is clearly a case to be made that whilst Napier clung to the 'ideals' of a previous era, he was more than prepared to embrace new 'ideas' if they helped him in his work.

Although a stern disciplinarian he showed great care for his men. This was perhaps more than simply the traditional paternalistic care of the officer to his men, or the mere appreciation of them as 'soldiers' and the concern for their efficiency as such. Whilst his constant calls for better facilities and treatment for the men had, to an extent, to do with efficiency it would be wrong to think that was all there was to it. There was a humanitarian side to Napier that was only occasionally seen.

This would even lead him to take a rather questionable course of action at one point in his career. In 1874 there was criticism of the Napier Cantonment system, largely on the grounds

---

80   The letter was written after the 1882 Egyptian campaign, and what was considered Wolseley's crowning achievement. On leaving Gibraltar in January 1883 Napier had travelled to Egypt and had walked the battlefields of that campaign. See H.D. Napier, Letters of Field Marshal Lord Napier of Magdala (London: Simpkin & Marshal Ltd, 1936), pp. 69-70. The letter was actually addressed to Major General Martin Dillon, Assistant Military Secretary to the Commander in Chief the Duke of Cambridge. However, it was clearly intended for the Duke to read.

that the size of them was inefficient. As we have already seen Napier had proved that by having space for clean air to move about there was a dramatic decrease in the spread of disease. Dr Cunningham, the Inspector General of Cantonments in India, had recently proposed decreasing barracks from 70 feet to 57 feet, along with numerous other measures which Napier thought would harm the men and increase the spread of disease. To help fight his case Napier contacted Miss Florence Nightingale, after reading her book *Life or Death in India*. As a soldier Napier could not really take his struggle public. However Miss Nightingale, as a public figure and renowned campaigner, certainly could. To this end Napier took the great risk of sending her confidential minutes on the subject which as he himself said to her, '...I have no business to send you, but I know I can safely do so, and that you will consider it confidential.'[81] This act of indiscretion, done at great risk to his own career and future, helps to demonstrate the real and profound care that Napier had for his men. This was beyond concern for them as soldiers and demonstrated a humanitarian side that was so often lacking in senior officers of this era.

This leads us on to another such paradox. Napier was ahead of his time in terms of conservation and preservation of wildlife. Almost unknown for the age, he was opposed to hunting for sport, although protocol often called for him to engage in such activities when visiting with Indian nobility. Indeed, one story exists that when out of a 'shoot' with the Maharaja of Kashmir, Napier informed His Highness of his reluctance to kill animals. The Maharaja's response was to kill extra animals himself so that they could be credited to Napier and thus preserve his 'honour'![82]

We can therefore see that Field Marshal Robert Napier, 1st Baron Napier of Magdala was an unusual combination of the traditional and the modern. Perhaps this is fitting as he was indeed a truly mid-Victorian General. Thus, he combined characteristics of the late Georgian and early Victorian with the late Victorian ideals that would lead into the early years of the twentieth century. Napier died on 14 January 1890 at his London residence, 63 Eaton Square. He had caught influenza and after a few days of illness had succumbed at the age of seventy-nine. His widow received letter of condolence from around the world including Queen Victoria, the Prince of Wales, the Princess of Wales, Emperor Wilhelm II of Germany, the Dowager Empress of Germany, the Duke of Cambridge, the Duke of Connaught, and Lord Roberts.[83] At noon on the 21 January 1890 Napier received a state funeral. Although Queen Victoria did not attend, the Prince of Wales, Prince George of Wales, and the Duke of Cambridge were present. The large crowd, including the entire War Office senior staff and numerous retired Generals, gathered to pay their last respects to Napier, before he was interned in the crypt of St Pauls. Sadly, and to chagrin of many, there had not been time to organise an official presence from the Bombay Army.

As per his instructions the Royal Engineers took centre stage along the route to St Pauls and in the escorting and carrying of the coffin, despite the presence of the large number of Guards and Household Cavalry present. There is something fitting about an 'unfashionable' regiment being given centre stage ahead of its more illustrious counterparts. In many ways that spoke to the career of Napier himself, from lowly East India Company subaltern to Field Marshal.

81 Napier, *Letters of Napier of Magdala*, pp. 36-37.
82 Napier, *Napier of Magdala*, p. 272-3.
83 I am grateful to Mrs Amanda Gore and her husband Tim for their assistance in providing copies of Lady Napier's correspondence.

4

Major-General Sir John Charles Ardagh (1840-1907)

Edward Gosling

> *The truth is that he is a hard worker and a great reader. He is a man in whom one instinctively puts confidence as being equal to any fate, and assuredly he has borne himself well in whatsoever his hand hath yet found to do.*[1]

Major-General Sir John Charles Ardagh K.C.I.E., C.B., R.E., was one of twenty-four Victorian generals to be featured in 'Our Army Chiefs', a series in *Lloyd's Weekly Newspaper* which ran from November 1895 to April 1896; his portrait and a brief biography followed the illustrious personages of General Sir Redvers Buller, Field-Marshal Lord Roberts and Lieutenant-General Sir Henry Brackenbury. In April 1896, Ardagh just had been appointed Director of Military Intelligence at the Intelligence Division of the War Office. It was the culmination of a career which had seen service across the globe in the Caribbean, Europe, the Balkans, Egypt and the Sudan and India and in as varied a capacity. Having entered the British Army as a Royal Engineer, John Ardagh would forge a career as one of the most capable intelligence officers in the British Army as well as a gifted topographer, administrator, lawyer and diplomat whose service would extend well beyond the War Office.

Ardagh was a highly intelligent and intuitive soldier, with astute abilities which ranged from military engineering to strategic planning. Physically, he was described by associates as, "about middle height, with a slight and graceful figure … He did not say much but what he said was always to the point. With a gentle smile and manner he held his own".[2] But his slight figure hid an athleticism and a steely determination. As a junior officer he spent several weeks in the field conducting surveys and supervising defence construction in the mountains of Bulgaria or the outskirts of Alexandria with a "conscientious energy and zeal" which compelled the efforts of

---

1   C. W., 'Our Army Chiefs: Major-General Sir John Ardagh, K.C.I.E., C.B.', *Lloyd's Weekly Newspaper* (London), 26th April 1896, issue 2788.
2   Susan, Countess of Malmesbury (Lady Ardagh), *Life of Sir John Ardagh* (London: John Murray, 1909), p. 14.

his subordinates.³ And to his subordinates, his quiet manner simply amplified the mystery of the officer who could inspire a mixture of respect, curiosity and awe.⁴ This chapter explores the career of John Ardagh, his rise and, arguably, his fall.

Early Life and Career 1840-75

John Charles Ardagh came, not from military family, but a religious one. The second son of the Reverend William Johnson Ardagh, vicar of Rossmire and his wife Sarah Cobbold of Ipswich, he was born at Comragh House, Co. Waterford, in Ireland on the 9 August 1840. His mother died soon after and the infant was raised by his father and his maternal aunt. From an early age, Ardagh seemed destined to take holy orders and pursue a career in the church. Whilst not demonstrating any particular talent which might suggest a military career beckoned however, Ardagh developed in his formative years many of the skills and attributes which would later render him an invaluable officer in the British Army and military intelligence.

From the age of ten Ardagh attended Waterford School, run by Dr Price. According to one erstwhile school friend, "no one could touch him at mathematics, and with all his cleverness he was as modest as he was generous".⁵ Having finished top of his school and head of the 'big boys' dormitory', Ardagh entered Trinity College Dublin (TDC) at the age of seventeen in 1857. There he enjoyed further academic success, gaining a prize in Hebrew and honours in Mathematics.

It was during his time at university that Ardagh's thoughts first turned to soldiering. Despite working towards a life in the church the prospect had lost its appeal, in part because of the "hard-and-fast dogmas" and "abstract truths" which characterised the church's governance in

Major-General Sir John Ardagh.

3   Lord Dufferin to Lord Granville, 29 November 1881, in Malmesbury, *Life of Major-General Sir John Ardagh*, pp. 140-141.
4   Fergusson, T. G., *British Military Intelligence 1870-1914: The Development of a Modern Intelligence Organisation* (Frederick, Maryland: University Publications of America, 1984), p. 106.
5   Extract from the testimony of 'an old school fellow' in Malmesbury, *Life of Sir John Ardagh*, p. 2.

Ireland during the mid-century.⁶ The presence of Sir William (then Major) Palliser, a neighbour of the Ardaghs', may also have had some influence; his experiments in artillery which he carried out close-by encouraged the young man's interest in military science. Further to his academic interests, Ardagh developed an aptitude for horse riding which he was taught by his father. He also showed an early penchant as an artist and was encouraged to draw by Louisa, Lady Waterford, who gave the boy his first paint-box.⁷

Despite his initial intentions towards the church therefore, John Ardagh's formative years endowed him with a fortuitous combination of talents particularly well suited for the career he would go on to forge. His artistic and mathematical skills would serve him well in his endeavours as a Royal Engineer and as a cartographer. His relationship with fellow and younger schoolmates was based upon authority through arbitration rather than dominance in a manner distinctly reminiscent of his tenure as Director of Military Intelligence. Moreover, the tensions he undoubtedly encountered growing up the protestant son of a vicar in Ireland and a student at the protestant Trinity College [TCD] as opposed to the Catholic University College in Dublin further instilled a sense of diplomacy and negotiation which he was to draw upon repeatedly in his encounters with several of the most noted military and political leaders of late nineteenth-century Europe. It would seem, Ardagh's future as a soldier-diplomat, engineer, mapmaker and General was well provided for in his early life.

Having taken the decision to try for a commission in the Royal Engineers (he had passed first place in Galbraith's preparatory class whilst at TCD), Ardagh attended the entrance examinations at the Royal Military Academy in Woolwich in 1858, passing in second. A year later, on the 1 April 1859, he passed out first in his cohort and was gazetted second lieutenant in the Royal Engineers.⁸ From Woolwich he proceeded to the School of Military Engineering at Chatham. He was a careful and diligent student, keeping detailed notes and neat sketches on subjects such as the costal defences - military and storm – across southern England and techniques in bridge-building and fort construction.⁹ Following Chatham, Lieutenant Ardagh's skills were quickly tested as he was sent to Pembroke to superintend the design and construction of Fort Popton, which, alongside Fort Hubberstone, was intended to defend Milford Haven. Popton and Hubberstone were part of the widespread Palmerston Forts, commissioned in response to fears of invasion from the French and initiated as part of the Royal Commission on the Defence of the United Kingdom in 1860. It was a task he seemingly found himself equal to and was officially commended in reports to the Inspector-General of Fortifications, Field-Marshal Sir John Burgoyne.

The early years of Ardagh's career can boast some unusual feats which earned the young Lieutenant a growing reputation. The first of these took place at sea, aboard the transport *Victoria* in 1861. Amid tensions between Great Britain and the United States over the *Trent* affair, Ardagh was despatched with a party of sappers and a considerable quantity of telegraph wire destined for St John's, New Brunswick in Canada.¹⁰ The steamship, rotten and built for sailing

---

6   Malmesbury, *Life of Major-General Sir John Ardagh*, pp. 3-5.
7   Malmesbury, *Life of Major-General Sir John Ardagh*, pp. 3-5.
8   Ardagh's commission as Lieutenant, R.E., is dated 30 October 1860.
9   The National Archives (hereafter TNA): PRO 30/40/5: Journals and Notebooks 1867 – 1878.
10   The Anglo-American crisis surrounding the *Trent* affair took place in November 1861 during the American Civil War. A Federal naval officer boarded the RMS *Trent* and arrested two of her passengers,

in the Pacific and Indian Oceans, was unsuited to Atlantic voyages to begin with. Following an initial, abortive effort, which saw the *Victoria* encounter storms with gale force winds and a considerable number of the crew subsequently desert, they embarked again from Cork Harbour in the February of 1862. The harsh Atlantic conditions caused further problems for the *Victoria* as it was blown nearly up to Iceland and then down to the Azores. As one witness recalled, the new crew were not of a high standard and it took the efforts of Ardagh and his engineers working solidly for three days to repair and maintain the ship's engines and pumps to get the *Victoria* seaworthy enough to reach Fayal Harbour in Portugal.

The *Victoria* enjoyed a few hours respite at Fayal to send home despatches and to avoid a Confederate steamer which was running a blockade from New Orleans, but during which time the Royal Engineers slaved tirelessly over the ship's engine. The vessel then finally returned to Plymouth three months after it had left Ireland and some distance further from its intended destination. Without Ardagh's endeavours, Captain Reid notes, the vessel may well have sunk.[11] Despite the group's failure to attend to their objectives in Canada, the Royal Engineers were credited with saving the ship. Ardagh's conduct was highly praised, bringing him to the notice of senior officers such as Sir William Jervois. He was thanked on parade by H.R.H the Duke of Cambridge, the Commander-in-Chief.

After a further short spell at Chatham, Ardagh was ordered to Newhaven, where the twenty-two year old Lieutenant was given responsibility for designing and building the Newhaven Fort. It was during this appointment, which commenced in 1862, that the young engineer was able to demonstrate his talents for military engineering and innovation, inventing and patenting for use in his fort the 'equilibrium' drawbridge. His design employed a system of counter weights, housed within the outer wall and behind the entrance way, thus enabling the bridge to be raised and lowered fully so when vertical it sealed the fort entrance making attack more difficult.

Ardagh's fort was also the first military structure to use concrete, which was made from shingle sourced from the beach some 120 feet below, and built around the contours of the cliff top, as opposed to flattening the ground prior to construction, helping the building blend with its milieu. In charge of the Newhaven Fort throughout its construction, Ardagh spent spells in Portsmouth and the Isle of Wight working on the southern defences there and at Spithead. He established his headquarters at Brighton where he remained until July 1867 when he took two months leave to travel to Iceland with a friend, Mr. Lawton, on his yacht the *Sappho*.

Following Ardagh's two-month excursion on the *Sappho*, during which time he enjoyed a varied and active existence mountain and hill climbing, sightseeing, nature watching and sailing across Scotland and Iceland, he returned to Newhaven Fort and a burgeoning social circle in Brighton which included his future wife and biographer Susan Hamilton and the future Prime Minister William Gladstone. This final stint at Newhaven was followed by a new appointment, on the recommendation of Field-Marshal Sir John Burgoyne, as Secretary to Admiral Sir Frederick Grey's Committee on Fortifications.

The Fortifications Committee, which Ardagh joined in April 1868, was established to inquire into the state and progress of the fortifications recently or currently under construction under

---

Confederate envoys bound for the United Kingdom, actions which caused diplomatic outrage in Britain.
11   Malmesbury, *Life of Major-General Sir John Ardagh*, pp. 7-9.

the Defence Act of 1860. The committee brought Ardagh into contact with some prominent individuals including Sir Lintorn Simmons (with whom Ardagh would later work in connection with the Eastern Crisis in Berlin), Sir Collingwood Dickson, Sir John Hawkshaw and Colonel Elwyn. Ardagh's work on the committee was well received and commended by Admiral Grey, further enhancing his reputation as a capable and reliable officer and an insightful engineer. As Sir William Jervois later recounted, "everyone connected with that committee spoke in the highest terms of [Ardagh's] ability and industry. The elaborate report [he] prepared for that committee is of itself a testimony to the value of [his] exertions while thus employed".[12]

Consequently, Ardagh was requested by the then Colonel Jervois to accompany him on his inspection of the fortifications at Halifax and Bermuda. Despite their work in Bermuda lasting only a short time, Ardagh established a good rapport with Colonel Jervois who, writing to Ardagh some ten years after the event, recalled the reputation for hard work and ability which the young Lieutenant had established for himself. "It is no exaggeration to say that there is no one amongst the number of engineer officers who have served under me whose ability, industry and judgement I value more highly than I do yours."[13] It was this reputation which led Sir William to request Ardagh for the mission, and Ardagh had evidently lived up to his expectations.

Upon their return from Bermuda, Ardagh was appointed Secretary to the Committee on Coast Defences which was established in light of the rumbles of the approaching Franco-Prussian War. As part of his duties, the Foreign Office sent Ardagh to Belgium and Holland in connection with the defence plans they were developing should their neutrality be violated. On the 26 February 1871, Ardagh was granted permission from the War Office to travel to the continent to view the French and German armies and the advance of the latter into Paris. Whilst in Paris he carefully observed the reaction of the Parisian public and authorities to their occupation and the diplomatic climate that existed amongst the officials there present. It was an approach he seemingly always took when visiting a foreign region, officially observing points of topographical or technical military interest but, unofficially, registering the reaction and response of peoples and States to the situations they were in. He demonstrated an astute reading of the French situation, noting the violence displayed towards the German troops by Parisians and the near anarchy which occasionally threatened. "These brutal excesses might easily be prevented, but a country in which there is so much licence and little liberty, as under such weak governments as may lead France for many years, they seem inevitable."[14] It was a tendency which would serve him well in his future work in military intelligence and the heavy reliance on written memoranda on any subject which formed the mainstay of the intelligence officer's productivity.

Officially, Ardagh inspected the fortifications of Paris, which had been stripped of their guns for use by the *communards*, and also of their fittings and materials by the local populace, in view of the German advance. He also attended the German high command at Versailles, and

---

12 General Sir William Jervois to Captain J. C. Ardagh, 1878, in Malmesbury, *Life of Major-General Sir John Ardagh*, pp. 30-31.
13 General Sir William Jervois to Captain J. C. Ardagh, 1878, in Malmesbury, *Life of Major-General Sir John Ardagh.*, p. 30.
14 TNA PRO 30/40/5: Notes on Paris, Besancon, Belfort, Strasbourg.

witnessed the preliminary peace papers, signed and sealed, awaiting submission.[15] He observed carefully the procedures the French employed in the final stages of their evacuation, down to the methods they used in spiking the guns. Following his stay in Paris and having obtained licence to travel as far as the 3rd Army, Ardagh headed east through France to Strasbourg in the Alsace, inspecting as a matter of routine the fortifications at Besançon, Pontarlier, Neuchatel, Mulhouse and Belfort *en route*.[16] Having already exceeded his leave period, Ardagh then made for home, travelling via Cologne and the Rhine and witnessing the jubilant celebrations of the German victors.

Following a short stay in Brighton, Ardagh was sent abroad once again, this time to Malta, where he was employed on the fortifications there. His stay was short-lived however as, after three months, he succumbed to his long working hours and to the sun and heat exposure commonly referred to by troops stationed there as 'Malta fever'. He returned to London by August 1871. Once home Ardagh appeared before a medical board and was granted six months sick-leave. He spent this period visiting Scotland and Ireland as well as Field-Marshal Sir John Burgoyne, for whom Lady Ardagh notes, he had a "great reverence and affection", before taking a tour of Germany.[17] He re-joined Chatham on the 25 February 1872 where he would serve for a year acting as Adjutant to Colonel Leahy R.E., Commandant at Wouldham Camp, Acting Brigade-Major at Chatham and as *Aide de Camp* [ADC] to General Browning commanding the division during the autumn manoeuvres. It was in the summer of 1872 that Ardagh was promoted to Captain.[18]

Since embarking for Malta, Ardagh had also been working towards gaining entrance to the Staff College. Twice he applied, failing on the first attempt on account of his youth and but passing the entrance examinations on the second in 1872. Passing in in second place, having lost out on first to Captain Hare R.E. by but a few marks, Captain Ardagh joined the Staff College in February 1873. He completed his final examinations in December 1874 with Military History as his special subject, Geology (in which he obtained a special mention), German and Experimental Sciences as his voluntary subjects and Italian and Landscape as his extra subjects. In the April of 1875, Ardagh was attached to the Intelligence Branch of the War Office.

The Eastern Crisis: The Balkans, Congress of Berlin and Boundaries Commissions, 1875-82

The world of intelligence into which John Ardagh entered in the spring of 1875 was in a fledgling form from the essential component of the military and State machine it would soon become. The Intelligence Branch [IB] could claim as its roots the Topographical Branch of the Quartermaster-General's Department which was itself created in response to the problems of the Crimean War in 1854-56. The 1870-71 Franco-Prussian conflict had further highlighted for the British the limited knowledge they possessed of the belligerent armies and their positions.

---

15 From Lt. Ardagh's diary, March 1871, in Malmesbury, *Life of Major-General Sir John Ardagh*, pp. 22 - 23.
16 TNA PRO 30/40/5: Notes on Paris, Besancon, Belfort, Strasbourg.
17 It is also noted that this was the last meeting the two men had as Sir John Burgoyne died in the October of 1871; Malmesbury, *Life of Major-General Sir John Ardagh*, p. 28.
18 Ardagh was promoted to Captain on the 3rd August 1872.

The IB was as a result established in earnest under the Sir Patrick MacDougall on the 23 February 1873.

From the outset, the IB was able to boast as a considerable strength its formidable wealth of information, in the form of a vast and ever-expanding library and a complement of gifted and dedicated officers. This strength was also a major hindrance however as, in spite of the authority with which its officers could present information to any department – both civil and military – which might request it, they did not have the authority to advise that department nor to influence its policy. Sturridge notes that, "the department as a whole was neglected by both the civil and military authorities", describing attitudes as, "suspicious and stingy, regarding the Intelligence Department as a short step from a General Staff and unfettered militarism".[19] As a result, the IB came quickly to be viewed as a convenience, there to be availed upon by ministers and officials for information yet for their recommendations and findings to be readily dismissible with a polite 'read and noted'. The branch was further isolated by its separation from Horse Guards; the IB headquarters was Adair House, at St James Square, just off Pall Mall, until 1884 when it transferred to Queen Anne's Gate.

Despite struggling with its status as something of a 'Cinderella section' of the War Office, the IB enjoyed rapid growth in strength and capability during the early 1870s, a progression Beaver attributes to the, "young captains and majors with experience and expertise beyond their years", whose input may not have influenced policy directly but certainly affected it.[20] Gradually, the IB became the first port of call for not only military issues but also queries from the Foreign Office [FO], Colonial Office [CO] and Indian Office [IO] whose minutes increasingly ended, "Presume you have asked the [IB]", to which the reply would come, "Done".[21] Fundamentally, this was a contradiction. This willingness to defer to the IB came in part from the "remarkable efficiency" of the Prussian General Staff which by providing the German army with coordinated strategic planning, fulfilled a similar role.[22] It was the prospect of a genuine British General Staff which dissuaded wholesale investment by the military and civilian authorities however. The first major steps in the IB's evolution into a respected, though abused, department came with the Eastern Crisis and the events which culminated in the Congress of Berlin in 1878. It was a development in which Ardagh was at the fore.

When Ardagh joined the IB in 1875 he work for nine months under Deputy Quartermaster-General for Intelligence, Major-General Sir Patrick MacDougall in London. In January-February 1876, Ardagh was employed in the Netherlands on intelligence duties before returning to become Deputy Assistant Quartermaster General [DAQMG] for Intelligence under Sir Patrick MacDougall and Sir Archibald Alison on the 13 July 1876. In that same month, Ardagh was made Head of the Ottoman Section (E).[23] He was immediately sent to the Turco-Serbian frontier.

---

19 Surridge, Keith, *Managing the South African War 1899-1902: Politicians v. Generals* (Woodbridge: Boydell Press & RHS, 1998), pp. 20-21.
20 Beaver, William, *Under Every Leaf: How Britain Played the Greater Game from Afghanistan to Africa* (London: Biteback Publishing, 2012), p. 2.
21 Beaver, *Under Every Leaf*, p. 2.
22 Fergusson, *British Military Intelligence 1870 – 1914*), p. 26.
23 The Ottoman Section (E) had been small and poorly resourced but with some careful bolstering from the Russian Section (D) it began to yield valuable information of the near East.

The root causes of the Eastern Crisis ran deep. For Great Britain and Russia, the tensions were part of 'the Great Game' and conflicting ambitions of Russian imperial expansion and British interests in India. The British had two schools of thought, *close frontier* and *forward frontier*, the former pertaining to defensive precautions to be taken on the Indian borders ensuring a concentrated and localised resistance to Russia, the latter preferring to meet any Russian attack on other territories, mainly Persia and Afghanistan, thus creating a buffer. The Ottoman Empire had by 1876 become a key pawn in the Great Game. It had been brought into the European diplomatic landscape at the Treaty of Paris which closed the Crimean War. Though ostensibly intended to remedy Turkey's diplomatic ostracism resulting from its not fighting in the Napoleonic Wars and therefore not being present at the Congress of Vienna (1815), the move was deliberately intended to limit Russian expansionism.[24]

The Ottoman Empire was crumbling, or so it was thought by the British and Russian powers who hoped to manipulate the weak Turkish regime to their own ends. However, as Ferris has argued, this was rather "fantastical", the Turkish state was "twenty years into a renaissance".[25] Despite the diplomats' misreading of the region, Turkey played a significant role in the aspirations of the European imperialists. It was the eruption of rebellion and insurrection among the Balkan states against the Turks over increased taxes in the face of famine which gave rise to such European opportunistic alarm, first in Herzegovina in the summer of 1875 and later in the May of 1876, in Bulgaria. The outrage caused by the brutal manner in which the Ottomans and the Bashi-Basooks had supressed the disturbances, coupled with the misrule by the Sultan Abdul Aziz and his nephew Murad and their deposition, further deepened concerns over their stability. By June 1876, Serbia and Montenegro also had launched offensives and it was the success of the Ottoman armies in repulsing these assaults which led to appeals to the Powers for arbitration.

For Great Britain, the crisis in the Balkans required careful handling and precise reading. War with Russia or with Turkey was to be avoided at all costs. Diplomacy and perhaps a show of strength were the tools to be relied upon by the Prime Minister Disraeli and his Foreign Secretary the Earl of Derby. Central to the diplomatic process was the presence and application of boundaries. Boundaries were already a key component of diplomacy across the globe in the nineteenth century as non-western nations moved towards asserting precise frontiers in order to adopt western methods and gain the benefits of regulated arbitration that accompanied it: a position Western colonial powers further exploited to enhance their influence.[26] In the case of Russia, which was growing ever more likely to declare war on Turkey in response to the Serbian difficulties, and the Balkans more generally, this was ever-more acutely the case. What the British Government needed to conduct such their strategy effectively, however, was intelligence on the Balkans.

It was in fulfilling the government's needs in this context that the Intelligence Branch were particularly successful and demonstrated for the first time its value and importance. The Foreign Office's knowledge of the Balkans was poor and as the diplomatic situation worsened,

---

24   Black, J., *A History of Diplomacy* (London: Reattion, 2010), p. 158.
25   Ferris, John, Robert, 'Lord Salisbury, British Intelligence and British Policy toward Russia and Central Asia 1874 – 1878' in Ferris, J. R., *Intelligence and Strategy: Selected Essays* (London and New York: Routledge, 2005), p. 14.
26   Black, J., *A History of Diplomacy*, p. 158.

the government's ability to predict and plan for the next step was hindered as both the FO and the IO failed to gather, share and process information effectively. As Beaver notes, "it was in this befuddled state that the Intelligence Branch found its niche".[27] The IB's involvement was encouraged by Lord Salisbury, then at the India Office, who regarded intelligence as the answer to the Eastern Question. Relying on the Secret Service Fund of only £25,000, the IB was put to work acting as the eyes and ears of the British Government in the Balkans.[28] The IB had responded quickly, transferring resources to the Ottoman Section (E) which by the October of 1875 had gathered sufficient material to publish three papers and confirm that, "the Ottoman forces were in a lamentable state and that the Russian advances in the Balkans were gathering pace".

From the outset the IB proved its worth. It collected efficiently and effectively 'news' and information from around the world, using reliable methods and modern means of communication. Furthermore IB officers analysed the information they were gathering thereby presenting the FO and the Prime Minister not with raw facts but "full blown intelligence" with which to formulate the government's operations. What was more, the IB had its own press, which enabled the information it processed to be rapidly and effectively disseminated with an efficiency not before available.[29] The Eastern Crisis was to constitute the coming of age of the IB.

Ardagh was ordered to proceed to Nisch to join the Turkish Army headquarters. The journey took almost four weeks to complete during which time Ardagh was able visit a number of towns *en route*, including Salzburg and Vienna and observe several of the fortifications and the temporary hospitals established to receive the Turkish wounded. The terrain was mountainous and difficult and the roads poor, and Ardagh noted the irregularity of the highly armed "rascals" who formed the guard sent to receive his party at the summit of the Sveti Nicola Pass some 4,000 feet above the town of Vidin. As he traversed Bulgaria, Ardagh bore witness to the scars of the conflict raging around him and noted the condition of the Turkish entrenchments at Vischok.

Upon his arrival at Nisch on the 24 September 1876, Ardagh observed the received etiquette and met with numerous Turkish officials, drinking copious amounts of coffee and smoking several cigarettes.[30] He reported to the British Military Attaché to the Turkish Army Sir Arnold Kemball and observed the Turkish positions at Hafiz and Suleiman Pasha on the west bank of the Morava with Lieutenant Maitland-Dougall R.N., the ADC to Sir Arnold. Ardagh also noted the presence of Russian volunteers – officers and men – amongst the Serbian forces, the likes of which were even commanded by Russian generals. He reported back to Maitland-Dougall who shared Ardagh's concern that the presence of the Russians, both as active military personnel and but also instrumental in the ceasefire, had led to "bad faith" on the part of the

27 Beaver, *Under Every Leaf*, pp. 67 – 68.
28 Wade, Stephen, *Spies in the Empire: Victorian Military Intelligence* (London: Anthem Press 2007), pp. 56-57.
29 Beaver, *Under Every Leaf*, p. 68.
30 Malmesbury, *Life of Major-General Sir John Ardagh*, p. 39.

Serbians and had prevented the Turkish forces from consolidating on their successes over the Serbs.[31]

Whilst Ardagh had been travelling to Nisch, the diplomatic situation had been progressing rapidly and gravely. Attempts by the powers at orchestrating a peace conference had proved unproductive as the Pasha refused to acquiesce to conditions which did not recognise Turkey as the aggrieved side in the conflict. The conflict which Great Britain was keen not to become physically embroiled in was in danger of leaving it little alternative. Disraeli therefore sought a different tactic, one which might demonstrate a show of strength whilst offering some material insurance also. On the 30 September 1876, the Prime Minister settled upon a military occupation of Constantinople as the means by which Britain would make a stand. Seeking the requisite intelligence on the city and what was needed to conduct such an operation, he turned to his Secretary of State for War, Gathorne-Hardy and demanded the relevant information on the state of fortifications and the force which would be required to capture and hold the Constantinople.

This presented a problem for the War Office since intelligence on Constantinople was incomplete. Without this information, the government's plans were impeded. The IB set about the task rapidly. Evelyn Baring produced a twenty-page document entitled, *Memorandum on the Probable Course of Action which would be adopted by the Russians in the Event of their attempting to occupy Bulgaria and March on Constantinople* in which he asserted that Britain could effectively support Turkey if the Royal Navy could control the Black Sea and defend the Bosphorus and the Dardanelles. Further knowledge was required however, of Constantinople and its vicinity in order to ensure, "timely forethought… be the means of averting defeat, or of paving the way to victory".[32]

Meantime, Ardagh had received his orders by late September to proceed to Constantinople and report on the city's defences. This he did, with astonishing pace and efficiency. In fifteen days, he produced surveys and sketches of 150 square miles including the position of Buyuk-Tchekmedjé-Derkos line (the peninsula between the Black and Marmora seas), and proposals for the defence of the Dardanelles and the Bosphorus, the Bulair lines and Rodosto. So rapid was the execution of the IB's efforts that the Foreign Office's minute, "further information required" given 16 October was answered with "Done. 25th October".[33] Ardagh was eventually joined by a party led by Lieutenant Colonel Home R.E., which was sent on the 25 October to gather further information on the region including its defence, the availability of supplies, landing grounds and any other details the British would require to conduct operations there. Upon reporting to Home as his superior in the field, Ardagh delivered his material which the Colonel confirmed was highly accurate.

It was at this time, as Beaver suggests, that the Intelligence Branch began to exert some influence over strategy and policy, providing a reliable source of intelligence and enabling forward planning and preparation to a scale never before achieved. "The IB had entered the machinery of decision making. The IB's entrée was made entirely upon its ability to supply

---

31 From a letter written by Captain Maitland-Dougall R.N., 1884, in Malmesbury, *Life of Major-General Sir John Ardagh*, p. 41.
32 Beaver, *Under Every Leaf*, p. 71.
33 Beaver, *Under Every Leaf*, p. 72.

'significant information' and interpret it in ways which made sense."[34] Ardagh, with Home and Fraser, proceeded to elaborate and develop upon the initial reports they had delivered in the October. Throughout November they braved the bitter conditions to survey and observe, finally compiling a three-hundred page intelligence report, *Reports and Memoranda Relative to the Defence of Constantinople and other positions in Turkey, and also Routes into Romelia* to be returned to the IB for publication and dissemination.

As the group's efforts were received back in London, their resources were increased, both financial and personnel, and the depth and scope of their recommendations followed a similar trajectory. Soon, Home's proposals outpaced the aspirations of the political masters. Gathorne-Hardy, upon receiving further requests for men and material in aid of the defence of Constantinople, nervously deferred the issue to Disraeli. For the Prime Minister, the huge cost of such an intervention was becoming apparent and he abandoned the plan in favour of a further peace conference. The IB had achieved success in delivering for the government an efficient system of intelligence sufficient to enable a course of action to be decided upon. Their energy drew criticism however as their proposals ceased to be realistic, leading Disraeli to unkindly suggest the branch be renamed the "Department of Ignorance".[35]

For Ardagh, the month spent working with Home in the region of Constantinople was tough. With both men fighting fever, Captain Edwin Collen, an Indian Intelligence Branch officer there to observe the methodology of his colleagues in the Balkans, praised the skill and accuracy of their work and remarked in his report that they operated under, "circumstances of the greatest physical difficulty, under great pressure and involving the deepest responsibility".[36] Despite his failing health, Ardagh continued to produce reports for the Foreign Office on operations in Herzegovina and Montenegro and in the December was despatched north, to Tirnova in Bulgaria, to assess claims of violence in the region. At the close of his efforts, which were praised by the Foreign Office for their value and accuracy, he succumbed to his fever and was forced to spend nineteen days in bed.

Having regained his strength, Captain Ardagh applied for a two month furlough. In the February of 1877 he embarked for Egypt. He visited the cities of Cairo and Alexandria, travelling on a Nile steamer, before making for Greece and Eleusis, Salamis, Pentelicus, Marathon and Corinth and Patras. He passed the time with his customary sketching and note-taking on the areas he encountered. From Greece, he travelled to Corfu and then onto Italy before returning to England through France. He re-joined the Intelligence Branch in the April and resumed his standard duties, including completing a report on the sea defences of the Lewes and Laughton levels. In late November, Ardagh visited Lord Halifax at Hickleton near Doncaster. A useful social excursion, he met with several high ranking political and military individuals including Lord Cardwell, the erstwhile Liberal Secretary of State for War and great army reformer and Colonel, later Field Marshal, Evelyn Wood, as well as former Chancellor Lord Selborne and Lord de Grey, the ex-War Secretary who had sent Ardagh to Canada during the Trent Affair.

A few days later, Ardagh was sent abroad on special service for the Foreign Office once again, this time to Italy. He reached Rome in the late December of 1877, arriving in the midst of a ministerial and papal crisis. The Italian cabinet was in the process of a major reshuffle and the

---

34   Beaver, *Under Every Leaf*, p. 72.
35   Beaver, *Under Every Leaf*, p. 77.
36   Beaver, *Under Every Leaf*, p. 75.

Pope was gravely unwell, both of which delayed Ardagh's progress in making his connections with the Italian authorities. He was successful in meeting Sir Augustus Paget, the Ambassador-Extraordinary in Rome from whom he received his orders: an alarming list of questions to which the diplomat commented, "Well! *Your* work is cut out for you if you answer all these!"[37]

The mission to Italy was a test of Ardagh's diplomatic skills. Against the chaos of political upheaval and the seasonal *festas*, he was required to gather a large quantity of information on the military establishment in Rome and Northern Italy. After an initial delay, Ardagh was successful in securing transfer from the office of the War Minister to the Chief of Staff General Bertole-Viale, and to gain access to Italian Artillery and Engineer Committees. A few days later he was placed *en rapport* with an Italian staff officer, Lieutenant Gigioli, with whom he was able to share mutually beneficial information on their respective armies. Ardagh's investigations also took him out of Rome and after some persuasion to be permitted access, he returned to familiar territory inspecting the fortifications around the city before proceeding to the Col di Tenda frontier and the Alpine passes and then to the Riviera costal defences. The breadth of Ardagh's research was considerable. He explored every aspect of life in the Italian military, down to the design and conditions of their barrack facilities, which he noted, lacking adequate heating, were rather cold.[38] His investigations were completed with a review of the religious and moral state of the Italian military and the methods for religious and social (largely regarding temperance) instruction they employed. Once his investigations were complete, Ardagh returned to London, arriving in March 1878.

Ardagh's return to London was short-lived once more however, for on the 8 June 1878 he received orders to accompany Field-Marshal Sir Lintorn Simmons as technical military delegate to support the British Government at the Congress of Berlin. Tensions in the near East had not been diffused upon Ardagh's retirement from his posting there in the winter of 1876. The continuing unrest among the Balkan states and public opposition to Turkey in both Russia and Britain following alleged atrocities against Christians in the region had encouraged a general consensus amongst the British, Austrians and Russians that change was needed. Therefore, a further peace conference was held at Constantinople in the January of 1877.[39] Alleged Turkish atrocities had stoked fervent opposition against them across Europe and it was clear that the promise of administrative reform on the part of the Ottoman rulers was necessary if negations and support for their cause was to be accepted back home.

As the British Government grappled with the question of how to convince the Porte that reform was in his interests and that British support was not guaranteed without it, it was Ardagh who offered a solution. He suggested the "appointment of foreign commissioners, Judges or officials [who] would [he] apprehended excite no opposition amongst the people, but rather the reverse for the Turk often suffers just as much as the Christian from maladministration of justice, and official corruption".[40] The proposition was well received by the British and the other powers and became the core of their proposals. It was not as popular with the Turkish however

---

37 From Ardagh's Diary c. 20 December 1877 in Malmesbury, *Life of Major-General Sir John Ardagh*, p. 50.
38 TNA PRO 30/40/5: 'Rome Fortifications etc.' in Notebook 1877.
39 A course of action particularly favoured by Disraeli after the IB had demonstrated the magnitude involved in any military intervention by the British in the Bosphorus.
40 Beaver, *Under Every Leaf*, p. 78.

and once again, efforts at negotiation failed. Neither Britain nor Austria were able to prevent armed escalation and three months later in April 1877, Russia had declared war on Turkey.

When Ardagh returned to the Eastern Question in June 1878, the Russo-Turkish war had been over for three months. The British remained determined to maintain a Turkish presence in the Dardanelles and preserve their buffer against the Suez Canal, whilst Russia and Austria had established an understanding at the Budapest Conventions which they had signed in secret in the spring of 1877 and which sought to annex the Turkish territories in Europe and the Asia Minor between them. It was acknowledged that the defeated Sultan could expect a considerable reduction in his authority and as the defeated party Turkey would lose out. Tensions between the British and the Russians remained severe. Each power, as Medlicott has termed it, had "a minimum programme for which it felt bound, in any circumstances to fight, and a maximum programme of ambitions which it would, under sufficiently favourable conditions, attempt to realise by more powerful means".[41] The words and actions of the delegates at the Congress, therefore, would require some careful handling.

Ardagh attended the Berlin Congress as a military delegate attached to the special embassy which included among its number Disraeli and the Marquis of Salisbury as the two British Plenipotentiaries and the British Ambassador to Berlin Lord Odo Russell as one of four secretaries. The abilities of the IB and the vital role it had played in the crisis up to that point had been noted; Salisbury, as Foreign Secretary had requested an officer of the IB for the role of technical advisor. Ardagh had been chosen for the position. His expertise of the region, through personal experience and access to the department's files and new maps, many of which he himself had drawn, made him the ideal choice. Although the first choice for the appointment as technical and military advisor, Ardagh attended only as the junior, under the orders of General Sir Lintorn Simmons. The appointment of Simmons as a delegate was made after the fact, following outrage at Horse Guards that the Foreign Office and the IB had bypassed them.

The role Ardagh performed at the Congress of Berlin was crucial. As usual in nineteenth century diplomacy, boundaries and the demarcation of borders lay at the heart of the negotiations. Ardagh's expertise were invaluable for the British, not only in advising their own delegates but in ensuring others, most notably the Russians, were unable to use 'creative' ways of winning the debate, by exaggerating or misrepresenting the nature of border-lines to their advantage. As Beaver has highlighted, Ardagh was "key in combating Russian chicanery over numerous technical, military and cartographic issues" and ensured that the existing and new borders in Serbia, Montenegro and Novi Bazar were all recorded to the highest accuracy. He was the only delegate to trace the boundaries of the new Bulgaria and Eastern Roumelia.[42] It was an intense month during which time Ardagh was involved in countless and continuous meetings during the daytime and customary dinners and entertainment in the evening. He described the event as, "a most anxious one, from the great interests and serious responsibility connected with it".[43]

The Treaty of Berlin was signed on the 13 July 1878 and the British delegation returned home triumphant. Captain Ardagh, for his 'able and valuable services during the Congress of Berlin and previously in the scene of war', was made a civil, rather than military, Companion of the Bath

---

41   Medlicott, W. N., *The Congress of Berlin and After: A Diplomatic History of the Near Eastern Settlement 1878-1880*, (London: Frank Cass & Co. Ltd., 1963), p. 4.
42   Beaver, *Under Every Leaf*, p. 91.
43   Beaver, *Under Every Leaf*, p. 91.

[C.B.], an uncommon accolade for a soldier.[44] He received scores of letters of congratulation and good wishes from friends, family, acquaintances and brother officers. His old friend and mentor General Sir William Jervois wrote with particular pleasure to congratulate him on receiving such an award:

> I take this first opportunity of congratulating you – as I do most sincerely on your having gained the first steps in "the Bath". Being a civil C.B. myself, I may venture to say I think the honour is worth a great deal more than some of our military brothers think. A man may, and sometimes does, get a military C.B. for nothing, but he must have done something to get a civil order.[45]

With the military and diplomatic matters settled, the new borders and boundaries which had been agreed upon during the Berlin Congress required demarcation and confirmation. Colonel Home had been appointed British member of the International Commission for the Delimitation of the Frontiers of the new Principality of Bulgaria. Ardagh was attached to Home's contingent to assist him in his duties and they departed for Constantinople, arriving on the 20 September 1878. The commission of which they were to be a part had two main objectives. Officially, their task was to create accurate borders. Less officially, their intention was to ensure the Turkish had the maximum military advantage in the lay of their borders in the face of any future Russian aggression. They were to take care not to separate villages from their food and water supplies and ensured the Turks were afforded every topographical advantage.[46]

Upon their arrival in Turkey the group were delayed by local Ramadan celebrations but were able to contact several other members of the commission with whom they would be working. They hosted a dinner party for their group, which counted in its number French, Italian, Russian, Austrian and Turkish officers. Ardagh was able to examine the defences of Constantinople, the design of which he had contributed a great deal towards, during the initial days of his stay there, meeting up with Baker Pasha, the former British cavalry officer and hero of Tashkesan, now a military advisor to the Turkish army. The construction of the city's defences had suffered considerably from Turkish mismanagement and an absence of engineers. Ardagh was indignant at the neglect by which the lines had been treated on the part of the Turkish Government and officers, angrily noting that, "If crucifixion and impalement were still in vogue… Suleiman, Mahmoud, Damat, Redif and a host of others merit these punishments for their infamous mismanagement".[47]

On 15 October, Ardagh was ordered by Sir Henry Layard to head to the west of Constantinople to Rodosto, to inquire into the reports of brigandage in the Tekir Dagh and outlying mountains to the north. Having taken a Mahoussé steamer, he landed in Rososto that same evening and was struck by the extent to which the absence of the Russian forces, recently withdrawn from the region (the status of which Ardagh had also been briefed to report on), was felt by the

---

44 The terms Disraeli used to present Ardagh's involvement to the Queen', in Malmesbury, *Life of Major-General Sir John Ardagh*, p. 55.
45 TNA PRO 30/40/1: General W. Jervois to Capt. J.C. Ardagh, 18 September 1878.
46 Beaver, *Under Every Leaf*, p. 94.
47 Extract from Ardagh's Diary, 7 October 1878, in Malmesbury, *Life of Major-General Sir John Ardagh*, p. 62.

local population. The Russians, he surmised, had been successful in maintaining order and bolstering trade and commerce for the locals and easing tensions between Christian and Muslim inhabitants and refugees.

By 25 October, the Boundaries Commission had established the time and location for their rendezvous, the Bulgarian town of Silistria on the north-east border with Romania. Silistria was to be the north-western point of the Dobrudscha Frontier heading down to Mangalia on the Black Sea, the precise course of which the commission was tasked with establishing. Ardagh and Lieutenant Chermside R.E. began the long journey north, aiming initially for Varna on the East coast. *En route*, the engineers were joined by a squadron of Cossacks with orders to escort them to their rendezvous. They were also accompanied by a plague of fleas. Fleas not-withstanding however, Ardagh's party arrived safely in Silistria on the 31 October.

After an initial few days during which Ardagh was required to await the arrival of the members of the Commission to have travelled via steamer from Rustchuk, preparations began for the work they were to undertake. Poor weather gave the Commission the opportunity to pause and establish the point at which the new boundary was to commence. In the meantime, Ardagh set to work conducting surveys of the vicinity in preparation for the expedition. Initially, Ardagh had been selected as director of the topographical operations, however, following jealous protestations from other members of the Commission, (in his diary he claims), a French officer Commandant Lemoine was placed nominally in charge. The whole Commission marched on the 7 November.

For Ardagh and Chermside, the operation was tough going. The topographers set out at dawn and returned at dusk, taking lunch in the saddle and covering up to twenty miles on foot and twenty miles on horseback each day, all the while with threat of attack from marauders or brigands reputedly in the region. The greatest challenge they faced was locating camp at the end of the day, having not finished surveying until after dark and particularly since the camp was liable to relocate whilst they were out. The weather was favourable however, and aside from some protestations from the Russian Colonel Bogoliubow, the Boundary Commission as a whole enjoyed a smooth run.

The Commission eventually regrouped at Varna on the 19 November, where Ardagh and Chermside had headed the previous day to ensconce themselves into a hotel and prepare their work for submission. From Varna they returned south to Constantinople and worked around the clock to prepare a complete map of the new frontier from the combined efforts of the Russian, Turkish, Romanian and English officers employed therein. Ardagh was later rather scathing of his international collaborators, complaining that the Russians, whilst producing a good quality sketch did so with half a dozen men whilst the Turkish and Romanian efforts were of a poor standard. Despite their differences however, the group were able to overcome variations in topographical style and produce one satisfactory map from thirty-four individual sketches (of which Ardagh and Chermside contributed twenty).[48]

The Commission met again on the 29 and 30 November and with the twelve-foot map successfully produced, new orders were assigned.[49] Colonel Home was despatched to Cyprus, Chermside was to remain in Turkey and Ardagh was to return to Britain. Before he could

---

48 Extract from Ardagh's Diary, 26 November 1878, in Malmesbury, *Life of Major-General Sir John Ardagh*, pp. 70 - 71.
49 On the 30 November 1878 Captain Ardagh was promoted to Brevet Major.

leave however, Ardagh, was ordered to make eight traced copies of the map to attach for the Protocols for the Powers and for Romania. On the 17 December, the Commission met to sign the documents and plans but were delayed by the opposition of Colonel Bogoliubow, alleging discrepancies in the map and partiality on the part of the Commission. The Russians' opposition and alleged machinations had led to fierce debate throughout the consolidation stages, against which Ardagh had been robustly pitted. Repeatedly, Ardagh checked attempts by the Russian members to manoeuvre the frontier to their advantage, on one occasion even surveying thirty miles in one day between Tchain and Kouron in order to present a superior sketch which was accepted over his competitors' version.[50] The morning following their initial abortive attempt to sign off on their work, the Commission returned and all but Bogoliubow signed. The Commission was then adjourned until spring and Captain Ardagh was thenceforth despatched for London, taking with him the original sketches from which to prepare a more accurate version for the IB back at Adair House.

In November 1878 Ardagh was promoted brevet Major. Unhappily, Colonel Home, whom had been suffering from Typhoid towards the end of 1878, died in the New Year. He was replaced as HM Commissioner by Major-General Hamley C.B., who accompanied Ardagh and a new group of officers; Captain Elles, RA; Captain Jones, RA; Captain Everett, 33rd; Lieutenant Hare, RE; Dr Exham and two Royal Engineer non-commissioned officers of Engineers, when they returned to Constantinople in late March 1879. Ardagh was to spend the majority of 1879 engaged in work for the Bulgarian Boundary Commission, delimitating the boundaries of the Balkan states. The work was harder than in northern Bulgaria, with much of the journey mountainous and the weather cold and bleak. Ardagh proceeded, diligently conducting surveys and recording the boundary lines starting in April with the Rhodope mountain range and through the Shipka Pass. The work of the Boundary Commission was finally concluded at the end of September 1879 after which Ardagh took a tour of the Crimean battlefields before visiting Odessa, Moscow and St Petersburg and returning to London via Finland.

Following a few months at the IB headquarters in Adair House, Ardagh returned to Germany as a Military Technical Delegate to another Berlin Conference in June 1880 to negotiate a new frontier between Turkey and Greece. The Powers succeeded in arbitrating between the two countries and in encouraging Turkey to cede a small corner of territory northwest along the Abyssinian Border. Ardagh was also promoted to regimental Major on the 22 September 1880. On the success of Berlin, the new boundary to the West of the Epirus was negotiated at a Convention between the Six Great Powers and the Sublime Porte on the 24 May 1881 in Constantinople. Ardagh was appointed the British Commissioner to the new Turco-Greek Boundary Commission which gathered on 14 June 1881. During a series of initial conferences during late June and July in Constantinople, the Commission members gathered to plan their operations. Ardagh was forceful in those initial meetings, strongly opposing the general inclination of the other representatives that a sketch of the new boundary would suffice, arguing, "a survey, based upon regular triangulation, was not only preferable but indispensable".[51] Ardagh and his assistants, Captain de Wolski and Lieutenant Leverson were entrusted with the

---

50 Beaver, *Under Every Leaf*, pp. 94 - 95.
51 TNA PRO 30/40/8: 'General Report by Major Ardagh on the Delimitation of the Turco-Greek Border'. p. 8.

topographical work required and the Commission proceeded to their starting point on the River Arta (now Arachthos).[52]

On average, Ardagh and his team surveyed in excess of 20 square mile a day.[53] It was a difficult and drawn out process. They experienced considerable obstruction from the Ottoman officials who refused to allow masts for triangulation to be erected. At one stage the party was delayed by fifteen days in Janina when the Ottoman Commissioner received orders to halt the Commission's work.[54] There were also frequent diplomatic issues with which they had to contend as they sought to ensure predominantly Greek or Turkish populations were positioned on the correct side of the border. The same problem applied to roads and passes causing further complications, as Ardagh reported to Lord Granville at the Foreign Office:

> Numerous instances exist of roads which follow clearly the line of the frontier, and pass, now on one side of it, now on the other. This arises from the fact that the line of crest usually offers fewer obstacles to movement along it, at the top, than on the slopes of the mountain, which are often interceded by raises and lateral features. The maintenance of a strict cordon along the line of the new frontier would therefore occasion much inconvenience to the inhabitants on both sides, by impeding traffic along both roads so situated; and some arrangement between the Turkish and Greek authorities upon the subject may become requisite.[55]

Moreover, the Commission's work brought with it considerable danger. The countryside was over-run by armed peasants or brigands, some issuing threats that throats would be cut if the Commission did not withdraw; one officer was killed by a man suspected to be a local farmer or shepherd. Ardagh, concerned for the men under his command, was forced to march to Metsovo to remonstrate and appeal with the Turkish Commissioner there for additional guards, in response to which half a battalion was awarded.[56] With heavier support, the party climbed 7,000 feet above sea level, through the Kakardista and Djumerka ranges before heading west towards the summits of Mavrovouni and Pade Skunta.[57]

The final observations and sketches of the Turco-Greek Boundary Commission were completed on the 15 October 1881. Ardagh reported back to the Foreign Office that the survey comprised of a line 370 kilometres (230 miles) long and at least 5 Kilometres (in excess of 3 miles) wide. The total area surveyed was 2,500 square kilometres (1,000 square miles), an

---

52 TNA FO 32/537 - Frontier Rectification Boundary Commission, Major Ardagh, Captain de Wolste (1881).
53 Malmesbury, *Life of Major-General Sir John Ardagh*, p. 132.
54 TNA PRO 30/40/8: 'General Report by Major Ardagh on the Delimitation of the Turco-Greek Border'. pp. 9 - 10.
55 TNA PRO 30/40/8: Ardagh to Lord Granville, 31 October 1881.
56 TNA PRO 30/40/8: 'General Report by Major Ardagh on the Delimitation of the Turco-Greek Border', p. 10.
57 TNA FO 32/537 - Frontier Rectification Boundary Commission, Major Ardagh, Captain de Wolste (1881).

average of 33 square kilometres (13 square miles) per day. Ardagh proudly reported that none of the delays suffered were due either to his officers or the surveying.[58]

Egypt, the Sudan, Mobilisation and India 1882-96

For a short while, Ardagh appeared to be set to return to the United Kingdom for a lengthier posting. In the February of 1882, he was appointed Instructor in Military History, Law and Tactics at the School of Military Engineering at Chatham. Having returned to a more familiar environment for a Royal Engineer, Ardagh was able to turn his attentions once more to such topics which excited his interest, in particular the feasibility in both construction and defence of a channel tunnel. He remained in that position for only five months however, for on the 5 July he was sent to Egypt.

For the British and the Prime Minister William Gladstone, involvement in North Africa was not greatly desired, except for the one irresistible economic and strategic game-changer, the Suez Canal. Egypt, itself a province of the Ottoman Empire, was struggling under debts it owed to the French banks, enabling Britain to acquire a junior-partner ownership of the canal with the French. High taxes had already weakened the Khedivate's grip over Egypt and its territories and when in June 1881 Muhammed Ahmad ibn Abdallah, a charismatic Islamic cleric announced himself the Mahdi and launched a jihad against the Sudanese's Egyptian colonial masters, the tide of rebellion began.[59] In April 1882 Islamic and Arab nationalist protests opposing Ottoman/European domination led by Colonel Ahmad 'Arabi Pasha, a renegade officer of the Egyptian army, forced the Khedive to retreat to Alexandria. Riots and unrest in the city had forced the European and Egyptian inhabitants to evacuate and the nationalist militia seized control of Alexandria's defences. With the objective of quelling the riots and preventing the threatened massacre of the Coptic Christians, the British ordered a naval bombardment which began on the 11 June and succeeded in securing Arabi's withdrawal on the 14 June 1882.[60]

Ardagh was appointed Commanding Royal Engineer under Major-General Sir Archibald Alison when he landed in Alexandria on the 17 July 1882.[61] He immediately began inspecting the condition of the defences of Alexandria and preparing to re-establish the city as a habitable and defensible location. Having established that the most serious problem requiring attention was the breach at the fort Kom-ed-Dyk, the interior redoubt of the city, Ardagh took charge of the two companies of Royal Engineers, the 36th and 17th and gave them their orders. The Royal Marines and Ardagh's Royal Engineers set to work plugging the major gaps in the city defences between the mouth of the Mahudié Canal, Bab-el-Gedid station and the old fortifications. Ardagh had received his orders under the strictest secrecy. The British sought to attempt a feint encouraging the Arabi's forces to prepare for an advance from Aboukir Bay whilst the British

---

58 TNA PRO 30/40/8: 'General Report by Major Ardagh on the Delimitation of the Turco-Greek Border', p. 18.
59 The Mahdi is an Islamic prophet.
60 Although initially a joint Anglo-French expedition, the French navy left for Port Said prior to the bombardment
61 The IB had despatched Major Tulloch to Alexandria in June where he established an intelligence and information network publishing in Arabic. He later proceeded to the Sweet Water Canal. Other intelligence officers despatched included Captain Gill, who went into the desert to work with the Bedouin Tribes, and Major-General Alison was placed in overall command of the Expedition.

approached from Port Said and Ismailia instead.⁶² For the present however, Alexandria received full priority.

In addition to directing the restoration work of Alexandria's defences, Ardagh was also responsible for ensuring the stores and water supply were adequate. The water-works were of particular significance since Arabi had dammed the Mahudié Canal. The Alexandria Water Works required some refurbishment with several ancient tanks in need of sealing and sanitising for use as reserve supplies. Ardagh also ordered a coffer damn be constructed across the canal itself to further secure the fresh water supply and prevent sea water from entering. Having set to order the requisite works to sure up Alexandria's defences, Ardagh rode out to Ramleh, on the Cairo railway to reconnoitre Arabi's position, which was strong. Ardagh established a defensive position with the newly-arrived 60th, two 7-pounders and 30 Royal Engineers at the principle reservoir of the water-works located there.⁶³

As more British troops landed in Alexandria, Ardagh was forced to divide his attention between reconstructing the city defences, excavating defensive trenches, bridging the canal and attending to the water-works and outer defensive positions at Ramleh. On the 26 July Ardagh joined a commission comprising of Admiral Sir Beauchamp Seymour, Sir Auckland Colvin, Captain Molyneux, R.N. and the Chief Engineer of the Alexandria water-works, Mr Cornish, to inspect the water-works and general water supply at Ramleh. The reservoir was now well defended with the 60th, 38th and Royal Engineers barracked at the site although, as with Alexandria, a shortage of working parties slowed the works. Ardagh had at his disposal four 4-pounder guns, six 9-pounders, two Gatling guns, 1,500 infantry and 40 Engineers.⁶⁴

On the night of the 29 July Ardagh led a working party consisting of two companies of Royal Engineers comprising of one officer and twenty men each, two companies of Royal Marines and a company of Rifles on a night-time mission to repair the railway. The line had become broken by the British bombardment and from sabotage by the rebels. Despite the close proximity to the enemy the group worked successfully and restored the line by 1am without incident, allowing a train of some thirty trucks pass from Gabbari onto the Moharrem Bey line. By the final days of July, Ardagh and his men had managed to secure the Ramleh outpost from raiders in preparation for the battle of Kafr-el-Dawar (5 August 1882). The men at the picket received sporadic contact with the Arabi's men but such skirmishes were short-lived and without great bloodshed.

Ardagh's engagement at Alexandria/Ramleh came to an end on the 24 August 1882, the day on which the Arabi's dam which had been starving Alexandria of fresh water was captured and destroyed. With orders to proceed to Port Said, Ardagh left the following day and reached Ismailia at the mouth of the Suez Canal on the 29 August. At Ismailia, British preparations were well underway for the planned advance to Cairo and confrontation of Arabi's forces; the feint which sought to deceive the Egyptian forces into expecting an attack on Cairo from Alexandria had succeeded allowing Wolseley to re-embark the British troops and land at Port Said and launch his operations from the canal. Upon his arrival, Ardagh further assisted in the restoration of the rail network which was so crucial to the British operations. He was present

---

62 Malmesbury, *Life of Major-General Sir John Ardagh*, p. 145.
63 Ardagh's Diary, 23 July 1882, in Malmesbury, *Life of Major-General Sir John Ardagh*, p. 150.
64 Extract from Ardagh's Diary, 26 November 1878, in Malmesbury, *Life of Major-General Sir John Ardagh*, p. 151.

at the battles of Tel-el-Mahuta and Kassassin which saw the Egyptian assaults quickly repelled and fall back to the village and military camp of Tel-el-Kebir. He was ordered by Wolseley to complete a survey of the terrain in and around Tel-el-Kebir in preparation for the impending battle there.[65]

Ardagh joined General Wolseley and his staff at the Battle of Tel-el-Kebir just before dawn, having travelled up by railroad on an iron-plated gun train, and entered the trenches with the Highland Brigade.[66] The British forces marched on Tel-el-Kebir overnight and assaulted the enemy positions under the cover of the early dawn. Ardagh and the Headquarter Staff were halted by an advanced Egyptian redoubt which held them once the breaking dawn illuminated their position for the Egyptian forces. The combat lasted little over an hour. As soon as the camp was taken, Ardagh set to work organising water carts for the Egyptian wounded.[67]

After the British victory at Tel-el-Kebir, the Egyptian Government were forced to take back Khedive Tawfiq as nominal ruler and Ahmed Arabi was banished to Ceylon (modern day Sri Lanka). Ardagh remained at Tel-el-Kebir as Senior Officer for the Railways. The ensuing eight days are recorded as one of physical and logistical hardship for Ardagh and the Railway Department. Staff and resources shortages added great strain upon a workforce already suffering from limited food and respite from the sun. The work of the Royal Engineers and the Railway Department was vital in ensuring the British Army's advance was successful. Few beasts of burden and low water levels in the canal limited alternative means of transportation and placed ever greater reliance upon the rail services to cover the twenty-five miles between Ismailia and Kassassin. Ardagh finally left Tel-el-Kebir for Cairo on the 21 September 1882 where he joined the rest of the Headquarter Staff and witnessed the return of the Khedive on the 24 September. On the 30 September the British Army of Occupation at Cairo held a review at Abdin Palace where medals for the recent action were conferred by the Khedive; Major Ardagh received the Fourth Class Order of the Osmanieh and later the Khedive's bronze star. He also received the British war medal with clasps for Tel-el-Kebir and was promoted to brevet lieutenant-colonel on the 18 November.

The pace of life for Ardagh eased after the Egyptian Expedition. He resided for six months in Cairo with the three other officers of the Headquarters Staff, General Dormer, Colonel Grenfell and Major Sandwith, serving as deputy assistant adjutant general to the British army of occupation. The social life of Cairo appealed greatly to Ardagh, who noted in his diary his wonderment that the region was not more popular as a winter retreat and observed that an enduring link would now exist between England and Egypt for some time.[68] In the April of 1883 Ardagh spent a fortnight's pilgrimage to Jerusalem. He found General Gordon there and the two pondered the future of the Turkey and Russia.

On return to Cairo, Ardagh remained there until the middle of July. Having obtained further leave until the 10 September, he embarked for Plymouth but upon reaching British shores caught news that cholera, which had erupted in Damietta and rapidly spread to Port Said and Mansura,

---

65   Malmesbury, *Life of Major-General Sir John Ardagh*, p. 157.
66   The Battle of Tel-el-Kebir, 13 September 1882.
67   From an account by Lord (then Colonel) Grenfell, in Malmesbury, *Life of Major-General Sir John Ardagh*, pp. 158-159.
68   Extract from Ardagh's Diary, Cairo, 1 January 1883 in Malmesbury, *Life of Major-General Sir John Ardagh*, pp. 164-165.

had reached Cairo. Disappointed at the loss of his holiday and frustrated at his wasted journey, Ardagh deemed it his duty to return and assist in the relief efforts. He set his affairs in order at home and headed on the 31 July for Cairo which he reached on the 9 August. Once in Egypt, Ardagh assisted administratively in the campaign to control the epidemic which by the 24 August had claimed 5,664 lives.[69] Once his leave period was at an end, Ardagh returned to his primary duties which took him away from Cairo frequently to carry out extensive surveys and revisions of previous inspections, however, he continued to assist in the city when he was able.

On the 12 February 1884, Ardagh received orders to join Sir Gerald Graham's expeditionary force to relieve Baker Pasha at El Teb. The Egyptian garrison at Tokar had been attacked by Sudanese Mahdi forces led by Osman Digna and suffered heavy losses. General Baker's relief force was routed *en route*. On the 14 February Ardagh was appointed Commanding Royal Engineer and Chief of the Intelligence Branch with Captain Slade, R.A., and Major Schoefer (Egyptian Suppression of the Slave Trade Department) as his staff of the Intelligence Department. With Colonel Stewart and Sir Redvers Buller commanding the cavalry and infantry brigades respectively, the force departed for Suakin at 8 a.m. on the 15 February 1884.

Having sailed down the Suez Canal to Suakin, on the Red Sea, the expedition then proceeded to Trinkitat. Once anchored off Trinkitat, Ardagh set to work reconnoitring and sketching the surrounding country from an anchored tall ship, the *Carysfort* and the gathering forces began disembarking. The Royal Engineers were busied building landing stages to traverse the marshy canal banks and constructing roads and means for transporting stores. A week later, Ardagh and the British force advanced from Trinkitat to Fort Baker and bivouacked there before marching on the Arab entrenchments the following morning, the 29 February. The battle of El Teb was bloody with 34 British soldiers killed and 155 wounded and over 6000 Arab casualties, an estimated 2,340 of whom were killed. Ardagh survived the battle unhurt. The following day, when the British forces advanced to Tokar, he was tasked with evacuating the 700 Egyptian civilians to Trinkitat.[70] Having achieved the relief of Baker Pasha's forces, the British re-embarked, on the 5 March, for Suakin. Once encamped there, one of Ardagh's customary reconnoitres revealed a concentration of Arab troops at nearby Tamai; the decision was taken to attack.

On the evening of 11 March Graham's force left Suakin for a zareba, or barricaded encampment, Baker Pasha had built nine miles to the south-west.[71] The following morning Ardagh was sent to reconnoitre the enemy positions with eighty British and thirty-five Abyssinian mounted infantry. Having located the enemy and estimated their strength, Ardagh sent a report back to General Graham who proceeded to advance the whole force in their direction. The heat slowed the pace of the march and by the time they reached the original position the Sudanese had moved into a ravine. The order was given to build a zareba at Osman Dinga's original position. That night Arab riflemen took long-distance shots at the British encampment, without great effect. The following morning Graham attacked Osman Dinga, killing 2,000 and forcing the remainder of his force to flee. It was not an impressive victory however, and General Graham was criticised for heavy losses of his own (5 officers, 104 men killed and 8 officers and 104 men

---

69   From the Conseil Sanitaire d'Egypte, in Malmesbury, *Life of Major-General Sir John Ardagh*, p. 157.
70   Malmesbury, *Life of Major-General Sir John Ardagh*, pp. 174 - 175.
71   A zareba is a camp enclosed and protected by a ring of prickly mimosa. Whilst ineffective against firearms, it offers good protection against the naked attacker.

wounded) which were "generally attributed to the vacillation of General Graham, who is said to have needlessly changed the formation of his troops during the enemy's attack, thus creating great confusion".[72]

Ardagh's experiences in the Sudan and at the Battle of Tamai offer an unusual insight into his interaction with the ordinary ranks of the army. By the nature of his work throughout his career, Ardagh operated in small groups of sappers, other intelligence officers or on his own; he rarely found himself in command of large numbers and the officers under him were generally engaged in equally independent tasks. Following the Battle of Tamai, Ardagh recorded something of the relationship he conducted with the men under his command. Ardagh makes reference to the morale of the British force as a whole, reflecting in his account on the poor motivation in the British soldiers to fight the Sudanese:

> The troops seem to have little interest in the war. The valour of the enemy, as compared with Egyptians, and the want of a clear understanding of what they are fighting for, tends to raise sympathy for the Arabs and physical fatigue, combined with scant water-supply, is a cause for depression.[73]

Ardagh's reflections indicate a sensitivity to both the physical and moral wellbeing of the men he commanded. It was not a sensitivity which translated into leniency, however. He continued:

> I myself attribute the unsteadiness of the men to the entire absence of any efficient means of enforcing obedience to orders. In all other armies but ours officers are required to shoot or cut down those who refuse to obey orders in action and this is a power we must sooner or later resort to; the sooner the better.[74]

The energy and depth of resources which characterised Ardagh's approach to soldiering extended to the expectations he held of the men under his command. In relation to individual soldiers however, Ardagh demonstrates an appreciation of the men with whom he lived and worked in a tone rather more akin to the concern and investment he demonstrated for his fellow officers. In his personal account of the Sudan Campaign, Ardagh mentions the death of his draughtsman shortly after the battle of Tamai. He laments bitterly Private Moffatt's loss, noting, "Poor Moffatt was an excellent draughtsman and I was just about to make him a corporal. He was quiet and popular and I miss him very much".[75]

The British force returned to the coast on the 13 March. A few days were taken to recover from the exhaustion of the battle, the march and to reassemble the stores and bury the dead. With Suakin as a base of operations, cavalry reconnaissance patrols were conducted, searching for Osman Digna's troops and encouraging offers of friendship and shelter to local wavering

---

72 Baker to Granville, 13 March 1884, in Shibeika, Mekki, *British Policy in the Sudan 1882-1902* (London, New York, Toronto: Oxford University Press, 1952), p. 209.
73 From Ardagh's Diary, March 1884 in Malmesbury, *Life of Major-General Sir John Ardagh*, pp. 180 – 182.
74 From Ardagh's Diary, March 1884 in Malmesbury, *Life of Major-General Sir John Ardagh*, pp. 180 – 182.
75 From Ardagh's Diary, March 1884 in Malmesbury, *Life of Major-General Sir John Ardagh*, p. 180.

tribes. From Suakin, Ardagh established his intelligence network and proceeded to conduct spies and agents from the camp reporting back on the enemy's actions, a task at which they quickly became adept. There was an evident learning-curve in this operation however, Ardagh notes the proficiency of his informants improved as they identified the questions they should be asking, in particular, the names of the tribal chiefs, the districts they came from and the number of their followers.

Further to establishing regional allies amongst the tribes, the British Army and Ardagh's Intelligence Officers were concerned with opening the road to Berber which ran inland a little short of three hundred miles. The road was viewed by the Army as the key of the Sudan, a route which would allow a short-cut between Upper and Lower Egypt. Major Wood and Major Chermside were sent to Handub, ten miles north-east of Suakin, to represent the Intelligence Department there and converse with the Sheikhs in the region. A zareba (No. 4) had been constructed a few days previously by the 75th and on the 25 March the whole force at camp in Suakin marched the ten miles to the new camp. Major Chermisde commanded a native contingent of one hundred Sudanese tribesmen co-operating with the British against Osman. On the following day the force marched to Tamanib and engaged a small number of Sudanese troops located there before withdrawing.

The Intelligence Branch reported that the Berber Road was a practical route and one it advocated, however, the government rejected the proposition, primarily attributing their decision to the scarcity of water available for troops undertaking the journey. Ardagh argued that there were ten or twelve watering places at twenty-five to fifty mile intervals and that with camels and rationing for troops alone, it was possible to supply sufficient water. Despite his assertions, however, the thirty-three day march was considered too great and the route was rejected. Despite the efforts of Ardagh and his officers, the British withdrew from the Sudan on the 3 April 1884 for the Suez. For his service during the Eastern Sudan Expedition, Ardagh received the military Companion of the Bath (C.B.).[76]

Ardagh returned to England in May 1884 to begin a spell of leave. Having abandoned his furlough the previous year to attend to the Cholera epidemic in Cairo, his time was occupied by a full social calendar and country retreats. He returned to Cairo on the 8 September 1884. Matters in Khartoum, where General Gordon's efforts to resist the Mahdi siege which had begun in the March, were becoming ever-more grave and discussion of a relief expedition dominated the minds of the military in Egypt. With the Suakin-Berber route abandoned, thoughts were turned to how best to reach Gordon. A sum of £300,000 had been voted in by Parliament on 7 August to fund a relief expedition, with the Nile selected as the route to be taken and Field Marshal Lord Wolseley in overall command. On the 26 September Colonel Ardagh was appointed Assistant Adjutant and Quartermaster-General and Commandant of the Base of the Nile Expedition.

The Nile Expedition departed Cairo on the 27 September 1884 and Ardagh accompanied them as far as the base at Assiut. The need for an officer with excellent skills in diplomacy was a key factor in the appointment of Ardagh as the base commandant. As he noted in a letter to a friend in November, his task was "rather a delicate one… inasmuch as the arrival of Lord Wolseley and the flood of officers the latter brought out with him (to the disjointing of all our

---

76 Malmesbury, *Life of Major-General Sir John Ardagh*, pp. 187 – 189.

noses here) produced a certain amount of bitterness between the old garrison and the new arrivals".[77] Ardagh was required to mediate between the two factions of officers and ensure the expedition ran smoothly. It was a challenge he was well suited to given his experience in the Balkans and the Berlin Congress in particular, forging a connection with Wolseley which, though not bringing him into 'the Wolseley Ring', a group of reform-minded officers connected to the future Commander-in-Chief, would last for the remainder of Ardagh's career.

The primary responsibilities of his role spoke further to his strengths in organisation and logistics: the base commandant was required to oversee a great deal of the needs and wants of the expedition and Ardagh received telegraphs on a regular basis for all manner of demands including battalions but also blankets, groceries, camels, locomotives and coffins.[78] The experience tested Ardagh's ingenuity and patience to a considerable degree. The staff of the Assiut base camp were faced with a bewildering array and volume of requests. Moreover, the means of transporting the materials, in particular letters and parcels, presented a challenge and required Ardagh to organise a postal system to accommodate the volume and distance they were required to support. Arduous though the task was, however, Ardagh and his staff were successful in operating the base and supporting Lord Wolseley's Nile Expedition, much to the gratitude of the officers and men. They received several letters of thanks, including one from Brigadier-General Sir Henry Brackenbury, the future head of the Intelligence Branch, who wrote, "you have had a lot of hard work… It has been a great rest to our minds to know we had so trustworthy a man to look after our wants at base".[79]

Ardagh remained in Egypt until the summer of 1885 when he received his brevet-colonelcy and returned to England for light (recruiting) duties. The Nile Expedition had infamously failed to rescue General Gordon from Khartoum in the January and the force had partially withdrawn from the Sudan. Followers of the Mahdi had continued to launch attacks on the Anglo-Egyptian fortifications along the Nile and established a base at Kosheh, south of Akasheh. And so Ardagh returned to Cairo in the autumn as Assistant-Adjutant and Quartermaster-General and Chief Staff Officer to the Anglo-Egyptian forces under Sir Frederick Stephenson in preparation for the Second Nile Expedition, which departed Cairo on the 19 December. They found General Grenfell at Akasheh and advanced up the Nile in a gig, half a dozen whalers and two *nuggars* to Dal Cataract and from thence to Kosheh. On the morning of the 30 December, the Anglo-Egyptian force engaged the Mahdist troops at the Battle of Ginnis. A British Victory, the enemy retreated from Koyeh that same day by *nuggars* on the Nile. Ardagh came perilously close to serious injury during the battle as a bullet passed through his helmet. He escaped with minor grazing to the skin and a slight deafness which would remain with him for the rest of his life, however, as Ardagh later noted, with slightly misplaced priorities, "Another quarter of an inch would have ended my career".[80]

---

77 Col. Ardagh to a friend, 7 November 1884 in Malmesbury, *Life of Major-General Sir John Ardagh*, p. 194.
78 Col. Ardagh to a friend, 7 November 1884 in Malmesbury, *Life of Major-General Sir John Ardagh*, p. 194.
79 H. Brackenbury to J. Ardagh, Tuesday 18 November 1884 in Malmesbury, *Life of Major-General Sir John Ardagh*, pp. 200 – 201.
80 Malmesbury, *Life of Major-General Sir John Ardagh*, p. 209.

For a week following the Battle of Ginnis, the expeditionary force established camp at Abri. From that base the army of occupation organised rations, in part from grain and arms seized on four *nuggars* at Said Effendi, and supplied the garrisons still manning the garrisons left behind. The wounded were attended to and Ardagh assisted in the efforts to take stock of current position. He made repeated surveying trips of the battle field and surrounding terrain. By the 7 January 1886 the Expedition was advancing back down the Nile. On the 9 January Ardagh joined General Grenfell and Sir Frederick Stephenson on board Grenfell's dahabieh, the *Pharaon*. By 11 January they had reached Abu Simbel and Ardagh sketched the temples there before they continued on to Assuan which they reached on the 14 January 1886.[81]

Upon Ardagh's return to Cairo he turned his attentions to the additional duties assigned to him when he returned to Egypt in 1885. Principally, Ardagh was tasked with adjusting the financial arrangements between the United Kingdom and Egypt, acting as a member of the Commission for the Reform of the Monetary System and the System of Weights and Measures in Egypt.[82] In December 1886 Ardagh received his promotion to regimental Lieutenant Colonel RE. He also received, with permission of Queen Victoria, the Order of the Mejidieh Third Class from the Khedive. The affairs of the Anglo-Egyptian finances occupied Ardagh's attentions fully for several months; Egypt was close to bankruptcy and the Foreign Office had entrusted Ardagh with adjusting the claims made by the Egyptian Government against the military authorities in Egypt since 1882. The complex accounts required Ardagh to calculate the amounts the British Government owed for the various military operations it had conducted, including the Nile Expeditions. He was unable to complete this considerable task however, for at the end of June, when Ardagh had returned to England for leave, he received an order from Sir Frederick Stephenson that his service in that country had concluded on the 14 June 1887.[83]

For the Intelligence Branch back in London, things had been developing slowly in Ardagh's absence. Arguably, momentum had been lost since Sir Archibald Alison became head in 1878 in place of Sir Patrick MacDougall. The impetus for change and expansion gained from the memory of the strategic blunders of the Crimean War and the alarm caused by the Franco-Prussian War had been lost. Furthermore, the crises in Egypt and the Sudan had, at their height, taken four of the six section heads – Ardagh included – overseas and away from their intelligence duties.[84] In January 1886, Major-General Sir Henry Brackenbury became head of the Intelligence Branch. The following June, he became the first Director of Military Intelligence [DMI] with the Intelligence Branch becoming re-designated the Intelligence Department [ID]. Brackenbury had been dismayed at the absence of permanent officers on his staff; the majority of intelligence officers were only attached and therefore, were expected to fulfil their regimental duties in addition to their intelligence work. It was on this basis that Ardagh was brought back into the ID, now based at Queen Anne's Gate.[85] He was appointed Deputy Assistant Adjutant General [DAAG] and Brackenbury's deputy.

---

81 Malmesbury, *Life of Major-General Sir John Ardagh*, pp. 210-216.
82 Malmesbury, *Life of Major-General Sir John Ardagh*, p. 225.
83 Malmesbury, *Life of Major-General Sir John Ardagh*, p. 226.
84 Brice, C., *The Thinking Man's Soldier: The Life and Career of General Sir Henry Brackenbury 1837-1914* (Solihull: Helion & Co., 2012), p. 164.
85 The Intelligence Branch had relocated from Adair House to Queen Anne's Gate in 1884.

Since the spring of 1886, Brackenbury had been grappling with "the preparation and maintenance of information relevant to the defence of the Empire and mobilisation of the Army".[86] He had drawn attention to the absence of a scheme for mobilisation when he had assumed control of the ID. The then Secretary of State for War, W. H. Smith, appointed Brackenbury and the Permanent Undersecretary at the War Office Sir Ralph Thompson to produce plans and recommendations to develop such provision. Brackenbury had produced his plans in December 1886. He had struggled with severe limitations in the Army's capacity to support the rapid mobilisation of two army corps, noting that civilians and soldiers alike had failed to grasp the need for strong commissariat, transport, medical, ordinance and equestrian services. Despite these limitations, however, Brackenbury was able to draw up plans for the mobilisation of the army for home defence, and for a single army corps for deployment abroad.[87]

With ground work complete, the mobilisation schemes still required further development to make the mobilisation of two army corps a reality. In the absence of a General Staff, the task fell to the ID, however, the other demands and responsibilities Brackenbury shouldered as DMI prevented him from dedicating further time to the question, and he did not wish his officers to be taken from their primary intelligence duties. He therefore requested permission to establish a separate mobilisation section, highlighting that since his arrival, the Deputy Assistant Adjutant General position, the *de facto* deputy to the DMI and head of the central section, had been vacant. There was, therefore, a pre-existing vacancy in the department for an additional officer who could assume the responsibilities of a new section.[88] He obtained sanction for the establishment of a mobilisation section from Lord Wolseley and Sir Ralph Thompson in October 1887 and the new section was formed the following month with Ardagh at its helm.

Ardagh's mobilisation section operated out of the main War Office buildings in Pall Mall. The original basis of the mobilisation scheme had been enlarged and Ardagh prepared plans for the deployment of two Army Corps for overseas service and to examine the use of the Forces of the Crown in home defence. He was assisted by Captain Percy Lake, Colonel Macgregor, Captain Fleming R.A. and Captain Codrington of Coldstream Guards. A preliminary survey of the requirements for mobilisation had been undertaken by Colonel Home in 1875, although primarily Ardagh suggests, in order to highlight the deficiencies in the national provision. In the case of home defence in particular, Ardagh examined what was once considered adequate to defend Britain against invasion, noting that in 1804, the combined forces of the United Kingdom numbered 718,000, 163,865 men greater than the current provision in 1888. Advances in weaponry, in particular increased naval power were also considered, highlighting that previous coastal defences such as the Martello Towers built between 1804 and 1810 and a majority of the small scale coastal fortifications then in service, would not stand up to the modern ship's guns and armour. Defensive positions would need to be established further in

---

86 Brackenbury to Quartermaster-General Arthur Herbert and Lord Wolsely, April 1886, in Brice, *The Thinking Man's Soldier*, p. 168.
87 Brackenbury and the War Office had anticipated plans for two corps to be deployed overseas but the limits in support services restricted their ambition. Brackenbury had hoped that the absence of a second corps would highlight the need for greater investment in the military support services, noting that in any case, the procedure would only need duplicating to produce a second or third corps.
88 Brice, *The Thinking Man's Soldier*, p. 172.

shore, it was advised, with only a small number of modern fortifications and armaments (too expensive to be employed extensively) to be built at key coastal locations.[89]

In the case for home defence in particular, with the estimated period between the declaration of war and likely attack or invasion revised from six weeks (by Colonel Home's estimation in 1875) to three or four days or less if conducted clandestinely, the pace of mobilisation was paramount and railroads were key to Ardagh's schemes. Three army corps were based in the south east of England, primarily in Surrey, Sussex, Kent, Essex and Norfolk. Overall, Ardagh surmised that it was possible to field three Army-Corps of which two would be entirely Regulars and the third partly regular and partly militia. There would be three more army corps of Volunteers, complete with Artillery; and in front three Cavalry divisions of Regulars, each with a Yeomanry Brigade attached but, as Brackenbury had found, 'the auxiliary departments are incomplete'.[90]

Fearing the wealth of the capital might tempt an invader, the Mobilisation Committee singled out London for further consideration.[91] Again, Ardagh examined past approaches to the defence of the city, the economics required especially in light of current armaments and naval strength, the availability of the militia and volunteers and the location of entrenched camps and forts, some temporary, in London and on the Thames.[92] By the end of 1888, Ardagh and the mobilisation section had submitted their plans. They were somewhat theoretical, not least since Ardagh knew parliament would never countenance the investment they would require, which stood at £3,000,000 for London alone.[93] Nevertheless, in March 1890, they were presented to the House of Commons by the Secretary of State for War Edward Stanhope and further developed by Colonels Coleridge Grove, Neville Lyttelton and Stopford into a protocol the War Office could follow in the event of major war.[94]

In April 1888, Ardagh was selected to succeed Colonel Albert Williams, R.A., in joining the HRH Duke of Cambridge's personal staff as an *aide-de-camp* (A.D.C.). It was a distinction he would hold until 1895, however, in reality only on an honorary basis as in October, Ardagh was offered the position of private secretary to the Marquess of Lansdowne, soon to become the Viceroy in India. Though welcome, the opportunity gave rise to mixed emotions for, as he later wrote to his friend Senator Sir James Gowan, Ardagh lamented leaving his, "most interesting work at the Horse Guards where [he] enjoyed the friendship and confidence of many from whom [he] was loath to part; and it was a severe wrench to tear [himself] away in the middle of numerous wide-reaching plans just assuming shape and substance".[95]

It is perhaps a testament to the reputation Ardagh had established, not only as a soldier but as a diplomat and an administrator that Lord Lansdowne approached Ardagh directly to ask whether he would assume the position of his private secretary, though the two men had never met. Ardagh sought the blessing of the Duke of Cambridge, Lord Wolseley and Edward Stanhope in order to be released from his obligations to them; the Duke offered to

---

89 TNA WO 106/6289: Ardagh, Col. J. C., *Defence of England: Mobilization of the Regular and Auxiliary Forces for Home Defence*, 17 April 1888.
90 TNA WO 106/6289: Ardagh, Col. Sir J. C., *Defence of England*, p. 8.
91 Spiers, Edward, M., *Late Victorian Army 1868-1902* (Manchester: Manchester University Press, 1992), p. 227.
92 TNA PRO 30/40/13: Ardagh, Col., Sir J. C., 'Defence of London', p. 2.
93 Spiers, *The Late Victorian Army*, p. 227.
94 Malmesbury, *Life of Major-General Sir John Ardagh*, p. 230.
95 TNA PRO 30/40/2: Ardagh, Sir J. C., to Senator Sir James Gowan, 21 January 1889.

retain Ardagh as an additional ADC despite his absence and Wolseley consented to Ardagh's departure advising him to take the opportunity and purportedly telling him that, "he had to part from his friends only too often; that he was never so sorry to lose anyone as [Ardagh] but that he would not stand in his way".[96]

Lord Lansdowne and Colonel Ardagh assumed their new positions in India on the 10 December 1888. Ardagh resided in Government House in Calcutta and in the Observatory at Simla, close to the Viceregal Lodge. So great were the demands placed upon the private secretary to the Viceroy, it was necessary for Ardagh to remain always in close proximity to Lord Lansdowne, should he be required.[97] Ardagh readily acknowledged the extent to which his new post dominated his time, noting that it was the Private Secretary's responsibility to be at the Viceroy's "beck and call" and to "devote every moment to his work".[98] His duties were numerous and sometimes unpredictable. Though free from assisting in Lansdowne's private correspondence, the large quantity of semi-official communiqués to pass through the Viceroy's office from across India found its way first to Ardagh's desk, where he redistributed it to the relevant department or dealt with it directly, under the Viceroy's orders. As Private Secretary, Ardagh was also responsible for supervising expenditure and auditing the accounts, as well overseeing any official appointments and honours, keeping lists of recommendations and recipients. More broadly, Ardagh received any matters of business before they were submitted to the Viceroy, refining the details to ensure they were as accessible as possible before they were in Lord Lansdowne's lap.[99]

Further to his office-bound administrative duties, Ardagh was also required to accompany Lord Lansdowne on the Viceroy's annual Autumn Tour of India. Each trip, which would last from between four to six weeks somewhere over October to December, was minutely planned, day by day and hour by hour. Ardagh departed each year with a full itinerary laying forth every detail from the transport schedule and locations of venues, accommodation and receptions to ceremonial procedures and routines the Viceroy was expected to observe. Ardagh completed the journey every year he was private secretary from 1888 to 1893.[100]

Ardagh only took one spell of leave during his time in India, despite even Lord Lansdowne advising him that overwork was unhealthy. Eventually, the pressure of his position and inability to escape the relentless onslaught of a workload only punctuated by equally demanding social engagements, combined with the altitude and climate of India, overcame his resolve. With his health failing, Ardagh was ordered by his doctors to take some leave, which he did in March 1892 when he returned to England and then to Germany to recuperate. He spent the summer in England, observing the summer manoeuvres and visiting Sir Evelyn Wood, then commanding at Aldershot and attending the Duke and Duchess of Devonshire's wedding. In order to completely recover his health and to further his tour of the world, Ardagh returned to Calcutta via America, Japan and China. *En route*, he demonstrated his characteristic eye for military detail, noting rather unkindly that, based on the number of troops armed with bow and arrow, the Chinese forces did not present an immediate threat to peace in Europe but also that with

96 TNA PRO 30/40/2: Ardagh Gowan, 21 January 1889.
97 Malmesbury, *Life of Major-General Sir John Ardagh*, p. 240.
98 Malmesbury, *Life of Major-General Sir John Ardagh*, p. 239.
99 Malmesbury, *Life of Major-General Sir John Ardagh*, pp. 235 - 236.
100 TNA PRO 30/40/10: Viceroy's Autumn Tour.

regards to the Indian frontier, their assistance in Kashgar, Tibet and Yunan would be valuable in opposing Russia.[101] Ardagh returned to Calcutta on the 19 November 1892.

The role of private secretary to the Viceroy of India was undoubtedly a challenging one. It was one which Ardagh was well qualified to fulfil. The important attributes required of him, "good health, an inexhaustible capacity for work, sound judgement, common sense and tact", had been well provided for by his prior military experience.[102] His inexperience of India worked in his favour to some degree, for though he lacked local knowledge and was reliant on other departments to compensate for him in that regard, he was also free from pre-existing obligations or prejudices and was well acquainted with public and parliamentary opinion back in Britain. Ardagh remained with Lord Lansdowne until the conclusion of his term as Viceroy in January 1894. He served for a few weeks with Lansdowne's successor, Lord Elgin, before relinquishing his position as private secretary and departing India in April. For his services in India, Ardagh was made a Knight Commander of the Indian Empire (KCIE), having already been made Companion of the Order of the Indian Empire (CIE) in 1892.

From his Indian departure in 1894 until the following April 1895, Ardagh enjoyed a rare period of extended leisure. He went on half-pay and joined a party on-board Sir John Pendar's steam yacht *Electra* at Genoa, bound for the Crimea, which included in its number Sir Evelyn Wood and Lord Wolseley. Revisiting very familiar territory for Ardagh, the *Electra* sailed on to Constantinople and then to Athens before returning to Genoa where the group separated. Upon his return to England, Ardagh continued his social touring, visiting among others, Lord Wolseley again, then Commander-in-Chief in Ireland at Dublin. In March 1895 Ardagh returned to London and one month later was appointed Commandant of the School of Military Engineering at Chatham.[103]

Intelligence Division 1896-99

Ardagh spent only a year as commandant at Chatham. On the 1 April 1896, he began the appointment to which his career had seemingly been building for almost forty years, succeeding Major-General Edward Chapman as the Director of Military Intelligence [DMI].[104] Promoted to the temporary rank of Major-General, as DMI, Ardagh was responsible for overseeing the wide array of operations the Intelligence Division was expected to perform, from matters relating to the preparation for national and imperial defence to the collation and dissemination of military, geographical and geo-political information.[105]

By this stage in his career, Ardagh had developed a considerable reputation as the "foremost politico-military officer" in the British Army.[106] It carried considerable weight for the DMI for, as the November 1895 order in council memorandum which had prescribed Ardagh's duties

---

101 Malmesbury, *Life of Major-General Sir John Ardagh*, p. 253.
102 Malmesbury, *Life of Major-General Sir John Ardagh*, p. 237.
103 Malmesbury, *Life of Major-General Sir John Ardagh*, pp. 263 - 267.
104 Chapman had been DMI since Henry Brackenbury's departure in 1891.
105 The Intelligence Department, which had previously been the Intelligence Branch until June 1887 was re-designated the Intelligence Division in April 1888 when Brackenbury was promoted to Major-General.
106 Fergusson, *British Military Intelligence 1870-1914*, p. 104.

had stated, the DMI, "conducts correspondence with other departments of state on defence questions, and is authorised to correspond semi-officially with them on all subjects connected to his duties".[107] Ardagh had, by the mid-1890s, worked with or for the Foreign Office, the Colonial Office and the Admiralty and was close with the Secretary of State for War Lord Lansdowne following their service together in India, and with Lord Wolseley.

When it worked, the ID enjoyed almost a symbiotic existence alongside offices such as the FO and the CO; the ID presented a reliable and effective source of information either from its considerable library, or from the capabilities of the talented young officers employed in London or overseas. In return, the ID relied heavily on the information those departments themselves could impart, gathering intelligence from Ambassadors, Consuls, Governors, Agents and a range of other sources which composed the world-wide network the British Government maintained.[108] It was a situation which offered little choice for the ID. The funds allocated to the section were tiny leaving little to no allowance to cover additional intelligence gathering or production. It was a short fall which would become painfully apparent to all at the opening of the South African War in 1899. For the DMI therefore, the ability to maintain cordial relationships was essential.

Part of the reason for the vast remit of the ID can be found in the absence of a general staff in the British Army. Despite the 1890 Hartington Commission recommending the creation of a general staff with a chief of staff as its head and the establishment of a War Office Council to officially advise the Secretary of State for War, any attempts to implement such a reform were blocked. Primarily this was due to the proposal to abolish the office of the Commander-in-Chief, then HRH the Duke of Cambridge and from 1895 onwards Lord Wolseley. As a result there was not a body within the higher echelons of the British Army responsible for devising a combined strategy and advice to the Secretary of State for War derived from individual departments or from the restricted and infrequent Defence Committee of the Cabinet.[109] Ardagh himself perceived the ID to be the forebear of a general staff, noting in his memorandum *The Intelligence Division* that it was a role his department already performed:

> The name of "Intelligence Branch" was originally given to a small branch for the collection of information about foreign countries. As necessities arose it has gradually been extended over a much larger field, and the original designation is now somewhat of a misnomer, as the expansion has included many of the subjects dealt with by the "general staff" of other armies; and it is my opinion very advisable that further development should take place in the same direction, and that it should eventually take that position, and become the authoritative advisory and consultative branch of the War Office.[110]

Despite having only limited influence in terms of policy and strategy decisions - the DMI was not usually invited to the Defence Committee meetings for instance - the fundamental information required for the Defence Committee and the government was provided for by the

---

107 Fergusson, *British Military Intelligence 1870-1914*, p. 108.
108 Fergusson, *British Military Intelligence 1870 – 1914*, p. 107.
109 Fergusson, *British Military Intelligence 1870 – 1914*, p. 108.
110 TNA PRO 30/40/14: Ardagh, Maj. Gen. Sir J. C., *The Intelligence Division*.

ID. This greatly limited the influence the DMI could exert, even one with Ardagh's connections. It was a 'clipping' which would cost the British Army dearly in South Africa.

Upon Ardagh's return from India and just prior to his appointment as DMI, the question of the Duke of Cambridge's successor as Commander-in-Chief had been dominating the minds of Britain's military. Ardagh, connected as he was with both the Secretary of State for War Lord Lansdowne, and the next Commander-in-Chief, Lord Wolseley, he became, for a time, something of a king maker. Privately, he mused over the appointment. He was not opposed to a royal candidate if a strong Adjutant General was in place. The Duke had patronised the Army well, but he recalled tales of favouritism in first half of the century. He supported Wolseley over General Roberts reasoning, Roberts (though publicly popular) had spent his whole career in India and was not familiar with the English Army, system or parliament.[111] It was fortunate Ardagh had applied himself to the matter for, aware of the close relationship to exist between Ardagh and Lansdowne, Wolseley sought his influence. When approached by Lansdowne for his advice, Ardagh concluded, "Whilst many might be called, the British Army would prefer Wolseley".[112]

When Ardagh took over as DMI, the re-conquest of the Sudan was dominating the War Office. It was an all too familiar issue, with several of the major concerns, such as the need to lay railroad to assist an expeditionary force's advance, stemming from the mid-1880s when Ardagh was Commanding Royal Engineer with the first Nile Expedition.[113] Furthermore, the government was caught between two rival advocates for command of an advance, on the one side Lord Wolseley and Horse Guards and on the other Kitchener and the Egyptian Army and the Consul-General of Egypt, Lord Cromer. Memories of the British experiences in the Sudan in 1884-5 still occupied the minds of Salisbury's Conservative government and an unease and caution dominated their attempts to divide Kitchener's and Wolseley's demands and decide how and when an expedition would be launched and by whom it would be led. The FO turned to Ardagh. Ardagh advised them that, "there was no rush. The retaking of the Sudan could 'come when it would'".[114]

Despite acknowledging that an advance up the Nile was necessary, patience was a constant recommendation in Ardgah's assessment of the options for the British. In his memorandum, *Advance up the Nile*, Ardagh dissected carefully yet concisely the pertinent facts required for the War Office and the British Government to reach a decision on such an expedition.[115] At the core of his recommendation was the manner of route the force would take, noting details of local knowledge such as times when the Nile was impassable as well as drawing attention to the continued construction and corresponding delay of the railway line between Wady Halfa and Abu Hamed. With careful calculations noting the pace at which the line might be laid, rest days

---

111 TNA PRO 30/40/13: Ardagh, Notes on next C-in-C, 6 August 1895.
112 Beaver, *Under Every Leaf*, pp. 269-271.
113 Despite commanders on the ground, Ardagh included, advocating the construction of a railway between Halfa near the banks of the Nile and Berber almost three hundred miles inland, the decision back in London had been taken to abandon their efforts through fears, primarily, of a water shortage *en route*.
114 Beaver, *Under Every Leaf*, p. 243.
115 TNA PRO 30/40/14: Ardagh, Major-General Sir J. C., *Advance up the Nile from Dongola: Forecast for 1897-8*, 15 March 1897.

and potential disruption from storms, accidents and other interruptions, Ardagh estimated the line would be complete by June 1898, coinciding with the high Nile.[116]

Ardagh offered further suggestions for once the expedition force had proceeded up the Nile, further recommending the manner in which the advance should be made, how far it was necessary to take up fortified positions and the severity of the opposition, based upon intelligence on the morale and equipment of the Sudanese troops. Overall, Ardagh advised, an advance should be withheld until the next year (1898), when the railroad and climatic conditions would be most favourable. It was a stance the Prime Minister also shared, dismissing even Lord Wolseley's impassioned demands for a sizable force to be assigned to him as soon as possible. Kitchener eventually advanced, reaching Omdurman in September 1898.

The Sudan dominated Ardagh's output as DMI in 1896-97. As well as his decisive memorandum *The Advance up the Nile from Dongola*, Ardagh published memoranda on more specialised issues such as the Sudanese railway extension, Kassala, and the Suez Canal Convention of 1888. He also published several wider-reaching memoranda however, on related and unconnected issues, for instance, Egypt, the Italian Army, the Uganda-Congo State Boundary, the Somalia Protectorate and the Eastern Question and Constantinople.[117] The range of the subject matter to pass across his desk was considerable, reflecting the entire remit of the ID, as demonstrated by his personal compendium of memoranda which runs to two volumes. During the five years Ardagh was DMI, he wrote on domestic and military topics, such as the 1897 pieces, *Home Defence: Army Services Loan; Authorised Scheme of Defences; Defence of London* and *Magazine Rifles and Single-Loaders*.[118] Later he presented assessments of *Expanding Bullets* and *Deficiency of Field Artillery* in 1899 and *Statutes on Calling out the Reserves* in 1900.[119] The major issues affecting British foreign, colonial or military policy were also extensively covered, for example between 1896 and 1901, South Africa and Boer related matters were featured in no fewer than four memoranda. He also wrote on the United States and Spain, France, and the future of China, drawing assessments on the probable course potential tensions and conflict between regions and nations might take and their impact on British policy.

Ardagh's past career continued to greatly support his service as DMI. As his work at the Berlin Congress had developed greatly his skills in diplomacy for instance, the majority of issues his memoranda covered were directly related to ongoing problems in which he had direct experience. British control of the Suez, Egypt and north-east Africa, the condition of the Ottoman Empire, the delimitation of the Balkan borders and the defence of the frontiers of India and of the United Kingdom all arose in the course of his service as DMI. His responsibilities as DMI ranged beyond writing memoranda, however. As surviving letters in his hand demonstrate, there was a public element to the role, where the skilful diplomacy and intimidating nature of the intelligence chief were employed in encouraging a civilian compliance with military expectations of secrecy and accuracy. In November 1899 for instance, Ardagh wrote 'privately' to Mr Moberly Bell, of *The Times* in Canada. A recent article to feature in that publication had, "excited a good deal of attention at the War Office". Ardagh informed him chillingly, "I have

---

116 TNA PRO 30/40/14: Ardagh, *Advance up the Nile from Dongola*, p. 3.
117 TNA PRO 30/40/14: *Sir John Ardagh's Memoranda 1896-1901, Vol. 1*.
118 TNA PRO 30/40/14: *Sir John Ardagh's Memoranda 1896-1901, Vol. 1*.
119 TNA PRO 30/40/14: *Sir John Ardagh's Memoranda 1896 – 1901, Vol. 2*.

been asked to make a private representation about it".[120] Claims in the article that the British Government had been interfering in Canadian defences had induced outrage in London. In his letter Ardagh highlighted to Mr Moberly Bell the untruths and inaccuracies it contained in a reproachful tone, before concluding;

> We in the War Office feel much indebted to *The Times* for the example which it has given, of abstaining at the present juncture, from the publication of any information as to measures of precaution considered advisable in view of possible contingencies. Such information would of course immediately be telegraphed to the other side and might be of incalculable injury to us in the event of a rupture.[121]

The majority of Ardagh's correspondences were not so sinister however and the DMI's letters demonstrate the amicability with which he treated others. Several letters survive in which Ardagh writes to forward for consideration the names of young officers for new posts or promotions or to advise a fellow officer of rumoured problems in his command. In addition to warning off members of the press who crossed the War Office, Ardagh also conversed with civilians hoping to aid the army with ideas or suggestions in tactics or weaponry. On the 9 January 1900, Ardagh responded to the curator at "the museum" thanking him for his suggestions regarding the use of mechanised mirrors to blind enemy sharp-shooters, explosive rockets and the wireless detonation of mines and shields, conscientiously explaining the limitations of each concept.[122] Contrary to the modern notion of the intelligence chief as anonymous, aloof and secretive, the DMI was somewhat more public, well known in military circles and government and engaged in the wider work of strategy.

The responsibilities of the DMI were far from minor or trivial however and much of Ardagh's work brought him into contact with matters directly affecting the security, continued development and prosperity of Great Britain and her Empire. As his wife and biographer Susan, Lady Malmesbury, has termed it, "his strenuous labour covered a period in which the political sky was over-clouded, not once, but almost perpetually, by storm clouds gathering, or threatening to gather, now in this quarter, now in that, each entailing increasing vigilance on the part of the Intelligence Division".[123] The continued movement by the European powers to secure territories in Africa and to 'open up the dark continent' demanded continued attentiveness and caution on the part of the ID. Britain's never-ceasing anxiety and concern over the security of India and its territories in the East and the ocean ways linking them together provided a constant concern as other European nations sought power in those regions.

These tensions, and the multifarious ways in which they manifested themselves in Ardagh's work are particularly well highlighted by his position as senior officer on the Cable Landing Rights Committee. This inter-departmental committee, formed originally to advise the Board of Trade on the intricacies of Crown licences for cables, became increasingly concerned with

---

120 TNA WO 106/6291: Maj. Gen. Sir J. C. Ardagh to Moberly Bell, 3 November 1899, in DMI Out Letter Book Vol. 10 1898 – 1901.
121 TNA WO 106/6291: Ardagh to Moberly Bell.
122 TNA WO 106/6291: Maj. Gen. Sir J. C. Ardagh to 'Curator of the Museum', 6 January 1900 in DMI Out Letter Book Vol. 10 1898-1901.
123 Malmesbury, *Life of Major-General Sir John Ardagh*, p. 290.

the defence of those cables, once laid, in light of the ever-changing geo-political landscape. As early as 1896, Ardagh had expressed concern over the weakness of the Porte following Britain's disastrous management of Turkey which had forced the Ottoman's greater reliance on Russia. He advocated the strengthening of Alexandria as a port the Royal Navy could use to maintain control in the Suez and protection over the cable which ran there between Britain and India.[124] A report, published by the Interdepartmental Committee of Cable Communications into government policy on submarine cables in 1902, after Ardagh had departed the ID but upon which he was a signatory, advocated the laying of multiple cables. Some would run between British bases and colonies only and others through friendly or neutral territories to ensure a connection remained.[125] This complex issue demanded the input of members of six government departments and was examined for two years by the committee from 1900 until the 1902 report.

In 1898, Ardagh was made a substantive Major-General, the final promotion of his career. The following year, he attended the first Hague peace conference as a military technical advisor, alongside Sir John Fisher as the Admiralty's representative, to the British delegates, Sir Julian Pauncefote and Sir Henry Howard. The conference had been mooted by the Russian Government in August 1898 as an attempt to "investigate the best means of securing to the world a durable peace, and of limiting the progressive development of military armaments".[126] The suggestion was accepted almost universally and in January 1899 an agenda was composed by the Russian statesman, Count Mouravieff. His agenda encompassed, within a wider remit, the limitation of the effective strength of naval and military forces; restrictions in the development of new types of firearms and explosives and naval and aerial (balloon) explosive projectiles; and the safeguarding and preservation of humanitarian, neutral and aid movement and of international laws and customs of war.

Ardagh was particularly well qualified to attend the Hague conference. The role required well-honed skills in diplomacy, but also technical expertise in naval and military affairs. Responsibility for supporting the British delegation at the conference fell particularly upon Ardagh's shoulders. Of the composite departments of the War Office, the ID was the natural choice for offering advice on military issues. But the composition of the ID, based primarily upon geographical groupings, meant that no one section was well placed to respond to the range of issues the conference might raise. Ardagh therefore represented the War Office personally. In approaching the agenda set out by Count Mouravieff, the British delegates and their advisors were issued three categories as guidance for the subjects the government wished to see addressed. Of these, the third, "Those upon which the War Department can advise", applied to the military advisor.[127] Ardagh was tasked with considering aspects relating to the limitation in the strength of military and naval forces, the prohibition of new types of weaponry and the restriction in the use of explosives. He was also expected to address in its entirety point 7, the revision of the laws and customs of war, drawn up at the Brussels Conference of 1874. In relation to these points, Ardagh's approach to the conference was dominated by two key issues.

---

124 Beaver, *Under Every Leaf*, pp. 252 – 253.
125 TNA PRO 30/40/13: Interdepartmental Committee on Cable Communications.
126 Proposal by the Court of St Petersburg for an international peace Conference, in Malmesbury, *Life of Major-General Sir John Ardagh*, p. 303.
127 TNA PRO 30/40/15: Draft of Instructions for Peace Conference 1899.

The first was the limitation of British military forces. Ardagh had cleared with Lord Lansdowne and Lord Salisbury the stance he would promote, contending that the British Army was, in comparison to the other Powers, small. Moreover he claimed, when the extent of the territories to be defended and the value of the interests at stake were considered, the British Empire employed a smaller number of soldiers than any other nation besides the United States. With regards to expenditure Ardagh maintained that the greater expense of the British military was accounted for by the use of volunteer recruiting. With only the United States as a comparable example, the inducements required to maintain recruiting on a voluntary basis justified a higher monetary investment than in the conscripted continental armies.[128] The British delegates were successful in securing support on this issue.

The second issue which came to dominate Ardagh's contribution to the 1899 Hague Conference was the development and use of the expanding, or Dum Dum bullet by the British. The conference brought widespread criticism of the projectile, which was challenged at both the Sub-Commission on arms and explosives and in the Sub-Commission on the revision of the Declaration of Brussels. Opposition to expanding bullets was raised on the basis that they caused deliberate and undue injury and suffering. Ardagh staunchly defended the British position, arguing that the intention behind the Dum Dum bullet was not to inflict greater injury but to provide the stopping power lost in modern fully-encased projectiles. The defining feature of the Dum Dum bullet was a small hollow in the nose which, upon impact, created an air dilation, punching a larger hole in the target. This design had developed to counter the limited impact resulting from the small-calibre, fully encased projectile used in the British soldier's Lee-Metford rifle, which simply passed through the enemy without incapacitating them.

The British delegation protested strongly that the expanding bullet was no more inhumane than those used previously in the Enfield, Snider or Martini-Henry rifles but was intended to equal the damage caused by those bullets, not to exceed it. Furthermore, they protested, there was some confusion between the British Dum Dum bullet and the experiments on a similar bullet developed by the German Inspector General of the Military Hospital Corps Professor Bruns at Tübingen in 1898. This bullet incorporated a lead tip which flattened and spread on impact, causing wounds of, "an excessively severe and terrible nature".[129] For the British, Ardagh protested, the Dum Dum bullet, rather than being inhumane, was intended to protect British soldiers, ensuring their rifle offered them a sufficient defence. In a rather wry manner, and with more than a hint of irony, he explained,

> Your civilised soldier ... when he has had a bullet though him, recognises the fact that he is wounded, and knows that the sooner he is attended to the sooner he will recover. He mounts his cacolet or lies down on his stretcher, and is taken off the field to his ambulance, where he is dressed and bandaged by his doctor or his Red Cross Society, according to the prescribed rules of the game, as laid down in the Geneva Convention. But your fanatical barbarian, when he receives wounds of a like nature, which are insufficient to stop or disable him, continues to dash on, sword or spear in hand, and before you have had time or opportunity to represent to him that his conduct is in

---

128 TNA PRO 30/40/15: Draft of Instructions for Peace Conference 1899.
129 TNA PRO 30/40/15: 'Statement which the British Military Delegate Proposes to make at the Peace Conference', in Draft of Instructions for Peace Conference 1899.

flagrant violation of the understanding relative to the proper course for a wounded man to follow, he may have cut off your head.[130]

Ardagh proceeded to emphasise that such projectiles were designed not necessarily only for a "savage" warfare but also against a civilised foe and to discourage a bayonet or cavalry charge and that the safety of the rifleman was at the foundation of the development. Presumably, this worked on the theory espoused by Ardagh in an earlier sub-committee forecasting that the increasingly lethal nature of modern weaponry would precipitate greater use of cover and evasive tactics, and not larger scale slaughter.[131] Despite Ardagh's protestations, the strength of the opposition led by the Dutch and Russian delegates and the abhorrence created by the results of Professor Brun's experiments succeeded in carrying the resolution to prohibit the development and use of expanding bullets.

The mixed success of The Hague Conference in May 1899 was of some irritation to the DMI. Ardagh submitted an appeal three weeks later pressing again the necessity and validity of the expanding bullet, but to no avail. A third attempt was made at a conference held on the 15 July between M. de Karnebeek, the reporter of the committee and the team of British delegates at The Hague, Ardagh included. Further protests were levied, complaining that attempts to develop a modified bullet which satisfied both the military and humanitarian expectations had failed. Their efforts were in vein however and the British Government found itself bound to prohibitions on the Dum Dum bullet as well as explosives dropped from balloons and gas warfare for five years.

South African War and Closure of a Military Career, 1899-1907

Upon his return from The Hague, suffering from fever, Ardagh collapsed and was bedridden for several days. Writing to Senator Sir James Gowan, he complained bitterly, "it was clear that the majority which opposed us was much more anxious to inflict a wound on the Anglo-Saxon, and on England in particular, than to listen to evidence or be guided by reason".[132] The Hague Conference had presented greater frustrations for the DMI however, for it was a decidedly ill-timed distraction in light of the impending outbreak of the South African or Second Boer War in October 1899.

The Boer War delivered in its opening months shock and injury to the national psyche and military prestige of the British, the likes of which had not been experienced since the Crimean War almost half a century earlier. Following pre-emptive coordinated strikes against the British garrisons at Natal and Cape Colony, which succeeded in bottling up large proportions of the British Army, the Orange Free State (OFS) and the Transvaal declared war on the British Empire on the 11 October 1899. By the 14 October, the garrisons at Cape Colony and Mafeking were completely cut off and on the 2nd November General Sir George White's Natal Defence Force, the largest British contingent in the region, had been defeated at the battle of Nicholson's Nek and besieged at Ladysmith by the similarly sized Boer Army led by General Piet Joubert.

---

130 TNA PRO 30/40/15: *Memorandum by Sir J. Ardagh respecting Expanding Bullets*, p. 1.
131 TNA PRO 30/40/15: Draft of Instructions for Peace Conference 1899.
132 Sir J. Ardagh to Sir J. Gowan, 29 July 1899, in Malmesbury, *Life of Major-General Sir John Ardagh*, p. 324.

In response, the British despatched Sir Redvers Buller VC, Victorian soldier-hero, and a 47,000 strong force to restore order to South Africa, rescue the besieged armies at Ladysmith and Kimberley and recover some British pride. Sir Redvers opted to attempt a simultaneous rescue of both garrisons, dividing his force and personally leading one half to Natal in aid of General White.[133] What followed were a series of three devastating British defeats by the armies of the Boer Republics, dubbed Black Week, which resulted in considerable loss of life and equipment, further damage to British pride and the removal of Sir Redvers Buller from command. The first defeat came with the ambush of General Gatacre's force at Stormberg on the 10 December; the second saw General Methuen's attack crushed at Magersfontein over the 10-11 December; and finally the Boer victory over General Buller's force of 21,000 men at Colenso on the 15 December.

Incredulity and outrage in Great Britain ensued. Explanations were demanded and there was a rush to apportion responsibility. If the Boer armies, their size, strength and capability had been underestimated and if the British soldiers in South Africa were hindered by poor or incomplete maps and surveys, then the department responsible for the provision of that information, it was reasoned, must be to blame. Public scrutiny fell, as Fergusson highlights for the first time in its history, on the Intelligence Division and the DMI.[134] It was a difficult and unpleasant experience for the ID. Obligations to secrecy meant Ardagh was unable to present his defence until the Royal Commission on the South African War was held in 1902.[135] Until then, the ID had to grit its teeth and suffer public vilification. The formal charges against the ID set out in the Royal Commission were as follows:

1. That it had failed to assess correctly the numerical strength of the Boers.
2. That it was ignorant of their armament, especially their artillery.
3. That it had failed to fathom the Boers' offensive designs on Natal.
4. That in any case, no warnings to the above had been given to the government.
5. That the troops were left unfurnished with maps and were without proper topographical information.[136]

Though Ardagh was forced to wait to defend the ID and himself, defend he did. For the most part, he was able to prove that the ID had in fact been successful, or as far as it was possible with the provision they were allowed, in meeting the expectations of them. Writing to Lord Lansdowne's successor at the War Office St John Brodrick in January 1901, General Ardagh announced:

> The ignorant attacks made on the ID at the time of the early reverses have been entirely disproved by the capture and publication of our secret documents which show that we

---

133 Fergusson, *British Military Intelligence 1870 – 1914*, p. 108.
134 Fergusson, *British Military Intelligence 1870-1914*, p. 103.
135 *Royal Commission on the South African War:Minutes of Evidence Taken before the Royal Commission on the South African War*, 1904, [Cd. 1790], Vol. 1.
136 Malmesbury, *Life of Major-General Sir John Ardagh*, p. 333.

furnished full information on the numbers, armament and plan of campaign of our enemies and for many years had formed plans of campaign of our own.[137]

Ardagh, and his chief of Section B (responsible for among other things, South Africa) Major (later Lieutenant General) Edward Altham had produced a series of memoranda and special reports between 1896 and 1899 and the handbook *Military Notes on the Dutch South African Republics* in 1898 which was revised in 1899. In his first memorandum published on the 11 June 1896, Major Altham had stated his belief that the Boers would take the offensive. He set out his fundamental strategic points, such as the importance of the defence of the Orange River and the bridges spanning it to an advancing army, as well as criticising existing defensive positions such as Laing's Nek which he correctly argued was dangerously exposed and not worth defending.[138] This was followed by a memorandum by Ardagh in October 1896 which drew official attention to the possibility of conflict with the OFS, based in part on the knowledge that the OFS was blocking the Transvaal.[139] On the 15 April 1897, Ardagh had issued a further memorandum reiterating the danger posed by the OFS and the likelihood of 5,000 'Free Staters' joining and bolstering their number. He denounced further plans to position troops at Laing's Nek to dissuade invasion and provide a forward position from which to attack, pointing out as Altham had done, the remoteness and vulnerability of that position.[140] Major Altham published three further memoranda on the subject of possible war in South Africa (21 September 1898, 3 June 1899 and 8 August 1899) stressing the likelihood of military cooperation between the OFS and the Transvaal in the event of war and the numerical inferiority of the British in that scenario. Ardagh had also raised concern after the re-election of President Paul Kruger in the Transvaal and the increase in military spending there from £61,903 in 1895, to £256,291 in 1897.[141]

Upon re-examination, it was found that the information contained in Ardagh's and Altham's reports was remarkably accurate. *Military notes on the Dutch South African Republics*, which had estimated the total fighting force of the Transvaal at 53,000 men and the OFS at 32,000 had been out by only 200 men.[142] Their warnings had not been completely overlooked; the total British regular troops, which had a strength of 3,699 in 1895 had gradually increased to 8,500 by August 1899 and then to 20,000 before the war began.[143] However, throughout the three year period leading to the start of the Boer War, the ID competed with an unwillingness to review the situation by the government. Both Salisbury and Lord Lansdowne, for whom there was no reason to doubt the word of their intelligence chief, feared provoking war but also believed it would be more politically powerful to send two regiments to the Cape, 'where the danger was'.[144] Furthermore, there was an overwhelming belief in the military and the government in

---

137 Ardagh, Maj. Gen. Sir John, to St John Brodrick, 30th January 1901, in Beaver, *Under Every Leaf*, p. 281.
138 Surridge, Keith Terrance, *Managing the South African War, 1899-1902: Politicians v. Generals* (Woodbridge: Boydell Press & RHS, 1998), p. 22.
139 TNA PRO 30/40/16: Ardagh, Major-General Sir J. C., *Memorandum on the Orange Free State and the Transvaal*, October 1896.
140 Surridge, *Managing the South African War, 1899-1902*, p. 22.
141 Surridge, *Managing the South African War, 1899-1902*, p. 33.
142 Beaver, *Under Every Leaf*, p. 281.
143 Fergusson, *British Military Intelligence 1870-1914*, p. 113.
144 Surridge, *Managing the South African War, 1899-1902*, p. 22.

the strength of the imperial army and the weaknesses of the farmer Boers.[145] The Commander-in-Chief Lord Wolseley in particular proved problematic in convincing of the threat the Boers represented; "Wolseley envisaged an addition of about 3,500 men, two battalions of which (roughly 2000 men) would be positioned at Cape Colony, the rest at Natal ... this confidence in [the British] ability to overawe the Boers revealed Wolseley's contempt for the Boer military abilities".[146]

Against this, the ID battled with a decidedly meagre budget and a tiny staff. In comparison to the German military for instance, the ID's 20 officer complement was dwarfed by 250 German intelligence officers.[147] Financially, even in comparison with the Transvaal Intelligence Department which allocated around £94,000 per year, the ID's £2,000 for Section B or a maximum £20,000 overall budget was minute.[148] The sum necessary to provide a complete and accurate bank of maps and surveys, the Royal Commission was told, would have been £17,000, immediately highlighting the constraints within which Ardagh and his officers were working.[149] Despite these constraints, the ID had been faced with establishing a spy network within South Africa, with Altham spending several months there on 'special service' in 1896 and gathering information from an array of covert sources, such as British military and civilian officials, Customs House, official OFS and Transvaal publications and observations from British civilians. With regards to topographical intelligence, maps of South Africa were rare and the ID had every one in existence. From there further information had to be gathered by hand, in civilian clothes, risking causing further friction between the British and Boer States if caught.[150]

If there was one area in which the DMI had fallen short it was, as Fergusson has suggested, in appreciating the advantage the particular nature of the Boer armies gave them over the British. There were not extensive logistical contingents and guard details for the lines of communications in the Boer strength and with every soldier mounted and armed, 40,000 men meant almost 40,000 rifles in the firing line. This combined with tactics tailored to the terrain of South Africa and the ideological motivation of fighting on their home soil against a hated adversary gave them an added edge.[151] Despite the challenges Ardagh faced in terms of resources, manpower and raw intelligence however, the Royal Commission found that no blame lay with the ID. It was perhaps fortunate that the Boers captured a copy of Ardagh's *Military Notes on the Dutch South African Republics* from General Sir Penn Symon at the battle of Talana in November 1899. The information it contained was so accurate the Boers, astonished, reprinted it unchanged for their own use. After the war the handbook was reviewed by the British authorities and was found to support Ardagh's defence greatly. Combined with this and other supporting evidence, Ardagh maintained confidently that the ID had done all it could in preparation. The disasters of the war, and even the conflict itself, would not have taken place if the British presence in South

---

145 Wade, *Spies in the Empire*, pp. 189-190.
146 Surridge, *Managing the South African War, 1899-1902*, p. 21.
147 Wade, *Spies in the Empire*, p. 188.
148 *Royal Commission on the South African War: Minutes of Evidence Taken before the Royal Commission on the South African War*, 1904, [Cd. 1790], Vol. 1, p. 216.
149 Fergusson, *British Military Intelligence 1870-1914*, p. 114.
150 Fergusson, *British Military Intelligence 1870-1914*, p. 111.
151 Fergusson, *British Military Intelligence 1870-1914*, p. 115.

Africa had been greater and that the information necessary for such a decision had been made available by the ID for some time. The committee seemed to accept this argument.[152]

In 1901 the Intelligence Division, as part of the Headquarters Staff of the British Army, underwent a process of reorganisation under Lord Roberts. The mobilisation branch was integrated once again with the Intelligence Division into one department. As part of these changes, the chief of the new department was to be a Lieutenant-General. The transition also coincided with the end of Ardagh's five year term as Director of Military Intelligence and though he was consulted as to the changes taking place in the ID, his service in that role had concluded. Ardagh was in full support of the reorganisation of the ID, which with the inclusion of the new chief as a member of the Army Board and the Committee of Imperial Defence, constituted a sure step in the direction of a General Staff, the likes of which Ardagh had been seeking for some time. His only concern, he told the leaving dinner given in his honour at the Army and Navy Club, was that in his mind, it did not go far enough.[153]

Having left the War Office, Ardagh found that with no room for promotion within the Royal Engineers at that present time and having reached the age of 62 without attaining the rank of Lieutenant-General, he faced retirement. Despite his work in the Intelligence Division having come to an end however, Ardagh was still actively advising the government on several issues including negotiations over the western and southern borders of Abyssinia, the arbitration on the frontier between Chile and Argentina and the Code of Regulations for the use of British officers in accordance with the findings of the Hague Conference. The Foreign Office applied therefore for an extension in his period of active service which was granted. On the 29 April 1901, Ardagh was chosen by His Majesty's Government to act as an agent before a commission appointed to investigate claims of compensations by foreign nationals deported from South Africa by the military authorities.[154]

The Commission, of which the President was Mr. Milvain K.C., investigated 1,700 claims, reporting on 1,252 of them, between 30 April and 13 November 1901. The cause for many of the claims came from the response of the authorities in Johannesburg to suspicions that groups of foreign nationals were plotting acts of kidnap and sabotage. Some 450 individuals were arrested on the night of the 13 July 1900, their names cross referenced with the relevant Consuls and several deported to England and to their native countries. Whilst the authorities were justified in their concern and vigilance, it was rapidly decided by the WO and FO that without sufficient evidence, the expulsion of foreign aliens was not legitimate. With the majority of cases concluded, Ardagh was then sent by the FO to South Africa in December 1901 to represent the Government in the arbitration of claims exempted by the general settlement and submitted before the Central Claims Board in South Africa.[155]

The task awaiting Ardagh in South Africa was of a larger scale and more complicated than the commission's work in London. The Central Claims Board was processing 40,000 claims by a majority of British nationals, against military damage to property as well as civil cases. Concerned with the foreign claims only, Ardagh was still confronted with a potential bill of £700,000 from predominantly Germans who, he feared, would show much perspicacity

---

152 Royal Commission on the South African War, *Minutes of Evidence*, p. 217.
153 Malmesbury, *Life of Major-General Sir John Ardagh*, p. 351.
154 Malmesbury, *Life of Major-General Sir John Ardagh*, p. 372.
155 Malmesbury, *Life of Major-General Sir John Ardagh*, pp. 381-382.

in their cases.¹⁵⁶ The Central Claims Board oversaw the process of claims in several military sub-districts across South Africa, the officials of which had pre-existing duties in those areas. Ardagh therefore recommended that three new members, including a senior military officer, a lawyer and someone familiar with South Africa be appointed to lead the proceedings with the original members free to attend to their other duties or the claims as they saw fit. The progress was slow, quite apart from the fact that the cessation of hostilities was required in order for the claims to be finalised, the committee contended with the infrequency with which the Central Claims Board met, the length the foreign individuals could be detained and the fact that they were well within their rights to demand a further, non-military, committee hearing. Having completed a general survey of the important points bearing on compensation, and with no immediate prospect of arriving at a conclusion for the claims he was ordered to investigate, Ardagh returned to England, departing Pretoria in May 1902.

Ardagh did not stay at home for long, for on the 10 August he embarked once more for South Africa. A Martial Law Commission had been appointed by Joseph Chamberlain, then at the Colonial Office, to review the sentences given to rebels, many of whom had been handed severe punishments, including transportation to St Helena. With the conclusion of the Boer War in May 1902, it was deemed wise to review the punishments meted out. Ardagh's studies in military law, particularly whilst Instructor of Military History, Law, and Tactics at Chatham in 1883 and more recently, in assisting in the preparation of handbooks on the subject, made him a valuable addition to the commission.¹⁵⁷ Appointed with the temporary rank of Lieutenant General, Mr. Justice Bigham, a judge and fellow member of the Martial Law Commission praised Ardagh's conduct, noting the sensitivity with which he avoided recriminations and recognised the need for reconciliation and healing with the Boers; "His suggestions as to the remission or reduction of a sentence always inclined towards the side of mercy… Only in cases where the prisoner had offended more than once or had tempted others to rebel, would he show anything like severity".¹⁵⁸

Officially then, Major-General Sir John Charles Ardagh retired from military service on the 9 August 1902, aged 62. He continued to serve the British Government however, working in various capacities connected to both civil and military concerns. In October 1902, on the strength of his experiences in 1870s and early 1880s Balkan Boundary Commissions, he was appointed as a member of a tribunal, alongside Lord Macnaghten, Lord of Appeal and Colonel Sir Thomas Holdich, R.E., established to draft the text defining the frontier between Argentina and Chile, which had been a source of tension between the two nations for several decades. Whilst Ardagh did not travel to South America to perform the surveys required for the award to be made, it was on the strength of the reports which returned that he drafted his recommendations, which were accepted by all concerned.¹⁵⁹

Ardagh was also appointed as a Director of the Suez Canal in March 1903. This appointment, held until his death, saw Ardagh assisting in resolving issues relating to regulations on the company and levies on goods and transit which by 1903 had been building for some considerable

---

156 Malmesbury, *Life of Major-General Sir John Ardagh*, pp. 384-385.
157 Malmesbury, *Life of Major-General Sir John Ardagh*, pp. 390-391.
158 Bigham, Justice John Charles to Lady Ardagh, in Malmesbury, *Life of Major-General Sir John Ardagh*, p. 392.
159 Malmesbury, *Life of Major-General Sir John Ardagh*, pp. 395-396.

time. He made frequent trips to Paris to attend company meetings and also to Egypt in order to inspect new works, dredgers, coaling arrangements, workshops and other aspects of the company's operations. He also served as one of four British delegates at the revision of the Geneva Convention in 1906. He had been connected to the revision since 1903 when the Swiss Government first invited the powers to conference but despite having presided at eight meetings to consider and redraft the convention in that year, the conference was delayed until 1906, in part by the Russo-Japanese War of 1904-05.

A notable outcome of that conference was that the inverted Swiss flag, the Red Cross on a white background, was established as a symbol of aid and neutrality. Though unconnected, two years before, Ardagh had joined the National Aid Society which in 1905 became the British Red Cross Society. It was a movement with which he had had sympathy for several years, assisting in an official capacity during the 1884-5 Egyptian Campaign and, when DMI in 1897, instigating the formation of the British Red Cross Committee at the War Office and raising concerns over the absence of any rights for ambulances under the 1864 Geneva Convention. In June 1907 he attended the eighth International Conference of the Red Cross Society in London. The revisions of the Geneva Convention the previous year were discussed and the use of female nurses and neutral international aid in time of war encouraged. The Red Cross Society's conference was the last public appearance Ardagh would make. His health had been failing for several years from fatigue and attacks of fever. He died at Glynllifon, Caernarfon in September 1907 and was buried at Broomfield near Taunton.

Conclusion

The period 1868 to 1902 saw a fundamental change in the British Army, an institution struggling to cast off its Wellington mould and begin to embrace the nature of modern military organisation and warfare. John Charles Ardagh was an officer at the forefront of that transformation. It is a legacy which in retrospect seems somewhat fleeting perhaps; he was not a great military reformer like Edward Cardwell or Lord Wolseley, nor was he quite the trail-blazing scientific officer of Henry Brackenbury or culturally influential like Lord Roberts or General Gordon. And yet Ardagh was at the elbow of each of them. His talents extended across the spectrum of the military profession, and beyond.

As militaries and governments were becoming alive to the value and necessity of intelligence, in Britain, Ardagh was at the fore of that awakening. His topographical and diplomatic skills rendered him instrumental throughout the Eastern Crisis (1876-82) as he became HM Government's eyes in the Balkans, enabling Disraeli to decide between invasion and negotiation and ensuring the British remained in control at the Congress of Berlin. In Egypt and the Sudan, Ardagh's skills as an officer were invaluable, as a Royal Engineer and as a commander, ensuring the defence of Alexandria (1882) and successfully supporting as base commandant the first Nile Expedition (1884-85). Those experiences, combined with an astute political and administrative acumen honed through service as the private secretary to the Viceroy of India and joint-architect of the schemes for Britain's defence and mobilisation, culminated in his appointment as Director of Military Intelligence (1896-1901). There, Ardagh combined his talents to "gain the wholehearted confidence of the most cautious statesmen and officials, including those at the

Foreign and Colonial Offices and at the Admiralty" and ensure the impoverished and abused Intelligence Division remained a vital component of the military machine.[160]

The South African War constitutes something of a downfall for the prodigious Ardagh. Despite achieving vindication at the subsequent Royal Commission, the DMI was forced to fall on his sword and endure two years of vilification in silence before absolution could be achieved. The work of the ID was too sensitive to be discussed sooner. It may be for this reason that Ardagh is a forgotten Victorian general. The biography written by his wife, Susan Countess of Malmesbury shortly after his death, demonstrates the need for public rehabilitation. But Ardagh had no reason to seek forgiveness. The ID performed its duties to the highest standard it was able and it was a testament to his leadership as DMI that during a period of absence through illness immediately prior to the outbreak of the Boer War "the machinery which his brain had built up and the personnel he had trained to handle it… [should have continued] uninterrupted and unimpaired in his absence".[161] The intelligence the ID had produced under his direction was astoundingly accurate.

In reality, Ardagh's departure from the ID spelled the partial realisation of his aims; the position of DMI was elevated to encompass much of the influence in policy and strategy which he had been pressing for throughout his service at the Intelligence Division. It was the first steps towards the Army Council and a General Staff in the British Army. For Ardagh this achievement rather constitutes his legacy – a Victorian General forgotten in his own time.

---

160 Fergusson, *British Military Intelligence 1870-1914*, p. 106.
161 Malmesbury, *Life of Major-General Sir John Ardagh*, p. 326.

5

Sir Arthur Cunynghame
General Officer Commanding Her Majesty's Forces at the Cape of Good Hope (1873-78)

John Laband

What are the qualities which define a successful commander? In the estimation of early nineteenth-century British soldiers, none possessed them in greater abundance than the Duke of Wellington and Rory Muir has specified them in his recent biography of the great warrior. They include personal daring and courage as they must for every officer, along with the character to inspire the men he leads, and the human sympathy to care for their welfare. But even more is demanded of a senior commander. The vision to formulate effective strategy is essential, as is the meticulousness required to prepare for a campaign and to ensure that an army in the field is financed and supplied. Moreover, a general has to possess in large degree the political skills vital for cooperating with fellow commanders and for working with often mistrustful civilian authorities.[1]

It is against these demanding standards and attributes that we must measure General Sir Arthur Cunynghame as a commander. In later life Wellington often discussed his campaigns and battles.[2] Cunynghame too, as we shall see, was an extensive traveller and intelligent observer, the author of four books based on his military service and travels in China, North America, south Russia and South Africa. Yet the letter he wrote *The Times* in the early days of his retirement from the Army is decidedly surprising. After commanding the forces in South Africa during the recent Ninth Cape Frontier War (1877-78), it might have been expected of him that he would engage with aspects of conducting a difficult colonial campaign. Instead, he wrote from the privileged comfort of the Senior United Service Club to enquire whether there was such a thing as 'concentrated beer or porter' to which water could be added. Such a commodity, he was sure, '...would certainly be hailed with gratitude by the troops employed

---

1   See Muir, Rory, *Wellington. The Path to Victory, 1769–1814* (New Haven and London: Yale University Press, 2013), p. 165.
2   See Stanhope, Philip Henry, Earl, introduced by Elizabeth Longford, *Conversations with Wellington* (London: Prion, 1998).

in those distant countries where carriage for this bulky article…is so difficult to be obtained and so expensive to the State.'³ Unquestionably, conscientious Victorian officers were routinely concerned to improve the quality of food in the ranks.⁴ But this letter, in its undeniable quirkiness, is indicative of its author. For Cunynghame was no reforming, modern soldier of the Sir Garnet Wolseley type. He was a quintessentially aristocratic officer of the mid-Victorian mold, adventurous and intrepid, undoubtedly brave in combat but also dependent (like most other officers who had gained their commissions before the army reforms of the early 1870s) on purchase and patronage for accelerated promotion. He was also naturally conservative both socially and professionally, and his command in South Africa sorely tested his organizational, military, and political skills.

The Cunynghames of Milnecraig, County Ayr, a Scottish landed family since the early seventeenth century, claimed to be descended from the second son of the Earl of Glencairn. What is certain is that the first distinguished member of the family was Sir David Cunynghame of Milnecraig, a lawyer and member of the Scottish Parliament who was created a Baronet of Nova Scotia on 3 February 1702.⁵ Succeeding baronets pursued military or political careers and married into the Scottish aristocracy or gentry. Cunynghame's father, Sir David, the fifth baronet, married in 1801 Maria, one of the three daughters of the intimidating lawyer and politician, Edward, first Baron Thurlow of Thurlow (d. 1806), who had been Lord High Chancellor from 1778 to 1792. All three daughters, however, were born out of wedlock to Polly Humphries, the daughter of the keeper of Nando's Coffee House in London, with whom Thurlow lived openly.⁶ Because common law insisted on the rule of 'indelible bastardy', this meant that Maria and her sisters remained unambiguously illegitimate for life, and had no legal next of kin.⁷ Even so, canon law regarded it as a moral duty for parents to support their illegitimate children, and bastards could acquire property through family settlements or personal gifts, or could inherit under a parent's will. In this case relations remained close between Lord Thurlow and his daughters, and all five of Lady Cunynghame's sons had Thurlow as one of their forenames and were eager to boast of their descent from the Lord Chancellor.

Sir David and Lady Cunynghame's youngest son was Arthur Augustus Thurlow Cunynghame [henceforth Cunynghame], born on 12 August 1812.⁸ His mother died in 1816, when he was only four. His father, who remarried, died in 1854, and the baronetcy was inherited in turn

---

3   General A.T. Cunynghame, letter to *The Times*, 23 October 1879.
4   Spiers, Edward M., *The Army and Society 1815-1914* (London and New York: Longman, 1980), p. 27.
5   Pine, L.G. (ed), *Burke's Peerage, Baronetage & Knightage* (London: Burke's Peerage, 102nd edition, 1959), p. 598.
6   Pine (ed), *Burke's Peerage*, p. 2228; Ditchfield, G.M., 'Thurlow, Edward, first Baron Thurlow (1731–1806)', in *Oxford Dictionary of National Biography* (Oxford: Oxford University Press, 2004, online edition, January 2008) <http://www.oxfroddnb.com/view/article/27406> (accessed 31 January 2014).
7   Indelible bastardy was repealed by the Legitimacy Act of 1921 and retrospective legitimization made possible. See Finn, Margot, Michael Lobban and Jenny Bourne Taylor, 'Introduction: Spurious Issues', in Margot Finn, Michael Lobban and Jenny Bourne Taylor (eds) *Legitimacy and Illegitimacy in Nineteenth-Century Law, Literature and History* (Basingstoke: Palgrave Macmillan, 2010), pp. 2–3, 5–6, 21, n. 6.
8   For basic biographical information concerning Cunynghame's life and career, see the obituary of Sir Arthur Cunynghame, *Illustrated London News*, 22 March 1884; Chichester, H.M. and Rev. James Lunt, 'Cunynghame, Sir Arthur Augustus Thurlow (1812–1884)', in *Oxford Dictionary National Biography* <http://www.oxfroddnb.com/view/article/6940> (accessed 19 March 2012); and Worcestershire

during Cunynghame's lifetime first by his eldest surviving brother David,[9] then in 1869 by the latter's unmarried son Edward (whose dissipation and criminal activities brought shame on his family),[10] and finally in 1877 by Cunynghame's elder brother Francis who passed it down to his male descendants.

Sir David, the sixth baronet and Cunynghame's eldest brother, was educated for the army at Sandhurst Military College. In the early to mid-nineteenth century the majority of army officers were recruited from the aristocracy and gentry. Their claim to command was based on their high social caste, in which good breeding mattered more than professional expertise. For many officers soldiering was an honourable extension of the country pursuits of shooting and riding to hounds.[11] David Cunynghame served for a time in the cavalry in India, but as the heir to the baronetcy and the estate he retired while still a captain in the 12th Lancers.[12] Cunynghame was also destined for the army after being educated at Eton College, but without his eldest brother's prospects he had to earn a living. He consequently had little choice but to make a successful career of the gentlemanly profession of arms.

General Sir Arthur Cunynghame.

Regiment website, 'General Sir Arthur Augustus Thurlow Cunynghame, G.C.B' <http://www.worcestershireregiment.com> (accessed 2 March 2014).

9   Edward, the first-born, had died in 1825.
10 Sir Edward Cunynghame, the seventh baronet, was adjudicated a bankrupt in July 1874. He had his first serious brush with the law in September 1875 when he borrowed a sapphire ring from a jeweler to wear at a ball but neglected to return it. Far more seriously, he and two others were accused in January 1877 of conspiring to defraud a fourth person during a wild drinking-match. Before the case could come to trial in March 1877 Cunynghame died—presumably by his own hand—at a hotel in Covent Garden. He thus escaped being sent to jail with hard labour along with his two surviving co-conspirators. See *The Times*, 10 and 17 September 1875; and the *Illustrated London News*, 6 January, 27 January and 10 March 1877.
11 Spiers, *Army and Society*, pp. 1–2, 7–9, 25, 29; Spiers, Edward M., *The Late Victorian Army 1868-1902* (Manchester: Manchester University Press, 1992), pp. 2, 94-5.
12 *The Times*, 3 June 1854; obituary of Sir David Cunynghame, Illustrated *London News*, 27 November 1869.

Still, establishing Cunynghame in the army cost his family a considerable sum of money, and a private income, especially in fashionable regiments, was the essential pre-condition of a military career. A commission was usually by purchase until the abolition of the system by Royal Warrant on 1 November 1871 as part of the Cardwell Reforms that introduced competitive examination.[13] Each step up in rank to lieutenant colonel was also by purchase, the rationale being that officers who acquired promotion only through wealth and suitable patronage would have a conservative stake in country and so would never challenge the status quo. Purchase also allowed ambitious officers to exchange between regiments when there was not a higher vacancy in their current regiment. That enabled them to acquire the social status conferred by membership of a more prestigious or fashionable regiment, or to secure accelerated promotion through membership of a regiment on active service.[14]

Cunynghame was commissioned second lieutenant, by purchase, in the 60th (The King's Royal Rifle Corps) Regiment of Foot on 20 November 1830 at the cost of £450 and was made first lieutenant on 2 May 1835 for a further £250. He purchased his company in the 60th Regiment on 17 August 1841 for the considerable additional sum of £1,100,[15] and transferred as a captain to the 3rd (East Kent, The Buffs) Regiment of Foot on 3 December 1841. After serving briefly with his battalion in the Mediterranean, he secured the coveted staff appointment of aide-de-camp [ADC] to Major General the sixteenth Lord Saltoun of Abernethy who, in late 1841, received command of a brigade in what is alternatively referred to as the First Opium, China, or Sino-British War of 1839–42.[16] Saltoun, who had fought exceedingly gallantly in the Peninsular and Waterloo campaigns, was described by Wellington as a 'pattern to the army both as a man and a soldier', and Cunynghame duly honoured him as such.[17]

In understanding Cunynghame's career, it should be appreciated that his appointment as Saltoun's ADC was a matter not so much of merit as of what was still entirely customary patronage. Saltoun was the younger man's uncle through marriage to his aunt Catherine, his mother's sister and daughter of Lord Thurlow. Catherine, who died in 1826, would have felt close to the very young Cunynghame after his mother's death in 1816, and the childless Saltoun

---

13 The Cardwell Reforms were primarily designed to improve the efficiency of the army and reduce costs through organizational changes. They opened the way for a series of subsequent reforms. See Brice, Christopher, *The Thinking Man's Soldier. The Life and Career of General Sir Henry Brackenbury 1837–1914* (Solihull: Helion, 2012), pp. 22–4, 64. For a full discussion of the Cardwell Reforms, see Spiers, *Army and Society*, pp. 177–200; and *Late Victorian Army*, pp. 2–24.

14 See Spiers, *Army and Society*, pp. 16, 18 –19 for the intricacies and financial considerations involved in the exchange and purchase of commissions. Also Harries-Jenkins, G., *The Army in Victorian Society* (London: Routledge and Kegan Paul, 1977), pp. 24-5; Spiers, *Late Victorian Army*, pp. 93–4, 105–6.

15 See Spiers, *Army and Society*, pp. 11, 17: Table 1.6: Regulation of prices of commissions established by the Royal Warrant of 1821; Spiers, *Late Victorian Army*, p. 104. In terms of the Royal Warrant of 30 October 1871 Cunynghame might have chosen to be among those officers who arranged that the Treasury reimburse them the purchase price of their commissions and then retired, but since he decided to pursue his career and accept promotion, his substantial capital investment in purchase was lost. See Erickson, Arvel B., 'Abolition of Purchase in the British Army', *Military Affairs*, 23, 2 (Summer, 1959), p. 75; Spiers, *Army and Society*, p. 16.

16 The accepted names of colonial wars are constantly changing with the times.

17 Stephens, H.M. and Rev. James Lunt, 'Fraser, Alexander George, sixteenth Lord Saltoun of Abernethy (1785–1853)', *Oxford Dictionary of National Biography* <http://oxforddnb.com/view/article/10102> (accessed 31 January 2014)

doubtless looked on his personable nephew as the son he never had. As for his being selected for his staff by his uncle, there was as yet no such thing as formal training for young staff officers such as Cunynghame, and they were expected to pick up their duties as they went along. Only after the blatant failures of staff and command in the Crimean War would the decision be taken to establish the Staff College at Camberley in 1858.[18]

Later, in 1856, by which time he was himself a major general, Cunynghame felt constrained to respond to a personal attack in a letter to *The Times* by a decidedly disgruntled 'H.M.' who (somewhat inexactly) cited the major general's military career as an example of the unfair advantages of purchase and patronage.[19] Rather than argue the merits of purchase, Cunynghame in his reply took up a stance which justified his army career up to that time, and would hold equally good for the future:

> That I have availed myself of every opportunity of purchase to advance in the profession your correspondent has clearly shown, but he has omitted to tell your readers how equally I availed myself of every opportunity of tropical and other service as another adjunct to the advancement I have sought, and without which I am well aware I should not have obtained it.[20]

Indeed, as he further put it in his letter, his military service always had (and indeed would) call him 'to all four quarters of the globe' and he stated that between 1830 and 1856 he had spent thirteen years abroad and served in two major campaigns.

The first of these campaigns, the First Opium War, was from the British perspective essentially a conflict over free trade, while from that of China's ruling Qing or Manchu dynasty (1644–1912) it was a matter of exerting its waning authority over the Han or native Chinese merchants of southern China. The war took the form of sporadic British operations to seize strategic cities and destroy fortresses, and ended with the Treaty of Nanjing, signed on 29 August 1842, which relaxed trade regulations, opened five port cities for trade and ceded the island of Hong Kong to Britain. The war was never other than one-sided with the British deploying their modern steamships, ship-mounted shell guns, mobile artillery and percussion cap muskets against obsolete matchlocks, bows and arrows, polearms, swords and an inferior assortment of ordnance. A further Chinese weakness lay in the organization of their army. The Bannermen, the hereditary Manchu military caste, formed its nucleus of crack troops, while the more numerous and poorly trained native Han—the Troops of the Green Standard—were employed as garrisons. The Han troops proved reluctant to die for the Daoguang Emperor (r. 1820-50), and it was only towards the end of the war that the British encountered determined and motivated Bannermen.[21]

---

18 Clayton, Anthony, *The British Officer: Leading the Army from 1660 to the Present* (Harlow: England: Pearson Longman, 2006), pp. 109–10. It would not be until the 1890s that the Staff College gained real credibility. See Spiers, *Late Victorian Army*, pp. 109–12.
19 H.P., letter to *The Times*, 22 November 1856.
20 Major-General A.A.T. Cunynghame, letter to *The Times*, 26 November 1856.
21 For succinct accounts of the course of the First Opium War and Chinese military organization, see Elleman, Bruce A., *Modern Chinese Warfare, 1795–1989* (London and New York: Routledge, 2001), pp. 13–34; Graham, Gerald S., *The Chinese Station: War and Diplomacy 1830–1860* (Oxford: Clarendon Press, 1978), pp. 198–229; Haythornthwaite, Philip J., *The Colonial Wars Source Book* (London: Caxton

Cunynghame recorded his experiences during the final stages of the war in China in his first book, *An Aide-de-Camp's Recollections of Service in China*, published in 1844 and dedicated to Lord Saltoun.[22] Following the conventions of the time, it was part travelogue, part war diary, and aimed above all at amusing readers with a sprightly account of adventures in faraway places.[23]

Saltoun's brigade formed part of the reinforcements, both British and Indian, bringing Major General Sir Hugh Gough's expeditionary force in China up to a strength of some 12,000 men. Gough's objective was to take control of the Yangzi River, capture the great city of Nanjing, and by closing trade along the Grand Canal enforce the Daoguang Emperor's submission. Cunynghame joined the army in Shanghai, which had fallen to the British on 19 June 1842. He was with the expeditionary force as the Royal Navy laboriously transported it up the Yangzi River on fifteen vessels of war through sandy shoals and dangerous currents as far as Zhenjiang, a walled city that commanded the southern entrance of the Grand Canal.[24]

'Thursday, July 21, must ever be to me a memorable day, as it was the first upon which I met the enemy on the field, and my feelings were naturally somewhat excited on that occasion,' Cunynghame wrote afterwards.[25] That day Gough's force assaulted the city. The 2 and 3 Brigades attacked the south-western and south-eastern walls intending to take them by escalade. Meanwhile, Saltoun's 1 Brigade of about a thousand men was given what appeared to be the more glorious mission of assaulting two entrenched Chinese camps on heights to the west of Zhenjiang, believed to be held by the main body of the garrison, some 2,000 strong. Saltoun divided his brigade into two columns to turn the Chinese position. The engagement commenced with the Chinese raising their 'usual wild yell' and opening 'a smart fire of round shot and grape.'[26] For Cunynghame, this was the first moment 'in which the real services' of his profession 'were brought into play.'[27] It proved an anti-climax, however. The moment the three British field pieces on their wheelbarrow carriages came into action the Chinese precipitately abandoned their position and fled, forsaking sedan chairs, banners, clothes and arms.

It was now nine o'clock in the morning and the heat was already so ferocious that many of Saltoun's men were succumbing to heatstroke.[28] But they were at least spared the unexpectedly tenacious defence of the city itself. About half of the 2,600 or so defenders were Manchu Bannermen. Once the walls were taken and the gates blown in, they fought desperately through

---

Editions, 2000), pp. 237–42. For a detailed contemporary military narrative, see Ouchterlony, Lieutenant John, *The Chinese War: An Account of All the Operations of the British Forces from the Commencement to the Treaty of Nanking* (reprint, New York: Washington and London: Praeger, 1970), passim. For a recent popular account, see Lovell, Julia, *The Opium War: Drugs, Dreams, and the Making of China* (London: Picador, 2011), pp. 1–240.

22 Cunynghame, Captain Arthur, *An Aide-de-Camp's Recollections of Service in China, a Residence in Hong-Kong, and Visits to Other Islands in the Chinese Seas* (London: Saunders and Otley, 1844).
23 One such place was Cape Town, where in March 1842 Cunynghame stepped ashore during his long voyage to the hinese theatre. He could not know it, but that is where, thirty-one years later, he would take up his South African command. Fortunately for the future, he was favourably taken by the place, its wines and its diverse inhabitants. See Cunynghame, *Service in China*, pp. 38–47.
24 Cunynghame, *Service in China*, pp. 113–62.
25 Cunynghame, *Service in China*, p. 164.
26 Ouchterlony, *Chinese War*, p. 358. See pp. 342–93 for his detailed account of the day's operations and the storming of Zhenjiang.
27 Cunynghame, *Service in China*, p. 166.
28 For Cunynghame's description of the attack on the Chines camp, see *Service in China*, pp. 164–70.

the streets and refused to surrender, finally killing their wives and children and then themselves. Saltoun's brigade was quartered outside the walls, but Cunynghame had many opportunities to visit the sacked and partially burned city with the dead still lying '… in all directions.' This was Cunynghame's first sight of the true horrors of war, and such scenes of desolation he hoped devoutly that he might never see again.[29] Nevertheless, his horror did not prevent him from participating in the soldier's age-old right to the plunder of a city taken by storm, and Cunynghame evinced no scruples in openly recording in his book that he helped himself to a warm cloak, jade ornaments, porcelain cups, a metal mirror and several richly inlaid and tasselled imperial 'battens of office.'[30]

Cunynghame took part in the subsequent investment of Nanjing but saw no further action as the campaign wound rapidly down. He continued as Lord Saltoun's aide-de-camp until 12 January 1844, when he resumed regimental duties with The Buffs. On 8 August 1845 he was promoted major by purchase (which would have cost him a further £1, 400). At 33 he was now at an age and sufficiently senior in the service for it to be socially desirable to take a wife,[31] and on 13 September 1845 he married the Hon. Frances Elizabeth Hardinge. They had two daughters, Emily and Lavinia, and two sons who entered the professions. Henry, born in 1848, would become a barrister and senior civil servant and be made Knight Commander of the Bath [KCB] in 1908; and Arthur, born in 1853, would earn his living as an auditor.[32]

Crucially for Cunynghame's career and essential network of connections in society and the army, his wife was the elder daughter of Lieutenant General Sir Henry Hardinge, the Governor-General of India (1844-48), raised to the peerage in May 1846 for his success in the First Anglo-Sikh War as Viscount Hardinge of Lahore. Her mother was Lady Emily Jane Stewart, the daughter of the 1st Marquess of Londonderry. Hardinge had been a staff officer of the Duke of Wellington in the Peninsular and had fought at Waterloo. Politically, he worked closely with Wellington, and in March 1852 would succeed him as General Commanding-in-Chief and be raised to Field Marshal in October 1855.[33] As with Saltoun, Cunynghame was once again drawn closely into the coterie of high-ranking officers who revered Wellington and his legacy, a circle that was not associated with ambitious officers advocating far-sweeping army reforms.

Once married, Cunynghame continued up the military ladder through exchange and purchase. On 28 August 1846 he exchanged into the 13th (First Somersetshire) (Prince Alfred's Light Infantry) Regiment of Foot preparatory to his appointment by purchase (for a further £1,300) as the regiment's lieutenant colonel on 3 November 1846. Then on 1 December 1846 he exchanged to captain and lieutenant colonel in the Grenadier Guards (an officer in the Guards possessed a concurrent regimental and higher army rank up to lieutenant colonel).[34] The Foot Guards

---

29 For Cunynghame's description of sacked Zhenjiang, see *Service in China*, pp. 176–83.
30 Cunynghame, *Service in China*, pp. 183–6.
31 Regarding marriage, the unwritten code was 'Captains may, Majors should, Colonels must.' See Clayton, *The British Officer*, p. 107.
32 Pine (ed), *Burke's Peerage*, p. 598; obituary of Sir H. Cunynghame, 'an unconventional civil servant', *The Times*, 6 May 1935.
33 Pine (ed), *Burke's Peerage*, p. 1058; Howlett, David J., 'Hardinge, Henry, first Viscount Hardinge of Lahore (1785–1856)', *Oxford Dictionary of National Biography* <http://oxforddnb.com/view/article/112271> (accessed 31 January 2014); obituary of the Dowager Viscountess Hardinge, *Illustrated London News*, 4 November 1865.
34 See Spiers, *Army and Society*, p. 18.

and Household Cavalry were the most fashionable and prestigious regiments in the army and accorded with Cunynghame's connections,[35] but the problem was that few regiments were as expensive as the Grenadiers where an officer might have to spend up to £900 a year above his pay.[36] Perhaps it was for that reason, or because of his undoubted desire to see the world and seek adventure (the evidence is lacking) that after spending just two years with the Grenadiers in London Cunynghame exchanged on 27 April 1849 into the 20th (East Devonshire) Regiment of Foot which was stationed in the Canadian provinces of Quebec and Ontario until 1850. As the regiment's commander in a peaceful Canada, he used his generous periods of leave to gather material for his next book, *A Glimpse of the Great Western Republic*. Published in 1851, this work presented his not unperceptive but necessarily superficial impressions of the United States.[37]

Stationed back in England with his regiment, on 2 April 1852 Cunynghame next exchanged into the 27th (Inniskilling) Regiment of Foot which he commanded in Ireland until placed on half-pay with the 51st (2nd Yorkshire West Riding, and later still The King's Own Light Infantry) Regiment of Foot on 16 December 1853.[38] The reason for this development was his enviable appointment as ADC to his father-in-law, Viscount Hardinge. As with Lord Saltoun, his family connections had helped secure him a plum staff position. However, he stayed on Hardinge's staff for only the briefest spell, for when in March 1854 Britain and France entered the Crimean War (October 1853–March 1856) on the side of the Ottoman Empire against Russia,[39] Cunynghame relinquished his post to join the army in the field. However, he did not do so as a regimental officer, but as Assistant Quartermaster General of the prestigious 1st Division which was made up of the Guards Brigade and two batteries of Royal Artillery. The divisional commander was Lieutenant General H.R.H. Prince George, the second Duke of Cambridge and Queen Victoria's first cousin.[40]

Cunynghame, who received the brevet rank of Colonel on 20 June 1854,[41] was with the 1st Division when it landed at Calamita Bay in the Crimea in September 1854. The allied expeditionary force then moved east along the coast with the intention of capturing Sevastopol, Russia's vital Black Sea naval base. The Russians unsuccessfully disputed their advance when

---

35 Between 1800 and 1849, 69 peers and peers' sons served in the Grenadiers. See Mansel, Philip, *Pillars of Monarchy: An Outline of the Political and Social History of Royal Guards 1400-1984* (London: Quartet Books, 1984), p. 78: Table I.
36 Clayton, *The British Officer*, p. 101.
37 Cunynghame, Lieut.-Col. Arthur, *A Glimpse of the Great Western Republic* (London: R. Bentley 1851).
38 Half-pay was the allowance officers received while marking time until they could return to active service, usually at a higher rank. See Spiers, *Army and Society*, pp. 14–15.
39 For a recent and stimulating analysis of the Crimean War, see Figes, Orlando, *The Crimean War: A History* (New York: Picador, 2012), passim. For a succinct account see Holmes, Richard, 'Crimean War', in Richard Holmes (ed), *The Oxford Companion to Military History* (Oxford: Oxford University Press, 2001), pp. 23–40.
40 For the Duke of Cambridge see Spiers, Edward M., 'George, Prince, second duke of Cambridge (1819–1904)', *Oxford Dictionary of National Biography* <http://oxforddnb.com/view/article/33372> (accessed 6 October 2004).
41 Officers in the British Army held substantive rank in their regiment based on seniority, but they could concurrently hold one rank higher in the army when serving in a staff appointment, as Cunynghame was in the Crimea. They could also hold brevet rank for distinguished service in the field or when it became necessary on campaign to make them eligible to hold a more senior command. See Spiers, *Army and Society*, p. 19

they crossed the River Alma on 20 September 1854. The conscripted Russian infantry, deployed in dense battalion columns, were armed mainly with smooth-bore muskets accurate at no more than 150 paces, and expected to close with the enemy at bayonet point. Their artillery was much the superior arm. The British soldiers, who were volunteers, had on the whole much less battle experience than the Russians, but most (including the 1st Division) had the distinct advantage of being equipped with the Enfield-pattern Minié-type muzzle-loading rifle-musket which was accurate over 300 yards and was good for volley-fire up to 1,000 yards. This was just as well because the standard British battle formation was still the thin line of infantry which brought maximum firepower to bear but was vulnerable to being outflanked or broken.[42] The Alma was the first test for the 1st Division. Cunynghame had been under fire at Zhenjiang, but it hardly prepared him for the ferocity and intensity of this encounter. His commander, the Duke of Cambridge, was undoubtedly valorous, but he had never seen action before and had no experience of field command. His troops eventually crossed the river, scaled the opposite slope and drove the Russians out of their redoubt, but under his uncertain command their advance had been a hesitant, stop-go affair.

The Allies began their investment of Sevastopol on 25 September 1854. Cunynghame was present on 25 October 1854 when the Russians unsuccessfully attempted to seize their supply base at Balaklava, and again the following day when a Russian sortie from Sevastopol was beaten back at the Chernaya River (Little Inkerman). On 5 November, the Russians made a determined effort to raise the siege, but were finally repulsed in the scrambling, hand-to-hand battle at Inkerman, fought for the most part in dense fog over difficult terrain. The outnumbered British were taken by surprise, and despite their dogged defence would most likely have finally been overwhelmed had not the French moved up in support.[43] The 1st Division was in the thick of the fighting at the Sandbag Battery which was the key to the British position and lost nearly half their men engaged. Cambridge himself had his horse shot under him and was nearly cut off by the advancing Russians. It was in this frantic fighting that Cunynghame demonstrated his coolness under fire and leadership qualities. His old regiment, the 20th, was positioned to the right of the Coldstream Guards. It was part of Sir George Cathcart's 4th Division, but before it could join in his advance, its colonel was wounded. Let Kinglake, the famous Victorian historian of the war, take up the tale:

> A staff officer chanced to ride up who proved to be Colonel Cunynghame, an 'old Twentieth man.' Lieutenant Dowling accosting him said: 'Colonel, all our mounted officers are killed, or wounded. Where shall we go?' Cunynghame accepted the leadership thus cast upon him by the chance of battle, caused the troops to form a well-knit line, marched them down to within a hundred yards of the enemy's column, and then, halting them, opened a fire which forced the battalion to yield. The halt of these 'Twentieth' men was not long maintained. When Cunynghame left them, they not only advanced in pursuit, but 'drove the Russians like sheep,' and were soon far below

---

42 Mercer, Patrick and Graham Turner, *Inkerman 1854: The Soldiers' Battle* (London: Osprey Military, 1998), pp. 21–26. Knight, Ian, *Go to Your God like a Soldier: The British Soldier Fighting for Empire, 1837–1902* (London: Greenhill Books, 1996), pp. 172–81.
43 For the part played by the 1st Division in the battle, see Mercer and Turner, *Inkerman*, pp. 56–64.

the crest, some getting down close to the spot where Cathcart sat in his saddle, and in this fortuitous way rejoining the commander of their own division.[44]

In his official despatch of 11 November 1854 on Inkerman, the Commander-in-Chief, Field Marshal Lord Raglan (who had been Wellington's military secretary in the Peninsular and had lost his arm at Waterloo), wrote that Cambridge 'reports most favourably of the exertions' of seven officers, among whom he listed Cunynghame.[45]

But Cambridge had himself had enough. Doubtless brave and popular with the troops he was nevertheless suffering from nervous exhaustion brought on by the overwhelming weight of his command and by his acute dismay at the slaughter of his division at Inkerman. On 25 November 1854 he quit the Crimea.[46] Cunynghame, by contrast, stayed on through the winter of 1854–55, sharing in the hardships of the siege of Sevastopol. His services were recognized, and in March 1855 he was appointed to the local rank of major general. This was a preliminary step to his taking up his first divisional command in May 1855—not of a British formation, but of a Division of the Turkish Contingent, paid, fed, clothed, and officered by the British.[47]

The Turkish Contingent is much neglected in the historiography of the Crimean War. For one thing, the Turks do not like to remember that 20,000 Ottoman soldiers were placed under the command of Christian officers and were in the pay of a Christian state; for another, the Turkish Contingent had no opportunity to show its mettle in battle or to affect the outcome of the campaign in any significant way. It had its origins in the British realization that with only 13,000 British troops in the Crimean as opposed to 70,000 French it was impossible to take the initiative in planning the campaign or in influencing the Sublime Porte (as the Ottoman government was known). The British ambassador to the Porte, Viscount Stratford de Redcliffe, came up with the idea of addressing the disparity by hiring a large force of Ottoman soldiers of all arms detached from the regular Ottoman army. Sultan Abdülmecid I could not afford to feed his own armies and approved the proposal. The agreement was signed on 3 February 1855. All officers above the rank of sergeant were to be British—even though they required Turkish interpreters to address their troops—and Major General Robert John Vivian, a British East India Company officer, was to be commander.[48] Inevitably, the British officers selected for service with the Turkish Contingent were attracted by the opportunities it offered. Not only would they receive more pay, but Vivian, now promoted lieutenant general, submitted a roll of officers on 28 August 1855 recommended for promotion in the Ottoman army. This meant several steps up in rank for British officers. Vivian himself was made *mushir*, or full general, and

---

44 Kinglake, A.W., *The Invasion of the Crimea: Its Origin, and an Account of its Progress down to the Death of Lord Raglan* (Edinburgh and London: William Blackwood and Sons, 1888), vol. VI, p. 236.
45 Official Despatches: Lord Raglan to the Duke of Newcastle, 11 November 1854, supplement to the *London Gazette*, 2 December 1854.
46 St Aubyn, Giles, *The Royal George 1819–1904. The Life of H.R.H. Prince George Duke of Cambridge* (New York: Alfred A. Knopf, 1964), pp. 87–101.
47 For the Turkish Contingent, see Baden, Candan, *The Ottoman Crimean War (1853-56)* (Leiden and Boston: Brill, 2010), pp. 52, n. 18, 245–7, 249, 257–63, 265–8; Slade, Rear-Admiral Sir Adolphus, *Turkey and the Crimean War: A Narrative of Historical Events* (London: Smith, Elder, 1867), pp. 378–85; and 'Turkish Contingent' <http://www.ottman-uniforms.com/anglo-turkish-contingent-1855-till-1858/> (accessed 11 February 2014).
48 See *Illustrated London News*, 23 June 1855.

among dozens of further promotions five officers were given the rank of *ferik*, the equivalent of general of division or lieutenant general.

One of these *feriks* was Cunynghame who had been made Commander of the Bath in July 1855 for his earlier service with the 1st Division, and who now also received the personal thanks of the Sultan for his service with the Turkish Contingent. Nevertheless, the truth was that the Turkish troops and their British officers were finding it difficult to work together. Ottoman officers chafed at being superseded by infidels and, as Rear-Admiral Slade acidly noted, British officers who had previously served in India were 'accustomed to rule haughtily a subject race, were not the men…to act judiciously with a dominant race, imbued with traditions of military renown.'[49] Cunynghame had no such Indian record and service with the Turkish Contingent was his first experience commanding troops who were not British. For lack of specific evidence, it is hard to say how well he worked with them. What is known is that the Turkish Contingent troops in general had no major complaints about their British officers and were generally satisfied with their treatment.[50]

Nevertheless, it was many months before Müşir Ömer Lütfi Pasha, the Ottoman Generalissimo, thought the Turkish Contingent ready for action. By the time Cunynghame and his Division reached the Crimea by way of Varna from their training camp at Büyükdere on the shores of the Bosphorus, Sevastopol had already fallen on 9 September 1855, and tentative peace talks had begun. General Sir James Simpson, in command of the British forces in the Crimea since mid-1855, had no use for the Turkish Contingent. As Slade put it, 'the dilemma was, where to send it?' Eventually, after much havering, Kerch 'was fixed upon as being a neutral out-of-the-way place.'[51] Kerch, at the eastern extremity of the Crimean Peninsula, had been seized on 24 May 1855 by Sir George Brown with 7,000 French troops, 3,000 British and 5,000 Turks with the objective of outflanking the Russians in Sevastopol. The operation was proving ineffective, but the allies were continuing to hold Kerch. Cunynghame sailed there in October 1855 with some 10,000 of the Turkish Contingent to reinforce the garrison and assisted in holding the place during the winter of 1855-56. Unfortunately, for lack of cavalry the Turkish Contingent remained behind their fortified lines at Kerch until the end of the war in March 1856.

For his services in Kerch with the Turkish Contingent (mundane as they were) Cunynghame was advanced to the Third Class (Commandeur) of the Légion d'honneur and the Second Class of the Ottoman Order of the Medjidie which was limited to 150 recipients.[52] As for British honours, besides being mentioned in despatches, he received the Crimean Medal with four clasps.

The Duke of Cambridge succeeded Lord Hardinge, Cunynghame's father-in-law, as General Commanding-in-Chief on 15 July 1856, a post he would hold throughout Cunynghame's lifetime, only finally retiring under pressure on 31 October 1895. Well acquainted with the Duke through serving on his staff during the Crimean War and with an excellent record of service in that war, Cunynghame could feel assured of his future patronage at the Horse Guards. This

---

49 Slade, *Turkey and the Crimean War*, p. 380.
50 Candan, *Ottoman Crimean War*, p. 268.
51 Slade, *Turkey and the Crimean War*, p. 383.
52 The Order of the Medjidie was instituted in 1851 by Sultan Abdülmecid I for outstanding service to the state by foreign nationals.

was essential, for Cambridge (who was made field marshal on 9 November 1862) exercised his authority at the pleasure of the Crown and doggedly maintained his grip on matters of command, discipline, appointments, and promotions. He was extremely jealous of these prerogatives and resented and resisted the interference of civilians—including the imperial cabinet—in military affairs. Vitally for Cunynghame's career, the Duke continued to champion seniority and social suitability as criteria for promotion over the selection by merit later introduced through the Cardwell Reforms.[53]

There is no doubt Cunynghame benefited from the Duke's patronage. From 21 July 1856 to 2 March 1860, he was given the command of an Infantry Brigade at Dublin, with the temporary rank of major general. Then, on 28 March 1860, he was given a divisional command of the forces of the Bombay Presidency in British India with the local rank of major general. Cunynghame's reasons for accepting an Indian command are not known but can be inferred. The lavish outlay expected of a general officer at a home command could well have been straining his resources. More generous pay and allowances were to be gained by service in India, and officers like Cunynghame with aristocratic connections but limited pockets could better support the standard of living expected of their high social status there. Besides, in British India's rigidly hierarchical society due deference was paid to someone of Cunynghame's rank and standing.[54] Nor must it be forgotten that his wife was the daughter of Lord Hardinge, a former governor-general, and this would have given Cunynghame entrée to the highest circles. There were other considerations too. Cunynghame clearly enjoyed serving abroad and seeing more of the world. But he would also have been aware that distinguished service in action was the surest way to accelerated promotion, and while a home command did not provide the opportunity, India might well. Meanwhile, his career advanced routinely through seniority, and on 20 April 1861 he was promoted to the rank of major general in the British Army. Then, doubtless through his connections, on 10 May 1862 he was moved on to the more prestigious divisional command of troops in Bengal, a post he held until 24 February 1865.

The India where Cunynghame held his commands was still reeling in the aftermath of the Indian Rebellion of 1857-59, known to the contemporary British as the Indian Mutiny. By the Government of India Act of 1858, the ruling powers of the East India Company had been transferred to the British Crown. The army, many of whose Indian troops, or sepoys, had mutinied, was being reformed, a process complete by 1863. In Philip Mason's memorable image, it was a 'Gothic cathedral of an army; it had been gutted by fire and rebuilt, not on some orderly and logical concept, but by making use of what could still safely stand up.'[55] The basic premise was that there should be a ratio of two Indian soldiers to one British, or 125,000 Indian

---

53 Spiers, *Army and Society*, p. 194; Spiers, *Late Victorian Army*, pp. 3, 5–8, 31–2, 109. For its part, the War Office had responsibility for financing the army, for the disposition of troops and for political decisions concerning its deployment. The War Office Act of 1870 confirmed this unwieldy division of authority between the general commanding-in-chief and the secretary of state for war, even though Cambridge was now officially subordinated to the War Office. See Spiers, *Army and Society*, p. 185; Brice, *Thinking Man's Soldier*, pp. 20–1. The fullest account of Cambridge as Commanding-in-Chief during the period of Cunynghame's career is to be found in St. Aubyn, *Royal George*, pp. 112–229.
54 See Holmes, Richard, *Sahib: The British Soldier in India 1750-1914* (London: Harper Collins, 2005), pp. 146–77; Spiers, *Late Victorian Army*, p. 105.
55 Mason, Philip, *A Matter of Honour* (New York, Chicago and San Francisco: Holt, Rinehart and Winston, 1974), p. 327.

to 62,000 British troops. The army in the Bombay Presidency (where Cunynghame had held his initial Indian command) and in the Madras Presidency had stood fast during the Mutiny, so it was agreed not to change them for the present. But the Bengal Army, which was the largest of the three, and which had most notably 'betrayed' its British masters, was radically reorganized. The new doctrine was that only the 'martial races', such as the Ghurkhas and Sikhs, would make good soldiers, and the bulk of the Indian troops comprising the new line regiments in the Bengal Army consequently came from the Punjab.[56] Cunynghame evidently threw himself energetically into the rehabilitation of the Bengal Army. He later wrote:

> During the period of my command, I incessantly traversed every portion of my divisional district, my home being my moveable camp, which for months I occupied, and…became sufficiently acquainted with their language to converse readily with the natives of all classes. I was intimately acquainted with many of the native Rajahs, as well as the Maharaja of Cashmere…[57]

Cunynghame served at a time when there were no more enemies left to fight in India itself. But this was a period when the 'Great Game' was on and Russia, then advancing into Central Asia, was seen to be threatening Afghanistan and British India. Cunynghame later wrote that he believed the Russian threat to be 'very much exaggerated', and that his personal knowledge of the passes over the Himalayas led him to believe that it was 'simply impossible' for a Russian army to attack India over the mountains.[58] Nevertheless, it remained axiomatic that Russia must be kept out of Afghanistan, and that the unruly mountain tribes along the undefined border between Afghanistan and the Punjab be kept under control.[59] Because the Indian government did not believe it had the wherewithal to pacify this savage region known as the North-West Frontier, it remained content with what Mason characterized as a 'barren policy of keeping the tigers in their game reserve.'[60] This meant punishing a raid with a destructive counter-expedition to deter further raids, and an interminable system of frontier wars arose along this wild and mountainous strip of territory, about 400 miles long and 100 wide.

No sooner was the Indian Army reorganized and Cunynghame in his Bengal command than they were confronted by the small, but viciously fought Ambela campaign of October to December 1863 against the local Pashtuns.[61] Known to the British as the 'Hindustani Fanatics' because of their intransigent Muslim fundamentalism, they called themselves the *Mujhaddin*, or Warriors of God. They had been defeated at the battle of Sitana in 1858 and had fallen back to establish a new mountain base at Malka from where they raided British territory and those

---

56 For the reform of the Indian Army and the Bengal Army in particular, see Mason, *Matter of Honour*, pp. 314–15, 317–20, 325–7, 340.
57 Lieutenant-General A. T. Cunynghame, letter to *The Times*, 16 May 1872.
58 Lieutenant-General A. T. Cunynghame, letter to *The Times*, 2 November 1872.
59 There was no settled frontier between the Punjab and the border tribes, imperfectly controlled by the Amir of Afghanistan, until the Durand Line was drawn in 1894. See Mason, *Matter of Honour*, pp. 334–6. See also Spiers, *Late Victorian Army*, p. 274 for the 'overriding imperial mission' to defend the North West Frontier from Russian encroachment.
60 Mason, *Matter of Honour*, p. 337.
61 The Ambela Campaign is also known as the Umbeyla Campaign (the spelling used for the clasp of the India General Service Medal) or the Sitana Campaign. See Haythornthwaite, *Colonial Wars*, p. 110.

tribes who would not convert to their creed. Two brigades were sent against them, and while the troops fought desperately to break *Mujhaddin* resistance and that of their allies the Bunerwals, to burn Malka and temporarily to subdue the region,[62] Cunynghame played a necessary but unglamorous role. He remained at Lahore in command of the reserve of the Ambela Field Force, feeding reinforcements up to the front in December.

Cunynghame's Indian command came to an end in February 1865, and he returned to England. He did not long kick his heels on half-pay. On 1 October 1865 he was appointed to command the Dublin District in Ireland. This was no easy command because of the growing strength and revolutionary activities of the Irish Republican Brotherhood, or Fenians, who aimed at violently throwing off British rule. Informers kept the authorities abreast of their plans, so when in March 1867 the anticipated Fenian Rising broke out in Dublin and other places around Ireland, it was easily contained by the Irish Constabulary in a series of skirmishes.[63] Although British troops did not come into action, Cunynghame clearly carried himself well during the crisis, and received the thanks of the Irish executive. Only a few days after the failed uprising he was in the Viceroy's official party at Dublin Castle to attend the 'relieving of the guard parade' held annually to celebrate St Patrick's Day. Like others in the party Cunynghame was reported to be wearing a bunch of shamrock on his left breast, but to confirm his respect for the national saint he alone wore a St Patrick's Cross on his right breast in accordance with folk tradition.[64]

As a sign of the Horse Guards' approval, on 2 December 1868 Cunynghame was appointed Colonel of the 36th (Herefordshire) Regiment of Foot. This was an honour, because colonelcies were awarded to distinguished generals; but it was then also more than the ceremonial position it has since become. In the pre-Cardwell Reforms era, it was also a welcome sinecure because a colonel was in a position to make a profit on the funds the government allocated a regiment for equipment, supplies and uniforms. This extension to a general officer's income was particularly welcome when he was put on half-pay or retired. As a further honor, on 2 June 1869 Cunynghame was advanced to KCB. His command at Dublin expired on 31 July 1870, but as an additional sign of official approbation on 22 October 1870 he was promoted to lieutenant general.

Lieutenant General Sir Arthur Cunynghame was full of honours, but he was now fifty-eight years old and on half-pay. Pending a fresh appointment, in 1871 he took the opportunity to travel over many parts of southern Russia, including the Caucasus, Georgia, the Caspian Sea and the borders of Turkey and Persia. However, he did not do so as a simple tourist, but as an officer who was fully cognisant of the Great Game, and who used the opportunity to observe Russia's military dispositions in this volatile and strategically vital region. He concluded that

---

62 For full, eye-witness accounts of the campaign, see Adye, Colonel John, *Sitana: A Mountain Campaign on the Borders of Afghanistan* (London: Richard Bentley, 1867), pp. 1–101; and Lord Roberts of Kandahar, Field Marshal, *Forty-One Years in India from Subaltern to Commander-in-Chief* (London: Richard Bentley and Son, 29th edition, 1898), pp. 280–93. For comment, see Callwell, Colonel C.E., *Small Wars. Their Principles and Practice* (London: His Majesty's Stationary Office, 3rd edition, 1906), pp. 44, 49, 73.
63 See Takagami, Shin-ichi, 'The Fenian Rising in Dublin, March 1867', *Irish Historical Studies*, 29 (115) (May 1995), pp. 340–62.
64 *Illustrated London News*, 24 March 1866. The St Patrick's Cross is a red saltire on a white field worn in honour of the saint.

Russia was overstretched and posed no immediate threat to Britain's interests in India, and in 1872 published his conclusions in his third book, *Travels in the Eastern Caucasus*.[65]

In the summer of 1873 Cunynghame was again on his travels. Passing through the Baltic countries he was in Moscow in August when the telegram reached him that he had been given command of Her Majesty's forces at the Cape of Good Hope, Natal, and St. Helena, effective from 5 November 1873. He wasted no time, and on 15 October he was on board ship with his wife and staff—the most influential of whom was his military secretary, Lieutenant Colonel Forestier Walker of the Scots Guards—on his way to the Cape.[66]

South Africa promised welcome employment and fresh scenes for the incorrigibly globetrotting Cunynghame to explore. He was aware, though, that it was neither a significant nor a highly prized command. On account of the relative smallness of the imperial garrison it was earmarked for a lieutenant general and not a full general. Furthermore, a previous dearth of major conflicts in the region meant that the Horse Guards considered it safe to be entrusted to a well-connected if relatively undistinguished senior officer who lacked experience in conducting independent operations. Nor, for such a low-profile command, was it necessary to appoint a thrusting and innovative commander such as Sir Garnet Wolseley who was currently dazzling the public eye in the First Ashanti (Asante) War of 1873-74.[67]

When Cunynghame had first travelled to the Cape in 1842 on the way to China it had been in a sailing ship. This time it was by rapid steamer and the *Teuton* entered Table Bay on 15 November 1873. Cunynghame had no sooner first set foot on the quayside in Cape Town to take up his command when the harbour master handed him a packet of documents relating to the recent rebellion in the Colony of Natal, a British possession since 1843. The papers informed him of the ignominious rout on 4 November at the Bushman's River Pass of a small force of colonial troops under Major Anthony Durnford, Royal Engineers. They had been attempting to intercept Chief Langalibalele kaMthimkhulu of the amaHlubi as he and his adherents—who were attempting to escape the harsh jurisdiction of the Natal authorities—were fleeing over the mountains into neighbouring Basutoland which the British had annexed in 1868 and turned over to the Cape administration in 1871.[68] Cunynghame immediately ensured that a Cape colonial

---

65   Cunynghame, A.A.T., *Travels in the Eastern Caucasus, on the Caspian and Black Seas, especially in Daghestan, and on the Frontiers of Persia and Turkey, during the Summer of 1871* (London: John Murray, 1872). At John Murray's annual trade sale in November 1872, booksellers ordered 400 of Cunynghame's new book as compared to 1,000 copies of Lord Byron's perennial *Poetical Works* and 6,200 of Darwin's latest work, *The Expression of the Emotions in Man and Animals* (*Illustrated London News*, 16 November 1872).

66   Cunynghame, General Sir Arthur Thurlow, *My Command in South Africa 1874 –1878: Comprising Experiences of Travel in the Colonies of South Africa and the Independent States* (London, Macmillan, 2nd edition, 1880), pp. 1–2; *The Times*, 10 October 1873; Gon, Philip, *The Road to Isandlwana. The Years of an Imperial Battalion* (Johannesburg and London: Ad. Donker, 1979), p. 76.

67   Cunynghame, *My Command*, p. 371; Beckett, Ian F.W., 'Military High Command in South Africa, 1854 - 1914', in Peter B. Boyden, Alan J. Guy and Marion Harding (eds) *'Ashes and Blood': The British Army in South Africa 1795–1914* (London: National Army Museum, 1999), pp. 64-5. For Wolseley's reception in England after the Asante War, see Beckett, Ian F.W. (ed), *Wolseley and Ashanti. The Asante War Journal and Correspondence of Major General Sir Garnet Wolseley 1873–1874* (Stroud, England: The History Press for the Army Records Society, 2009), pp. 375–7.

68   Cunynghame, *My Command*, pp. 2–6; Laband, John, *Zulu Warriors: The Battle for the South African Frontier* (New Haven and London: Yale University Press, 2014), pp. 15–16, 20–6.

force under Colonel Charles Griffith, the Cape Government Agent in Basutoland and a tough frontiersman with considerable experience in commanding troops,[69] intercept Langalibalele. He and his followers were returned to Natal where he was found guilty of treason and sent to Robben Island while his people were dispersed.

At one level Langalibalele's 'Rebellion' was a small matter in which only three white mounted volunteers perished before colonial authority reasserted itself once more. But, at another, it had significant repercussions. For years now white settlers in South Africa had been feeling increasingly menaced by the growing numbers of firearms in African hands, the most modern of which migrant workers, especially those attracted to the Kimberley diamond diggings, acquired from unscrupulous colonial arms-dealers. Fears were growing too that the remaining independent African polities of the sub-continent, of which the Zulu kingdom was the most powerful, would join already subjugated Africans in white-ruled territories in rising up to extirpate the colonial presence. The Langalibalele Rebellion intensified these existing settler apprehensions and led to urgent calls for the formulation of a common policy in the sub-continent aimed at disarming all African before it was too late.[70] For Cunynghame, the Langalibalele Rebellion and its fallout—which occurred at the very moment of his arrival at the Cape—inevitably shaped his perception of the problems and dangers confronting his command and moulded his ideas on how best to meet them.

Because the Langalibalele Rebellion was so quickly extinguished, Cunynghame felt no immediate need to travel to Natal. Rather, he set up a court of enquiry into the affair. What particularly concerned him about its findings was the reported lack of co-ordination and confusion of command between the colonial and imperial forces deployed, and the failure of the Natal authorities to communicate with those in the Cape or Basutoland when planning the campaign. To Cunynghame's way of thinking, these breakdowns 'demonstrated clearly the want of combination in South Africa,' one that could easily have led to disaster.[71]

Cunynghame's disquiet concerning this 'want of combination' would have applied equally to his own position as General Officer Commanding [GOC] Her Majesty's Forces at the Cape. Certainly, at sixty-two he was still an excellent horseman and shot, and with his dashing mustachios and side-whiskers, strong nose and fine military bearing, along with an easy, bluff manner and disarming relish in his role, he superficially lived up to public expectations of a GOC.[72] Yet to what extent was he truly in command of his troops? The demarcation of British military authority in southern Africa had been a tricky one from the outset. After much indecision the imperial government had ruled that it reposed in the hands of the High Commissioner (who was always simultaneously the Governor of the Cape Colony, confirmed by the Final Act of the First Treaty of Paris of 9 June 1815 as a British possession).[73] In 1846 that official was designated Commander-in-Chief.[74] As the imperial agent in southern Africa

---

69 Laband, *Zulu Warriors*, p. 114.
70 Laband, *Zulu Warriors*, pp. 18–21, 26.
71 Cunynghame, *My Command*, p. 4
72 Gon, *Road to Isandlwana*, pp. 42–3.
73 By the Convention of London of 13 August 1814, the Dutch had ceded sovereignty of the Cape of Good Hope to the British who had occupied the territory since 1806.
74 See Sir Henry Pottinger's High Commission of 10 October 1846 quoted in Benyon, J. *Proconsul and Paramountcy in South Africa: The High Commission, British Supremacy and the Sub-Continent 1806-1910* (Pietermaritzburg: University of Natal Press, 1980), p. 353: Appendix A (1).

directly responsible to the Secretaries of State for both the Colonies and for War in London, the High Commissioner's office enabled him to assert British paramountcy over the interior of southern Africa beyond the Cape Colony, including African kingdoms and Boer republics. His authority also overrode that of governors or lieutenant-governors of other British colonies in South Africa, especially in frontier matters. Therefore, as Commander-in-Chief the High Commissioner could claim that the framing and implementation of defence policy throughout southern Africa was his preserve alone.[75]

Nevertheless, did this mean the High Commissioner exercised actual control over all military planning and operations, or did these fall within the sphere of the GOC? That officer, whose command extended beyond the Colony to encompass all the South African High Commission territories, was himself responsible to the Secretary of State for War who framed imperial military policy and had supreme control of the army. But (as we have seen), to complicate matters further, thanks to the unwieldy division of authority between the Field Marshal Commanding-in-Chief at the Horse Guards and the Secretary of State for War, the GOC was also answerable to the Duke of Cambridge. This is where a GOC's temperament and local standing came into play. Inevitably, if he were not a powerful personality in his own right, he would tend to lean on the High Commissioner for support when dealing with his superiors in London. This in turn could lead to the GOC effectively subordinating his autonomy to the High Commissioner who might then assume the lead in military planning and the conduct of operations.[76]

If these were not challenges enough for a GOC unsure of his footing, Cunynghame also had to contend with the civilian government of the Cape. William Gladstone's economizing first Liberal ministry (1868–1874) had recently urged responsible government on the Cape. Its belief was that with the colony's steeply rising revenues resulting from the discovery of diamonds and a boom in wool and ostrich feather exports, the Cape could now pay for its own defence and administration. Conveniently, this would relieve the over-stretched imperial government of the financial burden. A vociferous faction of colonists from the western regions of the colony under the leadership of John C. Molteno, the member for Beaufort West, was equally eager for responsible government since its attainment promised to give the settler elite control of their own affairs. Responsible government was duly instituted in June 1872 with Molteno as the Cape's first Prime Minister. Henceforth, the Governor of the Cape and GOC had to work with a colonial prime minister and his cabinet responsible to the elected Legislative Assembly.[77] This posed a fresh, untested question: what would be the proper respective spheres of military authority should the GOC and the Cape government—both of them effectively subordinate to the High Commissioner—come into dispute? It was Cunynghame's challenge that this conundrum would become a crucial matter of policy while he was in command at the Cape.

75 Harlow, V.T., 'Cape Colony, 1806 –1822', in Eric Walker (ed), *The Cambridge History of the British Empire, Volume VIII: South Africa, Rhodesia and the High Commission Territories* (Cambridge: Cambridge University Press, 1963), pp. 206–8; Benyon, *Proconsul*, pp. 7-11, 69-70, 212-13, 353 –5: Appendix A (1–4): commissions illustrating the growth and closer definition of powers, 1846–1877; 358 –9: Appendix B: diagram of the structure of imperial government.
76 Beckett, Ian, *The Victorians at War* (London and New York: Hambledon and London, 2003), pp. 95–6.
77 De Kiewiet, C.W., 'The Establishment of Responsible Government in Cape Colony, 1870-1872', in Walker (ed), *Cambridge History of the British Empire, Vol. VIII*, pp. 452, 455, 458.

If these complex questions of divided and overlapping command threatened to trip Cunynghame up, then he found himself potentially hamstrung by the sheer size of the territory his scattered and inadequate troops were supposed to defend. This was a problem Cunynghame had to confront and overcome if his tour of duty in South Africa were to be a successful one.

'Her Majesty's Troops,' wrote Colonel William Bellairs in early 1878, 'may be said to occupy South Africa (1) for the protection of Imperial interests, and (2) to assist the Colonials, who, from weakness in numbers may be unable wholly to protect themselves against native attacks.'[78] Indeed, since Britain had first occupied the Cape during the Napoleonic Wars, its significance in the imperial context had lain in its control of the route to India. The opening of the Suez Canal in 1869 did little to diminish its strategic importance, and although safeguarding the Cape had increasingly drawn Britain into the affairs of the South African interior, the primary function of the imperial garrison remained that of protecting its ports against maritime attack.[79] Nevertheless, that did not mean the security of the colonists, perennially threatened by the antagonistic and numerically preponderant African population, could be ignored. Thus, even though it had been British government policy since the 1860s to withdraw imperial garrisons from colonies of white settlement, the Cape garrison had been exempted.

Cunynghame would have understood these two closely intertwined defensive obligations of his new command well enough, and in May 1874 he embarked on the first of two back-to-back tours of inspection to see for himself how prepared his troops were to fulfil their strategic function. Predictably, he undertook these very necessary tours with the same combination of professional diligence and irrepressible curiosity about local conditions he had exhibited in India. Later, in retirement, he wrote of his leisurely travels over thousands of miles by carriage, ship, ox-wagon and horse in exuberant and overly digressive detail in his last book, *My Command in South Africa*, published in 1879 and aimed essentially at vindicating his reputation as a commander. The journeys gave him numerous opportunities to indulge in shooting the teeming local game—ever a favourite sport among officers with their passion for country pursuits—and to observe the highly varied countryside and its very diverse inhabitants, both black and white, whom he described in the ineffably condescending and racist terms of his class and generation. The book was not received without reservations. *The Times* described it as 'perfectly unsystematic,'[80] while another reviewer complained that 'five-sixths' of it was made up of a 'talentless' mix of mundane 'personal anecdotes and observations' and 'very crude political opinions.'[81]

Cunynghame's first tour took him to the Eastern Frontier of the Cape Colony, north into the Boer republic of the Orange Free State whose independence the British had acknowledged in 1854, then eastwards to mountainous Basutoland. In his second tour he travelled north up the coastal lands beyond the Cape Eastern Frontier through the still independent territory of the amaMpondo to Griqualand East (which came under British rule in 1874), and finally

---

78 The National Archive, Kew (hereafter TNA), War Office Papers (hereafter WO) 32/7680: Memorandum, Col. W. Bellairs to Sir Bartle Frere, 20 January 1878. Bellairs, a veteran of the Crimean War and an experienced staff officer, was Cunynghame's Deputy Adjutant-General in the Ninth Cape Frontier War.
79 Beckett, 'Military High Command', p. 60; Spiers, Edward M., 'The British Army in South Africa: Military Government and Occupation, 1877–1914', in Boyden et al. (eds), *'Ashes and Blood'*, p. 72.
80 *The Times*, 19 February 1879.
81 *Illustrated London News*, 15 March 1879.

through the Colony of Natal to the borders of the powerful Zulu kingdom to its north. There Cunynghame halted, not visiting the Swazi and Pedi kingdoms beyond the amaZulu. Nor, on this occasion, did he travel to the South African Republic or Transvaal [SAR], which the British had recognized in 1852 as an independent Boer state. The only British territory Cunynghame did not visit on his tours of inspection was Griqualand West, annexed in 1871 as a Crown Colony and the location of the recently discovered and fabulously rich Kimberley diamond diggings.[82]

Back from his second tour in Cape Town by October 1874 and dividing his time between his headquarters at the seventeenth-century Castle in Cape Town with its five bastions and his residence in the pretty village of Rondebosch on the verdant southern side of Table Mountain, Cunynghame could reflect ruefully on the difficulties of his command. To secure the vast territories he had inspected, he had available only the two battalions of British infantry. These were the 75th (Highland) and the 86th (Royal County Down) Regiments of Foot divided between the Cape Colony and Fort Napier in Pietermaritzburg, Natal, where a garrison had been stationed since 1843.[83] On paper, a battalion on service, the standard tactical units of the time, was made up of a headquarters and eight companies, or about 900 men. In addition, British generals of this period regarded the Royal Navy as a ready source of manpower and artillery in support of land operations. Cunynghame therefore knew that in an emergency he could always count on a Naval Brigade drawn from whatever warships might be in harbour at Simon's Town, (the Royal Navy's base in False Bay south-east across the peninsular from Cape Town), or might be anchored outside Durban Bay in Natal where large ships could not get over the sandbar.[84]

Otherwise, Cunynghame had to rely on whatever settler units or African levies could be raised locally. In the Cape, the most professional of these was the Frontier Armed and Mounted Police [FAMP], a para-military force which was the colony's only regular military unit, and which had operated against Langalibalele in Basutoland. Created in 1855 and numbering some thousand men on paper, but only about two hundred in peacetime, it accepted only whites into its ranks. Its men were armed with breech-loading Snider-Enfield rifles and were attired in loose suits of variously coloured Bedford cord and slouch hats. This costume was undoubtedly suitable for bush warfare but was deplored as disreputable by British regulars who still wore their uniform of scarlet frock or tunic, blue trousers and white tropical helmet. At Cunynghame's instigation an artillery unit was added to the FAMP's establishment in 1874, although this amounted only to one 9-pounder Rifled Muzzle Loader [RML] and two 7-pounder RML mountain guns mounted on poor, locally manufactured carriages that broke under the smallest strain. Cunynghame considered the FAMP's weapons training and discipline so seriously neglected over the last decades of peace that he despaired of their being effective in the field,

---

82 For Cunynghame's initial visits in the vicinity of Cape Town, see *My Command*, pp. 7–8, 22–7, 30–8. His two 1874 tours of inspection are to be found on pp. 39–99, 108–70.
83 For the detailed history of the Natal garrison, see Dominy, Graham, *Last Outpost on the Zulu Frontiers: Fort Napier and the British Imperial Garrison* (Urbana, Chicago, and Springfield: University of Illinois Press, 2016).
84 Knight, Ian, *Companion to the Anglo-Zulu War* (Barnsley, England: Pen & Sword Military, 2008), p. 145.

even if the settler raw material was strong and robust.[85] In Natal Cunynghame could call upon the white Natal Mounted Police, created in 1874, a small standing body of 170 quasi-military police in smart black corduroy uniforms that was stationed at various strongpoints in the colony to provide mobile defence.[86]

The dozens of exclusively white volunteer units of urban militia which had sprung up in Britain's South African possessions—as they had across much of the Empire—were of questionable military value. They were based on the British regimental system and were formed predominantly by English-speaking settlers. The first of such units in the Cape was raised in 1855, and by 1877 there were 49 of them. Unfortunately, most were little more than social clubs—often only several dozen strong—with few training sessions and low standards of drill and musketry. In Natal, the 750-strong Natal Volunteer Corps, which had been established in 1854 and consisted of one artillery, two infantry and 11 mounted corps mirrored the composition and training of the Cape volunteer units and was of equally questionable military value.[87] Nevertheless, the Cape and Natal units of mounted infantry were potentially invaluable for scouting, screening, and raiding across the limitless terrain since no British cavalry were stationed in South Africa.

Additional mounted infantry was available in the form of the commando system of essentially rural volunteers who mustered during emergencies. It had been first instituted in 1715 in the Cape when the Dutch East India Company sought mobile defence against African raiders, and it had been carried with the Voortrekkers to their short-lived Republic of Natalia (1838-42), and to their two republics on the highveld. The British inherited the system and attempted to formalize it in the Cape in 1855 and in Natal in 1863. However, these Burghers, as they were called, consisted predominantly of poorly armed rural Dutch-speaking settlers (and mixed-race men in the Cape) who resisted British-style military organization and discipline and were, at best, undependable.[88]

And then there were African levies. Since the late fifteenth century it had been the standard practice for the severely out-numbered colonial armies operating in Africa to raise African levies under the command of white officers for combat and logistical support. Cunynghame was of course familiar with the custom from his service with the Turkish Contingent in the Crimea and from his commands in India. For Africans, as for Turks and Indians, serving the colonial power militarily was a means of maintaining their warrior traditions and sense of masculine honour—as well as reaping the rewards of fighting on the winning side.[89] Such especially was case of the Mfengu people of the Eastern Cape frontier (and to a much lesser extent, the abaThembu) whom the colonial authorities rewarded with extensive grants of land taken from their defeated enemies, the amaXhosa people. The Mfengu first entered colonial service in the Sixth Cape Frontier War of 1834–1835 when they proved their worth as light troops operating

---

85 Cunynghame, *My Command*, pp. 49–52, 112, 306–10; Laband, *Zulu Warriors*, pp. 114–15.
86 Laband, John and Paul Thompson, *The Illustrated Guide to the Anglo-Zulu War* (Pietermaritzburg: University of Natal Press, 2000), pp. 23, 36; Laband, John, *Historical Dictionary of the Zulu Wars* (Lanham, Maryland, Toronto, Oxford: The Scarecrow Press, 2009), p. 176
87 Laband and Thompson, *Anglo-Zulu War*, pp. 23, 36; Laband, *Zulu Wars*, pp. 177, 182.
88 Cunynghame, *My Command*, p. 309; Laband and Thompson, *Anglo-Zulu War*, p. 23; Laband, *Zulu Wars*, pp. 52–3; Laband, *Zulu Warriors*, p. 115.
89 Laband, John and Paul Thompson, 'African Levies in Natal and Zululand, 1836–1906', in Stephen M. Miller (ed), *Soldiers and Settlers in Africa 1850–1918* (Leiden and Boston: Brill, 2009), pp. 49–50.

in bush fighting which white troops found difficult work. They subsequently fought in the Seventh (1846-47) and Eighth (1850-53) Cape Frontier Wars, carrying increasing numbers of firearms and confirming their expertise in irregular warfare and their mastery of remorseless scorched-earth operations. Besides their fighting skills, the Mfengu were more economical than white troops because they were paid less and were disbanded after each conflict. The British consequently raised more and more Mfengu levies in each succeeding frontier war, so that by the time Cunynghame took up his command he could expect that in case of war they would make up the majority of the Cape military manpower available to him.[90]

Cunynghame mulled over what he had seen and learned on his two tours of inspection. He came to a firm conclusion on how best to secure the scattered British territories of South Africa from attack and saw it as his 'duty as a soldier' to advise his superiors accordingly. He later summed up his arguments in *My Command* in a chapter succinctly titled 'Federation and Colonial Defence.'[91] Noting the lack of seasoned troops and the dangers facing British possessions from neighbouring independent states and the threat of African insurrection, he pointed out that in a crisis troops from one colony would have come to the aid of those from another. Yet the Langalibalele Rebellion had shown him that with the existing medley of colonial administrations such cooperation was unlikely. He therefore strongly held that 'Federation alone…would enable the country to take such military measures as, while they involved the least possible cost, would prove efficient to secure life and property.'[92]

The notion of bringing the British colonies and two Boer republics of southern Africa under unified British rule was not Cunynghame's brainchild, however, and he was merely falling in with the dominant policy initiative of the moment. Some form of federation had long been in the air, as had the idea that the dangerously warlike independent African kingdoms of the region should be disarmed and politically neutralized. Gladstone's administration had seriously toyed with the idea, but when the Earl of Beaconsfield's second Conservative ministry came to power in February 1874 it gained sudden momentum. The driving force was the new Secretary of State for Colonies, the Earl of Carnarvon, who in 1867 had overseen the creation of the self-governing Dominion of Canada. He believed that if a prosperous, stable dominion could similarly be established at the strategically vital tip of Africa, not only would that secure the route to India, but it would lead to the economic integration of the sub-continent and bring the endemic, expensive little wars of the region to an end. The new Dominium of South Africa would consequently be able to manage its own affairs and shoulder the costly burden of its own defence.[93]

Because the self-governing Cape was by far the largest and richest white-ruled territory in South Africa with twice the settler population of Natal and the two Boer republics combined, it would inevitably have to take up the chief burden of confederation.[94] And there was the rub.

---

90 Stapleton, Tim, 'Valuable, Gallant and Faithful Assistants': The Fingo (or Mfengu) as Colonial Military Allies during the Cape-Xhosa Wars, 1835 –1881', in Miller (ed), *Soldiers and Settlers*, pp. 15–36, 4 –47; Laband, *Zulu Warriors*, pp. 99–103, 118.
91 Cunynghame, *My Command*, pp. 100–7 (Chapter XI).
92 Cunynghame, *My Command*, p. 105.
93 For a brief but recent discussion of the mainsprings of the confederation policy, see Laband, *Zulu Warriors*, pp. 68–70.
94 Saunders, Christopher and Iain R. Smith, 'Southern Africa, 1795—1910', in Andrew Porter (ed), *The Oxford History of the British Empire, Volume 2: The Nineteenth Century* (Oxford: Oxford University

Carnarvon would have to persuade the prickly and parochial Cape Legislative Assembly to go along with him. Unfortunately for Carnarvon, the Molteno ministry did not share his imperial vision. There was no ignoring that Molteno was morbidly suspicious of British interference in the newly self-governing colony's affairs, even if he saw no contradiction in believing that it remained the obligation of the British garrison stationed in the Cape to defend the colony. It would be quite another matter, though, should the Cape find itself helping pay for the upkeep of the British garrison being maintained primarily to further the confederation project beyond the Cape's borders.[95]

At the beginning of 1875, the British garrison in South Africa was relieved. The 1st Battalion of the 24th (Second Warwickshire) Regiment of Foot arrived in Cape Town from Gibraltar in January. Its commander was the 44-year-old Colonel Richard Glyn, a veteran of the Crimea and of the Indian Mutiny whose passion was the hunting-field. Seemingly irascible, he was in fact a steady and dependable officer, if somewhat hide-bound and unadventurous and (like Cunynghame) a beneficiary of the purchase system. The 1/24th was followed into harbour by the 1st Battalion of the 13th (First Somersetshire) (Prince Alfred's Light Infantry) Regiment of Foot from Malta. While the Headquarters of the 1/13th proceeded to Fort Napier in Pietermaritzburg, the rest of the regiment—along with the 1/24th—remained stationed for the moment in the Cape.[96]

As for Cunynghame, while the policymakers began to clash pens over confederation, he was faced by the need for military action. The capital of the British Crown Colony of Griqualand West was the squalid, rough–and–ready boom town of Kimberley that in the last few years had sprung up around the diamond diggings. The white adventurers who had rushed from all over the world to stake their claims were tough and unruly and disputed the sketchy attempts by the lieutenant-governor, Richard Southey, to control them. Agitation was spearheaded by the Diggers' Mutual Protection Association [DMPA] led by Alfred Aylward, an Irish Fenian and militant republican. Fearing without much real justification that the DMPA was planning an armed rebellion, in March 1875 Southey requested the High Commissioner from 1870 to 1877, Sir Henry Barkly, for military assistance.[97] The Diamond Field Revolt was to be Cunynghame's first campaign in South Africa.[98]

Lieutenant Nevill Coghill of the 1/24th, who was appointed ADC to Cunynghame in August 1876, wrote describing him as 'a highly enthusiastic soldier' but—unsurprisingly considering the nature of his career and social contacts—'of the old school.'[99] In practice, this meant Cunynghame keenly, if not obsessively, set about putting all his experience about organization and logistics into practice. It was necessary to do so, because Kimberley was 700 miles away from Cape Town, and much of the route was over the semi-desert of the Great Karoo. He

Press, 2001), p. 606.
95 Lewsen, P. (ed), *Selections from the Correspondence of J. X. Merriman 1870–1890* (Cape Town: Van Riebeeck Society, 1960), p. 26; Gon, *Road to Isandlwana*, p. 107.
96 Gon, *Road to Isandlwana*, pp. 22 –3, 27; Knight, Ian and Adrian Greaves, *The Who's Who of the Anglo-Zulu War, Part I: The British* (Barnsley, England: Pen & Sword Military, 2006), pp. 104–5.
97 *British Parliamentary Papers* (hereafter *BPP*) (C. 1342-1), no. 23: Sir H. Barkly to Lord Carnarvon, 5 May 1875; Laband, *Zulu Warriors*, pp. 155, 162–3; Gon, *Road to Isandlwana*, pp. 31–42.
98 For Cunynghame and the Diamond Field revolt, see Cunynghame, *My Command*, pp. 171–93, 204–5; Gon, *Road to Isandlwana*, pp. 45–49, 59–61; Laband, *Zulu Warriors*, p. 163.
99 Gon, *Road to Isandlwana*, pp. 43, 76.

haggled determinedly with transport contractors for mule wagons since ox-drawn wagons—the normal transport in South Africa—were impracticable because oxen could not survive the lack of water and grazing. As it was, he would find the price of forage *en route* quite 'startling.'[100]

By 6 May the Army of the Vaal, as the newspapers grandiloquently named the little force of 250 men of the 1/24th and two 7-pounder guns, was ready to march under the command of Colonel Glyn.[101] Mounted men were lacking, but Molteno refused the services of the FAMP, so Cunynghame detached forty men from the 1/24th for training as mounted infantry. From experience he knew that picked infantrymen could be quickly turned into mounted men 'of the very best description' carrying carbines and forming a useful substitute for cavalry in colonial small wars where they undertook the work of reconnaissance, screening, sentry and escort duties. Indeed, after 1881 all infantry battalions in South Africa would be required to train one company in mounted infantry work.[102]

Cunynghame and his staff set off on 25 May to join Glyn's column on the gruelling march. Two months after leaving Cape Town the Army of the Vaal paraded through Kimberley on 30 June. All steam had rapidly evaporated from the simmering insurrection once its leaders learned that troops were on the way, and to the soldiers' disgust Barkly had already settled the insurrection from Cape Town by agreeing to an amnesty for everyone except the ringleaders. While they waited for the High Commissioner to visit Kimberley to settle affairs, Cunynghame camped his troops near the Vaal River well outside the town for fear his men would be seduced by the 'unbounded riches near at hand, which they were forbidden to see.'[103] On 14 July Cunynghame set off via the Orange Free State to inspect the troops stationed along the Cape Eastern Frontier,[104] but he remained anxious about the welfare of his troops left camped under canvas outside Kimberley during the bleak winter months. However, they stayed there until 10 October while Barkly dealt with Griqualand West, on 26 September 1875 appointing Major Owen Lanyon as Administrator with orders to ensure that the Crown Colony would soon be sufficiently stable to take its place in the structure of confederation.

Lanyon was one of Major General Sir Garnet Wolseley's reforming 'Ring' of officers who had served with him in the Asante campaign,[105] and his appointment to Griqualand West was an indication of his mentor's new-found influence in South Africa. For while Cunynghame was involved with the Diamond Field Revolt, Wolseley, as Lord Carnarvon's Special Commissioner to Natal, had been busy in that colony (which enjoyed limited representative government) pushing through constitutional amendments which would make it easier for Carnarvon to compel a sceptical Natal to go along with his confederation plans.[106] Wolseley also made recommendations to the War Office concerning the distribution and beefing up of the South African garrison. Cunynghame was accordingly instructed to reinforce the garrison in Natal and

---

100 Cunynghame, *My Command*, p. 190.
101 *BPP* (C. 1401), enc. 1 in no. 5: Cunynghame to Barkly, 2 July 1875.
102 Cunynghame, *My Command*, p. 175; Laband, *Zulu Wars*, p. 166.
103 Cunynghame, *My Command*, p. 191.
104 Cunynghame, *My Command*, pp. 205–17.
105 Laband, *Zulu Warriors*, p. 163.
106 Guest, Bill, 'Colonists, Confederation and Constitutional Change', in Andrew Duminy and Bill Guest (eds), *Natal and Zululand from Earliest Times to 1910: A New History* (Pietermaritzburg: University of Natal Press and Shuter & Shooter, 1989), pp. 157–62. The Natal Constitution Amendment Law came into effect on 24 December 1875.

despatched the 1/13th stationed in King William's Town, the administrative hub of the Cape Easter Frontier, to join its headquarters at Fort Napier in Pietermaritzburg. Two companies of the 1/24th were moved from Cape Town to King William's Town to take its place. An additional battalion, the 2/3rd, was landed in the Cape in November 1876 and took up position on the Eastern Frontier.[107]

Back in Cape Town during the winter of 1876, Cunynghame was facing a torrid time during parliament's debate on the Cape's defensive capabilities. He was convinced as a result of his tours of inspection that the colony would not be able to defend itself without maintaining an even larger imperial garrison. Furthermore, he advocated (and continued vigorously to do so) a 'proper system of colonial military organization.'[108] This was precisely what the Molteno ministry did not want to hear, and it was unfortunate that Cunynghame expressed his alarmist conclusions with military directness and in a politically tactless manner. Relations between him and Molteno over defence almost reached breaking-point, and a political crisis was only averted by that time-hallowed parliamentary manoeuvre, the appointment of a committee to enquire into the matter. Even then, Molteno might not have been prepared to accept this compromise had it not been for concerns about unfolding events in the SAR.[109]

In July 1876, the SAR went to war against the Bapedi, its independent African neighbours along its unsettled eastern frontier. The campaign was ill-managed and unsuccessful, and its repercussions were alarming to settlers around South Africa who predicted it would encourage widespread African resistance.[110] The Boers and the Bapedi signed an inconclusive peace treaty on 15 February 1877, but the Boer-Pedi War had already opened a new chapter in the affairs of the sub-continent.

The humiliation the Bapedi had inflicted on the anarchic and bankrupt SAR provided Carnarvon with an unforeseen but god-sent excuse to kick-start the stalling machinery of confederation into life once more. How better to reassure the Cape about troublesome frontier wars it might have to pay for than by annexing the SAR and then sending in British troops to deal conclusively with the Bapedi? This required parliamentary sanction in Britain which would be secured through the passing of the South Africa Act of 1877 (the Permissive Federation Bill), and the commissioning of a local agent who could be entrusted to put it into effect. Carnarvon found him in Sir Theophilus Shepstone, an experienced Natal colonial official. Shepstone entered the SAR in January 1877 with a small force of 25 Natal Mounted Police, and after negotiations annexed the SAR on 12 April 1877 as the British Transvaal Territory.[111]

At the same time, Carnarvon decided to entrust his revitalised plans for confederation to an imperial statesman capable of carrying them into effect, and to whom he would entrust considerable discretion to act as he saw fit. The instrument he selected was the great Indian

---

107 *BPP* (C. 1748), enc. in no. 191: Cunynghame to the Secretary of State for War, 26 November 1876; Gon, *Road to Isandlwana*, pp. 64–5.
108 National Army Museum, Chelsea (hereafter NAM), Chelmsford Papers 12: *Cape of Good Hope, Copy of Despatches which have Passed between the Right Honourable the Secretary of State for the Colonies and His Excellency the Governor since January Last. Printed by Order of the House of Assembly* (Cape Town: Saul Solomon, 1878) (hereafter *Cape of Good Hope*), p. 8: Cunynghame to Frere, 16 February 1878.
109 Cunynghame, *My Command*, p. 299; Gon, *Road to Isandlwana*, p. 71.
110 For the Boer-Pedi War of 1876, see Laband, *Zulu Warriors*, pp. 63–8.
111 Laband, John, *The Transvaal Rebellion: The First Boer War 1880 1881* (Harlow, United Kingdom: Pearson Longman, 2005), pp. 18–19.

Map 5: South Africa, 1877.

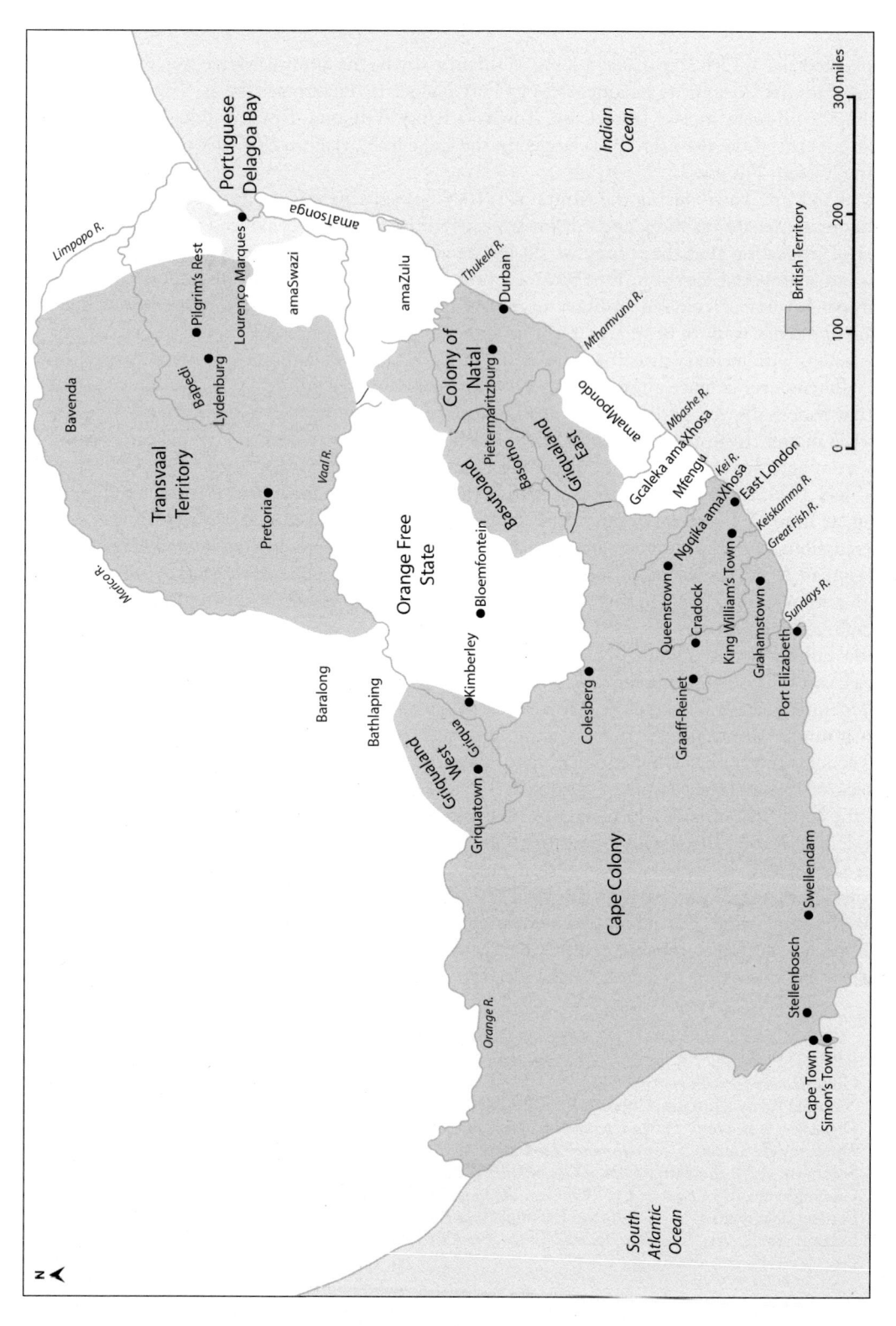

administrator, Sir Bartle Frere, a man of great intellectual powers, of forceful personality and a committed evangelical Christian who saw it as his moral duty to bring British civilization to benighted savages. To this high-minded proconsul of empire confederation was thus an exalted goal, one that he intended should crown his distinguished career with his appointment as the first Governor-General of the new South African dominion.[112]

On 31 March 1877 Cunynghame, who had been gazetted Lieutenant-Governor of the Cape on 5 March, welcomed Frere ashore at Cape Town.[113] The new High Commissioner's task in consummating confederation would not be an easy one. Even before he had arrived in South Africa the Cape parliament had rejected in principle the draft Permissive Federation Bill, and the Orange Free State would do likewise in May.[114] Even the annexation of the Transvaal would make his task harder because Molteno and his supporters in parliament came out against the legally dubious incorporation of their brother Afrikaners there by the perfidious British.[115] Stymied for the moment, Frere waited on events.

In military terms, the annexation of the Transvaal had an immediate ripple effect on the South African garrison and its deployment. With Frere vigorously at the helm, more troops were becoming available. The 1/13th marched out of Natal to occupy posts across the recently annexed Transvaal. The 2/3rd Regiment stationed at East London and the newly arrived 80th (Staffordshire Volunteers) Regiment of Foot replaced them at Fort Napier.[116] The 88th (Connaught Rangers) Regiment of Foot would arrive in Cape Town in July 1877 and free the companies of the 1/24th still there to join the rest of the regiment on the Eastern Frontier.[117] Backed up by Frere, Cunynghame insisted that the Transvaal garrison must have a unit of Mounted Infantry and at least a division of two 7-pounder guns.[118] The War Office concurred and undertook to send out more artillery so that Cunynghame soon had at his disposal in South Africa three batteries of 7-pounder RML Mk IV mountain guns and a battery of 6-pounder Armstrong RBL (Rifled Breech Loader) guns: a total of 23 pieces.[119]

With a greatly enhanced imperial garrison under his command, Cunynghame decided that he must embark on a fresh tour of inspection of Britain's new bases in South Africa.[120] As is made clear in *My Command in South Africa*, this was also an extensive opportunity for the

---

112 Benyon, John, 'Frere, Sir (Henry) Bartle Edward, first baronet (1815–1884)', *Oxford Dictionary of National Biography* <http://www.oxfroddnb.com/view/article/10171> (accessed 14 August 2014); Emery, F.V., 'Geography and Imperialism: the Role of Sir Bartle Frere (1815–84)', *The Geographical Journal*, 151 (2) (November 1984), pp. 342–50.
113 *Illustrated London News*, 10 March 1877.
114 Laband, *Transvaal Rebellion*, p. 19.
115 Gon, *Road to Isandlwana*, pp. 83–4.
116 *BPP* (C. 1776), enc. 1 in no. 92: Cunynghame to Sir Henry Bulwer, 28 February 1877; *BPP* (C. 1776), no. 88: Barkly to Carnarvon, 23 March 1877.
117 Laband, *Zulu Warriors*, p. 113.
118 *BPP* (C. 1776), enc. 1 in no. 109: Cunynghame to Frere, 10 April 1877.
119 *BPP* (C. 1776), no. 107: Major-General F.A. Campbell, Director of Artillery and Stores, to the Under Secretary of State, Colonial Office, 10 May 1877. Six-pounder Armstrong RBLs were introduced in 1859, but their breech closing mechanism proved unreliable, and there was a return to muzzle-loaders while an alternative was sought for. Seven-pounder RMLs came into service in 1865. See Hall, Major D.D., 'Artillery in the Zulu War—1879', *Military History Journal*, 4 (4) (January 1979), pp. 156–7.
120 Cunynghame, *My Command*, pp. 238–95; Gon, *Road to Isandlwana*, pp. 84–8. Gon's account is based on the diary kept by Cunynghame's ADC, Lt. Coghill.

GOC to go hunting game on the highveld of the interior, an occupation which kept him in excellent humour throughout his tour. On 3 May 1877 he sailed for Durban. There he found the Natal garrison under strength after reinforcing the Transvaal, and he ordered a half company of the 1/24th up from the Cape. Cunynghame then travelled to the little village of Newcastle in northern Natal, strategically important as a forward base for the Transvaal and the Zulu kingdom. He instructed the companies of the 80th stationed there to build a barracks and a permanent fortification (Fort Amiel) on the heights above the town.[121] At Standerton to the north across the Vaal River he set up a cavalry station in the healthy high country free from horse sickness. Journeying on to Pretoria, the capital of the Transvaal, Cunynghame ordered the establishment of a military cantonment consisting of barracks, a hospital, bathing houses and a fort. On 21 June he travelled to the Eastern Transvaal and its gold diggings. He inspected the area of operations of the recent Boer-Pedi War and acquainted himself with the villages and other bases from where in April 1878 the British would mount an offensive against the Bapedi.[122] He then turned back to Pretoria and going through the western Transvaal visited Kimberley.

During this tour, on 13 August 1877, he attained by seniority the rank of full General, gazetted on 1 October.[123] Technically, according to the rules of the service, in ordinary circumstances he was now of too high a rank to retain his command. However, it was 'intimated' to him that it was intended to leave him at the Cape to complete his period of a lieutenant general's command.[124] This was just as well, because in September Frere summoned him urgently to proceed to King William's Town in the Eastern Cape where trouble was brewing on the frontier.[125] At the age of sixty-five and after forty-seven years in the army, this was to be Cunynghame's first opportunity to demonstrate in a full-blown colonial campaign—and not a military promenade such as the Diamond Field Revolt had turned out to be—that he possessed the qualities of a commander.

The Eastern Cape frontier zone was an extensive, summer rainfall region, stretching between the Sundays River to the west and the Mbashe River to the east. Looming mountain chains covered by a thick mantle of forest and bush bounded it to the north, and to the south the lush coastal bush came down to the Indian Ocean. Numerous rivers and streams flowed erratically down to the ocean from the mountains and hilly uplands, and it was in the river valleys that possessed the best soils and pasturage where people preferred to settle.[126]

Between 1779 and 1853 eight increasingly destructive wars had been fought along this fluctuating frontier that pitted white settlers, along with British troops and their African allies, against the amaXhosa people.[127] Fatally for their ability to mount a unified armed response

---

121 For Fort Amiel, see Laband, J.P.C. and P.S. Thompson with Sheila Henderson, *The Buffalo Border 1879: The Anglo-Zulu War in Northern Natal* (Durban: Department of History, University of Natal, Research Monograph No. 6, 1983), pp. 88–9.
122 For the First Anglo-Pedi War of 1878, which would take place after Cunynghame left South Africa, see Laband, *Zulu Warriors*, pp. 188–94.
123 *Illustrated London News*, 6 October 1877.
124 Cunynghame, *My Command*, p. 374; *The Times*, 26 January 1878..
125 *BPP* (C. 2144), enc. in no. 102: memorandum by Cunynghame, 4 April 1878.
126 Peires, J.B., *The House of Phalo. A History of the Xhosa People in the Days of their Independence* (Johannesburg: Ravan Press, 1981), pp. 1–2.
127 Mostert, Noël, *Frontiers: The Epic of South Africa's Creation and the Tragedy of the Xhosa People* (London: Pimlico, 1993), p. 1249.

against the forces of colonialism, the amaXhosa never developed into a unified state akin to that of the amaZulu. The Xhosa paramount, instead of being a powerful monarch, was merely the accepted figurehead of the Xhosa nation, which was divided into two main chiefdoms, the Gcaleka amaXhosa east across the Kei River in the Transkei, and the Ngqika or Rharhabe amaXhosa to the west of the river in the Ciskei.[128]

The national weapon of the amaXhosa was the throwing-spear, but during the course of the nineteenth century they abandoned shields and added more and more muzzle-loading muskets to their arsenal.[129] Nevertheless, firearms played an uncertain role in Xhosa warfare because the amaXhosa remained tentative about their effectiveness and regarded them as ancillary to their conventional weapons, except for hunting.[130] Traditionally, the amaXhosa favoured pitched battles when they deployed into a central 'chest' and two enveloping wings with two further columns positioned in support on either flank. But by the time of the Sixth Cape Frontier War of 1834–1835 the amaXhosa knew better than to risk frontal attacks against the British with their superior firearms and were increasingly resorting to irregular warfare with ambushes and sudden raids. Finding it difficult to defeat the Xhosa warriors in the field, especially when they resorted to guerrilla tactics, the British and Cape troops increasingly adopted a brutal, total approach to frontier warfare that targeted the homes, livestock, fields, and lives of civilians in order to break the spirit of the amaXhosa and bring about their submission.[131]

In 1865, as part of his general settlement of the frontier after the devastations and mass expulsions of the Eighth Cape Frontier War of 1850-53 which opened up British Kaffraria (the territory between the Keiskamma and Great Kei Rivers) to white settlement, the Governor of the Cape, Sir Philip Wodehouse, settled the Gcaleka amaXhosa in a stretch of territory between the Great Kei and Mbashe Rivers. It was merely 80 miles long and about 35 miles across. This reserve constituted only a third of the former Gcaleka domain.[132] The Thembu chiefs, who had fought as British allies in the late war, were resettled in the northernmost third of the former chiefdom, to be known as Emigrant Thembuland. Wodehouse made over the central third to the main British allies in the late war, the Mfengu. Although not officially part of the Cape, Fingoland (as this territory was named) was placed under colonial military protection because it was accepted that it constituted a particular affront to the Gcaleka whose 'dogs' or vassals

---

128 Peires, *House of Phalo*, chapters 2 to 4; Switzer, Leo, *Power and Resistance in an African Society; the Ciskei Xhosa and the Making of South Africa* (Madison: University of Wisconsin Press, 1993), pp. 34–42; Iliffe, John, *Honour in African History* (Cambridge: Cambridge University Press, 2005), pp. 152–3.
129 For traditional Xhosa warfare, see Peires, *House of Phalo*, pp. 135–9; Soga, John Henderson, *The Ama-Xhosa: Life and Custom*, (Lovedale: Lovedale Press; London: Kegan Paul, Trench, Trubner, c.1932), pp. 65–81, 312–13; Knight, Ian, *Warrior Chiefs of South Africa* (Poole, Dorset: Firebird Books, 1994), pp. 179–86; Knight, Ian, *Queen Victoria's Enemies (1): Southern Africa* (London: Osprey Military, 5th impression, 2005), pp. 8–10; Milton, John, *The Edges of War: A History of the Frontier Wars, 1702–1878* (Cape Town: Juta, 1983), pp. 13–14; Iliffe, *Honour*, p. 153; Arndt, Jochen S., 'Treacherous & Merciless Barbarians: Knowledge, Discourse and Violence during the Cape Frontier Wars, 1834–1853', *The Journal of Military History*, 74 (3) (July 2010), p. 726.
130 Storey, William Kelleher, *Guns, Race, and Power in Colonial South Africa* (Cambridge: Cambridge University Press, 2008), pp. 55, 67–70, 72–3; Knight, *Warrior Chiefs*, pp. 183–4; Knight, *Victoria's Enemies*, p. 10.
131 Stapleton, Timothy J., *A Military History of South Africa from the Dutch-Khoi Wars to the End of Apartheid* (Santa Barbara, California: Praeger, 2010), p. 20; Storey, *Guns*, p. 54.
132 H.S. 'The Kaffir War. By an English Officer in South Africa', *Fraser's Magazine* (February 1878), p. 252.

the Mfengu had once been.[133] The Ngqika amaXhosa were squeezed into a reserve in British Kaffraria between the Kei River and the Amathole Mounains to its south, 50 miles long and 25 miles across at its widest point.[134] In 1866 Wodehouse incorporated British Kaffraria into the Cape Colony and with that declared the Cape frontier problem settled. It was not.

In the late winter of 1877, the worst drought anyone could remember had the Eastern Frontier in its grip, compounding the despair of the amaXhosa penned into their stifling reserves and inflaming their resentment of both settlers and their hated Mfengu neighbours. For their part, settlers in the Eastern Cape were becoming increasingly anxious about the lax regulations governing gun ownership and the number of firearms in African hands and were pressing for the amaXhosa to be disarmed for the future security of the colony.[135] Then, not altogether unexpectedly, on 3 August 1877 a fracas between some Gcaleka and Mfengu at a wedding feast led to spilt blood and the Cape authorities rushed to offer assistance to the Mfengu.[136]

Sir Bartle Frere believed that the spiraling restlessness on the Cape Eastern Frontier was hobbling his freedom to act elsewhere in southern Africa to implement his confederation policy.[137] So it was with an eye to imposing his own solution on this troublesome region that Frere left Cape Town for King William's Town. When he arrived there in early September 1877, he found the frontier in a state of heightened 'genuine apprehension and alarm.'[138] He decided that he had no other option left but to go to war with the Gcaleka. Sarhili, the Gcaleka chief and Xhosa paramount, reluctantly prepared for the unequal conquest, if only to maintain his honour.[139]

Frere established his headquarters in the barracks of garrison stationed in King William's Town and set up an informal war council to prosecute the campaign. Cunynghame, who had arrived in late September from Kimberley via the Orange Free State, was one of its members. The other two were colonial cabinet ministers who happened to be at hand, John X. Merriman, the Commissioner of Crown Lands and Public Works (and in practice the Cape minister of defence), and Charles Brownlee, Resident Commissioner of Native Affairs. As a seasoned imperial administrator Frere was accustomed to getting his own way, but he knew it would not be easy to manipulate Merriman. The latter was of like mind with Molteno, the prime minister of the Cape Colony, and the conduct of the looming war seemed destined to bring the simmering differences between the High Commissioner and the Cape administration to the boil. As GOC, Cunynghame could not hope to avoid being burned.[140]

---

133 Moyer, Richard A. 'The Mfengu, Self-Defence and the Cape Frontier Wars', in Christopher Saunders and Robin Derrincourt (eds) *Beyond the Cape Frontier: Studies in the History of the Transkei and Ciskei* (London: Longman, 1974), p. 121.
134 Milton, *Edges of War*, pp. 249–50.
135 Storey, *Guns,* pp. 199–200, 210, 227.
136 *BPP* (C. 1961), enc. in no. 83: Col. John Eustace to Charles Brownlee, 18 August 1877.
137 Benyon, *Proconsul*, p. 149.
138 *BPP* (C. 1961), no. 30: Frere to Carnarvon, 5 September 1877.
139 Milton, *Edges of War*, pp. 257–8; Mostert, *Frontiers*, p. 1249.
140 For useful summaries of the Ninth Cape Frontier War as they affected the question of command, see Lewsen, P., *John X. Merriman: Paradoxical South African Statesman* (New Haven and London: Yale University Press, 1982), pp. 65–8; Lewsen (ed.), *Merriman Correspondence*, pp. 26–7; Hummel, Chris (ed), *The Frontier War Journal of Major John Crealock 1878: A Narrative of the Ninth Frontier War by the Assistant Military Secretary to Lieutenant General Thesiger,* (Cape Town: Van Riebeeck Society, 2nd series, No. 19, 1989), pp. 10–11.

As he anticipated, Frere found it impossible to side-step the colonial cabinet ministers on his war council. The problem was that even although Gcalekaland was beyond the Cape frontier and the conduct of the war there consequently Frere's responsibility as High Commissioner, to wage a campaign in the Transkei required Cape logistical and military support.[141] To complicate matters, and to sour the meetings of the war council unnecessarily, Merriman followed Molteno in being contemptuous of General Cunynghame's military abilities and objected to his taking a leading role in operations. For his part, Cunynghame found Merriman of 'unbounded ambition… not over-courteous in manner or conciliatory in disposition, most difficult to reason with.' What particularly annoyed the GOC was Merriman's unconcealed 'contempt for every form of skilled or trained military experience.' He could only conclude that Merriman's 'ignorance of military matters was only surpassed by the obstinacy of his determination not to learn the principles of war.'[142]

It was the Cape government's contention that since it was the self-governing colony's duty to protect its own territory, imperial troops were not required against the Gcaleka. Both Frere and Cunynghame were decidedly sceptical of the Cape's military ability to handle a campaign on its own, but after much wrangling a compromise was hammered out. Cunynghame took formal command on 2 October 1877 of all the troops, imperial and colonial. However, it is evident—even though Cunynghame was at pains to deny such an arrangement—that an understanding was reached that his active role would be confined to military matters in the Ciskei, and that he would not control the colonial troops operating in the Transkei.[143] In the Ciskei he ordered Colonel Richard Glyn, who commanded the 1/24th stationed in King William's Town, to distribute his troops in military posts along the Kei River to secure the Cape frontier. Herein lay a problem. Glyn's lack of cavalry meant that he could not patrol between these post and intercept Xhosa raids, thus reducing his main objective, which was to hold open the lines of supply and communication to the Transkei.[144] To make matters worse, Cunynghame, that stickler for well-planned logistics, urged that the supply of the colonial forces operating in the Transkei should be entrusted to the officers of the Commissariat Department who had experience in such matters; but Merriman insisted that it be left in colonial hands, no matter how amateur. Cunynghame decried the arrangement, complaining about the deleterious competition in the market between colonial and imperial purchasers it would bring about, and foreseeing the inevitable breakdown of the colonial commissariat to the detriment of their campaign.[145]

The actual conduct of operations in the Transkei was also to be left exclusively to colonial troops. The main striking force would be the FAMP (of whose worth Cunynghame remained

---

141 For useful summaries of the Ninth Cape Frontier War as they affected the question of command, see Lewsen, *Merriman*, pp. 65–8; Lewsen (ed.), *Merriman Correspondence*, pp. 26–7; Hummel (ed), *Crealock*, pp. 10–11.
142 Cunynghame, *My Command*, pp. 310–11, 370, 374–5.
143 Cunynghame, *My Command*, p. 312; Gon, *Road to Isandlwana*, pp. 106–7; Gon, Philip, 'The Last Frontier War, *Military History Journal*, 5 (6) (December 1982), p. 209.
144 *BPP* (C. 1961), enc. 2 in no. 49: Cunynghame to Frere, 1 October 1877; *BPP* (C. 1961), no. 52: Cunynghame to Under Secretary of State for War, 10 October 1877; *BPP* (C. 2000), enc. in no. 19: Cunynghame to Secretary of State for War, 5 December 1877; *BPP* (C. 2144), enc. in no. 102: memorandum by Cunynghame, 4 April 1878; Cunynghame, *My Command*, p. 306; H.S., 'Kaffir War', p. 254; Smithers, A.J. *The Kaffir Wars 1779–1877* (London: Leo Cooper, 1973), p. 266.
145 Cunynghame, *My Command*, pp. 311–12, 314, 339–40, 375.

dubious); while the overwhelming bulk of the troops would be made up of African levies.[146] On 26 September 1877 Frere appointed Colonel Charles Griffith, the Cape Government Agent in in Basutoland who had fought in the Eighth Cape Frontier War, to command them. Cunynghame saved face by stating it was 'judicious not to tie the hands' of Griffith. Instead, he accorded the colonial commander wide discretion in 'the details of his operations' and agreed to confine his own role to making no more than strategic 'suggestions.' Of course, Cunynghame knew that if his 'suggestions' proved 'not palatable,' that had the merit of putting the onus for any failure on Griffith's shoulders. And to keep tabs on the progress of the colonial campaign, the GOC attached several staff officers to Griffith's forces to report back to him.[147]

The first clash between the Gcaleka and a patrol of FAMP and Mfengu levies took place at Gwadana (Mount Wodehouse) on the very day Griffith was appointed. The colonial troops panicked and bolted.[148] Brushing aside this embarrassing setback, Griffith established his fortified headquarters in a small trading store at Ibeka, only five miles from Holela, Sarhili's great place, and garrisoned it with 180 FAMP, their artillery section and 2,000 Mfengu levies.[149] Provoked as intended, on 29 September a Gcaleka army of 7,000 to 8,000 warriors armed with spears and muzzle-loaders, and under the command of the famous war-leader, Khiva, attacked Ibeka. The Gcaleka came on in their traditional array of densely massed columns, and not in the skirmishing order they had adopted in the previous frontier war. In two days of fighting, they were repulsed by the heavy fire laid down by the garrison and finally routed by a mounted counter-attack.[150] Following this crushing defeat Sarhili attempted to negotiate a settlement, but Frere decided that the time had come to annex Gcalekaland and include it in his South African confederation.[151] On 5 October he issued a proclamation demanding that Sarhili cease hostilities, relinquish his chieftainship and forfeit his territory.[152]

Preparatory to making good Frere's proclamation, Griffith augmented his forces at Ibeka until they stood at 500 FAMP, 1,000 white colonial volunteers (only English and Germans settlers came forward, and barely any Boers),[153] and 6,000 African levies. Most of the levies were Mfengu, but some were abaThembu who, after the battle of Ibeka, decided to join the war on the on the colonial side. On 18 October Griffith began his advance through Gcalekaland in three lightly equipped columns, devastating the reserve as they went.[154] They encountered little opposition because the Gcaleka warriors fell back with their families and livestock across

---

146 Cunynghame, *My Command*, p. 307.
147 *BPP* (C. 2000), enc. in no. 19: Cunynghame to Secretary of State for War, 5 December 1877; Cunynghame, *My Command*, p. 312; Hummel (ed), *Crealock*, p. 24, n. 14; Smith, Keith, *The Wedding Feast War. The Final Tragedy of the Xhosa People* (London: Frontline Books, 2012), p. 115.
148 *BPP* (C. 1961), enc. 2 in no. 102: Inspector C.B. Chalmer's report, 25 October 1877; H.S. 'Kaffir War', p. 252; Smith, *Wedding Feast War*, pp. 118–20.
149 Hallam Parr, Captain Henry, *A Sketch of the Kafir and Zulu Wars. Guadana to Isandhlwana* (London: C. Kegan Paul, 1880), p. 35; H.S. 'Kaffir War', p. 253; Milton, *Edges of War*, p. 259.
150 *BPP* (C. 1961), enc. in no. 61, Commandant C. Griffith to Military Secretary, 17 October 1877; H.S. 'Kaffir War', p. 253; Milton, *Edges of War*, p. 259; Stapleton, 'Fingo', pp. 37–8; Smith, *Wedding Feast War*, pp. 121–4.
151 Gon, *Road to Isandlwana*, p. 106.
152 *BPP* (C. 1961), enc. in no. 51: Proclamation of His Excellency the Governor, 5 October 1877.
153 H.S. 'Kaffir War', p. 254.
154 *BPP* (C. 1961), enc. 2 in no. 107: Cunynghame to Frere, 27 November 1877; Smith, *Wedding Feast War*, pp. 128–35; Stapleton, 'Fingo', pp. 38–9.

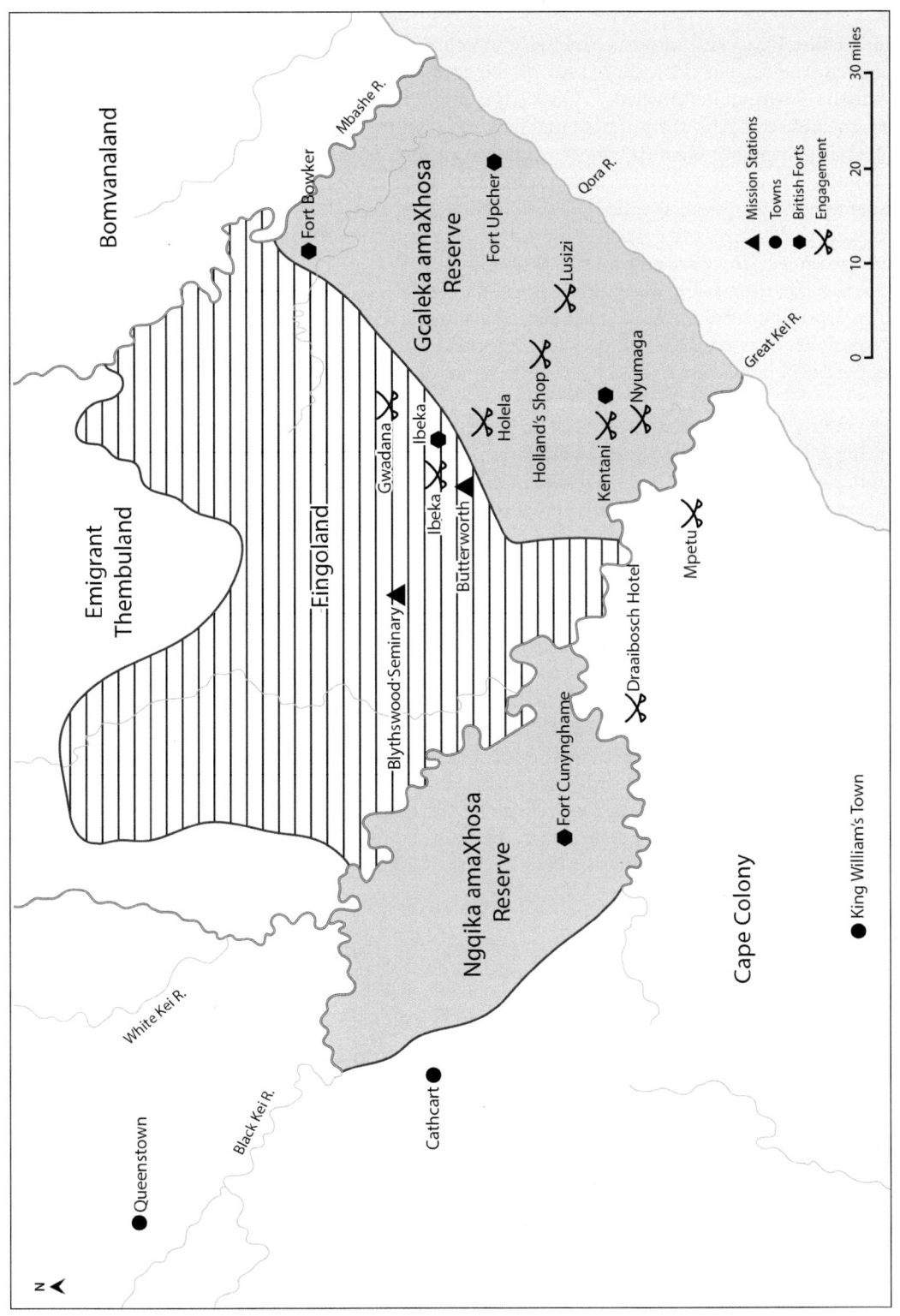

Map 6: Ninth Cape Frontier War, 1877.

the Mbashe River and into the sanctuary of neutral Bomvanaland beyond. On 1 November Cunynghame set out on a short tour of the area of operations and soon returned to King William's Town, quite satisfied.[155] On 29 November he left on another inspection tour in the opposite direction, this time of potential flashpoints in the Ciskei.[156]

In mid-November Griffith (whose commissariat had failed, as Cunynghame had predicted it would, and whose volunteer forces were 'returning spontaneously home' as Cunynghame disparagingly expressed it) called off the colonial campaign.[157] It seemed nevertheless to have achieved its objective, and a satisfied Frere designated conquered Gcalekaland a Cape magistracy on 1 December. The war, it seemed, was over.[158]

In fact, far from being extinguished, the flames of war were about to burst into a furious blaze. During Griffith's campaign in Gcalekaland, some Gcaleka had sought sanctuary in the Ciskei. Frere decided these refugees on Cape soil must be disarmed and targeted Makinana, a chief of the Ndlambe amaXhosa who was harbouring them.[159] When a FAMP patrol attempted to enforce Frere's order, Makinana and his followers took flight to the nearby Ngqika location. Responding to settler panic that this action might trigger an Ngqika uprising, and without waiting to consult the prickly colonial authorities, Cunynghame attempted to cordon off the Ngqika location with a thinly stretched line of imperial troops.[160] The Ngqika did not resort to arms as feared, but the military presence along their borders deeply unsettled them.[161]

Cunynghame kept his eyes on the agitated Ngqika, but it was the Gcaleka who struck first. Griffith, having disbanded the colonial volunteers and African levies, had only 500 FAMP available to patrol the long Mbashe River border with Bomvanaland.[162] On 2 December a thousand or more Gcaleka warriors slipped undetected over the Mbashe to attack an FAMP patrol at Holland's Shop. The skirmish was inconclusive,[163] but the over-stretched FAMP were near exhaustion and Griffith called for reinforcements.[164] All the colonial authorities could suggest in this crisis was to call out the Mfengu and Thembu levies again. At this juncture Frere decided he had had enough of colonial dithering and incompetence. Quite simply, he did not believe that the undisciplined colonial forces possessed the military capability to contain the mounting crisis. Ignoring colonial sensitivities, on 8 December Frere placed Cunynghame in active command of the imperial troops which he intended to send into the Transkei to deal with the Gcaleka. At the same time, he placed the GOC in direct command of the colonial troops which he pulled back to monitor the Ngqika in the Ciskei.

---

155 *BPP* (C. 1961), sub-enc. 1 in no. 107: Cunynghame to Secretary of State for War, 27 November 1877.
156 Cunynghame, *My Command*, pp. 318, 323–6, 328.
157 *BPP* (C. 2000), enc. in no. 19: Cunynghame to Secretary of State for War, 5 December 1877.
158 *BPP* (C. 1961), enc. 3 in no. 102: Proclamation by Sir Bartle Frere, 21 November 1877; Milton, *Edges of War*, pp. 261–2.
159 This was the chiefdom founded by Ndlambe, regent of the Rharhabe amaXhosa during his nephew Ngqika's minority.
160 Cunynghame, *My Command*, pp. 331–2; Gon, *Road to Isandlwana*, pp. 116-17; Gon, 'Frontier War', pp. 209–10.
161 Mostert, *Frontiers*, p. 1250; Smith, *Wedding Feast War*, pp. 138–41.
162 Milton, *Edges of War*, p. 264.
163 *BPP* (C. 2000), enc. 1 in no 22: Inspector J.H.W. Bourne's report, 3 December 1878; Gon, *Road to Isandlwana*, pp. 117–19; Milton, *Edges of War*, pp. 262–4.
164 *BPP* (C. 2000), enc. in no. 27: Cunynghame to Secretary of State for War, 12 December 1877; Smithers, *Kaffir Wars*, p. 267.

Richard Glyn, the Colonel of the 1/24th, whom Cunynghame characterized as 'a straightforward man of great energy, and good common sense', was gazetted Commander of the Army of the Transkei with the acting rank of Brigadier General, and Cunynghame instructed him to take his battalion to Ibeka.¹⁶⁵ To assist in his planned offensive, Cunynghame further ordered six companies of the 88th Regiment, which was stationed in Cape Town, to be shipped to East London on H.M.S. *Active* along with a Naval Brigade consisting of 196 men (42 of them Marines), two rocket tubes and a new-fangled Gatling gun which had first come into service in 1871.¹⁶⁶ There was scant response from colonists for volunteers, so Frere ordered Major Henry Pulleine, an officer of the 1/24th popular with the settlers, to raise a unit of 400 volunteer infantry, or Rangers, answerable only to the GOC. Pulleine gathered up the dregs of railway gangs, diamond diggers and the like to form a notorious unit of roughnecks known sourly as 'Pulleine's Lambs'.¹⁶⁷ Lieutenant Frederick Carrington, another 1/24th officer, was recalled from the Transvaal to raise a force of 200 mounted volunteers, the Frontier Light Horse [FLH]. These rough colonials had no specific uniform, but usually wore yellow or buff corduroy with black trimmings and a low-crowned, broad-brimmed Wideawake hat with a red puggaree. Under Major Redvers Buller, who succeeded Carrington in command, they became a tough and efficient unit, invaluable for scouting and raiding.¹⁶⁸

Only too aware of how previously Griffith's inadequate logistical arrangements had hobbled the colonial Transkei campaign, Cunynghame felt strongly that he must avoid a similar 'disgrace' by making proper preparations. As he rather luridly expressed it, he would have 'ill performed' his duty if he were to have sent his troops across the Kei 'wildly, without transport, ammunition or guns, into a dense bush, across a river running through stupendous ravines.' He gained Frere's support in insisting that the supply and transport of all the forces, whether imperial or colonial, be placed under British officers under the command of Deputy Commissary General Edward Strickland, a veteran of the Crimean War and Second Maori (Taranaki) War of 1863 –1866.¹⁶⁹ Sir Michael Hicks Beach (Carnarvon's successor at the Colonial Office from

---

165 *BPP* (C. 2000), enc. in no. 27: Cunynghame to Secretary of State for War, 12 December 1877.
166 *BPP* (C. 1961), no. 55: Admiralty to Colonial Office, 12 November 1877; *BPP* (C. 2000), enc. in no. 27: Cunynghame to Secretary of State for War, 12 December 1877; *BPP* (C. 2000), no. 66: Commodore Sullivan to the Secretary of the Admiralty, 19 December 1877; Cunynghame, *My Command*, pp. 327– 8, 340–1; Gon, 'Frontier War', p. 210; Norbury, Fleet Surgeon Henry F., *The Naval Brigade in South Africa during the Years 1877–78–79* (London: Sampson Low, Marston, Searle and Rivington, 1880), p. 88. The Naval Brigade left its six 12-pounder Armstrong guns on board.
167 Milton, *Edges of War*, p. 264. For lurid memories of trying to discipline these roughs, see Hamilton-Browne, Colonel George, *A Lost Legionary in South Africa* (London: T. Werner Laurie, 1912), pp. 36–42.
168 *BPP* (C. 2000), no. 63: Cunynghame to Secretary of State for War, 19 December 1877; Laband, *Historical Dictionary*, p. 100. The FLH was finally disbanded in December 1879 after service against the amaZulu and Bapedi as well as the amaXhosa.
169 *BPP* (C. 2000), enc. in no. 19: Cunynghame to Secretary of State for War, 5 December 1877; *BPP* (C. 2000), enc. in no. 27: Cunynghame to Secretary of State for War, 12 December 1877; *BPP* (C. 2000), no. 63: Cunynghame to Secretary of State for War (G. Gathorne -Hardy), 19 December 1877; *Cape of Good Hope*, p. 28: Strickland to the Surveyor-General of Ordnance, 16 January 1878; *BPP* (C. 2100), enc. in no. 40: Cunynghame to Frere, 23 February 1878; *BPP* (C. 2144), enc. in no. 102: memorandum by Cunynghame, 4 April 1878; Cunynghame, *My Command*, pp. 338–10; Laband, John (ed), *Lord Chelmsford's Zululand Campaign 1878–1879* (Stroud: Alan Sutton Publishing for the Army Records Society, 1994), p. 282.

23 January 1878), later ringingly endorsed this decision, writing that his government could not 'in any way acquiesce in a policy which allows operations to be undertaken on the line of the communications of the troops independently of the Officer in Command of the Regular Military Forces.'[170]

On 21 December 1877 Cunynghame left King William's Town for Ibeka, where he intended to set up his headquarters. He left all forces in the Ciskei under the trustworthy command of his Deputy Adjutant General, Colonel Bellairs, a veteran of the Crimea with considerable staff experience in the West Indies, Ireland, Canada and Gibraltar. The GOC remained in regular contact with him through the telegraph.[171]

While Colonel Glyn, on Cunynghame's orders, waited at Ibeka for reinforcement and concentrated his supplies, Khiva, the Gcaleka general, slipped past his forces and into the Ciskei.[172] On 22 December Khiva eased through the British cordon still surrounding the Ngqika location. He brought a message from Sarhili begging Sandile, the Ngqika chief, to bring all his people into the war. Despite misgivings, Sandile took the terrible plunge.[173] The day after Christmas Day his war parties broke out of their location to raid and ambush settlers as well as Mfengu, and some went on to blockade the forts along the Colony's side of the Kei. Thrown into panic, the white farmers and their families fled to military posts in the Ciskei for protection.[174]

Cunynghame, meanwhile (as he sententiously informed the Secretary of State for War since 1874, Gathorne Gathorne-Hardy),[175] had 'been detained' at his headquarters in King William's Town using his 'utmost exertions to perfect...the objects which [he] had in view under the recognized military principles', and had arrived at Ibeka on Christmas Day 'to superintend their being put into execution.'[176] He had had a narrow squeak on the way when he and his small escort had only just evaded an encounter with Khiva's force on its way to the Ngqika location.[177]

Aware that the Ciskei was bursting into flame behind him, Cunynghame decided that the best way of containing the conflagration was to deploy his troops in the Transkei in such a way that they would prevent the Gcaleka from joining hands with the Ngqika in the Ciskei.[178] The conservative strategy he devised to achieve this objective was nothing other than a repetition of that pursued by Griffith in October: three columns would drive to the coast, and then swing east to the Mbashe. Glyn advanced his troops on 27 December but, as with Griffith, the offensive proved a futile exercise. For two weeks Glyn's columns, wilting badly in the heat of midsummer, traversed most of Gcalekaland but made little contact with the enemy, killing only 120 Gcaleka and capturing a scant 2,000 cattle. Presuming that the Gcaleka warriors had fallen back into Bomvanaland, as they had during Griffith's campaign, Glyn had a series

---

170 TNA, WO 32/7683: Sir Michael Hicks Beach to Frere, March 1878 [sic].
171 Cunynghame, *My Command*, pp. 341; 357–8; 365; Laband (ed), *Chelmsford's Zululand Campaign*, p. 273.
172 *BPP* (C. 2000), enc. in no. 27: Cunynghame to Secretary of State for War, 12 December 1877.
173 Milton, *Edges of War*, pp. 265-6; Gon, 'Frontier War', p. 210; Smith, *Wedding Feast War*, pp. 148–50, 155.
174 *Illustrated London News*, 16 February 1878, p. 139; Milton, *Edges of War*, pp. 266; Smith, *Wedding Feast War*, pp. 151–5.
175 Gathorne-Hardy was raised to the peerage in 1879 as Viscount Cranbrook.
176 *BPP* (C. 2000), no. 63: Cunynghame to Secretary of State for War, 19 December 1877.
177 Cunynghame, *My Command*, pp. 341–2.
178 *BPP* (C. 2000), no. 63: Cunynghame to Secretary of State for War, 19 December 1877.

of earthworks constructed along the Mbashe intended to keep them safely bottled up east of the river. But while Glyn's columns were grinding east towards the Mbashe, the main body of Sarhili's forces slipped past them in the opposite direction, crossed the Kei, and joined forces with the Ngqika. Precisely what Cunynghame had planned to prevent had disconcertingly occurred. The combined Xhosa army was now concentrated to Glyn's rear in the densely wooded Tyityaba valley where it kept the scattered British forces in the area fully occupied. Guarding the approaches to Bomvanaland had been rendered embarrassingly pointless. Badly wrong-footed and his campaign a failure, Cunynghame had no choice but to order Glyn to pull his columns back to Ibeka. From there he was to prepare for a new offensive down the Transkei side of the Kei to engage the combined Xhosa forces.[179]

It was at this tense juncture that Molteno, the Cape premier, arrived at Frere's headquarters in King William's Town on 8 January 1878. He immediately declared that he was unsatisfied with Frere's military dispositions, not least because he had no faith in British as opposed to colonial troops, considering them slow, clumsy, unnecessarily costly and unsuited to local conditions. As for Cunynghame, he and Merriman both found the GOC over-cautious as a commander and an unbearable old chatterbox to boot. The main issue, however, was the question of colonial self-government, and both men intended to assert it by assuming full responsibility for the Cape's defence and prising it out of Frere's interfering hands.[180]

They would have been even more agitated if they had known that Cunynghame, abetted by Colonel Bellairs, had been pressing Frere urgently for imperial reinforcements, not only for the Cape campaign, but to stabilize the situation on the borders of Natal and the Transvaal Territory.[181] Frere had required little prodding. On 31 December 1878 he wrote to Carnarvon strongly requesting that two regiments be sent out immediately to the Cape as a reinforcement or a relief for the regiments slated to return home, and that a battery of field artillery accompany them for service in the Cape, Natal and Transvaal.[182] The Colonial Office responded with the immediate despatch of the 90th (Perthshire Light Infantry) Regiment of Foot. Carnarvon firmly believed he had to act to rescue the confederation project from the 'black conspiracy' which he imagined being stirred to violent life by the unresolved war on the Cape Eastern Frontier.[183] He nevertheless made clear that he was severely disappointed that the Cape had proved unable to shoulder its military burden as a self-governing colony, and made it an 'imperative condition'

---

179 *BPP* (C. 2079), no. 23: Cunynghame to Secretary of State for War, 15 January 1878; Cunynghame, *My Command*, pp. 343, 355–7, 359–61; Gon, *Road to Isandlwana*, pp. 124–6; Gon, 'Frontier War', p. 210; Milton, *Edges of War*, p. 266; Smith, *Wedding Feast War*, pp. 196–201.
180 Lewsen, Phyllis, 'The First Crisis in Responsible Government in the Cape Colony', in *Archives Year Book for South African History, 1943 (2)* (Pretoria: Government Printer, 1943), pp. 242–5; Lewsen, *Merriman*, p. 66; Hummel (ed), *Crealock*, p. 12.
181 *BPP* (C. 2000), enc. 6 in no 78: Cunynghame to Frere, Ibeka, 29 December 1877. See also *BPP* (C. 2000), enc. in no. 27: Cunynghame to Secretary of State for War, King William's Town, 12 December 1878; *BPP* (C. 2000), no. 63: Cunynghame to Secretary of State for War, 19 December 1877; TNA, WO 32/7680: Memorandum from Bellairs to Frere, 20 January 1878; Cunynghame, *My Command*, pp. 327–8.
182 *BPP* (C.2000), no. 78: Frere to Carnarvon, 31 December 1878.
183 *BPP* (C. 2000), enc. 6 in no 78: Cunynghame to Frere, Ibeka, 29 Dec 1877; *BPP* (C. 2000), no.78: Frere to Carnarvon, 31 December 1878; *Cape of Good Hope*, pp. 11–12: Cape of Good Hope No. 482: Carnarvon to Frere, 30 January 1878.

that the colonial government must make monthly payments into the Treasury Chest to cover the cost of supplying troops in the field.[184]

Meanwhile, unaware that imperial reinforcements were on their way to the Cape, Molteno pursued his political war against Frere and Cunynghame. In lengthy, stormy meetings he rejected Cunynghame's sole command over all the forces on the Cape frontier. On 11 January he insisted that the colonial forces must undertake their own independent military campaign in the Ciskei under Griffith's separate command, and duly appointed him Commandant General on the 15 January.[185] Molteno made it insultingly clear to Frere that 'the burgher forces would not willingly submit to military control, nor cordially co-operate with regular troops; that they would only act and fight in their own way and under their own leaders.'[186] Bellairs railed that Molteno's motives in appointing Griffith Commandant General was entirely political.[187] Frere deplored Molteno's principle of two separate commands in the same area of operations, and made the point to Carnarvon on 24 January that 'without staff or military experience' Commandant Griffith was unlikely 'to organise effectively the incongruous materials at his command.' The consequences of Molteno's 'totally uncalled for interference with the General's proceedings at the eleventh hour' would, he direly predicted, 'imperil' the entire campaign.[188] In a further despatch of 30 January he lamented that he had been unable to persuade Molteno that 'two independent generals commanding in the same field is not only a professional but a practical impossibility.' He indignantly added that Merriman was acting '...in ostentatious disregard of all authority of the Governor and Commander of the Forces as a kind of minister at war and general commanding in the field...without professional knowledge or any professional staff.'[189]

Cunynghame, who had turned over direct command in the Ciskei to Glyn before returning to his headquarters in King William's Town on 27 January specifically to find out exactly what the new Commandant General was up to, weighed in cautiously.[190] He informed Gathorne-Hardy, that 'the Civil Government has taken upon itself the conduct of military operations over a large area of country within my command: this they have done without giving me any information of the principles by which they were guided, or the system upon which they are conducted.' Nevertheless, he declined to state his own opinion as the issue of the divided command was properly a matter for the High Commissioner, and his duty (as he saw it) was to use his 'utmost diligence' to carry out Frere's policy in his military arrangements.[191]

---

184 *Cape of Good Hope* pp. 11-12: Cape of Good Hope No. 482: Carnarvon to Frere, 30 January 1878. See also *BPP* (C. 2000), no. 46: J.C. Vivian to Under-Secretary of State for War (Ralph Thompson), 22 January 1878.
185 Molteno fully laid out his principle of 'separating the Command and direction of Colonial Forces, from that of Her Majesty's troops' in a long memorandum dated 19 January 1878 (TNA, WO 32/7680: copy of Molteno's memorandum). *BPP* (C. 2079): Frere to Carnarvon, 16 January 1878; Cunynghame, *My Command*, pp. 362–3.
186 *BPP* (C. 2079): Frere to Carnarvon, King William's Town, 16 January 1878.
187 TNA, WO 32/7678: Bellairs to Secretary of State for War, 16 January 1878.
188 *BPP* (C. 2079), no. 42: Frere to Carnarvon, 24 January 1878.
189 TNA, WO 32/7683: Frere to Carnarvon, 30 January 1878.
190 *BPP* (C. 2079), no. 66: Cunynghame to Secretary of State for War, 30 January 1878; *BPP* (C. 2144), enc. in no. 102: memorandum by Cunynghame, 4 April 1878; Cunynghame, *My Command*, p. 368.
191 TNA, WO 32/7680: Cunynghame to Gathorne-Hardy, 30 January 1878.

This indeed was the crux of the matter, for Molteno was effectively denying Frere's authority over the Cape forces. As Frere later explained to Hicks Beach, Carnarvon's successor at the Colonial Office, he strongly believed that it was 'the constitutional duty of the Governor and Commander-in-Chief to guard against such a dangerous anomaly as a divided command of military forces...in one area of operations.'[192]

Yet more was at stake than the constitutional question of where the command of the Colonial troops lay, essential though it was in Frere's mind that he maintain absolute control over both them and the Cape garrison.[193] He and Cunynghame remained adamant that the imperial reinforcements they had called for were required to defend both the Colony (since Gcalekaland was not yet entirely subdued and the colonial troops were ineffective), and to implement the wider confederation policy. Indeed, Frere went so far as to insist that he would be '... fitter for a lunatic asylum' than governor if he thought otherwise.[194] Still, when Molteno finally learned of Frere's request for reinforcements he and his ministers were predictably appalled that the High Commissioner had proceeded without prior consultation. They bluntly refused to pay for them, contending as always that the colonial troops were sufficient for the current campaign.[195]

Far away from the political wrangling in King William's Town, Glyn's campaign in the Transkei was not going too badly. On 13 January about a thousand Gcaleka and Ngqika attacked the camp of Glyn's Right Column near a small river called the Nyumaga, four miles to the south-west of Glyn's headquarters at Ibeka.[196] For its defence Glyn had two infantry companies (one each of the 1/24th and the 88th), two troops of FAMP, 50 bluejackets of the Naval Brigade along with Royal Marine rocket launchers and two light 7-pounder field guns. Critically, these white troops were augmented by Mfengu levies. In deploying his small force for battle, Glyn was acting in the spirit of the new flexible battlefield training adopted by the War Office and printed in the 1877 edition of *Field Exercise and Evolution of Infantry*. The key to the 'bush-fighting' of small wars was, according to this manual, loose skirmishing order in an extended firing line with the troops making the most of the terrain and natural cover since they could kneel or even lie down with their breech-loading, single shot Martini-Henry Mark II rifles, introduced in 1874.[197] At Nyumaga Glyn inaugurated an apparently winning tactical formation. The infantry was positioned in skirmishing lines on either side of the fixed anchor of field guns with a second line in support. The mounted troops hovered on the flanks to foil an enemy attempt to envelope the formation and to act as a mobile force in counter-attack and

---

192 *BPP* (C. 2079), no 86: Frere to Hicks Beach 21 May 1878.
193 *BPP* (C. 2079), no. 86: Frere to Hicks Beach 21 May 1878; Benyon, *Proconsul*, p. 151.
194 *Cape of Good Hope*, p. 5: Minute from the Governor in Answer to Minute of Mr. Molteno, dated February 2nd, 1878, 6 February 1878; *BPP* (C. 2079), enc. 4 in no. 86: Cunynghame to Frere, 3 Feb 1878.
195 TNA, Colonial Office Papers (henceforth CO) CO 48/485, Cape 1782, minute, 13 February 1878; J.X. Merriman to Mrs J. Merriman (mother) 25 Feb 1878 in Lewsen, *Merriman Correspondence*, 42.
196 For the engagement at Nyumaga, see Smith, *Wedding Feast War*, pp. 201–4; Smithers, *Kaffir Wars*, pp. 270–1; Gon, *Road to Isandlwana*, pp. 131–2; Milton, *Edges of War*, pp. 266–7; Stapleton, *Military History*, pp. 59–60; Cunynghame, *My Command*, pp. 351–5.
197 Great Britain, War Office, *Field Exercise and Evolution of Infantry* (London: Her Majesty's Stationary Office, pocket edition, 1877), pp. 53–4, 93–4, 96 –9, 210–41; Laband, *Zulu Warriors*, p. 125; Laband, *Zulu Wars*, p. 151.

pursuit.¹⁹⁸ It remained to be seen, though, whether a thin skirmishing line, even at point-blank range, could develop the necessary volume of fire to stop a determined charge. At Nyumaga it did, and in what became essentially a fire-fight the amaXhosa were routed and dispersed into the bush of the Tyityaba valley.

Follow-up operations achieved very little despite some sharp skirmishes, notably at the head of the Mnyameni valley on 30 January, and the amaXhosa easily eluded the plodding British who were overcome by the summer heat. With no resolution in sight, Cunynghame decided to suspend operations until Glyn had built up more supplies and reinforcements had arrived.¹⁹⁹

Meanwhile in the Ciskei, Griffith's colonial forces opened their campaign on 14 January. They swept over the Ngqika location plundering and burning homesteads, driving off cattle and killing all they encountered.²⁰⁰ The colonial forces then became involved in a distracting extension to the war. On 24 January the local magistrate of Queenstown to the north of Griffith's area of operations called on him to help subdue a revolt led by Gungubele, chief of the Tshatshu abaThembu. On 4 February after three days of heavy fighting Griffith succeeded in dispersing Gungubele's army. But the violence that had been unleashed could not be contained and spread to Emigrant Thembuland where the colonial forces proved unable to subdue Sitokwe Tyhali, the disaffected chief of the Vundhle abaThembu.²⁰¹

Frere, who was seething at Molteno's denial of his authority as High Commissioner over the Cape forces, was incensed that these very same forces were botching the unnecessary 'Tambookie' campaign, as he called it. In this he had Cunynghame's emphatic support. The General insisted to Frere that he was personally 'entirely irresponsible' for Griffith's operations and protested that they were 'an infringement of his position and command, as laid down in the Queen's Regulations and his commission as General Commanding in the Colony.'²⁰²

Entirely convinced that it was essential to exercise full control over both the Cape garrison and the colonial troops through the GOC's uncontested command of both,²⁰³ Frere decided to have done with his recalcitrant ministers. Matters reached a head at a stormy meeting on 31 January.²⁰⁴ Molteno and Merriman belligerently refused Frere's demand that they resign, insisting they were accountable only to the Cape parliament. So Frere dismissed the ministry

---

198 Knight, Ian, *Zulu Rising. The Epic Story of Isandlwana and Rorke's Drift* (London: Macmillan, 2010), p. 353.
199 Smith, *Wedding Feast War*, pp. 204–6.
200 *BPP* (C. 2079), no. 10: telegram, Frere to Carnarvon, 29 January 1878; Milton, *Edges of War*, p. 270; Smith, *Wedding Feast War*, pp. 181–3.
201 Smith, *Wedding Feast War*, pp. 183–9. For operations by the colonial forces in the 'Tambookie Location', see *BPP* (C. 2079), no. 80: Frere to Carnarvon, 16 February 1878, and enclosure.
202 *BPP* (C. 2079), enc. 1 in no. 86: Cunynghame to Frere, 30 January 1878; minutes by W. Littleton of the meeting of the Executive Council, King William's Town, 1 February 1878.
203 *BPP* (C. 2079), no. 86: Frere to Hicks Beach 21 May 1878.
204 Lewsen, *Merriman*, 69, 73; Lewsen, 'Responsible Government', p. 250; *BPP* (C. 2079): enc in 86: Memorandum by Frere on Molteno's memoranda of 19 and 22 January 1878, 26 January 1878.

on 6 February.²⁰⁵ The ministers were exceedingly angry,²⁰⁶ but Cunynghame rejoiced to Gathorne-Hardy that the 'sort of Military Dictatorship' that the Cape ministers had delegated to Merriman, and which he had exercised in defiance of Frere's authority, was over, and that the command of the combined imperial and colonial forces had been restored to him.²⁰⁷

Back in London, both the War and Colonial Offices had no hesitation in endorsing Frere's dismissal of the Cape ministry, and the Under-Secretary at the Colonial Office went so far as to minute contemptuously that the Cape ministers' ignorant and arrogant 'notion of conducting separate & independent operations on either side of a small river traversable by the enemy is ridiculous even to one not a soldier.'²⁰⁸ More than that, he knew he was calling the Molteno ministry's bluff when he added that the 'Colony must be made to say whether they want the assistance of HM's forces or not … If they do not want them they must at whatever risk to the Colony be withdrawn.'²⁰⁹

The very day after Frere dismissed Molteno, on 7 February 1878, the Gcaleka were knocked out of the war. At the end of January Glyn had decided to establish a forward supply and operations base deep in Gcaleka territory to support further sweeps across the Transkei. Captain Russell Upcher of the 1/24th was placed in command and pitched his camp on some high ground 300 yards from the southern slope of a high hill called Kentani, 12 miles southeast of Ibeka. To defend the position Upcher laagered his wagons and built a strong earthwork surrounded by trenches and rifle-pits. The 600 white troops who held the defences consisted of 200 British regulars of two companies of the 1/24th, 25 bluejackets of the Naval Brigade, 90 mounted men of the FAMP and 70 of Carrington's Frontier Light Horse. They also had two guns—a 7-pounder and a 9-pounder—and a rocket tube. Some 560 Mfengu levies were deployed on the flanks outside the defences.²¹⁰ Glyn had advance word that a Xhosa attack was imminent but being unsure whether it would be on Ibeka or Kentani, with good strategic foresight he positioned a strong reserve column of infantry, horsemen and guns at the mission station at Tutura, midway between the two bases.

Early on the misty morning of 7 February a joint Gcaleka and Ngqika Xhosa army of about 5,000 warriors advanced on Ketani. The Gcaleka under Kiva attacked as they had at Nyumaga in traditional formation and were again cut down by the defenders' disciplined firepower. The mounted troops turned their withdrawal after only 20 minutes into a rout. The Ngqika

---

205 *BPP* (C. 2079), enc.in no. 86: Minutes of Executive Council, King William's Town, 2 February 1878; *BPP* (C. 2079), no. 54: Frere to Carnarvon, 5 February 1878; *BPP* (C. 2079), encs in no 63: Frere to Molteno and Merriman, 6 February 1878; *BPP* (C. 2079), no. 63: Frere to Secretary of State for Colonies, 12 February 1878.
206 Lewsen (ed), *Merriman Correspondence*, p. 38: J.X. Merriman to his father, Bishop N.J. Merriman, 19 February 1878.
207 TNA, WO 32/7680: Cunynghame to Gathorne-Hardy, 6 and 13 February 1878.
208 Laband, John, 'The Direction of the Whole of the Forces Available': The Disputed Spheres of Military and Civil Authority in the Eastern Cape (1877 –1878), Natal (1879) and Zululand (1888)', *Scientia Militaria, South African Journal of Military Studies*, 41 (2) (2013), p. 66.
209 TNA, CO 48/485, Cape 2672, minute by Mr. Malcolm, 1 March 1878.
210 For the battle of Kentani, see TNA, WO 32/7681: Cunynghame to Secretary of State for War, 15 February 1878; *BPP* (C. 2709), no. 81: Frere to Carnarvon, 20 February 1878; and *BPP* (C. 2709), no. 81, enc. 1 with official depatches and reports of the engagement; Hallam Parr, *Wars*, pp. 83–5; Smithers, *Kaffir Wars*, pp. 268–70; Gon, *Road to Isandlwana*, pp. 134–40, 145–6; Milton, *Edges of War*, pp. 267–9; Stapleton, 'Fingo', p. 40; Switzer, *Ciskei Xhosa*, p. 74; Smith, *Wedding Feast War*, pp. 207–13.

contingent came on next in skirmishing order but believing that the British reserves at Tutura were marching towards the battlefield, they broke off the engagement hotly pursued by the British mounted troops. The British lost only two Mfengu and four horses killed in the battle, along with nine men wounded. In stark comparison, an estimated 400 amaXhosa perished, mainly of the Gcaleka contingent.

The triumphant British celebrated Kentani as a model action and testimony to the effectiveness of breech-loading rifles. As for the Gcaleka, their fighting spirit was utterly broken by their rout at Kentani, and they would never appear again in the field deployed as an army. Quite daunted, Sarhili fled over the Mbashe to the sanctuary of Bomvanaland. This left the Ngqika alone in the field to carry on the war. Their forces were as yet relatively unscathed, and they pulled back across the Kei to pursue their tried and trusted guerrilla tactics in the Amathole Mountains to the south of their reserve in the Ciskei.[211]

Despite his troops' victory at Kentani, General Cunynghame would not long remain in charge of the Ciskei campaign. For a few heady days he believed he was set to crown his career by subduing the Ngqika. The promised reinforcements were marching in: the 90th Regiment had already arrived in the Ciskei; the 2nd Battalion of the 24th was on its way; and the 200-strong Diamond Fields Horse had cantered in from Griqualand West. With a line of posts established along the railway line that now connected King William's Town to East London, Cunynghame was ready to march.[212] But politics would trip him up.

Frere had wasted little time in appointing the prominent Eastern Frontier politician, J. Gordon Sprigg, to replace the meddling Molteno as prime minister. The High Commissioner at last had a ministry he could rely upon to espouse the cause of confederation, to insist on African disarmament, and to be sensible about military matters.[213] Indeed, to Cunynghame's considerable satisfaction Sprigg made it clear that his first priority was to coordinate military operations once more under a single command, and that in this he had found himself 'nobly seconded' by the General with his 'courteous manners and conciliatory demeanour.'[214] Of course, it was easy for Cunynghame to recall his manners when dealing with a prime minister who agreed with him. But the sacking of the Molteno ministry had caused a great stir in the Colony, and Cunynghame knew only too well that he had earned an embarrassing public record of 'want of cordiality' with the ministry over the direction of military policy.[215] Nevertheless, he did not anticipate the dire consequences for his career.

The General's political masters back in London, now that the point of undivided military command had been gained, were anxious to appease ruffled colonial opinion. It seemed politic, therefore, to offer Cunynghame up as a placatory sacrifice. If Cunynghame had proved himself to be an outstanding commander it might have been different, but as a merely adequate one he was dispensable. Unbeknown to Cunynghame, as early as 1 February and at Carnarvon's

---

211 Milton, *Edges of War*, pp. 267–9; Gon, 'Frontier War', p. 211.
212 Smithers, *Kaffir Wars*, p. 271.
213 Storey, *Guns*, pp. 239–40. Vindication would come on 18 June 1878 when the Cape parliament voted to confirm the authority of the High Commissioner 'as constitutional head of all armed forces of the Colony'. See *BPP* (C. 2144), no 101: Frere to Hicks Beach, 18 June 1878.
214 *BPP* (C. 2100), no 56: Frere to Hicks Beach, 16 March 1878, quoting from Sprigg's demi-official letter of 27 February 1878.
215 *BPP* (C. 2144), enc 1 in no. 102: Memorandum by Cunynghame, HMS *Hamalaya*, at sea, 4 April 1878.

insistence during his last days in office, the British government had already decided on his recall in favour of a junior lieutenant general.[216] On 25 February 1878 Sir Frederic Thesiger—who would succeed his father as Baron Chelmsford in October 1878—arrived in Cape Town. On 2 March he officially superseded Cunynghame in command of the troops in the Cape, Natal, Transvaal and St. Helena with the local rank of lieutenant general and proceeded to headquarters in King William's Town.[217]

Despite his deep chagrin, Cunynghame carried himself very correctly. Earlier, on 27 February, he had dutifully written to Gathorne-Hardy that he would 'make it my study to place upon him [Thesiger] all the information which I possess' regarding the South African territories, 'all of which countries,' he could not resist adding, 'are personally known to me.'[218] In company with Frere he gave Thesiger 'a cordial welcome' when he arrived by special train in King William's Town on 4 March.[219] In his General Order of the same day Cunynghame was punctilious in thanking all the units that had fallen under his command, whether imperial soldiers, colonial troops or African levies, along with sundry officers and officials, not forgetting members of the Railway Department who had assisted with his all-important logistical arrangements.[220]

All the same, Cunynghame had suffered a mortal blow to his self-esteem. As he bitterly expressed it in a lengthy memorandum written while on board HMS *Hamalaya* on the way back to England in April 1878, he could not forgive the government for superseding him 'when on the climax' of his military success against the amaXhosa 'with no explanation whatever for so cruel an act.' He declared that his officers were as 'astonished' as he was, and concluded rather pathetically with the hope that he would 'yet regain the position which has been torn from me, in the consideration of the army, my Queen, and my country.'[221] It was no consolation that the Duke of Cambridge himself assured him on his return to England that in his opinion he had committed 'no fault whatsoever,'[222] and had earlier gone so far as to write to Gathorne-Hardy in support of his 'poor old friend.'[223] Once back in London Cunynghame penned a second, nineteen-page-long memorandum outlining his record in South Africa which appears not to have been sent.[224] In it he once again vented his dismay at being thrown to the political wolves,

---

216 Goodfellow, C.F., *Great Britain and South African Confederation (1870-1881)* (Cape Town: Oxford University Press, 1966), p. 155.
217 BPP (C. 2100), no. 56: General Order by Col. Bellairs, 11 March 1878; *Illustrated London News*, 6 April 1878; Laband, John, 'Lord Chelmsford', in Steven J. Corvi and Ian F.W. Beckett (eds) *Victoria's Generals* (Barnsley, England: Pen & Sword Military, 2009), p. 97.
218 TNA, WO 32/7684: Cunynghame to Gathorne-Hardy, 27 February 1878.
219 Hummel (ed), *Crealock*, p. 22: entry, 4 March 1878.
220 BPP (C. 2100), no. 56: General Order by Cunynghame, 4 March 1878. Two days earlier Cunynghame wrote Gathorne -Hardy lauding the services of the Natal Brigade (*BPP* (C. 2100), no 18: Cunynghame to Secretary of State for War, 2 March 1878).
221 BPP (C. 2144), enc. in no. 102: memorandum by Cunynghame, 4 April 1878.
222 BPP (C. 2144), enc 1 in no. 102: Memorandum by Cunynghame, HMS *Hamalaya*, at sea, 4 April 1878. NAM, Cunynghame Papers 7805-42: Memorandum by Cunynghame, Queen Anne's Mansions, Westminster, 6 May 1878.
223 Cambridge to Gathorne-Hardy, 30 January 1878, quoted in Goodfellow, *Confederation*, p. 155.
224 Similarly, when Chelmsford was fighting disgrace on his return to England after the Anglo-Zulu War, he also drafted a long memorandum rebutting his critics which he never sent. See Laband (ed), *Chelmsford's Zululand Campaign*, pp. 220–6: memorandum by Maj.-Gen. Lord Chelmsford, February 1880.

and insisted on his need for recompense. As he put it in the indignant summation: 'I look with confidence therefore that every consideration should be shown to me; for the grievous injury which has been placed upon me that of being superseded by a junior officer in command of an army in the field when in the midst of a successful command.'[225]

Thesiger, that junior officer, was of much the same social and military background as Cunynghame, with a similar military career.[226] Fortunately for him, he was able to report that with the approval of the Sprigg ministry he enjoyed 'the entire direction of the Colonial as I have already of the Imperial troops.'[227] Yet once he began operating against the Ngqika in the Amathole Mountains, he followed Cunynghame's conservative strategy of sending in several strong columns with the intention of surrounding the enemy and bringing them to battle. In five offensives between March and May 1878 he failed to entrap the Ngqika. It was only then that he took the advice of colonials better versed then he in irregular warfare. In May he divided the area of operations up into 11 zones, each patrolled by a mobile mounted force, which harried the Ngqika and denied them supplies. Even so, it took until mid-1878 before the war was over.[228]

Cunynghame, meanwhile, as with anyone whose career comes to an unexpected and jarring halt, could not suddenly throw over the concerns that had been occupying him for the past four years. To his mind, he wrote Frere, the abiding threat of Africans to white rule in South Africa had to be addressed comprehensively, and that to make it '…clear to their minds that they *are* an inferior race, and must be guided by civilization, it is necessary to put down all opposition to our arms within our own borders.' To that end he advocated mounting strong military demonstrations along the borders of the Zulu kingdom to cow King Cetshwayo.[229]

Frere was after a far more definitive end to the perceived Zulu menace, however. Once Thesiger had concluded his counter-insurgency operations in the Cape, Frere sent him in August 1878 to establish his headquarters in Pietermaritzburg. There he was to prepare for the campaign against the Zulu kingdom which the High Commissioner was determined to fight (despite the acute misgivings of his governments) as a means of finally clinching confederation. Ironically, the ensuing Anglo-Zulu War of 1879 was to prove anything but the easy military promenade it was expected to be. It destroyed both Frere's and his general's careers and led to the final collapse in 1881 of the painstakingly raised structure of confederation following the successful Transvaal Rebellion.[230]

Cunynghame could only follow these developments from afar. The Queen honoured him on his return from South Africa by inviting him and Lady Cunynghame to a dinner at Windsor Castle on 16 May 1878 for the Crown Prince and Princess of Germany.[231] But there was no disguising that his military career was over, and being made Knight Grand Cross of the Order of the Bath in June 1878 was an empty honour and scant consolation.[232] He was still Colonel-Commandant to his old corps, the 1/60th (on 2 February 1876 he relinquished his Colonelcy of

---

225 NAM, Cunynghame Papers 7805-42: Memorandum by Cunynghame, Queen Anne's Mansions, Westminster, 6 May 1878.
226 Laband, 'Chelmsford', pp. 92–7.
227 *BPP* (C. 2100), enc. in no 43: Gen. Thesiger to Secretary of State for War, 12 March 1878.
228 Laband, *Zulu Warriors*, pp. 138–45.
229 *BPP* (C. 2100), enc. in no. 65: Cunynghame to Frere, 15 March 1878.
230 Laband, *Zulu Warriors*, pp. 145, 148 –9, 191, 282–4; Laband, *Transvaal Rebellion*, pp. 237–8.
231 *The Times*, Court Circular, 17 May 1878.
232 *Illustrated London News*, 22 June 1878.

the 36th Regiment because only one colonelcy could be held at a time), but in 1879 he retired from the Army. He and his wife took up residence at the substantial Hurlingham Lodge in Fulham, London.[233] In 1879, in recognition of her august Indian connections, and as a sign of the Queen's favour, Lady Cunynghame was appointed a Member of the Imperial Order of the Crown of India.[234] Unsurprisingly, Cunynghame continued to travel, and he died on 10 March 1884 whilst at sea. He left his personal estate (exclusive of the property in settlement) to an amount 'exceeding £16,000' to wife for life, then to his four children.[235]

How then to assess Cunynghame as a commander? He was inextricably a man of his aristocratic class and period, sharing the assumptions and pastimes of that conservative social milieu. His promotion in the army through purchase, patronage and seniority was conventional enough for a man of his connections and means, and it was almost inevitable that he became closely associated with the Duke of Cambridge's old-school military circle. At the same time, as the battle of Inkerman indicated, he more than possessed the expected courage in the field and the personality to encourage men to follow him. Yet, for all that, he was not an entirely conventional officer. His inquisitive fascination with foreign places, peoples and occupations, his extensive travels, his desire to serve in exotic postings in the Americas, Asia and Africa, his preparedness to command 'native' Turkish and Indian troops—all of this marks him as somewhat different from the general ruck of senior officers. Like many fellow officers of the period, he wrote books about his experiences, and in their rag-bag organization they reveal much about his impulsive, enthusiastic and somewhat unsystematic approach to life.

It was as a conscientious (if largely untried), elderly general officer that he was appointed to the Cape. That 'safe' command at a time when the policymakers were spurring on the confederation of South Africa proved far more testing than anticipated and involved military intervention in the Transvaal, Griqualand West and the Eastern Cape. Cunynghame saw no combat, and all the actual fighting in the Ninth Cape Frontier War was undertaken by his field commander, Colonel Glyn. As GOC, Cunynghame's role was to formulate strategy and plan logistical support. He was almost obsessively thorough concerning logistics, but his approach to strategy was ploddingly conventional and lacking in vision, and he never contemplated the option of irregular operations against an elusive foe. Instead, he fell back on the usual procedure—familiar to him from operations on the North West Frontier of India—of mounting cumbersome sweeps through enemy territory, seeking decisive pitched battles and building lines of fortifications to contain the foe. He was fortunate that the disastrous decision by the Xhosa commanders to force a resolution through pitched battle played into the hands of his field commander and made victory in the Transkei against the Gcaleka amaXhosa possible. Yet, if Cunynghame had used the identical conventional methods against the Ngqika amaXhosa in the Ciskei he would have failed, as did Thesiger, and one can only suppose he would have been eventually constrained, as was his successor, to mount flexible counter-insurgency operations.

233 The distinguished brick and stucco house still stands in Hurlingham Road, London SW6.
234 Obituary of Frances Lady Cunynghame, *The Times*, 10 July 1894; Duckers, Peter, *British Orders and Decorations* (Oxford: Shire Publications, 2011), p. 37. The order was instituted by Queen Victoria in 1878 on becoming Empress of India and was conferred only on British and Indian women who had rendered distinguished service of benefit to India.
235 *Illustrated London News*, 29 November 1884. Lady Cunynghame died on 9 July 1894.

Cunynghame's real challenge in South Africa concerned the politics of command rather than command in the field, and with the newly self-governing Cape Colony that required tact and finesse. Cunynghame clearly thought little of colonial volunteer soldiers or parliamentarians and had no time for their parochial sensitivities. He had his eyes on the big, imperial picture and adhered wholeheartedly to Frere's confederating mission, joining him in the call for military reinforcements to make it feasible, and dismissing the military capabilities of the Cape government as amateur and inadequate. As the High Commissioner's obliging military instrument, he saw it as his duty to carry out Frere's policy in his day-to-day military arrangements and made no significant decisions without consulting him. It also meant that when (with considerable justification) he joined Frere in vigorously opposing the Cape ministry's push for a division in command between colonial and imperial troops, that he was inevitably drawn into the political limelight. It speaks to the political naivety of this bluff soldier that he did not see how his strongly expressed views would make him an embarrassment to his masters in London who were trying to mend fences with the Cape government. Certainly, he never imagined that his loyal support of the High Commissioner could lead to his supersession at the very moment his troops won their decisive battle in the Transkei. Cunynghame was devastated by this act of apparent unfairness which terminated his career, and never quite grasped that dealing effectively with political problems was as much part of a commander's brief as was winning battles.

6

Field Marshal Sir William Nicholson, 1st Baron Nicholson (1845-1918)

Paul M. Ramsey

Introduction

Reflecting on the military preparations made by the War Office for the organisation of the British Army before the First World War, Richard Burdon Haldane, the Secretary of State for War between 1905 and 1912, alluding to the work of the General Staff under General Sir William Nicholson wrote that,

> Much of what we did owe for the excellence of the Expeditionary Force, such as it was in point of size, and much of what we have since owed for the excellence of the great armies that we subsequently raised, was due to the unbroken work of the fine Administrative Staff ... I often regret that when the nation gave its thanks through Parliament to the army, the splendid contribution made by those who prepared the administrative services was not adequately recognised. But this arose from the old British tradition under which fighting and administration were not distinguished as being quite separate and yet equally essential for fighting. The public had not got into its head the reality of the process of defining the two different functions with precision, and of confiding them to different sets of officers differently trained.[1]

William Nicholson was one of the most remarkable soldiers of the late Victorian and Edwardian army. Yet, the tendency noted by Haldane to focus on command in battle at the expense of administrative control in war and peace diminishes the great development and importance of staff work in the British Army before the First World War. Through the preparation of strategic and operational plans staff officers played an essential role in preparing the military for the next conflict. As arguably the leading staff officer of his generation, Nicholson excelled throughout his military career in positions of administrative control. Although 'not by nature a

---

1 Haldane, Richard B., *Before the War* (London: Cassell and Company, 1920), p. 176.

soldier in the field', and with little command experience, Haldane thought "... Nicholson was one of the cleverest men (he) ever came across, both in quickness of mind and in capacity for expressing it."[2] In 1908 Nicholson became the second chief of the recently formed General Staff and he applied his unmatched administrative experience and great intellectual capacity with considerable effect, shaping the British Army that entered the First World War.

Nicholson's contribution to the organisation of the British Army is largely forgotten. However, his contemporaries recognised his exceptional abilities and his close colleagues relied heavily on his methodical and tireless work. General Sir Frederick Roberts and General Sir William Lockhart were the first to recognise that Nicholson was an officer of 'brilliant abilities' whose assistance contributed greatly to their own success.[3] Nicholson was one "...of the best men in the Army", noted the Conservative politician and journalist Leo Amery in his multivolume history of the South African War, with "...great experience of staff work, whose cautious critical judgment and skilled pen Roberts had long since learned to value in India."[4] The leading British military thinker of the period Professor Spenser Wilkinson wrote that "Lord Nicholson excelled his contemporaries of the Army in exactitude of knowledge and statement, in clear thinking and exposition, and in cool and level judgement....I think that if he had had the chance he would have been a great minister of war."[5] This assessment was echoed by Haldane who recalled, "I use to tell him, laughingly, that he was born to be a lawyer, and that if he had gone to the Bar he might have become Lord Chancellor. But he had a great power of grasping military principles and applying them."[6] These opinions were widely shared. Referring to Nicholson's work with the General Staff and the Staff College, and despite initial reservations about his personality, Reginald Brett, the 2nd Viscount Esher, one of the most influential political figures on military and foreign affairs, wrote in December 1909 that, "He certainly is an underrated man – and no one will ever know what a large debt of gratitude is due to him for his hard work, patience, and good sense." Esher thought he was the "... cleverest soldier he had yet seen."[7] Indeed, Nicholson dominated the War Office in the first decade of twentieth century until his retirement in 1912. According to *The Times* military correspondent Colonel Repington, his influence was so great that the efficiency of the War Office declined by half after the departure of Nicholson and his close colleague Haldane.[8] More recently, however, Nicholson's reputation has suffered with some prominent historians accepting the views of a few notorious critics.

2   Haldane, Richard B., *Richard Burdon Haldane: An Autobiography* (Garden City, N.Y.: Doubleday, Doran, 1929), p. 212.
3   See Hutchinson, H. D., *The Campaign in Tirah, 1897-1898* (London: Macmillan, 1898), p. 28 for Lockhart's on Nicholson and Roberts, F. S., *Forty-One Years in India: from Subaltern to Commander-in-Chief* (London: Macmillan, 1898), p. 521 for Roberts' comments.
4   Amery, Leo S., *The Times History of the War in South Africa, 1899-1902* (London: Sampson Low, Marston and Company, 1900), Vol. IV, p. 93 and Vol. III, p. 337.
5   Bodleian Library (hereafter Bod. Lib), Spenser Wilkinson newspaper cuttings, 2229 c.4 v.39, p. 43, article in The Times, September 15th 1918, titled 'Lord Nicholson: An Appreciation'.
6   Haldane, Richard B., *Richard Burdon Haldane: An Autobiography* (Garden City, N.Y.: Doubleday, Doran, 1929), p. 212.
7   Brett, Maurice V. (ed) *Journals and Letters of Reginald Viscount Esher, Vol. II., 1903-1910* (London: Ivor Nicholson & Watson, 1934), p. 431a; Atwood, Rodney, *Roberts*, p. 235.
8   Gooch, John, The *Plans of War: The General Staff and British Military Strategy c. 1900-1916* (London: Routledge & Kegan Paul, 1974), p. 124.

The pioneering historians of British strategic policy were unable to reach a consensus about Nicholson's importance in the administration of British defence before the First World War. Scholars like Samuel Williamson and Nicholas d'Ombrain thought the 'irascible, salty-tongued' Nicholson and his attitude towards the Admiralty created "...confusion in national policy for war."[9] Nicholson was all "...wit and words", d'Ombrain asserted, rather than "...demonstrable talent."[10] Yet, neither description gave Nicholson the credit he deserved. Providing a more balanced view of Nicholson's abilities, John Gooch showed how he was the most powerful personality in the Edwardian army and 'a formidable figure' in British defence policy.[11] However, Gooch maintained that his character was questionable, concluding that Nicholson was, "... addicted to lurid language and possessed a rich vein of caustic humour, as well as what seems in retrospect to have been a visceral loathing of the navy."[12] These assertions were restated in Nicholas A. Lambert's powerful analysis of the Royal Navy's strategic planning during Admiral Sir John Fisher's time as First Sea Lord from 1904 to 1910. Lambert argued that Nicholson "...antagonised almost everyone with whom he came into contact. Cooperation with such a man was quite impossible."[13] This was based largely on the hostile opinion of Sir John Fisher who thought 'Sir William Beelzebub' was, "... so hateful to the Admiralty." Accepting Fisher's opinion, Lambert concluded that Nicholson's contribution to the ongoing strategic debates was unimportant.[14] Although Nicholson was undoubtedly difficult, to which he fully admitted comparing himself to "...gout, which like me though not violent is very persistent", his view of the Admiralty was never so simplistic.[15]

At a serious disadvantage, Nicholson never wrote an autobiography or handed down a set of private papers, the criticisms of his more famous opponents whose priorities and plans he hindered have dominated the historical narrative. In addition to Sir John Fisher, several other prominent figures strongly disliked or were suspicious of Nicholson, including Sir John French, Sir Henry Wilson, Lord Kitchener and Sir Ian Hamilton. French, for example, who had little time for Nicholson, said he "... was born to be a damned nuisance to everyone."[16] Wilson, who

---

9   Williamson, Samuel R., *The Politics of Grand Strategy: Britain and France Prepare for War, 1904-1914* (Cambridge: Harvard University Press, 1969), p. 190; d'Ombrain, Nicholas, *War Machinery and High Policy: Defence Administration in Peacetime Britain, 1902-1914* (London: Oxford University Press, 1973), pp. 43, 100-110.
10 d'Ombrain, Nicholas, *War Machinery and High Policy: Defence Administration in Peacetime Britain, 1902-1914* (London: Oxford University Press, 1973), p. 210
11 Gooch, John, The *Plans of War: The General Staff and British Military Strategy c. 1900-1916* (London: Routledge & Kegan Paul, 1974), p. 98; Gooch, John, *The Prospect of War: Studies in British Defence Policy, 1847-1942* (London: Frank Cass, 1981), p. 108.
12 Gooch, John, '"A Particularly Anglo-Saxon Institution": The British General Staff in the Era of Two World Wars', in French, David & Holden-Reid, Brain (eds) *The British General Staff: Reform and Innovation c. 1890-1939* (London: Frank Cass, 2002), p. 197.
13 Lambert, Nicholas A., *Sir John Fisher's Naval Revolution* (Columbia, SA: University of South Carolina Press, 1999), p. 170.
14 Fisher to Esher, October 1907 and January 17 1904, in Marder, Arthur J. (ed) *Fear God and Dread Nought, The Correspondence of Admiral of the Fleet Lord Fisher of Kilverstone* (hereafter FGDN), 3 vols (Cambridge, MA: Harvard University Press, 1952-1959), ii. p. 145 and i. p. 298
15 National Archives of Scotland (hereafter NAS), John Spencer Ewart military papers, GD527/1/1/67/2, Nicholson to Ewart, 24 August 1909.
16 French to Esher, 2 June 1906, in Holmes, Richard, *The Little Field-Marshal, Sir John French* (London: Jonathan Cape, 1981), p. 111.

worked under Nicholson as commandant of the Staff College and director of military operations (D.M.O.) in the War Office, wrote that "I doubt if, in the whole time he has been C.I.G.S.(Chief of the Imperial General Staff), he has done a single thing to prepare the Army for war." Wilson's depiction of Nicholson was 'typically sweeping', as were most of his comments about his time at the War Office.[17] Kitchener and Hamilton were similarly ambiguous in their criticisms and cited issues including interference, promotion, jealousy and mischief-making.[18] Although Nicholson disliked Kitchener, he was oblivious to Hamilton's paranoid enmity. Nicholson had been friends with Hamilton since their time working under Lord Roberts in India. Taking their lead from French, Wilson, Kitchener and Hamilton, historians have characterised Nicholson as a distinguished but opinionated reactionary. One scholar for example, noted "...the folly of placing Fisher and Nicholson, Kitchener and Henry Wilson, or Nicholson and French, side by side at the C.I.D. (Committee of Imperial Defence) [This] ought to have been obvious, one would think."[19] However, as another more recent historian pointed out, Nicholson and French appear to have worked well together, despite French's antipathy.[20] Indeed, there is a good deal of evidence to show that Nicholson worked well with most colleagues, including those from the Admiralty, politicians and the General Staff officers in the War Office.

Unlike most of the aforementioned contemporaries, Nicholson was uninterested in acclaim and largely uninterested in exhibition. As Spenser Wilkinson remarked, "He always made a point, in forwarding work prepared by a subordinate, of calling attention to the fact that it was the subordinate's work and to see that its author received credit for it."[21] Moreover, Nicholson operated an efficient collaborative War Office and the accusations of interference and mischief-making are at odds with this evidence. The challenges faced by Nicholson's rivals were in fact intellectual, since their arguments and analysis needed to be strong enough to withstand his repeated incisive examinations. According to Major-General Sir George K. Scott-Moncrieff, who served at the War Office with Nicholson, "Men might fear him, or dislike him, but all were imbued with the respect that is commanded by capacity, decision and impartiality."[22] Indeed, Nicholson was feared and disliked by those officers for whom the questioning intellectual capacity he commanded caused difficulties. Furthermore, intellectual authority after 1900 was increasingly essential to the exercise of command and administrative control in the War Office. The coherence of the Army's strategic plans before 1914 cannot be understood in isolation from the direction provided to the General Staff's planning process by the C.I.G.S. Wilson's claim that Nicholson had done nothing to prepare the Army for war is absurd. By taking a notoriously

---

17 Jeffrey, Keith, *Field Marshal Sir Henry Wilson: A Political Soldier* (New York: Oxford University Press, 2008), p. 102.
18 For an example of this in practice see Lee, John, *A Soldier's Life: General Sir Ian Hamilton, 1853-1947* (London: Macmillan, 2000), p. 232 and Bond, Brian, *The Victorian Army and the Staff College, 1854-1914* (London: Eyre Methuen, 1972), p. 300.
19 d'Ombrain, *War Machinery and High Policy*, p. 122 n. 16
20 Beckett, Ian, '"Selection by Disparagement": Lord Esher, the General Staff and the Politics of Command, 1904-1914', in French, David & Holden-Reid, Brain (eds) *The British General Staff: Reform and Innovation c. 1890-1939* (London: Frank Cass, 2002), p. 55.
21 Bod. Lib, Wilkinson cuttings, 2229 c.4 v.39, p. 43, *The Times*, September 15th 1918, 'Lord Nicholson: An Appreciation'.
22 Scott-Moncrieff, G. K., 'Memoir: Field Marshal Lord Nicholson, G.C.B., Colonel Commandant, R.E.', *The Royal Engineers Journal*, 28:6 (December 1918), p. 247.

pejorative group of officers at their word, historians have overstated the extent to which Nicholson obstructed the development of British strategy, underestimating his intellectual and administrative contribution to the organisation of British defence policy. Comparable to Fisher at the Admiralty, Nicholson was the central figure in the evolution of War Office planning between 1901 and 1912.

Building on his thirty years of experience in field, administrative and staff positions in India and South Africa, Nicholson's work in several important positions in the W.O., including as chief of the Imperial General Staff, shaped the British Army that entered the First World War. It is impossible to fully understand the reorganisation of the British Army or the development of British strategy before the First World War without studying Nicholson's career. Along with Fisher and Esher, Nicholson was at the centre of events from 1900 to 1914. As the director-general of mobilisation and military intelligence, Nicholson established a proto-staff system that began the process of studying and developing British operational and strategic plans. The decision of the 'infamous' Esher Committee to dismiss Nicholson in 1904 in an unceremonious manner had wide ranging and lasting effects for the development of British strategy.

With the British Army rudderless, Nicholson was brought back into the War Office and appointed quartermaster-general of the forces (Q.M.G.) in 1905 to guide the Army Council. Nicholson was de facto chief of the General Staff (C.G.S.), which he was appointed officially in 1908. During this time Nicholson was central in organising and establishing the General Staff on a functioning basis as well as making key contributions to the debates about invasion and Haldane's territorial scheme. Nicholson pushed for Imperial integration, which he increasingly achieved through shrewd accommodation of Dominion partners at numerous Imperial conferences. Nicholson set the agenda for British strategy as a member of the important 1909 invasion sub-committee and the well-known August 1911 meeting of the Committee of Imperial Defence (C.I.D.). Nicholson was a model staff officer and as C.I.G.S. became the exemplar head of the Army. In preparing to fight a modern conventional war, the W.O. required more officers and generals like Nicholson and less like the Victorian warrior heroes Roberts, Wolseley or Gordon. Nicholson's appointment as C.I.G.S. represented a break with those who had previously been head of the Army and largely built their reputations through success in command. Nicholson was undoubtedly one of the most intellectually gifted soldiers ever to be head of the British Army and he demonstrated his ability through success in administrative control. Nicholson's leadership of the W.O. before the First World War deserves more attention than it has hitherto received.

Early Life and Career

The youngest son of a Yorkshire landowner, William Gustavus Nicholson, 1st Baron Nicholson, was born on 2 March 1845 at Mansion House, Roundhay Park, Leeds. Nicholson attended Leeds Grammar School, where he received a classical education. Trained in Latin and well-rehearsed in classical texts, he was always ready with a quotation from Ovid or Vergil. An accomplished writer, with a talent for incisive language, his intuitive and decisive expressions could be damning, but he was no humourless pedant.[23] Nicholson enjoyed practical jokes and his demeanour with friends sometimes resembled that of an "...innocent boy and sometimes that of a clown."[24] Yet, Nicholson typically avoided intimate comradeship and developed a detachment from subordinates, giving him a capacity for clear decision-making.[25] Most officers when submitting a report to 'Roberts' golden pen' learned to expect 'a cynical note from [their] pen-loving Chief'.[26] Nevertheless, his education and abilities were suited to a military career.

From 1863 to 1865 Nicholson studied at the Royal Military Academy, Woolwich, where he passed out first in his term and was awarded the Pollock medal. Nicholson was commissioned into the Royal Engineers in March 1865 and he spent the next three years at Chatham, completing the course in military engineering and the usual regimental service. In March 1868 he was sent to the West Indies and served in Barbados until 1871, when his three-year tour ended and he returned to duty at home. In the same year he married Victoria, with whom he had a long and supportive marriage, but no children. Victoria was a keen golfer and Nicholson would travel with her to matches, but he

Field Marshal William Nicholson.

---

23 Moreman, T. R., 'Nicholson, William Gustavus, Baron Nicholson (1845-1918)', *Oxford Dictionary of National Biography* (hereafter DNB), Oxford University Press (2004); Heathcote, T. A., *The British Field Marshals, 1763-1997: A Biographical Dictionary* (South Yorkshire: Leo Cooper, 1999); Wilkinson, S., 'Lord Nicholson: An Appreciation', article in *The Times* (September 15 1918); Scott-Moncrieff, G. K., 'Memoir: Field Marshal Lord Nicholson, G.C.B., Colonel Commandant, R.E.', *The Royal Engineers Journal*, 28:6 (December 1918), pp. 237-249; These are the best sources for Nicholson's life and career. The latter work provides the most comprehensive overview upon which most other existing accounts are based.
24 Wilkinson, H. Spenser, *Thirty-Five Years, 1874-1909* (London: Constable, 1933), p. 153.
25 Scott-Moncrieff, G. K., 'Memoir: Field Marshal Lord Nicholson, G.C.B., Colonel Commandant, R.E.', *The Royal Engineers Journal*, 28:6 (December 1918), p. 249.
26 Atwood, Rodney, *The Life of Field Marshal Lord Roberts* (London: Bloomsbury, 2015), p. 174; Smith-Dorien, H. L., *Memories of Forty-Eight Years' Service* (New York, N.Y.: Dutton, 1925), p. 358.

never played himself. He thought St. Andrews offered little to the non-golfer and he lamented during his time at Rawalpindi that while "My wife is flourishing and plays golf assiduously" he was unable to find many new friends. During periods when Victoria was absent Nicholson found mixing more difficult and life 'somewhat dull' and he occupied himself with work.

Soon after marrying Victoria, Nicholson volunteered for service in India, beginning in October 1871. He worked first in the Public Works Department at Hyderabad and then as assistant engineer in the Punjab Irrigation Branch. In 1873 he transferred to the Military Works Department and was employed first at Rawalpindi and then at Peshawar on the usual barrack and road work. At Peshawar Nicholson worked on a major waterworks project, which improved greatly the local sanitary conditions. Employed around Peshawar in the foothills area near the Bara River, he became familiar with the tribes and conditions of the North West Frontier of India. Although his career remained unremarkable and his advancement was slow, only being promoted Captain on 16 March 1878, his experience while employed on frontier military works would soon prove invaluable.[27]

Afghanistan, Second Afghan War, 1878-80

Afghanistan in the 1860s was divided by revolts, coups and civil war. When Amir Sher Ali finally secured control of Afghanistan in 1869, he brought about a period of internal stability. During the 1870s Sher Ali obsessed increasingly about his own independence and the threat from the encroachment of Russia and Britain to Afghanistan's borders. British policy was to prevent a Russian annexation of Afghanistan. Moreover, Britain secured a border agreement with Russia in 1873, providing Afghanistan with a guarantee of territorial integrity. Yet, Sher Ali and the Government of India remained concerned as Russian expansion continued unabated, with Russia annexing the entire region north of Afghanistan by 1876. In response Britain was keen to offer support to Kabul. However, Sher Ali's strategy was to remain nonaligned until attacked, which strained Anglo-Afghan relations. Sher Ali accepted British arms, but refused to accept any offer that restricted his ability to act independently, refusing money and a military mission. Given this, the arrival of a Russian delegation in Kabul in 1878 appeared to the Government of India to signal a hostile intent and the Viceroy of India, Lord Lytton, demanded the establishment of a permanent British mission in Afghanistan. When Sher Ali refused, the Government of India, unable to accept a Russo-Afghan alignment, decided on intervention.[28]

---

27 Scott-Moncrieff, G. K., 'Memoir: Field Marshal Lord Nicholson, G.C.B., Colonel Commandant, R.E.', *The Royal Engineers Journal*, 28:6 (December 1918), pp. 238-239: provides the only account of Nicholson's early years in India and is largely the source for the details covering his early years in this narrative; The details of Nicholson's relationship with his wife are taken from letters to his friend Spenser Wilkinson, but also Lord Roberts. For the information presented here see: National Army Museum (hereafter NAM), Spenser Wilkinson Papers, OPT 13/13/35, Nicholson to Wilkinson, 10 October 1895; 13/13/40, Nicholson to Wilkinson, from Rawalpindi, 15 February 1897; 13/13/49, Nicholson to Wilkinson, 3 March 1901; See also for example, NAM, Lord Roberts Papers, 71-01-23-87, R52/43, Nicholson to Roberts, 10 January 1897.

28 Johnson, Rob, *The Afghan Way of War: How and Why They Fight* (Oxford: Oxford University Press, 2012), pp. 100-101; Robson, Brian, *The Road to Kabul: The Second Afghan War 1878-1881* (London: Arms & Armour, 1986), pp. 11-54; MacGregor, Charles Metcalfe, *The Second Afghan War: Office Account* (London: J. Murray, 1908), pp. 1-15.

For Nicholson the outbreak of the Second Afghan War was an overdue opportunity to show his abilities and move his career forward. During the campaigns in Afghanistan Nicholson established a reputation as a skilled engineering officer and he distinguished himself in several engagements. However, the decisive moment in his early military career came during the defence of the isolated Lataband Pass in December 1879. He assisted the commanding officer of the small garrison by undertaking the duties of a chief of staff, providing cool and intelligent support in the successful defence of the mountain pass. Nicholson's performance in this capacity did not go unnoticed and, "From then onwards he became more and more a staff officer", as a subaltern during the defence later remarked.[29] The Second Afghan War not only established Nicholson's reputation as an accomplished field engineer, but demonstrated his ability to be an effective staff officer.

The British advanced on three lines into Afghanistan in the autumn of 1878. Two field forces moved on Kabul, one on the northern route via the Khyber Pass and one on the central route via the Kurram Valley. Further south a third field force advanced through the Bolan Pass via Quetta towards Kandahar. Nicholson served as a field engineer in the 2nd (Quetta) Division under Major-General Michael Biddulph, which together with the 1st (Multan) Division formed the Southern Afghanistan Field Force, commanded by Lieutenant-General Donald Stewart. The main British thrust into Afghanistan, General Stewart's march through Baluchi territory was unopposed by the local tribes. However, the route to Kandahar from Multan via Quetta and through the Bolan and Khojak passes was difficult, as the geography presented serious logistical and engineering challenges.[30] Yet, the British had made no proper provision at Multan for an advance into Afghanistan and the southern force began the campaign deficient in transport and many necessary supplies, which needed to be hurriedly arranged. On 13 October 1878 General Biddulph set out for Quetta, instructing Nicholson to remain behind and organise an engineers' park, with orders to follow on as soon as possible. Nicholson completed the task with 'remarkable celerity' and when he joined Biddulph in Quetta in November, he brought with him a field mule train loaded with entrenching tools, implements for blasting, and large quantities of hauling ropes and cordage.[31] Biddulph acknowledged the engineering difficulties the march presented, notifying his officers of the need to devote themselves to the works "... pointed out by the Engineer Officers."[32] The materials transported by the engineers' field park proved invaluable to the successful advance on Kandahar.

---

29 Scott-Moncrieff, G. K., 'Memoir: Field Marshal Lord Nicholson, G.C.B., Colonel Commandant, R.E.', *The Royal Engineers Journal*, 28:6 (December 1918), p. 241.
30 MacGregor, Charles Metcalfe, *The Second Afghan War: Office Account* (London: J. Murray, 1908), pp. 143-174; Johnson, Rob, *The Afghan Way of War: How and Why They Fight* (Oxford: Oxford University Press, 2012), p. 113; Hanna, Henry B., *The Second Afghan War, 1878-79-80: its causes, its conduct and its consequences*, three volumes (Westminster: Constable and Co., 1899-1910), ii. p. 326.
31 Biddulph, Michael, *The March from the Idus to the Helmund and Back, 1878, 1879* (London: R.U.S.I., 1880), pp. 19-20; Hanna, Henry B., *The Second Afghan War, 1878-79-80: its causes, its conduct and its consequences*, three volumes (Westminster: Constable and Co., 1899-1910), i. p. 302, especially fn. 1.
32 Biddulph, Michael, *The March from the Idus to the Helmund and Back, 1878, 1879* (London: R.U.S.I., 1880), p. 26.

During the march Nicholson worked building roads and in securing the water supply for the main columns.[33] On 12 December the 2nd Division commanded by Biddulph reached the Khojak Pass and he found the tracks were absolutely impracticable for laden camels and wheeled artillery. It was necessary to improve the road to the top of the pass and in the interim secure an improved water supply for the men and the transport animals. This was achieved by digging pools into the gorge, allowing the springs to trickle down to the side of the track. The water supply secured, Lieutenant-Colonel W. Hichens, the commanding officer of the Royal Engineers, was assisted by "Nicholson and his field park, [and] opened operations on the road-making of the pass" on 13 December. Remarkably, by the evening of 14 December the road was ready for the passage of infantry and cavalry and mountain guns and "… 450 baggage camels were marched over" with no problems. Yet, Colonel Hichens informed Biddulph that it would take a further two weeks to complete a road fit for the descent of the wheeled artillery. Instead, as Biddulph explained, they decided, "…to improve a tolerably straight gully into a ramp, and to let the guns down by ropes, which Captain Nicholson had brought with him." This 'slide' was completed on 18 December and on the next day the guns were lowered successfully, ready to continue to Kandahar.[34] The march over the Khojak Pass was the most difficult manoeuvre of the expedition. Nicholson and his engineers' field park made an important contribution to its success, which was recognised by his being mentioned in despatches.

On 8 January 1879 Nicholson entered Kandahar with the advanced troops of the Southern Afghanistan Field Force, after dispersing a small force of Afghan cavalry on a ridge outside the city. The garrison was established at Kandahar, but the larger force needed to reduce their consumption of local supplies. On 15 January General Stewart marched his 1st Division east to Qalat and on the next day 16 January Nicholson with the 2nd Division under General Biddulph set out for the Helmand River. The object was to open up new sources of supply, but Biddulph's "… instructions were to avoid all enterprises which might cause irritation to the inhabitants." It is likely the disinclined locals on realising this withheld food and fodder and the reconnaissance achieved little. The 2nd Division maintained its position on the Helmand until 23 February before returning to Kandahar, where it arrived on 1 March to be disbanded.[35] In February 1879 Sher Ali died in the north of Afghanistan after a severe illness. The Amir's strategy to obtain Russian support failed and the Afghan army was completely ineffective.

With their strategic objectives achieved the British resolved to withdraw their forces from Afghanistan before the start of the extreme Afghan summer.[36] The Government of India ordered General Biddulph to return to Multan with a reduced force via the unknown Tal-Chotiali route, due east from Kandahar into the Derajat region. Nicholson served as the field engineer on the headquarter staff for the Chotiali Field Force, the staff leaving Kandahar on 7 March. It was instructed to examine the route carefully, with a view to considerations for a military

---

33 Scott-Moncrieff, G. K., 'Memoir: Field Marshal Lord Nicholson, G.C.B., Colonel Commandant, R.E.', *The Royal Engineers Journal*, 28:6 (December 1918), p. 239.
34 Biddulph, Michael, *The March from the Idus to the Helmund and Back, 1878, 1879* (London: R.U.S.I., 1880), pp. 27-29.
35 Biddulph, Michael, *The March from the Idus to the Helmund and Back, 1878, 1879* (London: R.U.S.I., 1880), pp. 34-39, quote on p. 37; Johnson, Rob, *The Afghan Way of War: How and Why They Fight* (Oxford: Oxford University Press, 2012), p. 113.
36 Johnson, Rob, *The Afghan Way of War: How and Why They Fight* (Oxford: Oxford University Press, 2012), p. 102 and 114: see for an excellent discussion of the conflict from an Afghan perspective.

post, a possible military road and railway. Despite the advanced column of the force being attacked by up to 2000 men at Baghao, a punishing defeat of the tribesmen discouraged any further hostilities. Notwithstanding many difficulties, including 105-degree heat, according to Biddulph the men reached the Indus in better condition than when they started out from Kandahar. The success of the march was due in part 'to the energy and ability' of Nicholson. The march was completed in late April 1879 and Nicholson returned to duty at Simla, believing the Afghan War was over.[37]

In May 1879 the son of Sher Ali and the new Amir, Yakub Khan, signed the Treaty of Gandamack. Afghanistan was required to host a British Residency in Kabul and Major Sir Louis Cavagnari was selected as envoy by the Viceroy, Lord Lytton. However, Yakub Khan's control of Afghanistan was fragile. On 3 September 1879 disgruntled unpaid soldiers from Herat mutinied and attacked the Residency in Kabul. Major Cavagnari and his men were overrun, murdered and dismembered.[38] With hostilities renewed General Roberts was ordered to take command of the troops still occupying the Kurram Valley, move over the Shutargardan Pass and advance on Kabul. Nicholson was appointed field engineer on the Staff of the newly formed Kabul Field Force, which reached the Shutargardan on 27 September 1879.[39] However, Roberts' actions were limited by two considerations: firstly, the route via the Shutargardan would be closed by snow by the end of October or early November, and secondly, the force was severely deficient in transport. As Nicholson later recalled, "… the transport readily available in India was nearly exhausted during the first phase of the Afghan War' and this as Roberts explained presented difficulties that were 'greater than [he] ever … experienced in any former campaign."[40] The denuded transport provisions were unable to carry the supplies for the entire Field Force and it required Roberts to split his 6600 men into two parts. On 1 October Roberts moved with two thirds of the Force across the Shutargardan Pass, but its advance was blocked only 11 miles from Kabul at Charasiab on 5 October by a force of about 8,000 to 10,000 Afghans. The next day at the Battle of Charasiab Roberts' Force of about 4,000 men attacked and easily defeated the Afghan force. With the opposition dispersed Roberts occupied Kabul on 8 October and Yakub Khan abdicated his throne on 12 October.[41]

Although Roberts' risky advance with a weakened force succeeded, the smaller force that remained garrisoning the Shutargardan under Colonel G. N. Money to protect the line of communications and the movement of provisions, were left exposed to repeated attack by

---

37 Biddulph, Michael, *The March from the Idus to the Helmund and Back, 1878, 1879* (London: R.U.S.I., 1880), pp. 38, 40-46 and 49, for the march of the Chotiali Field Force; Scott-Moncrieff, G. K., 'Memoir: Field Marshal Lord Nicholson, G.C.B., Colonel Commandant, R.E.', *The Royal Engineers Journal*, 28:6 (December 1918), p. 239.

38 MacGregor, Charles Metcalfe, *The Second Afghan War: Office Account* (London: J. Murray, 1908), pp. 175-184 and 189-91; Johnson, Rob, *The Afghan Way of War: How and Why They Fight* (Oxford: Oxford University Press, 2012), pp. 114-115.

39 MacGregor, Charles Metcalfe, *The Second Afghan War: Office Account* (London: J. Murray, 1908), pp. 194-210; Scott-Moncrieff, G. K., 'Memoir: Field Marshal Lord Nicholson, G.C.B., Colonel Commandant, R.E.', *The Royal Engineers Journal*, 28:6 (December 1918), p. 240.

40 NAM, Wilkinson Papers, OPT 13/13/14, Nicholson to Wilkinson, 10 September 1893; MacGregor, Charles Metcalfe, *The Second Afghan War: Office Account* (London: J. Murray, 1908), pp. 195, 197, 212.

41 Hanna, Henry B., *The Second Afghan War, 1878-79-80: its causes, its conduct and its consequences*, three volumes (Westminster: Constable and Co., 1899-1910), iii. pp. 62-79; MacGregor, Charles Metcalfe, *The Second Afghan War: Office Account* (London: J. Murray, 1908), pp. 213-222.

hostile local tribesmen. On 14 October intelligence suggested that tribesmen were gathering in increasing strength and Colonel Money decided to withdraw the units stationed at outlying posts. However, Money soon learned that a relief force was necessary to aid a surrounded outpost, an action that required, "... every staff-officer ... to take his place in the fighting line", including for the first time in a major engagement, Captain Nicholson.[42] Money was able to disperse the tribesmen after intense fighting and return his entire force intact to the entrenched Shutargardan camp. The following day a strongly reinforced enemy occupied the ground overlooking the British position and Money "...order[ed] Captain Nicholson to see to the improvement of the defences and the laying of wire entanglements at their weakest points" to check any rush.[43] The defence of the Shutargardan camp was maintained until the arrival of a relief force under Brigadier-General Hugh Gough, whose approach was enough to scatter the enemy force before entering the camp in a violent snowstorm on 20 October. On 29 October the combined force abandoned the Shutargardan and marched unopposed to Kabul, where it arrived on 4 November. Roberts' united Kabul Field Force was left cut off from India and isolated in a hostile and resentful Afghanistan.[44]

The success of the expedition now relied on Roberts securing the Field Force's position in Kabul and the line of communications to India via the Khyber Pass route. On 1 November the Field Force moved into the Sherpur Cantonment on the edge of Kabul, "...which the Engineers had prepared for winter quarters", and Nicholson, with his reputation enhanced during the defence of the Shutargardan, was appointed by Roberts to superintend the construction of the road and telegraph line 20 miles on the Khyber route from Kabul to the Lataband Pass. To secure the Khyber route small posts were established at the Lataband Pass and at Butkhak, 11 miles from Kabul. The remainder of the road via the Khyber line was complete as far as Gandamak and the 50 miles from here until the Lataband Pass was to be completed by the Khyber column as it advanced under Brigadier-General Charles Gough.[45] Nicholson set about working on the two most challenging points on the route, the mile wide Logar swamp across the Logar river from Kabul and the difficult mountain pass of Lataband. Through the effective organisation of labour and supplies Nicholson quickly completed the drainage of the Logar swamp, gathered the materials for the construction of the numerous bridges and "...the winding tracks up the pass

---

42   Hanna, Henry B., *The Second Afghan War, 1878-79-80: its causes, its conduct and its consequences*, three volumes (Westminster: Constable and Co., 1899-1910), iii. pp. 106-108, see fn. 2, p. 108; Hensman, Howard, *The Afghan War of 1879-80* (London: W. H. Allen & Co., 1882), p. 96.
43   Hanna, Henry B., *The Second Afghan War, 1878-79-80: Its causes, its conduct and its consequences*, three volumes (Westminster: Constable and Co., 1899-1910), iii. pp. 109-110; Hensman, Howard, *The Afghan War of 1879-80* (London: W. H. Allen & Co., 1882), p. 98.
44   MacGregor, Charles Metcalfe, *The Second Afghan War: Office Account* (London: J. Murray, 1908), pp. 291-297, especially p. 296; Hanna, Henry B., *The Second Afghan War, 1878-79-80: its causes, its conduct and its consequences*, three volumes (Westminster: Constable and Co., 1899-1910), iii. pp. 110-112.
45   Roberts, Frederick S., *Forty-One Years in India: From Subaltern to Commander-in-Chief*, two volumes (London: Richard Bentley and Son, 1897), ii. pp. 253-254; Hanna, Henry B., *The Second Afghan War, 1878-79-80: its causes, its conduct and its consequences*, three volumes (Westminster: Constable and Co., 1899-1910), iii. pp. 132-135, see fn. 1, p. 134 for comment on Nicholson's appointment; Scott-Moncrieff, G. K., 'Memoir: Field Marshal Lord Nicholson, G.C.B., Colonel Commandant, R.E.', *The Royal Engineers Journal*, 28:6 (December 1918), p. 240.

were rapidly assuming shape."[46] Nicholson's earlier experience in road-making over the Khojak Pass to Kandahar proved invaluable to the work on the Lataband Pass. Despite the regular "... cutting [of] the telegraph-wires", which was as Roberts joked, "... a favourite amusement of the tribesmen", telegraphic communication with India was restored on 19 November, the road was progressing well and everything went smoothly for the rest of the month.[47]

In early December however tensions increased around Kabul as a reconstituted force of Afghan troops approached the city. On 11 December Roberts dispatched troops to disperse the Afghan force, but after several days of fighting the British re-entered the Sherpur Cantonment on 14 December. Inspired by an appeal for a holy war against the occupation local Kabulis and Afghan tribesmen assembled to join the Afghan force, which now occupied Kabul, cut the telegraph wire and besieged Roberts' force in Sherpur. Roberts had recalled the smaller posts on the line of communication including Butkhak to Kabul, but the small garrison on the Lataband under Colonel John Hudson was ordered to hold its position and await the arrival of a relief force under Brigadier-General Charles Gough. As Roberts explained, "... Lataband was the most important link in the chain of communication between Kabul" and India and it had sufficient supplies to last until Charles Gough's arrival.[48] When the serious fighting began around Kabul, Nicholson anticipated Roberts decision and ordered "... his subaltern at Butkhak to load up all his transport animals and send them at once to Lataband, under strong escort." Despite the addition of extra supplies, the post was provisioned only up to 23 December.

During this period Colonel Hudson relied heavily on Nicholson who was according to one fellow officer "... indefatigable also in the defence arrangements, and indeed in all matters connected with the safety and well-being of the garrison, and a sufficiently powerful counter-offensive against the enemy." The latter happened on 16 December when 'a furious attempt' was made against the post by 800 to 1,000 Afghans, who "...were dispersed with considerable loss, and not a single casualty occurred on the British side."[49] Nicholson's cool and intelligent support was vital to Hudson in the successful defence of the Lataband post, where Gough's relieving force arrived on 22 December. On 23 December the large Afghan force occupying Kabul attacked the Sherpur Cantonment and suffered heavy casualties before disbanding. The next day Hudson and Gough's combined force marched into Sherpur without opposition. Roberts re-imposed order in Kabul and in early 1880 put Nicholson to work building more permanent defences. Meanwhile the Kabul to Lataband road was completed "...and was the subject of a

---

46 Scott-Moncrieff, G. K., 'Memoir: Field Marshal Lord Nicholson, G.C.B., Colonel Commandant, R.E.', *The Royal Engineers Journal*, 28:6 (December 1918), pp. 240-241.
47 Roberts, Frederick S., *Forty-One Years in India: From Subaltern to Commander-in-Chief*, two volumes (London: Richard Bentley and Son, 1897), ii. pp. 257-258; Hanna, Henry B., *The Second Afghan War, 1878-79-80: its causes, its conduct and its consequences*, three volumes (Westminster: Constable and Co., 1899-1910), iii. p. 134.
48 Roberts, Frederick S., *Forty-One Years in India: From Subaltern to Commander-in-Chief*, two vols. (London: Richard Bentley and Son, 1897), ii. pp. 282-294, p. 287 for Roberts quote.
49 Scott-Moncrieff, G. K., 'Memoir: Field Marshal Lord Nicholson, G.C.B., Colonel Commandant, R.E.', *The Royal Engineers Journal*, 28:6 (December 1918), p. 241; MacGregor, Charles Metcalfe, *The Second Afghan War: Office Account* (London: J. Murray, 1908), pp. 279-280.

special report from [Roberts], eliciting from the Commander-in-Chief a letter of thanks to Nicholson", whose exceptional conduct had not gone unnoticed.[50]

By the summer of 1880 the British recognised Abdur Rahman, a nephew of Sher Ali, as Amir and were preparing to withdraw from Afghanistan. However, in early July Ayub Khan, a brother of the recently dethroned Yakub Khan and a formidable rival to Abdur Rahman, was appointed the leader of a large force marching from Herat on Kandahar. Major-General James M. Primrose despatched a small 2,500 strong force to the Helmand River under Brigadier-General George S. R. Burrows to oppose Ayub Khan's advance. On 27 July Burrows' vastly outnumbered brigade was isolated in the open at Maiwand and defeated in a shockingly bloody engagement with almost half of his force, 1,109 men killed, missing or wounded.[51] On the following day the news of the disaster at Maiwand was telegraphed from Kandahar to Simla and Kabul where, as Roberts described, it was received with "...a certain feeling of uneasiness" and a great anxiety.[52] Roberts resolved to march on the now besieged Kandahar and was given 'carte-blanche' to select the best available troops and transport for the relief column. Nicholson was appointed the field engineer of the 2nd Infantry Brigade in the 10,000 strong Kabul to Kandahar Field Force, which after more than a week of meticulous preparation on 9 August began the march that made Roberts' reputation.[53]

The march covered over three hundred miles at a relentless pace, but aside from fighting against the climatic conditions of an Afghan summer and the logistical challenges over difficult ground, Roberts encountered little opposition and entered Kandahar on the morning of 31 August. The following morning on 1 September Roberts attacked Ayub Khan's larger force just north of the city.[54] During the battle Nicholson was engaged in some of the most intense fighting and his prior knowledge of the ground was invaluable for the 2nd Brigade, which "...had been threading its way through the lanes and walled enclosures which lay in their line of attack ... the enemy being well protected by the high mud walls", reminiscent of the British experience of the Afghan conflict in the 21st Century; "The loss suffered clearing these enclosures was

---

50   Scott-Moncrieff, G. K., 'Memoir: Field Marshal Lord Nicholson, G.C.B., Colonel Commandant, R.E.', *The Royal Engineers Journal*, 28:6 (December 1918), p. 241, including on Roberts letter of thanks to Nicholson; MacGregor, Charles Metcalfe, *The Second Afghan War: Office Account* (London: J. Murray, 1908), pp. 321-325; Hensman, Howard, *The Afghan War of 1879-80* (London: W. H. Allen & Co., 1882), p. 269; Johnson, Rob, *The Afghan Way of War: How and Why They Fight* (Oxford: Oxford University Press, 2012), pp. 124-125.
51   Roberts, Frederick S., *Forty-One Years in India: From Subaltern to Commander-in-Chief*, two volumes (London: Richard Bentley and Son, 1897), ii. pp. 331-335; Johnson, Rob, *The Afghan Way of War: How and Why They Fight* (Oxford: Oxford University Press, 2012), pp. 126-135.
52   Hanna, Henry B., *The Second Afghan War, 1878-79-80: its causes, its conduct and its consequences*, three volumes (Westminster: Constable and Co., 1899-1910), iii. p. 463, see fn. 1 for the telegram dated 28 July 1880 from Kandahar informing Simla of Burrows' defeat; Roberts, Frederick S., *Forty-One Years in India: From Subaltern to Commander-in-Chief*, two volumes (London: Richard Bentley and Son, 1897), ii. p. 336 for Roberts' assessment.
53   Roberts, Frederick S., *Forty-One Years in India: From Subaltern to Commander-in-Chief*, two volumes (London: Richard Bentley and Son, 1897), ii. pp. 339, 341, 346; Hanna, Henry B., *The Second Afghan War, 1878-79-80: its causes, its conduct and its consequences*, three volumes (Westminster: Constable and Co., 1899-1910), iii. pp. 466, 469, 472.
54   Roberts, Frederick S., *Forty-One Years in India: From Subaltern to Commander-in-Chief*, two volumes (London: Richard Bentley and Son, 1897), ii. pp. 347-362

necessarily severe." Despite this stubborn resistance the Afghan force was quickly routed and Roberts' victory effectively ended the War in Afghanistan.[55] Yet, that the battle was fought and won seemed hardly to matter, as Roberts' march from Kabul to Kandahar was glorified in the contemporary press and celebrated by the British public.[56] In a speech at a dinner to commemorate the Kabul to Kandahar march 34 years later Nicholson recalled that

> Many of the daily marches covered a good many miles, but so excellent were the arrangements and so perfect was the organization that we found we had reached our next camping ground almost before we had time to realize how far it was from the last one. Everything worked without a hitch. There was no confusion and no friction. In fact, so far as my humble experience goes, I have never seen any other movements of troops on a considerable scale so smoothly and efficiently conducted.[57]

While Roberts was pleased to be feted, he was also disappointed that his "...difficult, more dangerous" operations in the War were overlooked.[58]

Most of Roberts' force soon left Kandahar for India and Nicholson took a period of short leave before he returned to duty at Simla. Nicholson was awarded a brevet majority for his services in Afghanistan and as the politician John Morley later remarked, he was forever "... full of Afghan experiences."[59] For Nicholson, the Second Afghan War was the most exciting and fulfilling period of his life. As he explained,

> ... we had then been trained for nearly two years in the best of all schools, that of field service, which is so greatly superior to any sort of peace training. We had learnt our own merits and shortcomings, our angularities had been rubbed down, the square men had got fitted into the square holes, and the the round men into the round holes.[60]

The 'school of field service' not only confirmed Nicholson's ability as an accomplished and resourceful field engineer, but importantly, established his reputation as a knowledgeable and effective staff officer. Indeed, his capacity for staff work was noticed by Roberts and Nicholson would soon be employed in several permanent staff positions.

---

55 MacGregor, Charles Metcalfe, *The Second Afghan War: War Office Account* (London: J. Murray, 1908), pp. 575-579, see p. 575 for the quoted description of the fighting.
56 Johnson, Rob, *The Afghan Way of War: How and Why They Fight* (Oxford: Oxford University Press, 2012), p. 131; Beckett, Ian F. W., *The Victorians at War* (London: Hambledon & London, 2003), pp. 45-52 for a chapter detailing the broader dynamics of Roberts' march from Kabul to Kandahar.
57 NAM, Lord Roberts Papers, 71-01-23-87, R52/135, William Nicholson's speech to the Kabul to Kandahar March Dinner, 9 June 1914.
58 Roberts, Frederick S., *Forty-One Years in India: From Subaltern to Commander-in-Chief*, two volumes (London: Richard Bentley and Son, 1897), ii. p. 377.
59 Morley, John, *Recollections*, two volumes (New York: The Macmillan Company, 1917), ii. p. 200
60 NAM, Lord Roberts Papers, 71-01-23-87, R52/135, William Nicholson's speech to the Kabul to Kandahar March Dinner, 9 June 1914.

Egypt, Egyptian Campaign, 1882 and Burma, Third Burmese War, 1886-87

In the 1880s Nicholson was summoned only twice to active field service, taking part in two short operations, first in the Egyptian campaign of 1882 and then in 1886 in the Third Burmese War. Nicholson enhanced his burgeoning reputation in the former as an energetic and resourceful field engineer and in the latter as the leading member of Roberts' Headquarter Staff. The Egyptian campaign began in the summer of 1882 when the British Government decided to send an expedition commanded by General Sir Garnet Wolseley to suppress a nationalist revolt led by Arabi Pasha, a Colonel in the Egyptian army, against the Khedive of Egypt. An Indian force under the command of Major-General Sir Herbert T. Macpherson was ordered from India. Commanding the Royal Engineers of the Indian Contingent was Colonel James 'Buster' Browne, with Nicholson appointed his chief field engineer. Sailing from Bombay on 9 August, Macpherson's force reached the town of Suez, at the southern end of the Suez Canal, on the evening of 20 August. Over the next two days the Indian Contingent secured control of and repaired the local railway line and fresh-water canal and moved north to Ismailia, at the centre of the Suez Canal, where the main British force had landed. Nicholson was put to work on road and canal repairs, and on making additional railway lines, in preparing for the concentration of the whole army at Qassasin, where the last troops arrived on 12 September.[61]

In the early hours of 13 September Wolseley's force attacked Arabi's army at Tell al-Kebir, advancing on the Egyptian forces directly through the desert north of the canal. Macpherson's Indian Contingent however, moved on the south side of the canal, the attached Naval Brigade marching on the northern bank, with the connection between them being maintained by 'some pontoons', under the charge of Browne, Nicholson and the Royal Engineers. Making a flanking movement on the left of Wolseley's force, the Indian Contingent cleared the entrenchments on the south bank and blocked the retreat of Arabi's defeated troops, who were trying to enter the village of Tell al-Kebir across the bridge from the northern side of the canal. Macpherson's brigade then marched on the important railway junction at Zagazig to keep the Egyptian forces dispersed throughout the Nile Delta from reforming. Nicholson and the engineers moved with the advanced guard formed by the 6th Bengal Cavalry, whose progress was delayed when it was found the canal sluices had been opened and needed to be closed to protect the local villagers. The column advanced next along the railway embankment and entered Zagazig as Egyptian troops were trying to escape by railway. One of the assistant field engineers Lieutenant G. Burn-Murdoch, shot the driver of the first train and Nicholson captured four trains under steam, out of the ten engines and over 100 carriages that were seized. A captured train was sent back down the line to help bring forward the rest of the Indian Contingent. The occupation of Zagazig opened the way for the surrender of Cairo and the defeat of Arabi Pasha the following day on 14 September. In October, the campaign a complete success, the Indian Contingent returned to India.[62]

---

61 Maurice, John Frederick, *Military History of the Campaign of 1882 in Egypt* (London: H.M.S.O., 1887), pp. 21, 35-36, 76-68, 106, 118-119; Scott-Moncrieff, G. K., 'Memoir: Field Marshal Lord Nicholson, G.C.B., Colonel Commandant, R.E.', *The Royal Engineers Journal*, 28:6 (December 1918), p. 242.
62 Maurice, John Frederick, *Military History of the Campaign of 1882 in Egypt* (London: H.M.S.O., 1887), pp. 77, 96-97, 100-101, 106; Scott-Moncrieff, G. K., 'Memoir: Field Marshal Lord Nicholson, G.C.B., Colonel Commandant, R.E.', *The Royal Engineers Journal*, 28:6 (December 1918), pp. 242-243.

Nicholson now made a choice indicative of the delight he took throughout his career in agitating authority. In the official list of brevets awarded appeared the name of an officer in the Royal Engineers who had originally been ordered to Egypt from India, but never left the Indian subcontinent owing to the reduction of the Indian Contingent. As one of his contemporaries recalled:

> This inexcusable blunder tickled Nicholson's sense of the ridiculous, and, as he enjoyed nothing more than a practical joke, he applied officially for the brevet, alleging that it was evidently a clerical error, and really meant for him. The application was refused, whereupon Nicholson appealed to the Queen under Sec. 42 of the Army Act [which relates to complaints by officers]. The flutter in official dovecots caused by this audacious act was exactly what he desired. When asked about the success of his appeal, he would reply with much laughter that the highest authorities at the War Office "were very peevish."[63]

The official history of the campaign published by the War Office retained the oversight, with the absent Major J. A. Armstrong, Royal Engineers, receiving the brevet of lieutenant-colonel, to the certain amusement of Nicholson.[64]

The Egyptian campaign of 1882 was the final time Nicholson was employed as a field engineer on active service. In his next campaign, the pacification of Upper Burma from late 1886 to early 1887, he served as assistant adjutant-general on Roberts' Headquarter Staff. In 1885 Lieutenant-General Harry Prendergast had overthrown the military forces of King Thibaw. The success was short-lived however, as disturbances spread throughout Burma. Indeed, strong reinforcements were despatched under Nicholson's previous commander in Egypt, General Macpherson, but shortly after arriving he died of fever. Roberts, who had been travelling and inspecting frontier hill stations with some of his staff, likely with Nicholson, was ordered to transfer his headquarters to Burma immediately. Roberts landed with his staff at Rangoon on 9 November confident of success, knowing he had "...taken great care in the selection of the brigade commanders and staff officers." Yet, the difficulty of the military situation had been underrated and further reinforcements were required. However, the operations were then so successfully carried out that Roberts and his staff were able to return to India in February 1887, as Burma gradually became quiet. Nicholson proved to be Roberts' most reliable advisor and for his services in Burma was mentioned in dispatches and awarded the brevet of lieutenant-colonel.[65]

---

63   Scott-Moncrieff, G. K., 'Memoir: Field Marshal Lord Nicholson, G.C.B., Colonel Commandant, R.E.', *The Royal Engineers Journal*, 28:6 (December 1918), pp. 242-243.
64   Maurice, John Frederick, *Military History of the Campaign of 1882 in Egypt* (London: H.M.S.O., 1887), pp. 124, 170.
65   Roberts, Frederick S., *Forty-One Years in India: From Subaltern to Commander-in-Chief*, two volumes (London: Richard Bentley and Son, 1897), ii. pp. 399-400, 413-417, see p. 415 for Roberts' comment; Scott-Moncrieff, G. K., 'Memoir: Field Marshal Lord Nicholson, G.C.B., Colonel Commandant, R.E.', *The Royal Engineers Journal*, 28:6 (December 1918), pp. 243-244.

India, the 'forward policy' and defence of the North-West Frontier

Following Nicholson's service in the Egyptian campaign of 1882, he served almost exclusively in staff positions with some degree of administrative control. As Spenser Wilkinson recalled, he was an uncommonly clear thinker and had a good memory, and "During many years' service he had acquired a familiarity with the Indian Army and its administration surpassed only by that of Lord Roberts", making him an ideal staff officer.[66] Over the next two decades, he acquired an intellectual authority on defence matters through the study and development of strategic plans for the defence of India against Russia on the North-West Frontier. In doing so, he perfected the skills that later served him well during his time at the War Office. Indeed, Russian expansion to the borders of Afghanistan was the primary strategic concern for the British army in India, and questions about Indian frontier policy were central to the broader strategic debates about British imperial and home defence.

The defence of the frontier became muddled after the Second Afghan War. Indeed, how Afghanistan was to be used as a 'buffer state' in the event of Russian aggression was fiercely debated. Those Indian army officers associated with Roberts broadly agreed on the necessity of a forward policy of defence into Afghanistan, which was to India, Roberts explained, what the English Channel was to Britain. Yet, the importance attributed by the 'Indian' school to frontier defence was rejected by Roberts' rival Wolseley and his 'ring' of supporters, as well as by Liberal politicians. The election of a Liberal administration in April 1880 appeared to signal the end of the 'forward policy', with Gladstone's Liberals favouring a policy of 'masterly inactivity'.[67] However, Roberts and Major-General Sir Charles MacGregor, author of *The Defence of India*, responded by stepping-up their advocacy for a direct involvement in Afghanistan.[68] Nicholson approved. Indeed, he thought the abandonment of the 'forward policy' jeopardised Indian defence. "Sooner or later", he warned pessimistically, "Britain would need to annex Afghanistan, [but] under far more difficult conditions than those existing in 1880."[69]

In 1884 Nicholson was selected to accompany Sir Charles MacGregor and Sir Robert Sandeman, the governor-general's administrator in Baluchistan, on a reconnaissance mission through Baluchi territory, to determine the practicality of several military works.[70] He was selected for his special knowledge, which was important, for very few officers had an equally excellent understanding of the geographical, engineering, and strategic problems of defending

---

66 Bod. Lib, Wilkinson cuttings, 2229 c.4 v.39, p. 43, *The Times*, September 15th 1918, 'Lord Nicholson: An Appreciation'.
67 Beckett, Ian F. W., 'Soldiers, the Frontier and the Politics of Command in British India', *Small Wars and Insurgencies*, 16:3 (December 2005), pp. 280-283; Johnson, Robert, 'Russians at the Gates of India'? Planning the Defense of India, 1885-1900 MacGregor', *The Journal of Military History*, 67:3 (July 2003), p. 714.
68 Johnson, Robert, 'Russians at the Gates of India'? Planning the Defense of India, 1885-1900 MacGregor', *The Journal of Military History*, 67:3 (July 2003), pp. 714-715; Preston, Adrian, 'Sir Charles MacGregor and the Defence of India, 1857-1887', *The Historical Journal*, 12:1 (1969), pp. 58-77; Charles Metcalfe, *The Defence of India: A Strategical Study* (Simla: 1884) MacGregor privately published and distributed this work to senior officers and politicians. It was then leaked to the press in order to influence Liberal policy.
69 NAM, Wilkinson Papers, OPT 13/13/14, Nicholson to Wilkinson, 10 September 1893.
70 Moreman, T. R., 'Nicholson, William Gustavus, Baron Nicholson (1845-1918)', *Oxford Dictionary of National Biography*, (Oxford: Oxford University Press, 2004).

the frontier between India and Afghanistan. To this end, when in early 1885 he returned to Simla, he was appointed assistant adjutant-general of the Royal Engineers in India, working as the secretary on the Defence Committee convened by Sir Donald Stewart, then commander-in-chief in India, to consider the defence of the North-West Frontier.[71] The significance of Stewart's Committee was increased by two events in 1885: first, in March, Russian and Afghan troops clashed at Penjdeh, appearing to signal Russian intentions to secure control of northern Afghanistan, and second, a new Unionist administration, which was in favour of a "... forward policy, replaced the outgoing Liberals."[72] Added to this, Stewart relinquished his command in December, before any of the Committee's recommendations could be given effect.[73] He was replaced by Roberts as commander-in-chief in India, the principle advocate of the 'forward policy', who penned twenty papers discussing his plans between 1877 and 1893. Roberts believed war with Russia was inevitable and that British authority needed to be extended over the tribal areas of the frontier, to control the vital entry points into Afghanistan, where his idea was to secure a 'scientific frontier', a defensive line along the Hindu Kush mountains.[74] In developing these plans further, Roberts studied the proposals of the Stewart Committee for the defence of India.

From 1885 until his departure from India in 1893, Roberts relied heavily on Nicholson. Although their work merged naturally together, Nicholson's contribution to the development of the 'forward policy' was important. Referring to the Defence Committee in 1885, Roberts praised Nicholson's involvement, writing in his autobiography that "It seemed to me that none of the members, with the exception of Sir Charles Macgregor and the secretary, Major W. G. Nicholson, at all appreciated the great change which had taken place in our position since the near approach of Russia."[75] However, an earlier draft of the chapter had made no reference to Nicholson, who then pressed Roberts to re-examine the proposals embodied in his note to the members of the Committee, which became largely the recommendations made to the Government of India. Indeed, "...the scheme in its inception was" Nicholson's scheme.[76] As Roberts explained, he disagreed with "...the majority of the members [of the Committee, who] laid greater stress on the necessity for constructing numerous fortifications, than upon lines of

---

71 Scott-Moncrieff, G. K., 'Memoir: Field Marshal Lord Nicholson, G.C.B., Colonel Commandant, R.E.', *The Royal Engineers Journal*, 28:6 (December 1918), pp. 242-243; Johnson, Robert, 'Russians at the Gates of India'? Planning the Defense of India, 1885-1900 MacGregor', *The Journal of Military History*, 67:3 (July 2003), pp. 724-726, for Stewart's 1885 Defence Committee.
72 Beckett, Ian F. W., 'Soldiers, the Frontier and the Politics of Command in British India', *Small Wars and Insurgencies*, 16:3 (December 2005), pp. 281 and 283; Johnson, Robert, 'Russians at the Gates of India'? Planning the Defense of India, 1885-1900 MacGregor', *The Journal of Military History*, 67:3 (July 2003), pp. 698, 717-718.
73 Roberts, Frederick S., *Forty-One Years in India: From Subaltern to Commander-in-Chief*, two volumes (London: Richard Bentley and Son, 1897), ii. pp. 402-403.
74 Johnson, Robert, 'Russians at the Gates of India'? Planning the Defense of India, 1885-1900 MacGregor', *The Journal of Military History*, 67:3 (July 2003), pp. 711-718 for a detailed coverage of Roberts' plans; Beckett, Ian F. W., 'Soldiers, the Frontier and the Politics of Command in British India', *Small Wars and Insurgencies*, 16:3 (December 2005), p. 284.
75 Roberts, Frederick S., *Forty-One Years in India: From Subaltern to Commander-in-Chief*, two volumes (London: Richard Bentley and Son, 1897), ii. p. 403.
76 NAM, Lord Roberts Papers, 71-01-23-87, R52/41, Nicholson to Roberts, 31 August 1896.

communication, which [Roberts] conceived to be of infinitely greater importance", for the rapid concentration of force into Afghanistan.⁷⁷

In response, Nicholson noted that, "Communications by railway and road [were] placed first in order of urgency." Therefore, his note had stated, "…concentration will be rendered rapid and easy at the points which are open to attack, or whence future offensive operations must be initiated." Moreover, the members of the Committee accepted this proposal without comment.⁷⁸ As Nicholson emphasised, he was not one of those, "…narrow-minded frontier officers who fancy that the world stands still because they are so stupid that they cannot see it move." Indeed, he had always insisted on the necessity from a military and political point of view of having the railway extend to Kabul and Kandahar.⁷⁹ Nicholson then addressed fortifications:

> if you refer to my note you will admit that I did not advocate more numerous entrenched positions than those subsequently approved and constructed, but rather the reverse. … You mention Sir C. MacGregor as the only member of the Defence [Committee] whose views met with your approval. But do you think, Sir, if you will take the trouble of again reading his remarks, that he showed much foresight or took a really comprehensive view of the situation? … However, in the letter to [the Government] … most of the additional fortifications were those recommended by Sir C. MacGregor.⁸⁰

While Nicholson made clear that MacGregor was responsible for the recommendation Roberts found most disagreeable, he was willing to admit the scheme was, "…in many respects faulty." It needed to be acceptable to the authorities to gain approval, including Gladstone, which made an already difficult task more problematic. Still, as Nicholson said subtly, Roberts had done "…scant justice to the Defence Committee."⁸¹ Undoubtedly, by stating he had "… recorded a strong opinion in opposition to the proposals of the Defence Committee", Roberts implied the defence of the North-West Frontier was taken seriously only after he became commander-in-chief in India.⁸² Yet, Nicholson was largely responsible for the Committee's proposals. By accepting the argument made by Nicholson to be listed as one the members of the Committee who appreciated the requirements of the 'forward policy', Roberts was admitting the Committee's scheme provided "…a useful starting-point for something better." Nicholson, however, would have preferred this had been made clear.⁸³

Notwithstanding the 1885 Defence Committee, most of their views on the defence of India were aligned. Moreover, Roberts trusted Nicholson's opinion, and he was retained from 1886 onwards, in the position of secretary to the Defence Committee. Roberts remarked that

---

77 Roberts, Frederick S., *Forty-One Years in India: From Subaltern to Commander-in-Chief*, two volumes (London: Richard Bentley and Son, 1897), ii. p. 404.
78 NAM, Lord Roberts Papers, 71-01-23-87, R52/41, Nicholson to Roberts, 31 August 1896.
79 NAM, Lord Roberts Papers, 71-01-23-87, R52/33, Nicholson to Roberts, 18 May 1895.
80 NAM, Lord Roberts Papers, 71-01-23-87, R52/41, Nicholson to Roberts, 31 August 1896.
81 NAM, Lord Roberts Papers, 71-01-23-87, R52/41, Nicholson to Roberts, 31 August 1896.
82 Roberts, Frederick S., *Forty-One Years in India: From Subaltern to Commander-in-Chief*, two volumes (London: Richard Bentley and Son, 1897), ii. pp. 403-409, see p. 406 for Roberts' statement.
83 NAM, Lord Roberts Papers, 71-01-23-87, R52/41, Nicholson to Roberts, 31 August 1896.

During 1887 and 1888 much useful work was got through by the Defence Committee ... As Commander-in-Chief I ... was fortunate in being able to secure as my [secretary an officer] of exceptional ability, Lieutenant-Colonel W. Nicholson, R.E., for defence [matters] ... It was in great measure due to Colonel Nicholson's clear-sighted judgement on the many knotty questions which came before us, and to his technical knowledge, that the schemes for the defence of the frontier, and for the ports of Bombay, Karachi, Calcutta, Rangoon and Madras, were carried out so rapidly, thoroughly and economically as they were.[84]

Nicholson made a prolonged tour of the North-West Frontier with Roberts' staff in December 1887. In the autumn of 1888 he returned and visited all the important military stations to assess how the new defences were advancing. This was repeated again in late summer 1889, as efforts were increasingly made to establish British influence over the frontier tribes.[85] Nicholson spent much of this time reading about the political and military history of British policy on the frontier, including parliamentary papers, intelligence department reports and official correspondence.[86] When the scheme proposed for the defence of the frontier was implemented, the effect was an increase in the number of useable roads and railways, an improved communications network, some improvement in relations with the frontier tribes, and the extension of British control over the "...strategic passes: the Khyber, the Bolan, the Khojak, and the Kurram."[87] As Roberts noted, Nicholson deserved to be praised for the remarkable administrative control he asserted over the Committee's proposal. Indeed, "The total cost of the coast and frontier defences amounted to the very moderate sum of five crores [million] of rupees, or about three and half millions sterling."[88] As Nicholson informed Roberts, this could only be achieved by not "... violating the true principle of military administration, i.e. the maintenance of a distinction between its military side and its financial side."[89]

In December 1889 Nicholson was offered the position as Roberts military secretary. He officially accepted the appointment in early 1890 and continued to work with Roberts on the defence arrangements for the Indian frontier, which was still their primary concern.[90] It was during this period Nicholson became friends with a number of officers, including Ian Hamilton, then assistant adjutant-general for musketry, and with politicians and military writers, including Spenser Wilkinson. Both men later became important for Nicholson's work. In particular, Nicholson was good friends and worked well with Hamilton, and while in India they collaborated

---

84 Roberts, Frederick S., *Forty-One Years in India: From Subaltern to Commander-in-Chief*, two volumes (London: Richard Bentley and Son, 1897), ii. p. 423.
85 Roberts, Frederick S., *Forty-One Years in India: From Subaltern to Commander-in-Chief*, two volumes (London: Richard Bentley and Son, 1897), ii. pp. 428-429, 422, 435-436.
86 NAM, Wilkinson Papers, OPT 13/13/18, Nicholson to Wilkinson, 15 September 1893.
87 Johnson, Robert, 'Russians at the Gates of India'? Planning the Defense of India, 1885-1900 MacGregor', *The Journal of Military History*, 67:3 (July 2003), p. 728; Roberts, Frederick S., *Forty-One Years in India: From Subaltern to Commander-in-Chief*, two volumes (London: Richard Bentley and Son, 1897), ii. pp. 408-409.
88 Roberts, Frederick S., *Forty-One Years in India: From Subaltern to Commander-in-Chief*, two volumes (London: Richard Bentley and Son, 1897), ii. p. 423.
89 NAM, Lord Roberts Papers, 71-01-23-87, R52/1, Nicholson to Roberts, 22 July 1889.
90 NAM, Lord Roberts Papers, 71-01-23-87, R52/2, Nicholson to Roberts, 19 December 1889.

on an article in response to a series of publications by Sir John Frederick Maurice, the military writer teaching at the Staff College, on the qualities of a good soldier. In 1890 Roberts went through a great deal of trouble and controversy in securing their promotions, which included writing letters to the Secretary of State for War. In 1891 Nicholson was promoted colonel and was awarded a CB, and Hamilton became the youngest colonel in the army.[91] In the autumn of 1892 Nicholson met Wilkinson for the first time, while the latter was Roberts' guest on a tour of the North-West Frontier. Wilkinson recalled their meeting, remembering that, "He struck me as the ablest member of the Headquarters Staff – an impression which Lord Roberts confirmed – and my acquaintance with him quickly ripened into a friendship."[92] Wilkinson accompanied the staff and was a guest of Nicholson and his wife in Meerut, where they discussed the frontier in every detail. By the time Wilkinson left Calcutta, he counted both Roberts and Nicholson as close friends, becoming their powerful ally in the press.[93]

Nicholson returned to England in 1893 with Roberts, who was succeeded as commander-in-chief in India by Sir George White. He used the time on the unemployed list studying and writing about military affairs, particularly, thinking about the reform of the army and the War Office. The question of these reforms, however, were complicated by government and War Office politics regarding strategy and senior appointments. Indeed, Nicholson acquainted himself closely with the politics of British defence policy. He was bemused by the sluggishness of the political process and the domination of domestic issues, especially when compared with the Indian system. Debates about Irish 'Home Rule' left little room in the public mind for defence. He told Wilkinson in one of his more colourful characterisations of the problem that

> I am getting a little annoyed with W. Gladstone and his subservience to the ill-bred and aggressive Irishmen who now govern Parliament and dominate the British nation. How the English and Scotch can put up with the present state of affairs I cannot understand. I have no objection to Home Rule, provided the Irish were left to stew in their own juice, but the Home Rule now proposed which would entail our stewing in Irish juice is to me, and I should hope to more Englishmen, quite intolerable.[94]

The reform of the British Army was doubtless an urgent requirement. Nicholson bemoaned that 'measures of parochial policy' and the continuation of the Duke of Cambridge as commander-in-chief of the Army, which confirmed the 'survival of the unfittest', stopped real progress.[95] Nicholson made every effort to support the arguments against the Duke of Cambridge remaining in office, sending Wilkinson information to use in his articles advocating reform. He also hoped the perceived poor treatment of Roberts, who was overlooked for Viceroy of India, would gain

---

91 Lee, John, *A Soldiers Life: General Sir Ian Hamilton, 1853-1947* (London: Macmillan, 2000), pp. 31 and 33-34; NAM, Wilkinson Papers, OPT 13/13/20, Nicholson to Wilkinson, 18 October 1893; NAM, Lord Roberts Papers, 71-01-23-87, R52/4, Nicholson to Roberts, 30 May 1891.
92 Bod. Lib, Wilkinson cuttings, 2229 c.4 v.39, p. 43, *The Times*, September 15th 1918, 'Lord Nicholson: An Appreciation'.
93 Wilkinson, H. Spenser, *Thirty-Five Years, 1874-1909* (London: Constable and Company, 1933), pp. 143, 153, 160, 168.
94 NAM, Wilkinson Papers, OPT 13/13/10, Nicholson to Wilkinson, 13 July 1893; See also, 13/13/6-9 for Nicholson's views on domestic politics.
95 NAM, Wilkinson Papers, OPT 13/13/11, Nicholson to Wilkinson, 5 September 1893.

public attention.⁹⁶ To this end, Nicholson drafted speeches for Roberts' many dinner speaking engagements, wrote articles against Wolseley and Sir Redvers Buller, and edited chapters for his autobiography.⁹⁷ Indeed, he hoped for the creation of a chief of the general staff to replace the commander-in-chief position and advised Roberts that when the Duke of Cambridge retired, he would be best placed under his rival Wolseley in the War Office, rather than in the undesirable Irish command. Nicholson joined the Navy League, established to advocate for the creation of a chief of the naval staff, which if successful, he thought, would make it "...impossible for the government to refuse a similar reform in Army administration."⁹⁸

Alas, the position of commander-in-chief was retained, but with reduced powers. When the Duke of Cambridge finally retired in 1895 under pressure from the government, he was replaced by Wolseley, who was succeeded in the Irish command by Roberts. Nicholson had an unfavourable reputation with the current Army regime. His association with Roberts' criticisms of the current War Office administration and the 'Wolseley ring', which he helped write, made getting a suitable staff appointment in the home army difficult. Indeed, Roberts tried unsuccessfully to get Nicholson an appointment to the Horse Guards as assistant-adjutant general under Buller. Nicholson agreed it was "...too much to expect that [Buller] should bring into his own office a man whom he naturally regards as an adherent of his most powerful rival."⁹⁹ As Buller admitted, Nicholson "...was exceedingly well qualified for [the] certain staff appointment [he] wanted, had it not been for [his] intimate association with Lord Roberts."¹⁰⁰ Nicholson disliked the idea of returning to India, but after more than a year unemployed at home, he reckoned on returning to military service shortly, or risk "...falling out of touch with military matters."¹⁰¹

Reluctantly, Nicholson returned to India in April 1895. He secured an appointment as the deputy-adjutant general of the Punjab Army, and was therefore chief staff officer, with the rank of brigadier-general, under the command of Lieutenant-General Sir William Lockhart. Nicholson led a 'somewhat solitary' and 'humdrum life'. His old friends had left India, new ones were difficult to make and he found the work uninteresting at the 'dull station'. As he explained, "I have had about enough of India and should prefer some responsible staff [appointment] at home."¹⁰² Indeed, his unhappiness was enough to send him into a depression, and he suffered from periodic stints of ill health, "...feeling a good deal out of sorts."¹⁰³ He even contemplated leaving the army. Repeating his dissatisfaction with the War Office administration to

---

96 NAM, Wilkinson Papers, OPT 13/13/13, Nicholson to Wilkinson, 9 September 1893.
97 NAM, Lord Roberts Papers, 71-01-23-87, R52/22, Nicholson to Roberts, 15 December 1894; R52/19, Nicholson to Roberts, 27 October 1984.
98 NAM, Lord Roberts Papers, 71-01-23-87, R52/14, Nicholson to Roberts, 18 June 1894; NAM, Wilkinson Papers, OPT 13/13/31, Nicholson to Wilkinson, 5 February 1895; 13/13/29, Nicholson to Wilkinson, 22 December 1894.
99 NAM, Lord Roberts Papers, 71-01-23-87, R52/18, Nicholson to Roberts, 26 October 1894; R52/22, Nicholson to Roberts, 15 December 1894.
100 NAM, Wilkinson Papers, OPT 13/13/28, Nicholson to Wilkinson, 12 December 1894.
101 NAM, Wilkinson Papers, OPT 13/13/31, Nicholson to Wilkinson, 5 February 1895.
102 NAM, Wilkinson Papers, OPT 13/13/32, Nicholson to Wilkinson, 24 June 1895; 13/13/33, Nicholson to Wilkinson, 28 July 1895; 13/13/42, Nicholson to Wilkinson, 6 June 1897; 13/13/40, Nicholson to Wilkinson, 15 February 1895.
103 NAM, Wilkinson Papers, OPT 13/13/35, Nicholson to Wilkinson, 10 October 1895.

Wilkinson, he declared that "...the only question for me personally is whether it is worth my while to continue in the service. This is a dull place, and though I fancy I run the staff business of the Punjab Army well enough I don't find it particularly interesting."[104] Nicholson considered a career on the stock exchange, but Wilkinson persuaded him to stick it out, since the alterative might be worse than his "...great weariness of India and of the monotonous official routine."[105] Nevertheless, his boredom soon ended.

Tirah Campaign, 1897-98

In the summer of 1897 the Pashtun tribes on the North-West Frontier revolted. The outbreak of serious insurrections and fighting resulted in the largest British operational deployment in India since the Mutiny of 1857-58.[106] British troops were sent to supress several individual risings, but the main campaign was directed against the Afridi Pashtuns located in the Tirah Maidan valleys, south of the Khyber Pass between Kohat and the Kurram River valley. Nicholson was appointed Chief of the Staff of the Tirah Expeditionary Force, which was commanded by Sir William Lockhart. Lockhart's plan for the expedition was to advance into Tirah Maidan and announce the British terms to the Pashtun *jirgahs* or councils, defeating the revolt decisively at the centre of Afridi territory. Maidan was only some 40 miles west of Peshawar but was about 6000 feet above sea level and the line of advance was through a series of difficult mountain passes, "...no European [had] ever been within 20 miles of the place."[107] Nevertheless, Lockhart was confident of success. He held Nicholson in the highest esteem, trusted his sound judgement and clear grasp of military affairs. Indeed, Nicholson's knowledge and experience of frontier warfare was invaluable, and as Chief of the Staff, he exerted a significant influence on the expedition. Moreover, as Lockhart's health deteriorated, the direction of the campaign became increasingly the work of Nicholson.[108]

Nicholson recognised when employed as Roberts military secretary that modern conditions in India had made small wars and defence against revolt more difficult. Moreover, he agreed there were serious limitations to the 'forward policy' on the North-West Frontier. As Nicholson explained to Roberts, he had "... grave doubts whether the improvement of communications has done as much as is commonly supposed to strengthen our position within India itself." He concluded that, "...the organization of [wide-spread] revolt is a much easier matter than it used to be ... [and] the existing means for rapid military concentration might be destroyed at any moment."[109] However, in Nicholson's view, these were military and political limitations, and he

---

104 NAM, Wilkinson Papers, OPT 13/13/34, Nicholson to Wilkinson, 7 September 1895.
105 NAM, Wilkinson Papers, OPT 13/13/35, Nicholson to Wilkinson, 10 October 1895.
106 Johnson, Rob, *The Afghan Way of War: How and Why They Fight* (Oxford: Oxford University Press, 2012), p. 149 for an excellent discussion of the expedition from a Pashtun perspective.
107 Hutchinson, H. D., *The Campaign in Tirah, 1897-1898* (London: Macmillan and Co., 1898), pp. 22-42; Johnson, Rob, *The Afghan Way of War: How and Why They Fight* (Oxford: Oxford University Press, 2012), pp. 156 and 164-167; NAM, Wilkinson Papers, OPT 13/13/44, Nicholson to Wilkinson, 3 September 1897.
108 Scott-Moncrieff, G. K., 'Memoir: Field Marshal Lord Nicholson, G.C.B., Colonel Commandant, R.E.', *The Royal Engineers Journal*, 28:6 (December 1918), p. 245; Bod. Lib, Wilkinson cuttings, 2229 c.4 v.39, p. 43, *The Times*, September 15th 1918, 'Lord Nicholson: An Appreciation'.
109 NAM, Lord Roberts Papers, 71-01-23-87, R52/6, Nicholson to Roberts, 11 September 1893.

rejected the idea that the Pashtun uprisings were caused by the 'forward policy'. The cause of the revolt, he thought, was not British frontier policy, but the weakness with which it had been implemented since Roberts left India. On the contrary, he argued, religious enthusiasm was the main cause:

> A general frontier rising has been unknown till now, although the occupation of the ... Punjab was at that time a forward policy, and though for years we have quietly occupied Baluchistan, the Kuram, and the Khyber. Some time ago while the Turkish envoy was at Kabul, the Amir [Abdur Rahman] summoned all the principle mullahs to his capital [Kabul] and is stated to have urged on them the duty of preparing for a religious war. What is termed a *jihad* or *ghaza*. ... Religion or fanaticism is the only thing that overpowers tribal discussions, and the result is that, for the first time in our experience, we have to meet a <u>general</u> tribal rising.[110]

Indeed, the Amir supplied the Pashtuns with arms and ammunition, and there was great concern that by calling for a holy war the Amir would encourage disturbances in India. The result showed "...the great fighting strength of the tribes when united", Nicholson concluded, "...and the consequent necessity for our having them under control."[111] Undoubtedly, as one historian argued, the cause of the uprisings was rooted in the internal dynamics of a society seeking to exclude foreign influences, and this needs to viewed in the context of the British 'forward policy'.[112] Yet, as Nicholson acknowledged, there were serious limitations to increased British control on the frontier. The 'forward policy' was often neither forward or an implemented policy. Perhaps, the weaknesses of the 'forward policy', as he argued, provided more encouragement to the Pashtun tribes.

Throughout the late summer of 1897 British forces were hampered by the indecision of 'incompetent civilians', and the inaction 'owing to the centralisation' of offensive planning at headquarters and in the Intelligence Branch in India. The punitive operations that were approved, some 45,000 troops were in the field in August, made slow progress in the intense summer heat.[113] Moreover, dealing with the uprisings across the frontier, against the Waziris in the Tochi Valley to the south, and the Mohmands, the Bajauris, and the Swatis to the north, absorbed some of the best troops, and significantly, a large proportion of the good available transport. Indeed, logistics were difficult and delayed the Tirah expedition. When Nicholson arrived at Kohat in early October he found the arrangements for the campaign were poor, "... hardly any of the Staff [had] turned up and [the] transport was in a rather chaotic state."[114]

---

110 NAM, Wilkinson Papers, OPT 13/13/44, Nicholson to Wilkinson, 3 September 1897.
111 Moreman, T.R., 'The arms trade and the North-West frontier Pathan tribes, 1890-1914', *The Journal of Imperial and Commonwealth History*, 22:2 (1994), pp. 192-195; NAM, Lord Roberts Papers, 71-01-23-87, R52/50, Nicholson to Roberts, 9 August 1897; R52/51, Nicholson to Roberts, 9 August 1897.
112 Johnson, Rob, *The Afghan Way of War: How and Why They Fight* (Oxford: Oxford University Press, 2012), pp. 150-151, 172-173.
113 NAM, Lord Roberts Papers, 71-01-23-87, R52/52, Nicholson to Roberts, 29 August 1897; NAM, Wilkinson Papers, OPT 13/13/43, Nicholson to Wilkinson, 31 August 1897.
114 Hutchinson, H. D., *The Campaign in Tirah, 1897-1898* (London: Macmillan and Co., 1898), pp. 43-47; NAM, Lord Roberts Papers, 71-01-23-87, R52/55, Nicholson to Roberts, 5 November 1897; R52/54, Nicholson to Roberts, 10 October 1897.

Nicholson explained later to a meeting of the Committee of Imperial Defence how the Tirah expedition placed a "…great strain on the transport resources of India." He stated that the transport consisted of mules and ponies, "…every animal they could possibly squeeze out of the Punjab", and these were "…of the worst quality I have ever seen."[115]

Nevertheless, the Tirah Expeditionary Force was slowly concentrated three marches from Kohat on the advanced base at Shinwari, where preparations were made for the advance into the Kanki Valley, including road building. The Samana Range needed to be crossed first at the Chagru Kotal, or summit, near the village of Dargai, where Orakzai and Afridi tribesmen, likely aware of the British plans, had gathered in strength.[116] On 18 October Lockhart dispatched a scouting force in an attempt to dislodge the tribesmen at Dargai. From a vantage point on the Samana Suk, Lockhart, Nicholson and the headquarters staff observed the difficulties the force encountered as it climbed up the steep mountain-side. Progress was slow, taking six hours before a frontal assault could be made on Dargai, which forced the Pashtun riflemen to retreat, fearing they might be outflanked. It was impossible to hold the ridge overnight and the small British force withdrew to Shinwari. The Pashtuns regained their defensive position and reinforcements rushed in from the neighbouring valleys.[117] On 20 October Lockhart's Force advanced on the strengthened Dargai heights, marching via the direct Chagru Kotal route into the Kanki Valley. The British forces attacked the heights and came under heavy rifle fire. Nicholson noted: "The enemy were well armed, strongly posted, had lots of ammunition, and shot with wonderful accuracy."[118] The Pashtuns fought the British to a standstill, but the British and Indian troops were determined to take the position at all costs, and their disciplined effort continued to press the tribesmen. Pinned down for three hours, a fresh assault gained the summit, just after 3 P.M., with the Pashtun riflemen retreating into the Kanki Valley, having exhausted their ammunition in the sustained engagement. The British suffered 200 casualties, whilst the tribesmen escaped with their own force largely intact.[119] The assault on the Dargai heights was the most difficult offensive operations of the expedition. As the renowned military theorist Sir Charles E. Callwell, author of *Small Wars: Their Principles and Practice*, explained in his dedicated study of the campaign, *Tirah 1897*, the morale effect of the resolute British attack meant the Orakzai Pashtuns never again offered any serious opposition.[120] Nicholson drew the same conclusion at the time: "The morale effect of the Dargai fights on the 18th and 20th [October] was very beneficial and did much, I think, to facilitate our further operations."[121]

---

115 Wyatt, Christopher M., *Afghanistan and the Defence of Empire: Diplomacy and Strategy during the Great Game* (London: I. B. Tauris, 2011), pp. 154-156.
116 Hutchinson, H. D., *The Campaign in Tirah, 1897-1898* (London: Macmillan and Co., 1898), pp. 48-50; Callwell, Charles E., *Tirah 1897* (London: Constable and Co., 1911), pp. 38-39.
117 Hutchinson, H. D., *The Campaign in Tirah, 1897-1898* (London: Macmillan and Co., 1898), pp. 57-66; Callwell, Charles E., *Tirah 1897* (London: Constable and Co., 1911), pp. 41-47.
118 NAM, Lord Roberts Papers, 71-01-23-87, R52/55, Nicholson to Roberts, 5 November 1897; Hutchinson, H. D., *The Campaign in Tirah, 1897-1898* (London: Macmillan and Co., 1898), pp. 69-73.
119 Callwell, Charles E., *Tirah 1897* (London: Constable and Co., 1911), pp. 48-52; Johnson, Rob, *The Afghan Way of War: How and Why They Fight* (Oxford: Oxford University Press, 2012), pp. 160-162.
120 Callwell, Charles E., *Tirah 1897* (London: Constable and Co., 1911), pp. 56-59; Callwell, Charles E., *Small Wars: Their Principles and Practice*, Third Edition (London: H.M.S.O., 1906).
121 NAM, Lord Roberts Papers, 71-01-23-87, R52/55, Nicholson to Roberts, 5 November 1897.

The next morning the British entered the Khanki Valley and advanced to the fortified village of Khangarbur, where after a short engagement the Afridis decided not to remain. A camp was set up near the village on a large plateau and the next two days were spent collecting supplies.[122] "The camp", Nicholson told Roberts, "was attacked in considerable force almost every night and there were a good many bullets flying about, but the position was a very strong one and well defended, and our casualties were not very heavy."[123] Meanwhile the delay allowed the Afridis time to strengthen the defences of the Sampagha Pass, the next obstacle for the British force, by "... building walls ... digging trenches and rifle pits."[124] On 27 October the Expeditionary Force began the final advance into Tirah. However, on 29 October the action anticipated at the Sampagha Pass never occurred, and the Afridi riflemen dispersed after a short bombardment of accurate artillery fire. The pass was captured by 11.15 A.M., just as Lockhart arrived at the summit with Nicholson and the rest of his staff.[125] The next day they entered the Mastura Valley and halted to rest and reconnoitre the way ahead. Only the Arhanga Pass, 5 miles away, now stood between the British forces and Tirah proper, "... the inviolate home of the Afridis."[126] However, the transport arrangements were under great strain. Yet, as Hutchinson noted, "...it was enough for General Nicholson, the chief of the Staff, to intimate what were Sir William Lockhart's wishes regarding the advance on the morrow for [the Transport Staff] to determine that, so far as [the] department was concerned, it could be arranged."[127] On the morning of 31 October the Expeditionary Force captured the Arhanga Pass, the gateway to Tirah Maidan, which proved to be an even easier task than the taking of the Sampagha Pass two days before. The troops advanced into the Maidan Valley and established camp.[128] While Lockhart awaited the outcome of the *jirgas* discussions, he pressed the Afridi fighters in the Tirah, selecting targets for his operations carefully, which included a difficult expedition to Saran Sar on 9 November against the strongest clan, the Zakka Khel Afridis. On 12 November Nicholson joined Lockhart as he received into camp the 'venerable old greybeards' of Orakzai *jirgas* to discuss their surrender. On 21 November the *jirgas* accepted Lockhart's terms, which included "'...fine, the restitution of property, the surrender of 800 rifles and a formal act of submission."[129] However, the Afridi tribesmen remained stubborn. Nicholson noted: "We have inflicted very heavy loss on the latter in the way of villages and forage besides killing and wounding a large number, but they still go on firing into [the Maidan] camp every night and attacking our convoys."[130] On 7 December, with the onset of the winter weather, Lockhart began the withdrawal of the Tirah Expeditionary Force, via two routes, through the Bara and

---

122 Hutchinson, H. D., *The Campaign in Tirah, 1897-1898* (London: Macmillan and Co., 1898), pp. 76-79.
123 NAM, Lord Roberts Papers, 71-01-23-87, R52/55, Nicholson to Roberts, 5 November 1897.
124 Hutchinson, H. D., *The Campaign in Tirah, 1897-1898* (London: Macmillan and Co., 1898), p. 80.
125 Hutchinson, H. D., *The Campaign in Tirah, 1897-1898* (London: Macmillan and Co., 1898), pp. 90-92; Callwell, Charles E., *Tirah 1897* (London: Constable and Co., 1911), pp. 69-70.
126 Hutchinson, H. D., *The Campaign in Tirah, 1897-1898* (London: Macmillan and Co., 1898), pp. 93-94.
127 Hutchinson, H. D., *The Campaign in Tirah, 1897-1898* (London: Macmillan and Co., 1898), pp. 96-97.
128 Callwell, Charles E., *Tirah 1897* (London: Constable and Co., 1911), pp. 74-76.
129 Johnson, Rob, *The Afghan Way of War: How and Why They Fight* (Oxford: Oxford University Press, 2012), pp. 164-167; Hutchinson, H. D., *The Campaign in Tirah, 1897-1898* (London: Macmillan and Co., 1898), pp. 129-132; Callwell, Charles E., *Tirah 1897* (London: Constable and Co., 1911), pp. 83-90.
130 NAM, Lord Roberts Papers, 71-01-23-87, R52/56, Nicholson to Roberts, 21 November 1897.

Bazar valleys. The retirement over tough mountain terrain was more difficult than expected. As Nicholson explained, "We had a pretty rough time marching down the Bazar Valley as rain was falling, the river had risen some 18 inches, and the tribesmen did not leave us alone for a moment." Indeed, he continued, "They seem to me to shoot better than our own troops … we got through all right, though our losses were pretty heavy, especially during the last two days, the 13th and 14th."[131] The final Afridi tribes submitted to the British terms in the spring of 1898.

The expedition against the Afridi tribesmen in Tirah Maidan was far more challenging than most observers understood, and a great deal of criticism was directed towards Lockhart and his Staff regarding the conduct of their operations. "The Indian newspapers, particularly *The Pioneer*, have now taken up an attitude quite opposed to the so-called forward policy and they severely censure the way in which the Tirah expedition had been conducted", as Nicholson informed Roberts, and "…the criticisms are almost invariably based on incorrect or inadequate information."[132] The criticisms, Nicholson thought, were groundless:

> The difficulties were enormous. First, a country probably one of the most difficult in the world, not one or two mountain passes and then level country, but a network of mountains, passes, and ravines, absolutely without roads through it, and with many of the hills covered with forest. Secondly, numerous transport animals, at least three-quarters of which were of a very inferior type. Thirdly, an enemy who made no stand in the open, but knew the ground perfectly, and were more active and better shots than our troops, while equally well armed.[133]

Nicholson also felt the expectations were unrealistic. Indeed, "Some badly-informed people both at home and in India seem to think that it ought to be the matter of a few weeks thoroughly to subdue a hardy race of well-armed mountaineers inhabiting one of the most difficult countries in the world. They have only to study history to arrive at a different conclusion."[134] Moreover, Nicholson was annoyed the criticisms were driven by service rivalry. Lord Methuen, a strong supporter of Buller as Wolseley's successor as commander-in-chief, went in a private capacity as an observer and accompanied the Staff during the Tirah campaign. Methuen wrote, as Nicholson pointed out, "…in a disparaging strain to Lord Wolseley and [other members of his 'gang']."[135] However, junior officers were also responsible for writing vilifying remarks about their commanders to the Indian newspapers. Nicholson remarked: "If success is less rapid and complete than these embryo Napoleon's think it ought to be, every senior officer in command or on the staff is to be characterized as either a fool or a coward."[136] The criticisms, Nicholson concluded, were the most unpleasant aspect of the whole campaign.

The criticisms were due largely to a lack of understanding of the geographical conditions in Afridi territory, and the difficulties of hill fighting and the conduct of small wars against an

---

131 NAM, Lord Roberts Papers, 71-01-23-87, R52/57, Nicholson to Roberts, 19 December 1897.
132 NAM, Lord Roberts Papers, 71-01-23-87, R52/58, Nicholson to Roberts, 10 January 1898.
133 NAM, Lord Roberts Papers, 71-01-23-87, R52/62, Nicholson to Roberts, 20 February 1898.
134 NAM, Lord Roberts Papers, 71-01-23-87, R52/60, Nicholson to Roberts, 23 January 1898.
135 NAM, Lord Roberts Papers, 71-01-23-87, R52/60, Nicholson to Roberts, 23 January 1898.
136 NAM, Lord Roberts Papers, 71-01-23-87, R52/62, Nicholson to Roberts, 20 February 1898.

irregular enemy with modern weapons. Few grasped how difficult the expedition had been, with the notable exception of the military theorist Sir Charles Callwell. Callwell recognised that the character of the operations were somewhat unique, and the second and third editions of his *Small Wars* book were updated to include the experiences gained in the, "... operations beyond the Panjab [sic] frontier in 1897-98", adding an entire new chapter on hill warfare.[137] Moreover, in his detailed study of the expedition, *Tirah 1897*, he devoted a chapter to the lessons of the campaign, and the analysis added important context the newspaper and individual criticisms had ignored.[138] Notably, his conclusions mirrored those of Nicholson: the "...expeditions were keenly and not always wisely criticized [sic]."[139] "The tribesmen of Tirah are admittedly brilliant exponents of partisan warfare", Callwell wrote, "...and unless full allowance is made for this in contests of this class, faulty deductions are likely enough to be drawn from their history."[140] Indeed, "... the campaigns of regular troops against hill-men fighting in guerrilla fashion" were "... the most trying which disciplined soldiers can be called upon to undertake ... the conditions of genuine hill warfare ... deserve to be considered as a subject quite apart."[141] Moreover, "... the dangers to which the forces of civilisation are exposed", Callwell explained in typical Victorian language, increased "... against savage antagonists armed with modern fire-weapons of precision."[142] These conditions made guerrilla warfare tactics far more difficult to oppose. Yet, as Nicholson noted, the British regiments were "... too young, [and] quite inexperienced in hill fighting."[143] For Callwell, the lesson was "... the importance of training our troops with a view to meeting the exigencies of this hill warfare", otherwise those troops "... engaged on operations of a new and uncanny kind" would be dangerously exposed.[144] The expedition also demonstrated the difficulty of communicating orders during action in hill warfare. "When the army engaged becomes broken up into very small units", Callwell argued, "Mistakes as regards orders have frequently caused difficulty and loss in hill warfare", when those forces misunderstand the intentions of the operations.[145] Nicholson agreed: "... in mountain warfare much has to be left to the judgment and capacity of officers commanding units or detachments, however small; and a petty mistake, such as the premature withdrawal of a picquet [picket] by the officer in charge of it, may produce the most serious results."[146] Moreover, the campaign confirmed the 'well-known principles' highlighted in the majority of small wars. In particular, the precept that offensive tactics were generally imperative to success. As Nicholson remarked, "With Asiatics [sic] never

---

137 Callwell, Charles E., *Small Wars: Their Principles and Practice*, 3rd Ed. (London: H.M.S.O., 1906), pp. 286-247, see also the preface to the second edition (1899), printed in the third edition.
138 Callwell, Charles E., *Tirah 1897* (London: Constable and Co., 1911), pp. 139-155.
139 Callwell, Charles E., *Small Wars: Their Principles and Practice*, 3rd Ed. (London: H.M.S.O., 1906), p. 346.
140 Callwell, Charles E., *Tirah 1897* (London: Constable and Co., 1911), p. 155.
141 Callwell, Charles E., *Small Wars: Their Principles and Practice*, 3rd Ed. (London: H.M.S.O., 1906), p. 286.
142 Callwell, Charles E., *Tirah 1897* (London: Constable and Co., 1911), pp. 151-152; Callwell, Charles E., *Small Wars: Their Principles and Practice*, 3rd Ed. (London: H.M.S.O., 1906), p. 289.
143 NAM, Lord Roberts Papers, 71-01-23-87, R52/56, Nicholson to Roberts, 21 November 1897.
144 Callwell, Charles E., *Small Wars: Their Principles and Practice*, 3rd Ed. (London: H.M.S.O., 1906), pp. 286, 320-321, 346-347.
145 Callwell, Charles E., *Small Wars: Their Principles and Practice*, 3rd Ed. (London: H.M.S.O., 1906), pp. 310-311.
146 NAM, Wilkinson Papers, OPT 13/13/45, Nicholson to Wilkinson, 2 March 1898.

await attack; continually harass them and keep them on the move."[147] The Tirah Expeditionary Force performed the assigned task, Nicholson concluded, "... in the face of unexampled natural difficulties", opposed by tribesmen unequalled in irregular and hill warfare. Callwell agreed: The Tirah campaign was one of the most 'arduous struggles' British troops had engaged in since the Indian Mutiny. "It is a little too much for the British public to be indignant", Nicholson thought, given the unprecedented difficulties the expedition encountered.[148]

The campaign in Tirah reinforced Nicholson's belief in the limitations of the 'forward policy'. However, as far as he was concerned, it had not resulted in the Pashtun uprising. Indeed, he thought the general lack of preparation for a conflict on the North-West Frontier had exposed the defence of India, which in turn, had encouraged tribal unrest. Moreover, the expedition to Tirah was given neither the time or the transport required to succeed fully against a resolute and effective enemy. This resulted in much undeserved criticism. Nevertheless, Nicholson was mentioned in despatches. He was "An officer of brilliant abilities, fertility of resource, and experience in war", Lockhart confirmed, "...the value of whose assistance it is difficult for me to acknowledge in adequate terms."[149] For his services he was awarded the frontier medal with two clasps and made KCB. Later in 1898 Lockhart helped Nicholson secure the appointment as adjutant-general in India.[150] He set about reforming the methods and organisation of the Indian Army but was stopped in this task before he really got started.

South African War, 1899-1902

The South African War has been well documented in a number of excellent works, so will not be detailed here.[151] Needless to say, Nicholson's work again merged with with that of his friend and former commander-in-chief in India. In December 1899 Roberts summoned Nicholson to meet him at Cape Town in South Africa, where he arrived on 18 January 1900. Roberts was sent to South Africa to recover the British position against the Boers, after a series of disasters in late 1899. Nicholson was originally appointed as Roberts' military secretary. However, in February he was appointed director of the transport department. He was tasked with reorganising transport as a centralised service, which could be distributed according to the requirements of each operation. Nevertheless, he continued to be employed by Roberts in a personal capacity for a variety of responsibilities and confidential duties, and during this period he was also employed on intelligence work. Indeed, he was one of the very few officers to whom Roberts' plan of campaign was made known. As Roberts' closest assistant, he was engaged in operations at Paardeberg, Poplar Grove, Driefontein, Vet and Zand Rivers, and participated in fighting near Johannesburg, Pretoria, and Diamond Hill in the Transvaal. For his services in the South African War he was mentioned in despatches and was promoted major-general. In

---

147 NAM, Lord Roberts Papers, 71-01-23-87, R52/52, Nicholson to Roberts, 29 August 1897; Callwell, Charles E., *Small Wars: Their Principles and Practice,* 3rd Ed. (London: H.M.S.O., 1906), pp. 150, 304-305.
148 NAM, Wilkinson Papers, OPT 13/13/45, Nicholson to Wilkinson, 2 March 1898; Callwell, Charles E., *Small Wars: Their Principles and Practice,* 3rd Ed. (London: H.M.S.O., 1906), p. 289.
149 Hutchinson, H. D., *The Campaign in Tirah, 1897-1898* (London: Macmillan and Co., 1898), p. 28.
150 NAM, Lord Roberts Papers, 71-01-23-87, R52/65, Nicholson to Roberts, 14 March 1898.
151 For example, see Pakenham, Thomas, *The Boer War* (London: Abacus, 2009); for Roberts, see Atwood, Rodney, *The Life of Field Marshal Lord Roberts* (London: Bloomsbury, 2015).

November 1900 he returned to India to resume his appointment as adjutant-general in India. He soon afterwards went on leave, and in February 1901 was called to London to meet with Roberts.[152]

The War Office, General Staff and Army Reform

Roberts was made commander-in-chief of the British Army in late 1900. In early 1901 he offered Nicholson the newly created position of director-general of mobilization and military intelligence at the War Office. "It is rather a wrench giving up India after having served there for nearly 30 years", Nicholson told Roberts disingenuously, "...but as your Lordship thinks it best for me to come to the War Office, I shall gladly meet your wishes. ... The pay, I understand, will be £2,100 a year."[153] Nicholson was promoted lieutenant-general and took office in November 1901. It was the first time since he was a junior subaltern that he had served in England. He spent most of the next 11 years reshaping the War Office. During this time, he directed the reform of the Army administration, prepared detailed defence plans and established the General Staff on a functioning basis, despite strong opposition. He achieved this using his knowledge from thirty years of experience in the field, and his important work under Roberts in several administrative and staff positions in India was especially valuable. He immediately made his mark as a powerful administrator.

When Nicholson became the director-general of military intelligence in 1901 he set about establishing a proto-staff system to study and develop British operational and strategic plans. Roberts had hoped Nicholson would have the 'department resuscitated'.[154] As noted by one historian, Nicholson "...was to prove an immense success, grasping the potential of his new department and willing to fight for it against all comers."[155] Indeed, Nicholson thought the department should be a directing and strategy making power, on whose recommendations the whole policy of the Army should be based. The broader policy needed to be outlined by the Cabinet, he thought, after which the Army Staff could work out all the details, to give military effect to the policy. To this end, he asked for the Government to define its foreign policy, but the Government informed him this was not at present possible.[156] Nevertheless, after only a week in his new appointment, he informed Roberts that "I have ordered a beginning to be made in preparing schemes of offensive and defensive operations, the first being to meet such a

---

152 Amery, L. S., *The Times History of the War in South Africa, 1899-1902*, seven volumes (London: Marston and Co., 1900-09), iii. p. 337; Scott-Moncrieff, G. K., 'Memoir: Field Marshal Lord Nicholson, G.C.B., Colonel Commandant, R.E.', *The Royal Engineers Journal*, 28:6 (December 1918), pp. 245-246; NAM, Wilkinson Papers, OPT 13/13/48, Nicholson to Wilkinson, 26 February 1901.
153 NAM, Lord Roberts Papers, 71-01-23-87, R52/72, Nicholson to Roberts, 16 January 1901.
154 Wessels, Andre, *Lord Roberts and the War in South Africa, 1899-1902* (London: Sutton Publishing for the Army Records Society, 2000), p. 170.
155 Gooch, John, *The Plans of War: The General Staff and British Military Strategy, c. 1900-1916* (London: Routledge & Keegan Paul, 1974), pp. 21-29.
156 Spiers, Edward M., *The late Victorian Army, 1868-1902* (Manchester: Manchester University Press, 1992), pp. 326-327; Hamer, W. S., The British Army: Civil-Military Relations, 1885-1905 (Oxford: Oxford University Press, 1970), pp. 191-192; Scott-Moncrieff, G. K., 'Memoir: Field Marshal Lord Nicholson, G.C.B., Colonel Commandant, R.E.', *The Royal Engineers Journal*, 28:6 (December 1918), p. 246.

contingency as a war with France and Russia combined."¹⁵⁷ Nicholson's increased responsibilities meant, he was not only a member of the War Office Council, but he also became accountable for the "... preparation and maintenance of detailed plans for the military defence of the Empire and for the organisation and mobilisation of the regular and auxiliary forces, ... and the collection and distribution of information relating to the military geography, resources, etc., of foreign countries and of the British colonies and possessions."¹⁵⁸

Demanding more staff Nicholson lobbied the Treasury for additional expenditure. He "... pointed to the immense resources of the German General Staff and warned that skimping his department was a false economy."¹⁵⁹ He tried to obtain Spenser Wilkinson as his assistant in the department to deal "...with matters of organization and intelligence", but the Treasury refused an increase in funds, and this along with some other plans were abandoned.¹⁶⁰ Nicholson fought a tough battle. The war in South Africa left Britain with a large debt, and military expenditure had risen greatly in the previous decade, there was much concern to keep the estimates down.¹⁶¹ The Chancellor of the Exchequer, Hicks Beach, informed Nicholson that the Intelligence Department should not be occupying itself with 'what at Oxford is called research', and no attention should be paid to such plans until war broke out. Nicholson responded bitingly that this was, "... entirely opposed to the teaching of military history and the experience of past wars." He struggled against these attitudes "...to maintain something resembling the General Staff, which he perceived was so necessary."¹⁶²

Nevertheless, his reforms were a great success. During his period as director-general of mobilisation and military intelligence, all military and government departments were able to call on the Intelligence Department to produce detailed papers and memorandums on every strategic issue of interest. He occupied a significant amount of his time writing these memos and he was aided in his efforts by some very able minds, including Charles Callwell.¹⁶³ Nicholson laid the foundation of his later work as chief of the Imperial General Staff.

The Esher Committee and War Office Reorganisation

In 1904 Lord Esher's War Office (reconstitution) Committee reported. The three-man committee, which included Esher, Sir George Sydenham Clarke and Admiral Fisher, was established to reform the War Office. The Committee decided the War Office required a 'clean

---

157 NAM, Lord Roberts Papers, 71-01-23-87, R52/87, Nicholson to Roberts, 8 May 1901; also quoted in Gooch, John, *The Plans of War: The General Staff and British Military Strategy, c. 1900-1916* (London: Routledge & Keegan Paul, 1974), pp. 21-23.
158 Spiers, Edward M., *The late Victorian Army, 1868-1902* (Manchester: Manchester University Press, 1992), pp. 326-327
159 Gooch, John, *The Plans of War: The General Staff and British Military Strategy, c. 1900-1916* (London: Routledge & Keegan Paul, 1974), pp. 22-23
160 NAM, Wilkinson Papers, OPT 13/13/50, Nicholson to Wilkinson, 16 March 1902.
161 Ehrman, John, *Cabinet Government and War, 1890-1940* (Cambridge: Cambridge University Press, 1958).
162 Gooch, John, *The Plans of War: The General Staff and British Military Strategy, c. 1900-1916* (London: Routledge & Keegan Paul, 1974), p. 24.
163 NAM, Lord Roberts Papers, 71-01-23-87, R52/110, Nicholson to Roberts, 18 December 1903.

sweep' and, "...agreed that [Nicholson] ought to go."[164] The objection to his remaining in the War Office was driven by Fisher, who observed Nicholson's antipathy to the Admiralty's strategic ideas during the invasion inquiries of 1903. He "...took a much more realistic view than some soldiers in the past of the likelihood of invasion." If Nicholson remained in the War Office, Fisher, Esher and Clarke reckoned, he would be a formidable obstacle to their defence plans. The Secretary of State for War, H. O. Arnold-Forster, sent a letter on 31 January to Nicholson confirming that his appointment was being discontinued in its current form, but the letter arrived after the newspaper accounts of the report on 1 February.[165] Nicholson was extremely disappointed. As he explained to Wilkinson, "I am handing over my functions temporarily … but I have received no formal indication that I am to do so … I know [only] by the newspapers."[166] Moreover, the report recommended the creation of a general staff and a permanent secretary for the new Committee of Imperial Defence. Indeed, Nicholson had "...put forward the idea of a fully-fledged General Staff on the German model' when interviewed by the Esher Committee. He was not the type of character to pull punches and stood little chance of endearing himself to what was effectively an informal selection committee. However, they were clearly happy to act on his suggestions, but not to have him implement the change.[167] Nicholson would soon be back in the War Office. In the meantime, he needed an appointment. He was offered a command at Gibraltar, but rejected it. The outbreak of the Russo-Japanese War provided a solution.

Chief British Military Attaché to the Japanese Army, 1904-05

Nicholson was appointed chief British military attaché to the Japanese Army in Manchuria in early 1904, and he remained in Asia for over a year. For Nicholson, the special duty as representative of the War Office was a great relief. As he told Wilkinson: "This is a good business and I am very pleased."[168] The journey via Canada was arduous, indeed, he returned on a different route, via India. "I arrived here [Tokyo] yesterday afternoon after a very stormy voyage across the Northern Pacific, preceded by an equally stormy one across the Atlantic", he explained, "and a journey across Canada during a spell of cold and snow which was quite exceptional in its severity." He spent most of the early part of the War at the Imperial Hotel, which was crowded with newspaper correspondents.[169] He had to wait until July to be allowed to join the Japanese Second Army, which he accompanied during the battle and capture of Liaoyang. The experience

---

164 Beckett, Ian, '"Selection by Disparagement": Lord Esher, the General Staff and the Politics of Command, 1904-1914', in French, David & Holden-Reid, Brain (eds) *The British General Staff: Reform and Innovation c. 1890-1939* (London: Frank Cass, 2002), pp. 44-50; Mackay, Ruddock F., *Fisher of Kilverstone* (Oxford: Oxford University Press, 1973), pp. 294-295.
165 Beckett, Ian, '"Selection by Disparagement": Lord Esher, the General Staff and the Politics of Command, 1904-1914', in French, David & Holden-Reid, Brain (eds) *The British General Staff: Reform and Innovation c. 1890-1939* (London: Frank Cass, 2002), pp. 47-50; Gooch, John, *The Plans of War: The General Staff and British Military Strategy, c. 1900-1916* (London: Routledge & Keegan Paul, 1974), p. 49.
166 NAM, Wilkinson Papers, OPT 13/13/55, Nicholson to Wilkinson, 11 February 1904.
167 Gooch, John, *The Plans of War: The General Staff and British Military Strategy, c.1900-1916* (London: Routledge & Keegan Paul, 1974), pp. 42-59.
168 NAM, Wilkinson Papers, OPT 13/13/53, Nicholson to Wilkinson, 6 February 1904.
169 NAM, Wilkinson Papers, OPT 13/13/56, Nicholson to Wilkinson, 28 March 1904.

was of great value, since the operations he witnessed were on larger scale than anything he had observed before. In observing the battle of Liaoyang, he praised the courage and patriotism of the Japanese soldiers, and he described the Russian entrenchments and the Japanese attack. The entrenchments "...had been so well designed, possessed so much overhead cover for the troops holding them, and their front and flanks were so well protected by wire entanglements", he described, "that but little effect was produced ...with heavy loss."[170] For his attachment to the Japanese Second Army, he was granted the war medal and was awarded the Grand Cordon Order of the Rising Sun. The whole experience, he thought, was very worthwhile.

Quartermaster-General of the Forces, 1905-08

The War Office had become somewhat dysfunctional since the Esher Committee's 'clean sweep' and there was a growing recognition that something had to be done to get the War Office back into shape. Esher and Clarke were forced to engage with the idea of bringing Nicholson back into the fold. However, a change of Government in December 1905 saw Richard Burdon Haldane become Secretary of State for War, and the decision was taken out of their hands. Haldane appointed Nicholson to succeed General Sir Hubert Plumer as quartermaster-general, restoring a balance at the War Office that had been missing since the Esher Committee's reconstitution. As quartermaster-general, he was now a member of the Army Council, and in a position to exercise direct influence on Army administration.[171] Haldane, "… was anxious to have [his] assistance … [and] when an opportunity occurred, [Haldane] would endeavour to make [him] Chief of the Staff."[172] It was widely acknowledged that Nicholson was the only answer to the problem of leadership on the Council, otherwise there was "… nothing but years of chaos in front of us."[173] Indeed, Nicholson was selected to help with Haldane's reforms "to ensure his proposals were as comprehensive as possible."[174] Moreover, Haldane "…virtually dispensed with the Army Council as an advisory body; only seeking assistance from the intellectually able, he relied upon individual members of the Council like Nicholson."[175] Nicholson assisted Haldane greatly in the Autumn of 1906 when they moved ahead with the reform of the reserve forces, and he also lent considerable support to the campaign to improve the organisation of the General Staff.[176] Haldane and Nicholson developed an excellent working relationship, and they became good friends, which was central to the major reforms of the British Army and British strategy from 1906 to 1912.

---

170 NAM, Lord Roberts Papers, 71-01-23-87, R52/113, Nicholson to Roberts, 10 October 1904.
171 Scott-Moncrieff, G. K., 'Memoir: Field Marshal Lord Nicholson, G.C.B., Colonel Commandant, R.E.', *The Royal Engineers Journal*, 28:6 (December 1918), p. 247.
172 NAM, Lord Roberts Papers, 71-01-23-87, R52/129, Nicholson to Roberts, 14 December 1905.
173 Gooch, John, *The Plans of War: The General Staff and British Military Strategy, c.1900-1916* (London: Routledge & Keegan Paul, 1974), p. 77.
174 Spiers, Edward M., *The Army and Society, 1815-1914* (London: Longman, 1980), pp. 265, 274-275.
175 Spiers, Edward M., *Haldane: An Army Reformer* (Edinburgh: Edinburgh University Press, 1980), p. 190.
176 Spiers, Edward M., *The Army and Society, 1815-1914* (London: Longman, 1980), pp. 274-275; Spiers, Edward M., *Haldane: An Army Reformer* (Edinburgh: Edinburgh University Press, 1980), pp. 195-196.

Chief of the Imperial General Staff, 1908-12

In April 1908 Nicholson succeeded General Sir Neville Lyttelton as chief of the General Staff and was made GCB the same year. To allay concern about the possibility of an inexperienced field commander leading the Army in the event of war, the position of the inspector-general of forces was made the real trainer of the army and its probable leader in any future conflict.[177] Nicholson's appointment, according to Wilkinson, breathed the breath of life into the General Staff: "He gave the General Staff its organisation and prepared the mobilisation arrangements of the Expeditionary Force which in 1914 were to prove of such value. He also worked out for the use of a future administration a scheme for the reorganisation of the Army on a national basis."[178] Moreover, the Territorial Force was organised for home service, and plans were made for a future compulsory national service. Indeed, he welded together the various personal elements of the General Staff, who supported their chief admirably.[179] Others allies were important too. In the same month as Nicholson was appointed chief of the general staff, he wrote to Winston Churchill, who he first met during the Tirah campaign: "… congratulations on your joining the Cabinet. In common with your many friends, I have watched your career with much interest and satisfaction, and far as you have gone already I hope and believe that you are destined to go much further."[180] When Nicholson was considering the question of compulsory service in connection with continental warfare, Churchill sent him a paper on national service and the organisation of the Army. Nicholson described it as having some 'original ideas' and being 'of value as suggesting alternative methods' of organisation. In response, Nicholson concluded: "I have never been able to appreciate the objection to employing conscript soldiers abroad as well as at home during a national emergency."[181] An important friend, Churchill became a member of the Committee of Imperial Defence in 1909.[182]

From 1908 onwards attention moved away from the traditional preoccupation with India and the dominions. The 1908-09 committee of imperial defence sub-committee on the military needs of the Empire as influenced by the Continent, considered the possibility of a European war. British resources were seen to be required in Europe and the Indian Army needed to become self-reliant and sustainable. Having an intimate personal knowledge of Indian conditions, Nicholson questioned the advisability of the armed forces of India being so organized as to be able to take the field in strength against a European Army.[183] Moreover, Nicholson influenced the proposals for British strategy in the event of a continental war. As Nicholson argued about the well-known 23 August 1911 meeting of the committee of imperial defence, which supposedly

---

177 Gooch, John, *The Plans of War: The General Staff and British Military Strategy, c.1900-1916* (London: Routledge & Keegan Paul, 1974), pp. 77-78.
178 Bod. Lib, Wilkinson cuttings, 2229 c.4 v.39, p. 43, *The Times*, September 15th 1918, 'Lord Nicholson: An Appreciation'.
179 Scott-Moncrieff, G. K., 'Memoir: Field Marshal Lord Nicholson, G.C.B., Colonel Commandant, R.E.', *The Royal Engineers Journal*, 28:6 (December 1918), p. 247.
180 Churchill Archives Centre (hereafter CAC), Churchill Papers, CHAR 2/37/20, Nicholson to Churchill, 13 April 1908.
181 CAC, Churchill Papers, CHAR 24/2, Nicholson to Churchill, 4 November 1910.
182 d'Ombrain, Nicholas, *War Machinery and High Policy: Defence Administration in Peacetime Britain, 1902-1914* (London: Oxford University Press, 1973), p. appendix, defence establishment chart.
183 Charteris, John, *Field-Marshal Earl Haig* (New York: C. Scribner's Sons, 1929), pp. 46-49.

established the continental commitment, the "... debate was a storm in a teacup because the continental strategy had been settled two years previously", in the conclusions of the 1908-09 sub-committee.[184] Nevertheless, Nicholson helped establish that an Expeditionary Force should be maintained for war overseas, and a Territorial Force should be organised for home defence.[185]

Nicholson pushed for Imperial integration, which he achieved through the shrewd accommodation of Dominion partners. "Among a small band of military reformers who had struggled to improve military education," noted the historian Brian Bond, "Nicholson was preeminent in urging the necessity for a coherent "School of Thought" which would in time create a sense of uniformity and harmony in the Army as a whole." Nicholson had pointed out that 'only Canada had been able to produce officers sufficiently well-educated to compete' for entrance into the Staff College at Camberley. He wanted to expand the number of places at the Staff College so that twelve to fifteen officers from the Dominions could enter annually.[186] Indeed, Nicholson drafted a scheme for coordinating the organisation of the local sections of each Dominion's General Staff, who should he thought, "...appoint officers who had a General Staff training at headquarters and in the Staff College." The plan was approved at the 1909 Dominion Conference on military affairs after Nicholson had satisfied Dominion concerns about the centralisation of authority in the War Office. "I could not have had finer help ...", Haldane remarked, "... than I got from [Nicholson]."[187] As the so-called chief of the Imperial General Staff, the reforms gave the title some meaning.

Nicholson played an important part in the reorganization of the British Army, in devising new strategic plans, and in the consolidation of the Territorial Force and of a modern Imperial General Staff. Nicholson shaped the British Army that entered the First World War. Despite this, and even among his contemporaries, Nicholson "...was less known to the army than many officers of incomparably less power and judgement." Wilkinson explained: "A few years ago [Nicholson] told me, with great delight, the following story." Nicholson

> ... had to go down, I think, to Salisbury to look at a cavalry barracks and was met at the station by the commanding officer and adjutant, who had been out with their regiment in the rain and were wet through. He told them to go home and change, as he could do the business without help. After he had finished his inquiries he went for lunch to the regimental mess, where he was treated as a distinguished guest, but was puzzled by the constant polite references made by the officers to the French Army in the course of their conversation. So he asked the question. 'Who do you suppose me to be?' and the answer was, 'We know who you are General Foch.' 'I thought you were mistaken,' he said. 'I am not General Foch.' 'Who are you, then?' 'The Chief of the General Staff.'

---

184 Strachan, Hew, 'The Continental Commitment', in French, David & Holden-Reid, Brain (eds) *The British General Staff: Reform and Innovation c. 1890-1939* (London: Frank Cass, 2002), p. 84.
185 Scott-Moncrieff, G. K., 'Memoir: Field Marshal Lord Nicholson, G.C.B., Colonel Commandant, R.E.', *The Royal Engineers Journal*, 28:6 (December 1918), p. 248.
186 Bond, Brian, *The Victorian Army and the Staff College, 1854-1914* (London: Eyre Methuen, 1972), pp. 237-238.
187 Haldane, Richard B., *Richard Burdon Haldane: An Autobiography* (Garden City, N.Y.: Doubleday, Doran, 1929), pp. 212-214.

Great consternation, and after lunch, as General Nicholson left for his train, the senior officer expressed the hope that their careers would not suffer from their error.[188]

Retirement

In the spring of 1912 Sir John French succeeded Nicholson as chief of the Imperial General Staff. He had been made an aide-de-camp general to George V when he came to the throne in 1910 and had been promoted field-marshal in 1911. On retirement from the Army Council in 1912, Sir William Nicholson was raised to the peerage as Baron Nicholson of Roundhay, Yorkshire. However, Nicholson had never been a hobbyist and instead wanted an opportunity for useful service. In 1912 he was appointed chairman of the Army in India Committee, consisting of Sir William Meyer, Sir Percy Lake and Sir Robert Scallon, created to inquire into the role and expenditure of the Indian Army. He returned to India in the summer of 1912 for one final visit, examining evidence there for about a year. He returned home and the Nicholson Committee's report was submitted in 1913.[189] The Nicholson Committee suggested the imposition of financial restrictions on the Indian Army. The Committee argued that "… with the Russian threat gone the most the Indian Army would have to face was the fierce but poorly armed tribesmen of the North West Frontier." The decision was justified, Nicholson thought, "…by the strategic requirements to prepare the British Army for the next likely war, on the Continent of Europe, which required all extra expenditure to spend towards that aim." Indeed, the report's conclusions should be seen in the context of all Nicholson's work while chief of the Imperial General Staff. However, the outbreak of the First World War stopped the somewhat controversial recommendations being carried into effect.[190]

The First World War

Nicholson continued to be a member of the Committee of Imperial Defence during the First World War. On the outbreak of the War, as one historian noted, the General Staff at the War Office was seriously weakened and faced enormous strategic problems. When Sir Charles Douglas, the chief of the Imperial General Staff, died from overwork in October 1914, Haldane recommended Nicholson to replace him. Lord Kitchener, now Secretary of State for War, ignored Haldane's recommendation. Kitchener had long since disliked Nicholson, for his apparent undoing of Kitchener's reforms to the Indian Army. Kitchener appointed General Sir James Wolfe-Murray instead, "… who was totally unfit for the post either in temperament or experience." Churchill referred to him as a 'sheep' and Nicholson had repeatedly exposed his limited abilities in several Army Council meetings.[191] During the War Nicholson was also

---

188 Bod. Lib, Wilkinson cuttings, 2229 c.4 v.39, p. 43, *The Times*, September 15th 1918, 'Lord Nicholson: An Appreciation'.
189 Scott-Moncrieff, G. K., 'Memoir: Field Marshal Lord Nicholson, G.C.B., Colonel Commandant, R.E.', *The Royal Engineers Journal*, 28:6 (December 1918), p. 248.
190 Heathcote, T. A., *The Military in British India: The Development of British Land Forces in South Asia, 1600-1947* (Manchester: Manchester University Press, 1995), pp. 196-197.
191 Bond, Brian, *The Victorian Army and the Staff College, 1854-1914* (London: Eyre Methuen, 1972), p. 300.

chairman of the Territorial Force Association for London and in 1916 he was appointed colonel-commandant of the Royal Engineers.[192]

Dardanelles Commission

Nicholson was a member of the commissions of inquiry that investigated the conduct of operations in the Dardanelles and Mesopotamia campaigns. General Sir Ian Hamilton was selected to command the Dardanelles force, but when it failed he was recalled. The Dardanelles Commission was set up in 1916 to establish what had gone wrong. However, Hamilton's main concern was not his defence of the conduct of the operations, but rather Nicholson's attitude as a member of the Commission. As Hamilton wrote, "Nick's [Nicholson's] appointment caused me to shiver. On the surface he has always been a friend; ... [but] his delight in mischief-making will certainly find scope in the Commission. ... he has been jealous of me and has always had a mischievous delight in trying to put a spoke in my wheel."[193] Nicholson appeared unaware of Hamilton's bitterness. Indeed, his correspondence with Roberts show that Nicholson viewed Hamilton as a good friend. Moreover, Nicholson was impressed by Hamilton's abilities. He remarked: "The Native Soldiers [sic], thanks to [Ian] Johnny Hamilton, shoots better as a rule than his British comrade."[194] Yet, Hamilton clearly established a deeply held resentment against Nicholson, who Roberts had favoured for promotion in 1890, delaying Hamilton's own advancement. Nicholson was again selected over Hamilton by Sir William Lockhart for his Chief of the Staff, and subsequently was appointed over Hamilton as adjutant-general in India.[195] Undoubtedly, the animosity was one sided. Hamilton was left exasperated again by Nicholson's appointment as chief military observer during the Russo-Japanese War. "Hardly is my back turned", Hamilton boohooed, "when Nick [Nicholson] steps forward and secures the very position he had taken pains to assure me I should get!"[196] Hamilton had mistaken Nicholson's awkwardness at having an officer of the same rank under his orders in Japan for unfriendliness. Nevertheless, Nicholson remained completely unaware of Hamilton's feelings.[197] When the Commission reported, Hamilton's concerns about Nicholson's intentions proved to be unfounded.

Conclusion

Nicholson died on 13 September 1918 at his home at 51 Pont Street, Chelsea, London. His body was interred four days later at Brompton cemetery. On his death the peerage became extinct.[198] "He cared nothing for the pomps [sic] and shows of military traditional", Wilkinson remarked,

---

192 Scott-Moncrieff, G. K., 'Memoir: Field Marshal Lord Nicholson, G.C.B., Colonel Commandant, R.E.', *The Royal Engineers Journal*, 28:6 (December 1918), p. 248.
193 Macleod, Jenny, *Reconsidering Gallipoli* (Manchester: Manchester University Press, 2004), pp. 37-38.
194 NAM, Lord Roberts Papers, 71-01-23-87, R52/67 Nicholson to Roberts, 18 January 1899.
195 NAM, Lord Roberts Papers, 71-01-23-87, R52/54 Nicholson to Roberts, 10 October 1897.
196 Lee, John, *A Soldier's Life: General Sir Ian Hamilton, 1853-1947* (London: Macmillan, 2000), p. 79.
197 NAM, Wilkinson Papers, OPT 13/13/60, Nicholson to Wilkinson, 22 September 1904.
198 Moreman, T.R., 'Nicholson, William Gustavus, Baron Nicholson (1845-1918)', *DNB*, Oxford University Press (2004).

"and his last wish was that he should be laid in his grave without the display or ceremony usually associated with his high rank."[199]

General Sir William Nicholson was made in the late Victorian army. He excelled throughout his military career in positions of administrative control. Nicholson's career demonstrates that although staff work in the late Victorian army was informal, the administrative work was not unsophisticated. Indeed, this assessment is far too simplistic. Moreover, Nicholson instigated a great development in staff work while at the War Office. It is impossible to fully understand the reorganisation of the British Army, or the development of British strategy before the First World War, without studying Nicholson's career. Nicholson was a model staff officer. As chief of the Imperial General Staff he became the exemplar head of the Army. Undoubtedly, 'Old Nick' was one of the most remarkable generals of the late Victorian and Edwardian army.

---

199 Bod. Lib, Wilkinson cuttings, 2229 c.4 v.39, p. 43, *The Times*, September 15th 1918, 'Lord Nicholson: An Appreciation'.

7

A Victorian Hero: Lord Wantage VC (1832-1901)[1]

Roger T. Stearn

Robert James Lindsay, from 1858 Loyd-Lindsay, and from 1885 Baron Wantage (1832-1901), was among the first recipients of the Victoria Cross, and is today remembered by students of military history primarily because of the 1892 Wantage Committee. A Victorian hero, eulogised by contemporaries, he was the subject of a panegyric by his widow, *Lord Wantage, V.C., K.C.B.: A Memoir* (1907*)*, still the main source for his life, but has received no subsequent biography other than the relatively short articles in the old and new *Dictionary of National Biography*. As his widow observed, "… his career was a varied one; he touched life at many points, as a soldier, a land-owner, a Member of Parliament, a Lord-Lieutenant, and a leader in works of public utility and benevolence."[2] The present chapter attempts an overview of his varied life, both military and civilian, in its context, focusing more on its military aspects. It considers his regular army service, including the Crimean War, and his roles as an MP concerned with the army and defence, as a Volunteer, as a leader of the Red Cross, and as a landowner and farmer. These roles were interrelated and overlapped chronologically but are here considered thematically. He experienced war as a young officer and later as a neutral observer but, like most Victorian generals, he never commanded a formation in battle. He was a peacetime Volunteer brigadier general. Although he was not a military theorist or policy-maker, his life now offers significant insights into aspects of the Victorian military and its interface with civil society.

---

1   I wish to thank Professor Ian Beckett, Dr Mark Curthoys, Ms Justine Taylor (Archivist, Honourable Artillery Company), Ms Jemma Lee (Archivist, British Red Cross), the staff of the Bodleian Library, Institute of Historical Research, National Army Museum Templer Study Centre, National Art Library, and especially my wife. I also wish to thank and to acknowledge my indebtedness to the authors of the books, articles and websites I have sourced.
2   Wantage, Lady, *Lord Wantage, K.C.B., V.C.; A Memoir* (London: Smith, Elder & Co., 1907) p. 1. The present chapter is partly based on this book, on Roger T.Stearn, 'Lindsay, Robert James Loyd-', *Oxford Dictionary of National Biography* (Oxford, Oxford University Press, 2004 and online) [hereafter cited as *ODNB*], and on the archives of the Honourable Artillery Company and the British Red Cross.

Early Life and Crimean War

Robert Lindsay came from an aristocratic and military family of Scottish descent. He was the younger son of Lieutenant-General James Lindsay (1793-1855), Grenadier Guards, of Balcarres, Fife – son of a nabob and grandson of the fifth earl of Balcarres – and his second wife Anne, co-heir of Sir Coutts Trotter, first baronet and banker. James Lindsay served in the Peninsula and was later a tory MP. Robert Lindsay, called Bob or Robin by his family, was born on 16 April 1832 and spent much of his boyhood at Balcarres. He loathed his private school: its headmaster was "…about the only man Lindsay ever thoroughly hated."[3] He enjoyed Eton, from 1846 to 1850, where he was a 'wet bob' and spent much time rowing. He was slim, handsome, blue-eyed, golden-haired, and, his father wrote, "… like a thoroughbred pony … a gentlemanlike, moral, good boy, beloved by masters and companions."[4] After Eton he was tutored for the East India College at Haileybury, where "…before the dawn of the Competition Wallah young Indian civil servants received their training", for a career under the East India Company, in which his family, like other Scots, had 'considerable interest'[5]. However, he preferred a military career and, through the influence of his 'fascinating' sister May's admirer, Colonel the Hon. Alexander Gordon, ADC to Prince Albert, in December 1850 was commissioned ensign and lieutenant by purchase in the Scots Fusilier Guards (from 1877 the Scots Guards); the regulation price was £1200, more than twice that for line infantry.[6]

As a young guardee Lindsay enjoyed ample leave, and he spent the winter of 1850-1 with his family in Italy. In Rome they became friends of Lord Overstone's family. Samuel Jones Loyd, Baron Overstone (1796-1883), another Etonian, was a successful banker and influential economist – a leader of the 'currency school' of monetary theorists – and was ennobled, on Lord John Russell's recommendation, in 1850.[7] He became a millionaire, one of the richest men in the country. He invested much of his money in land, at the time of 'high farming' when agriculture was profitable and owned more land than any other 'new man', though less than several dukes. He spent £1,670,000 buying land, and in the year of his death owned 30,849 acres, yielding £358,098 per annum.[8] In 1862 he built his grandiose country mansion, Overstone Park, near Northampton, later described by Mark Girouard as "…a terrible bastard Renaissance house … drearily asymmetrical, with two vamped-up Barry towers and much ornament."[9] Lord Overstone's son had died as a baby and his daughter Harriet Sarah (1837-1920) was his heiress.[10] She was fourteen when the Lindsays met her, governess-educated and shy. She was described

---

3   Wantage, *Lord Wantage*, p. 11.
4   Wantage, *Lord Wantage*, p. 11.
5   Anon, 'Lord Wantage', *Spectator*, 4 January 1908, p. 21.; Wantage, *Lord Wantage*, p. 12.
6   Bruce, Anthony, *The Purchase System in the British Army, 1660-1871* (London: Royal Historical Society, 1980), p. 177.
7   Reed, Michael, 'Loyd, Samuel Jones', *ODNB*; Mitchie, Ranald C., 'Income, expenditure and investment of a Victorian millionaire: Lord Overstone, 1823-83', *Bulletin of the Institute of Historical Research* LVIII (1985).
8   Rubinstein, W.D., *Men of Property: the very wealthy in Britain since the industrial revolution* (London: Social Affairs Unit, 2006), p. 264.
9   Girouard, Mark, *The Victorian Country House* (London: Yale University Press, 1979), p. 415.
10 T.A.B.Corley, 'Lindsay, Harriet Sarah Loyd', *ODNB*.

in 1854 as "... extremely modest in her manners and expression ... still kept in her washed-muslin dresses and considered a child."[11]

Following war between Russia and the Ottoman Empire from October 1853, in March 1854 Britain declared war on Russia, so entering what became the Crimean War.[12] British troop movements had already begun. Earlier in March the Scots Fusilier Guards, part of the Army of the East and reputedly the Queen's favourites, left England for the Mediterranean. In July they reached Varna in Bulgaria, then Ottoman-ruled. There cholera ravaged the British and French troops. Lieutenant Lindsay escaped it but was seriously ill with dysentery. In August he wrote home criticising the Varna hospital: "... nothing is worse managed than our Medical Staff."[13] In September the Allies landed unopposed on the Crimea to attack the Russian base at Sevastopol, the centre of Russian naval power. At the battle of the Alma, Lindsay, carrying the Queen's colour, distinguished himself. The Allies besieged and bombarded Sevastopol. In November at the battle of Inkerman Lindsay again distinguished himself. That month he was promoted captain without purchase, following the death of another officer. He endured the Crimean winter, and wrote home condemning British mismanagement of supply, and the resultant suffering of the troops. He wrote, "I can hardly refrain my indignation against all those who humbug Lord Raglan and soothe him in his fool's paradise."[14] His letters were shown by Overstone to the Duke of Newcastle, the secretary of state for war. However, Lindsay suffered less than the rank and file as his family sent him thigh boots and warm clothes, including, "... a large blue uniform coat, lined all through with flannel." In March 1855 General Sir

Lord Wantage VC.

---

11 G.E.C. *et al*, *The Complete Peerage* XII (London: St Catherine Press, 1959), p. 341.
12 From Alexander Kinglake's eight-volume *The Invasion of the Crimea* (1863-87) on, so much has been written about the Crimean War that it is here unnecessary to provide more than a brief outline, focusing on Lindsay's experience.
13 Wantage, *Lord Wantage*, p. 23.
14 Wantage, *Lord Wantage*, p. 67.

James Simpson, a Peninsula veteran and friend of Lindsay's father, arrived as chief of staff and appointed Lindsay his aide-de-camp. Lindsay's letters home continued critical; he stated that the British land transport was "… compared with the French, utterly trumpery." He admired Raglan and after his death in June wrote, "…he was a fine religious old man, a perfect gentleman, and all those that knew him well were wonderfully attached to him."[15] In August Lindsay became adjutant of his regiment. In September Sevastopol fell and in March 1856 the armistice was signed. While he was in the Crimea his father died, in December 1855; Lindsay inherited £6,000 and a £300 annuity. In June the Scots Fusilier Guards and Lindsay finally left the Crimea. He never forgot what he had experienced and witnessed there.

In June 1856 Lindsay returned with the Scots Fusilier Guards to England, and in December was promoted brevet major. He was soon 'a conspicuous figure in society'. A committed Anglican, he became an Evangelical and, with other young Guards officers, was influenced by Catherine Marsh,[16] and held Bible classes for soldiers. His widow wrote that, "… religious convictions and a serious view of duty remained with him through life, but the Evangelical phase proved a passing one."[17] Awarded the Crimea medal with four claps, the Legion of Honour, the Medijie 5th class and the Turkish medal, in February 1857 he was one of 111 Crimean veterans awarded the new Victoria Cross, which was for his conduct at the Alma (20 September 1854) and at Inkerman (5 November 1854).[18] In June crosses were presented to him and sixty-one others by Queen Victoria at a public ceremony in Hyde Park, before thousands of spectators. Lindsay's mother wrote that he 'looked particularly handsome'.

In the Crimea the British troops' Minié rifles had given them a significant advantage over the musket-armed Russians. Before the war, in 1853, the School of Musketry had been established at Hythe on the Kent coast, to instruct the army in rifle-shooting and to experiment with new weapons. In early 1858 Lindsay, with other Guards adjutants, attended a special ten-week course there, which he enjoyed. He wrote that, "…all sorts of new inventions are daily tried here; breech-loaders of every description and pattern, different-shaped bullets, and different degrees of powder, etc."[19]

Prince Albert meticulously, if unsuccessfully, planned his heir's education. In 1858 he arranged that Albert Edward, Prince of Wales, should have his own, but paternally-supervised, household at White Lodge, Richmond Park. Albert chose as his companions there 'three very distinguished young men' to be equerries in monthly rotation and provided 'a rigorous code of disciplinary rules' to be applied. He wrote of the equerries that from their "… more intimate intercourse I anticipate no small benefit to Bertie."[20] One of the three, to his surprise, was Lindsay. He had a long interview with Albert, who instructed him on training the young Prince. Lindsay was initially favourably impressed by the Prince and wrote that "…those about him hardly realise how intelligent he really is."[21] The appointment soon ended, in 1859, because

---

15 Wantage, *Lord Wantage*, p. 100.
16 See Timothy C.F. Stunt, 'Marsh, William', *ODNB*.
17 Wantage, *Lord Wantage*, p. 138.
18 Wantage, *Lord Wantage*, p. 457 prints verse by Lady Lindsay, 'V.C.', which calls the Victoria Cross 'the little cross of iron'.
19 Wantage, *Lord Wantage*, p. 140.
20 Martin, Theodore, *The Life of His Royal Highness the Prince Consort* IV (London: Smith, Elder & Co., 1879), p. 206.
21 Wantage, *Lord Wantage*, p. 142.

of Lindsay's marriage. He had failed to influence the subsequent conduct of the Prince of Wales, who notoriously preferred a different 'intimate intercourse' from that offered by the respectable Lindsay. Nevertheless the Prince apparently liked him and their relations continued cordial. Although his clubs included the Marlborough, he was never in the Marlborough House set. The Prince later appointed him colonel of the Honourable Artillery Company.

In June 1858 Lindsay became engaged to Lord Overstone's daughter and heiress, Harriet Jones-Loyd, and in October he changed his name to Loyd-Lindsay. In November they were married at St. Martin-in-the-Fields. Mrs Loyd-Lindsay was a keen horsewoman and a generous philanthropist.[22] She loyally helped her husband in his various activities, and they enjoyed a long and apparently happy, though childless, marriage. Loyd-Lindsay's marriage transformed his life. A younger son, though from a landowning family, he had himself owned neither land nor wealth. The land and other property given them by Overstone made the Loyd-Lindsays very rich and major landowners. Loyd-Lindsay's land and wealth conferred status and enabled his subsequent roles as a member of parliament and in the Volunteer Force and the Red Cross. In September 1859 he retired from the regular army with the ranks of captain and lieutenant colonel. His connection with the military was far from over, but thenceforth took a different form.

Despite his Scottish ancestry, at the time of the Victorian cult of the highlands – Walter Scott, Balmoral, tartans, bagpipes, John Brown, 'invented tradition', and German princes posing in kilts – Loyd-Lindsay took no part in it. Rather he saw himself as an English county magnate. He had an 'attractive personality' and 'personal charm'. He was 'not a great reader', pragmatic, a doer rather than a thinker. He believed in duty: "I must do something to justify my existence."[23] Like Prussian Junker officers, he combined social and political conservatism with willingness to innovate and enthusiasm for new technology. According to the *Spectator*, "…without any pretension to the tricks of the orator, he was a clear, forcible speaker, with a natural eloquence."[24] He was praised as "…the straightest man in the Army".[25] Devout, brave and philanthropic, he personified the Victorian chivalric ideal.[26] He was tall, handsome, with a 'noble face and head', fair-haired and blue-eyed. Like other Crimean veterans and civilians who copied them, he was full-bearded.[27] His widow wrote that 'stately in bearing and distinguished in manner, he realised the ideal of martial beauty and chivalry attributed to the knights of old'. His appearance was much admired by contemporaries. Julia Cameron, who photographed him, said he was the nearest to her ideal of King Arthur, and he was painted by Sir William Richmond, Lady Butler, Walter Ouless and Louis Desanges. He might, with hindsight, be regarded as an

---

22 Corley, 'Lindsay, Harriet'.
23 *LW*, p. 427.
24 *Spectator* 4 January 1908, p. 22.
25 Quoted, *The Times*, 11 June 1901, p. 8.
26 See Mark Girouard, *The Return to Camelot: chivalry and the English gentleman* (London: Yale University Press, 1981).
27 Trevelyan, G.M., *Illustrated English Social History* IV *The Nineteenth Century* (London: Reprint Society, 1963), p. 88. Oldstone-Moore, Christopher, 'The Beard Movement in Victorian Britain', *Victorian Studies* Vol.48, No.1 (Autumn 2005) disagrees with Trevelyan's claim of the Crimean War origin of the beard fashion, showing it antedated the war; arguably the article understates the impact of the Crimean soldiers. Loyd-Lindsay's was the first bearded generation since the 17th century. Loyd-Lindsay's beard may have contributed to his arrest in Paris in 1870.

example of 'Christian militarism' and of 'gentlemanly capitalism', and as a Wolseleyite, but such reductionism, if unqualified, is inadequate: "…the truth is in the detail."[28]

MP and Defence Issues

Loyd-Lindsay's retirement did not end his connection with the regular army. Thereafter it was political – as a member of parliament, minister and inquiry chairman – and personal, through his social, Volunteer and Red Cross contacts with senior officers, though his influence can only be conjectured. County MPs, the knights of the shires, were more prestigious than MPs for boroughs, some of which even after 1832 were still notoriously corrupt.[29] County MPs were traditionally major landowners or from major landowning families. The basic county franchise was still the historic forty-shilling freehold, excluding agricultural labourers, and voting was open. It was indicative of Loyd-Lindsay's landowning status that he was invited to stand not for a borough but for Berkshire: his widow wrote that he was "…naturally looked to as a future candidate." Both parties competed for him. Although his father-in-law and paymaster was a moderate Liberal, Loyd-Lindsay was from a Conservative family, and in 1860 he declared himself a moderate Conservative.

In 1864 he was proposed as a Conservative candidate and spoke largely on agricultural issues. The Liberals won the July 1865 general election but the three Conservatives won the Berkshire county election. Loyd-Lindsay was head of the poll with 2,227 votes. After the poll at Abingdon, the county capital, the successful candidates girded on their swords as knights of the shire. In the November 1868 general election again the Liberals won nationally but the Conservatives won Berkshire. Loyd-Lindsay rode from Lockinge to the poll at Abingdon escorted by mounted farmers, tenantry and yeomen. He continued MP until 1885. In the House of Commons he spoke largely on army issues, both regular and Volunteer. He was a member of the parliamentary Volunteer interest and a spokesman for the Volunteer movement.[30] While he spoke on various aspects of the regular army, he repeated one theme: transport and supply, what would later be called logistics. The Crimean War was a formative experience for Loyd-Lindsay and others of his military generation, as the Boer War was to be to a later generation. In the Crimea he had witnessed and endured the appalling breakdown of the supply system and the resultant suffering.

Gladstone's first ministry included Edward Cardwell, the greatest secretary of state for war of the century, who introduced the 'Cardwell reforms' of the army. The political elite of both main parties often met socially. Loyd-Lindsay knew Cardwell, who was an old friend of Overstone and a frequent guest at Lockinge. In 1870 Loyd-Lindsay was largely absorbed in Red Cross work during the Franco-Prussian War. In 1871, as a prominent Conservative military spokesman,

---

28 Anderson, Olive, 'The growth of Christian militarism in mid-Victorian Britain', *English Historical Review* LXXXVI, January 1971; Cain, P.J. and Hopkins, A.G., *British Imperialism: Innovation and Expansion 1688-1914* (London: Longman, 1993), chapters 1, 3.
29 Hanham, H.J., *Elections and Party Management: Politics in the time of Disraeli and Gladstone* (London: Longmans, 1959), chapter 13; Gwyn, William. B., *Democracy and the Cost of Politics in Britain* (London: Athlone Press, 1962), chapter 3.
30 Beckett, Ian F.W, *Riflemen Form: A Study of the Rifle Volunteer Movement 1859-1908* (Aldershot: Ogilby Trusts, 1982), pp. 154-6.

he was pressed to oppose Cardwell's proposal, in his Army Regulation Bill, for the abolition of purchase of commissions. This was a contentious issue, with abolition strongly opposed by aristocrats and army traditionalists.[31] In the Commons on 6 March 1871, Loyd-Lindsay moved his amendment and spoke against Cardwell's proposal.[32] He claimed abolition of purchase was the most important point of the Bill. It would cost far more than was anticipated: 'the cost of compensating officers in full he estimated at £12,000,000'. He alleged the army, unlike that of North Germany, was inadequately organized. It needed "… an organization consisting of staff, commissariat, transport, and medical departments", as the "… Army Service organization – which was now called the Control – was quite insufficient." He cited the Crimea, "…when there was a complete collapse of this department, and our Army was left to starve at a distance of only seven miles from its base of operations." He argued for expenditure on reforming transport and commissariat, not on abolition of purchase. He criticised competitive examinations: "… there were qualities required in an officer which no examiner could ever bring to light … by testing all men by one uniform standard of bookwork examination we ran the risk of shutting out the very men we should endeavour to bring into the service." He claimed purchase provided 'an excellent system of self-supporting retirement', which would be expensive to replace. In the non-purchase corps there was stagnation from want of promotion, and a system of pure selection meant favouritism. He cited the Duke of Cambridge, Hartington, and others against selection, and alleged that abolition would be an act of "… mistaken and mischievous extravagance." His speech was well received by his army friends. After further debate, advised by Disraeli he withdrew his resolution. According to Dr Bruce, he was much more concerned with preserving purchase than with allocating additional resources to the army.[33] The Bill passed the Commons but was rejected by the Lords, so in July 1871 the government abolished purchase by royal warrant.

Loyd-Lindsay, however, unlike most Conservative military MPs, supported Cardwell's other reforms: localisation – a 'territorial system' – association of Militia and Volunteers with regular battalions, short service and reserve. He continued to support them in subsequent years, and through this became associated with a group of army reformers which included Wolseley, Evelyn Wood and Henry Brackenbury.[34] He continued to advise and co-operate with them and, his widow claimed, his influence in military matters became increasingly felt. Although well aware of Indian defence, as the Wantage Committee Report showed, Loyd-Lindsay never visited India and the Indian army. He was a Wolseleyite and while not a member of the 'ring', a friend to its members. Looking back in 1901, Wolseley wrote of Loyd-Lindsay:

> Army reform with us was then sadly in want of friends willing to come forward and help; few had the moral courage to face the taunts of "society" … But he was not prevented by party politics from helping forward Army reform at a time when it was

---

31   The definitive study is still Bruce, *Purchase System*; a concise account is in Spiers, Edward M., *The Late Victorian Army 1868-1902* (Manchester: Manchester University Press, 1992), pp. 11-18.
32   *Hansard's Parliamentary Debates. Third Series* [hereafter cited as *Hansard*], CCIV (1871), 6 March, cc1397-1408; Wantage, *Lord Wantage*, pp. 208-9; Bruce, *Purchase System*, p. 129.
33   Bruce, *Purchase System*, p. 129.
34   Wantage, *Lord Wantage*, p. 210. On Brackenbury see Brice, Christopher *The Thinking Man's Soldier: the life and career of General Sir Henry Brackenbury 1837-1914* (Solihull: Helion, 2012).

very unpopular in certain quarters, and I know from personal experience how much the country owed to Lord Wantage then for the support he – a great Conservative – afforded those who then strove to modernise and make efficient our out-of-date Army system.[35]

Another military issue raised in Parliament was that of army manoeuvres. In 1871 Cardwell proposed they be held on the Berkshire Downs. In April Wolseley (recently returned from the Red River expedition) and other senior officers visited the area and were entertained at Lockinge. They reported favourably and plans went ahead for manoeuvres in September. In Berkshire Loyd-Lindsay strove to facilitate them. He formed a committee representing landowners, farmers and others from 36 parishes and villages, held meetings, and used his influence to persuade them to co-operate in enabling the manoeuvres. Suddenly in July Lord Northbrook, the under secretary for war, announced the manoeuvres were cancelled because of the lateness of the Berkshire harvest. The latter was widely believed only a pretext, and that the real cause was the inability of the Control Department to cope with the movement of the troops from Aldershot to Berkshire. There were questions in Parliament and on 31 July, after Cardwell insisted that the harvest was the cause, Loyd-Lindsay moved an adjournment to consider the subject.[36] He claimed there was an emergency, "… a matter of the greatest importance, involving … the very existence of the Army." The Berkshire farmers had not been consulted by the military about the harvest. He alleged "…the Control department had collapsed" and "could not move their army 30 miles from its base of operations." He claimed "…the feeding and transport of the Army were all important", and again cited the Crimea, "…where men were starving within seven miles of the base of their operations, because there was neither food nor transport." He insisted that "…if the Control department broke down, their Army was worthless." He alleged that ministers were deceived, "…just as much as Napoleon III was deceived when he imagined his Army was in first-rate order." Cardwell replied that the Control Department, introduced by the Conservatives in 1868, in peacetime had only 'the nucleus of a transport corps' which in war would be supplemented by transport from the country where they were campaigning. Nevertheless, Loyd-Lindsay's criticism may perhaps have contributed to the 1888 formation of the Army Service Corps.

The Conservatives won the February 1874 general election, and in Berkshire the three sitting members were returned unopposed. Disraeli formed his second ministry. Loyd-Lindsay hoped for a War Office appointment but was disappointed, and Disraeli wrote to him that it was, "…a matter of great personal regret" that he had been unable to arrange his appointment.[37] In 1876 and 1877 he was involved in organising Red Cross activity in the Turco-Serbian War. In August 1877, following the transfer of Colonel Stanley, Disraeli, since 1876 Lord Beaconsfield, appointed Loyd-Lindsay Financial Secretary at the War Office under Gathorne Hardy. Congratulatory letters to Loyd-Lindsay included one from General Sir Henry Brackenbury which suggested he should "…make the War Office remember that the Army is meant as an instrument of war, not merely to be kept clean and bright and exhibited on show like a piece of plate."[38] During

---

35 Wolseley to Lady Wantage, November 1901, quoted in Wantage, *Lord Wantage*, pp. 405-6.
36 *Hansard* CCVIII (1871), 31 July, cc545-9.
37 Wantage, *Lord Wantage*, p. 217.
38 Wantage, *Lord Wantage*, p. 252.

the eastern crisis of the Russo-Turkish War Loyd-Lindsay was involved in preparations for possible war with Russia; the planned expeditionary force was to be commanded by Napier, with Wolseley his chief of staff. Loyd-Lindsay argued for calling out the reserve, as consonant with the short-service system, rather than transferring soldiers from other regiments to those allocated to the expeditionary force.

Following the resignation of Lords Carnarvon and Derby and the resultant cabinet changes, Gathorne Hardy was succeeded as Secretary of State for War by Colonel Frederick Stanley, like Loyd-Lindsay formerly in the Guards. Loyd-Lindsay was involved with the Regimental Exchange Bill, the occupation of Cyprus, and boy enlistment, which he favoured. He proposed a scheme whereby adolescents, not under fourteen, would be enlisted, paid sixpence a day retaining fee while in civilian employment until seventeen, then join as boy recruits and engage to serve for twelve years. He hoped this would gain the army a 'superior class of men', but his scheme was not adopted. During the Zulu War he urged that Wolseley be sent to replace Chelmsford. Early in 1880 he addressed a large meeting at Newbury, contrasting the Crimean bungling and suffering with the present regime. The Conservatives lost the March-April 1880 general election but kept their Berkshire seats. In July 1880 Disraeli wrote to Loyd-Lindsay, "… ours was the most unlucky Government …Had we had decent harvests and fair trade we should probably have renewed our lease."[39] Loyd-Lindsay's War Office experience confirmed his support for the Cardwell system and 'Sir Garnet Wolseley and his school'. He continued to be in touch with and was consulted by the War Office. In Gladstone's new ministry his relative the Earl of Morley was undersecretary of state for war, and they met frequently and discussed army topics.

In the Commons army debates in 1881 Loyd-Lindsay continued to defend Cardwellian short service and reserve. He claimed that although long service produced a limited number of good soldiers, the losses on a long campaign such as the Crimea showed its disadvantage, and "… with long service we can have no Reserve."[40]

With his Crimean memories, solicitude for British soldiers, and Red Cross involvement, Loyd-Lindsay was concerned about medical provision on campaign. He had long known and corresponded with Florence Nightingale who, though a bedridden invalid – probably with brucellosis ('Crimean fever') – from her house at 11 South Street, Mayfair continued to promote the causes of nursing and army health.[41] She influenced largely behind the scenes, through significant men, especially, earlier, Sidney Herbert. Loyd-Lindsay was happy to help her. He criticised medical mismanagement in the 1881 Transvaal War and its quasi-exoneration by Evelyn Wood's committee. The 1882 Egyptian campaign was an impressive military victory but, with its typhoid death rate, apparently a medical failure.[42] Press and public criticism of the Army Medical department began during the campaign, and Loyd-Lindsay and others pressed for an inquiry. He was a member of the 1882-3 Army Medical Service Committee chaired by Lord Morley. It heard evidence from 140 witnesses including Wolseley, who bitterly criticised

---

39 Wantage, *Lord Wantage*, p. 266.
40 Wantage, *Lord Wantage*, p. 269.
41 Bostridge, Mark, *Florence Nightingale: the woman and her legend* (London: Penguin, 2009), pp. 281-2, 324-5.
42 Curtin, Philip D., *Disease and Empire: the health of European troops in the conquest of Africa* (Cambridge: Cambridge University Press, 1998), pp. 158-62.

the Medical Department. Loyd-Lindsay, her 'ally' worked closely with Miss Nightingale.[43] She suggested witnesses to him and sent him elaborate briefs for questioning them. She was given daily minutes of evidence, and when the committee was preparing its report sent successive papers of suggestions which Loyd-Lindsay submitted to the chairman. Loyd-Lindsay wrote to her in May 1883 about the report, thanking her: "...the best suggestions come from you." He wrote in June, "... how valuable your aid was to me during the enquiry. If the Secretary of State carries out the report, some of the most useful improvements will have originated with you."[44] The report, over 800 pages, covered the medical history of the Egyptian campaign, and recommended reforms including administrative changes, increased use of nursing sisters, and more medical training for medical officers. Some of these were later implemented.

Loyd-Lindsay and his wife sometimes travelled overseas. In 1883 his health was failing and 'a sea voyage' was ordered. With his wife's relation A.K.Loyd and his 'faithful valet' Cooper, in August he sailed to South Africa.[45] He met Rhodes and other politicians and travelled in Cape Colony. At Kimberly he found navy and army officers, "University men, Eton and Harrow men", and enjoyed "...a small but high-toned society composed of the best sort of Englishmen and English ladies." He wrote that, "... affairs in South Africa are in frightful confusion; Heaven knows whether they can ever right themselves without a desperate convulsion, perhaps a civil war, with a war of black and white races on top of it." He returned home in mid-October, and in December published in the *Nineteenth Century* a short article, 'A recent visit to the Boers'. His interests were never exclusively military, and he did not comment on the military aspects of the recent Transvaal War nor their lessons, but he noted the Boers' 'Old Testament bloodthirstiness towards their enemies', and British South Africans' resentment at Gladstone's agreement with the Transvaal, and the problem of, "... a population of black savages outnumbering the civilised community." He claimed the British caused the economic development and progress in South Africa, and he advocated the British government preventing further Boer expansion into Bechuanaland.

During the 1884-85 Gordon Relief Expedition several of Loyd-Lindsay's army friends were in Egypt and the Sudan: Wolseley, Buller, Brackenbury, Frederick Stephenson, Francis Grenfell and John Ardagh. In June 1885 Gladstone's government was defeated and Lord Salisbury formed his first ministry. He offered Loyd-Lindsay the oddly-misnamed post of surveyor-general at the War Office. W.H.Smith, the new war minister, urged him to accept, but he declined because of ill health. In July 1885, nominated by Salisbury, he became Baron Wantage of Lockinge and took his seat in the House of Lords. From 1886 he was lord lieutenant of Berkshire and from 1889 was also a Berkshire county councillor. He had been initiated into freemasonry in Malta before the Crimean War, and in 1898, nominated by the Prince of Wales, was appointed masonic provincial grand master of Berkshire. His electoral influence apparently continued.[46] Although the 1884 Reform Act enfranchised rural workers, it had less impact than the radicals hoped. Rural workers doubted the secrecy of the ballot and feared 'the screw', intimidation.

---

43   Cook, Edward, *The Life of Florence Nightingale* Vol II (London: Macmillan, 1913), pp. 337-8; Wantage, *Lord Wantage*, pp. 279-80.
44   Cook, *Life*, pp. 337-8.
45   On Loyd-Lindsay and South Africa from 'A visit to the Boers', *Nineteenth Century* XIV, December 1883, and Wantage, *Lord Wantage*, pp. 282-5.
46   Pelling, Henry, *Social Geography of British Elections 1885-1910* (London: Macmillan, 1967), p. 116.

The *Daily News* reporter, George Millin alleged Wantage's workers "… have no idea whatever that they are free electors." A local woman told him, "… they all votes Lord Wantage's way, of course. It wouldn't do for 'em to go again 'im."⁴⁷ Berkshire North continued a safe Conservative seat.

Lord Wantage maintained contact with the regular army partly through their manoeuvres. In 1890 some 3,000 cavalry manoeuvred on the Berkshire Downs, and Evelyn Wood, Baker Russell and their staffs were quartered at Wantage. The Duke of Cambridge, Wolseley, Buller and other senior officers were at Lockinge, where Wantage and his wife 'kept open house during the manoeuvre fortnight', culminating in a 'great ball' for officers and neighbours. The success of these manoeuvres led to more on the Downs. At the 1893 manoeuvres Wantage provided free beer for the Guards and was thanked by 'lusty cheers'. Also he and his wife frequently visited Evelyn Wood at Aldershot and rode with him at drills and field days.

As Dr Skelley has written, "… throughout the whole of the period 1856 to 1899, one of the biggest problems facing the regular army was to recruit men in sufficient numbers to meet its needs."⁴⁸ The late Victorian army had a chronic manpower shortage, and Wolseley and others urged that it be solved by improving rank and file pay and conditions. In 1891 Edward Stanhope, Conservative war minister in Salisbury's second ministry, responded by establishing the Committee on the Terms and Conditions of Service in the Army.⁴⁹ He appointed Wantage its chairman and it became known as the Wantage Committee. Its twelve members were mostly army officers, with also a hostile and obstructive War Office bureaucrat, Arthur Haliburton. A letter to *The Times* described him as representing, "… the powerful forces which for years have successfully obstructed the reform alike of the War Office and of the Army", and alleged he "… had been placed upon the committee in order to play the part of the dynamite charge controlled by clockwork and to wreck the ship at a given moment."⁵⁰ The committee heard evidence from Cambridge, Wolseley, Evelyn Wood, Buller and many other officers, but not from the rank and file. The witnesses agreed on the inadequacy of the home battalions, which Wolseley likened to squeezed lemons and Evelyn Wood alleged were 'only a nursery'. Wolseley insisted that a voluntary army had to be well paid: "…unless we can give a very high rate of pay, we shall always be obliged to take in "the waifs and strays"."⁵¹ The Committee Report was largely drafted by Wantage and expressed his strongly-held convictions. It recommended improvements in pay and conditions, including abolition of stoppages, a messing allowance, and more free uniform. Haliburton disagreed and wrote a long 'Dissent'. Although the Report was favourably received by the press, Stanhope disliked it and was angered by some of the senior officers' views, the government was unwilling to pay for the proposed changes, and allegedly Haliburton's malign influence acted against them: he was allegedly "…able to annul the whole proceedings and to

---

47 Special Commissioner of the "Daily News" (G.F. Millin), *Life in Our Villages* (London: Cassell, 1891), p. 110. Millin did not allege political pressure by Wantage and his agents ('Tories') but suggested the possibility.
48 Skelley, Alan Ramsay, *The Victorian Army at Home: the recruitment and terms and conditions of the British regular, 1859-1899* (London: Croom Helm, 1977), p. 235.
49 Wantage, *Lord Wantage*, pp. 335-41, 433-45; Skelley, *Victorian Army*, pp. 189-90; Spiers, *Late Victorian Army*, p. 138.
50 Letter from 'Reform', *The Times*, 14 December 1897, p. 9. Dynamite, patented by Alfred Nobel in 1867, was in the late 19th century used by terrorists.
51 Spiers, *Late Victorian Army*, p. 138.

stave off Army reform."[52] The Report had little immediate effect: only the recommendations on the issue of clothing were implemented and later some marginal improvements in pay.

Wantage continued to advocate army reform and defend the Cardwell system, especially what he considered three cardinal points: increased pay including the 'clear shilling', elasticity of terms of service, and the strengthening of the Reserve. He spoke in the House of Lords and at county meetings and wrote to *The Times*. In November 1897, during controversy on the army, he wrote to *The Times* disagreeing with H.O. Arnold-Forster's proposals and reasserting his own support for the short service, confirmed by the evidence to the Wantage Committee.[53] The Crimean War had shown the failure of long service and the necessity of a reserve. Under the conditions of modern warfare a reserve to enable expansion and reinforcement was an 'absolute necessity'. The system needed a proper balance of home and overseas battalions and so more battalions should be raised. To attract the required recruits, soldier' pay should be raised to 'the ordinary market rate of unskilled adult labour'. The present system had never had a 'fair or full trial', and if implemented as originally intended, with also better pay and other advantages, would work well. In 1899 Lord Lansdowne, the Unionist war minister Wolseley loathed, appointed Wantage chairman of the board of visitors of the military colleges at Woolwich and Sandhurst; after a year he resigned because of ill health.

Volunteer Force

In 1859 and 1860, in response to public anxiety about French invasion, the Volunteer movement swept the country.[54] By local initiatives numerous units were formed, drawing men who would normally never have joined the regular army or militia: middle class and artisans. Unpaid, distinctively and diversely uniformed often in grey, emphasising rifle-shooting, they were for the next half-century a crucial component of the auxiliary forces. Popular yet controversial, they were variously praised, mocked and derided. Historians have differed in their assessments. Sir John Fortescue, himself a former Yeomanry officer, in his classic *History of the British Army*, with aristocratic contempt for 'petty tradesmen', condemned the Volunteer Force, alleging "… it should not have been countenanced by the Government." He alleged it always had only a few efficient corps but "… a very great many who served no purpose except to inspire the negligent and ignorant with a false feeling of security."[55] Loyd-Lindsay was more positive. He was among the early participants and became a leading Volunteer and spokesman for the movement, until his formal retirement from the Volunteer Force in 1895. In October 1859 a Volunteer company was started at Reading, followed in 1860 and after by twelve more in various parts of Berkshire, and in 1860 they were formed into the grey-uniformed Berkshire Rifle Volunteer Corps, later the 1st Volunteer Battalion of the Berkshire Regiment, with Loyd-Lindsay colonel commanding. In October 1866 Loyd-Lindsay commanded over a thousand Volunteers on a visit to Antwerp,[56]

---

52 *The Times* 14 December 1897, p. 9.
53 *The Times* 25 November 1897, p. 8.
54 On the Volunteers largely from Beckett, *Riflemen Form*.
55 Fortescue, J.W, *A History of the British Army* XIII *1852-1870* (London: Macmillan, 1930), p. 528.
56 *Annual Register 1866* Part II, pp. 148-61; *LW*, pp157-60; A.F. Flatow, 'Volunteers in Brussels, 1866', *Journal of the Society for Army Historical Research* 44 (1966).

invited thither by King Leopold II.[57] They received a 'splendid reception' and, according to his fellow-officer Viscount Bury, 'Bob won all hearts in Belgium'.

In his Volunteer activities Loyd-Lindsay was supported by his father-in-law, Lord Overstone. In October 1859 Overstone gave evidence to the Royal Commission on National Defence. He warned against the disastrous effect of foreign invasion and declared 'it must never be'. Loyd-Lindsay's eminence as a leading Volunteer resulted partly from his military experience and reputation and partly from 'his position as a large county landowner'. Although a *nouveau riche* financed by another *nouveau riche*, he was of aristocratic descent and a traditional Conservative, to whom it was natural that the Volunteer rank structure should reproduce the social hierarchy. He chose officers from 'leading squires and county gentlemen'. With time this became more difficult but, his widow claimed, "...a high standard both of social position and efficiency was maintained among the officers."[58] He believed in the 'staying power' and potential for future development of the Volunteers, and that their superior intelligence and desire to learn fully compensated for the shortness of their training.

After his 1870 visit to the Franco-Prussian War for the Red Cross, he reported that the French *francs-tireurs* were different from the British Volunteers. The latter were from 'the most respectable classes', but the former were from "… the lowest … a curse instead of a protection to the country." If Britain were ever invaded the Volunteers should "… act as regular troops in divisions and corps d'armée."[59] He welcomed his Volunteers training on manoeuvres with regulars. He wanted massive expansion of the Force to provide national military training, believing this was "…the only real and effective alternative to conscription." He was praised for his 'liberality' to his Volunteers. Like other Volunteer and Yeomanry commanding officers, he subsidised his unit and provided facilities; their summer camps were held on his estate. He frequently visited the individual companies, entertained officers, and usually commanded the summer camps. His widow wrote that "…he was never happier than when handling troops, thoroughly enjoying the early morning drills and more extended field-days." Nationally the Volunteers were conspicuous, and their major events – reviews and sham fights – were popular events attended by thousands of spectators. Volunteers also participated in various public ceremonials. From the June 1860 Hyde Park review of some 21,000 Volunteers, to the 1887 Jubilee procession, Loyd-Lindsay's Berkshire Volunteers were on display. In summer 1889, with other units of the Home Counties brigade, they participated in a field day and sham fight at Aldershot, attended by Kaiser Wilhelm II who praised them.

In 1881 the 'coming of age' of the Volunteers was celebrated. Some of the oldest and most eminent officers were awarded honours; in May Loyd-Lindsay was appointed KCB. James Knowles, the founder, proprietor and editor of the *Nineteenth Century*, invited Loyd-Lindsay to contribute an article on the Volunteers. The *Nineteenth Century*, founded in 1877, was a monthly journal whose eminent contributors included Gladstone, with fifty-five articles and reviews, and Cardinal Manning. Successful and influential, it was an ideal vehicle for reaching the educated and political classes. Loyd-Lindsay's 'The coming of age of the Volunteers' was published in

---

57 Leopold II (reign 1865-1909) was later notorious for his quasi-genocidal exploitation of his Etat indépendant du Congo (Congo Free State). After he visited Germany the Kaiserin had the rooms he stayed in exorcised.
58 Wantage, *Lord Wantage*, p. 271.
59 Wantage, *Lord Wantage*, p. 192.

August 1881. In it he argued his case for the Volunteers and stated his views on the Force and its future. He claimed that although the government's attitude towards the Volunteer Force had always been one of reserve, the Force had progressed and improved and become 'a great national army' with a much higher reputation than formerly. The Boers in the recent Transvaal War had shown the British public the importance of rifle-shooting and "... how very formidable unprofessional soldiers may become when they thoroughly understand its use." It was rifle-shooting more than anything else which kept the Volunteer Force together and made it popular. Volunteer riflemen would be effective in war, and trenches would be crucial: "...the spade is therefore destined to become an implement second only in importance to the rifle."[60] The Force was accepted because of its "... thoroughly non-political character." The Volunteers recruited from men "... unknown to the agents of the regular army ... men of greater intelligence ... the superior class of men". They were 'the pick of the nation'. The Volunteers should be incorporated into the regimental localisation scheme and should join the army reserve. More retired regular officers should serve with the Volunteers. In future the Force should become more efficient, gain ancillary services, and be "... a lasting guarantee for the safety of our native shores." The article's positive assessment was unsurprising from a leading Volunteer spokesman, but later Victorians would have questioned its omission of seapower and the Navy. The Volunteer movement, like 'Palmerston's follies', was predicated on alleged naval inadequacy. A few years after the 1881 article came 'The Truth about the Navy', revived popular navalism, and major naval construction. The Volunteer Force continued apparently regardless.

Edward Stanhope, Secretary of State for War in Salisbury's Conservative government, did more to define a role for the Volunteers and so to develop their organisation than any previous war minister.[61] In 1888 he formed Volunteer brigades from those battalions' not allocated garrison duties in the new mobilisation scheme. Loyd-Lindsay was appointed brigadier-general commanding the Home Counties Brigade, comprising the Berkshire, Buckinghamshire, Bedfordshire and Oxfordshire regiments, with headquarters at Reading. Indicative of the fragmentation of the auxiliary forces, the county Yeomanry regiments were not included in the scheme. Loyd-Lindsay welcomed the change and "... threw himself zealously into the duties of his extended command." In September 1891, with other Volunteer officers, he attended the German army manoeuvres in the Erfurt area. He was impressed by popular enthusiasm for the young Kaiser, and by the 'prodigious scale' of the manoeuvres. He considered the German cavalry and artillery horses inferior to the British, but that "... German soldiers can outmarch the present British soldiers." In 1895 he resigned from his command and retired from the Volunteer Force. His regiment presented him with a silver gilt cup and a portrait by Briton Rivière of Lady Wantage. Nevertheless he continued actively interested in the Berkshire Volunteers.

An enthusiast for mounted infantry, Loyd-Lindsay in 1860 at Overstone, his father-in-law's estate, raised from farmers and members of the Pytchley Hunt, the 1st Northamptonshire Light Horse Volunteers. Their uniforms were scarlet Norfolk jackets and grey breeches, and he trained them in the park at Overstone. However, the unit lasted only until 1869. He also attached a company of mounted riflemen to his Berkshire Volunteer regiment. To encourage

---

60   Robert Loyd-Lindsay, 'The Coming of Age of the Volunteers', *Nineteenth Century* X, August 1881, p. 210. Today the trenches statement might seem proto-Bloch, but they were probably influenced by the Ottoman 1877 defence of Plevna, and perhaps also by memories of the Crimea.
61   Beckett, *Riflemen Form*, p. 135.

mounted firepower he donated from 1873 the Loyd-Lindsay prizes at the National Rifle Association meetings at Wimbledon and Bisley, competed for by teams from the Yeomanry, Light Horse Volunteers, mounted rifles and mounted infantry.[62] The teams had to ride about three-quarters of a mile, jumping two hurdles, and fire five rounds dismounted at 200 and 400 yards, using service rifles and ammunition; later the distances were increased and the qualifying time shortened. Loyd-Lindsay continued to advocate mounted infantry. In August 1881 in the House of Commons he moved that 'to meet the requirements of modern warfare' mounted infantry corps should form part of the Army establishment in future.[63] Presumably partly to placate the cavalry, he stated that he did not want a new branch of the army established, but the infantry to be more mobile. He argued the value of mounted infantry in the Indian Mutiny and the Second Afghan War, and quoted leading generals – Roberts, Wolseley, and Evelyn Wood – on the necessity of mounted infantry. The reply by Hugh Childers, the Secretary of State for War, was favourable but noncommittal, and it was not until 1888 that mounted infantry were formally added to the regular army.

The Yeomanry Cavalry, not the Volunteers, were the preferred auxiliary force of the landocracy and social-climbing plutocracy. Yet the Yeomanry were controversial. They were long loathed for their repressive role, epitomised in the 'Peterloo Massacre', although they had last been used in support of the civil power against food rioters at Exeter in November 1867.[64] Latterly, unreformed and with declining numbers, the Yeomanry were criticised as militarily useless, and some, including Cardwell and Wolseley, favoured their conversion to mounted rifles. In March 1872, in the House of Commons debate on the army estimates, Loyd-Lindsay praised the Volunteers and criticised the Yeomanry, alleging they were, "…servile imitators of the worst faults of the cavalry", and that if any corps had to be disbanded, none would be better spared than the Yeomanry.[65] He agreed they should be trained to use their carbines dismounted, and he hoped to see "…great reforms promptly instituted." A further example of criticism was the May 1885 Commons debate on army issues, when the radical Burnley M.P., Peter Rylands, alleged the Yeomanry were, "…a sham Force … absolutely useless for fighting" and "…not worth the money spent upon them." In the same debate Loyd-Lindsay criticised the old-fashioned cavalry as 'tight trousers and spurs', and "…the worst trained … and the worst armed in the world", and he recommended that they be changed to mounted rifles.[66] He regretted that so many county gentlemen went into the Yeomanry rather than the Volunteers: 'he wanted to see them joining the Volunteers'. Lord Hartington, replying for the government, alleged that mounted infantry had been unsuccessful and were unpopular. He claimed the Yeomanry were popular and potentially valuable, and conversion to mounted infantry would reduce their popularity.

While he enjoyed commanding in Berkshire, Loyd-Lindsay also had a less congenial involvement in London with the Honourable Artillery Company.[67] It was about a battalion

---

62 *The Times*, 11 June 1901, p. 8.
63 *Hansard* CCLXIV (1881), 4 August, cc853-6.
64 Beckett, Ian F.W., *The Amateur Military Tradition 1558-1945* (Manchester: Manchester University Press, 1991)), p. 192.
65 *Hansard* CCIX (1872), 11 March, c1828.
66 *Hansard* CCXCVII (1885), 7 May, cc1939-40.
67 On the HAC largely from Court Minutes, Honourable Artillery Company Archives, Armoury House, London; Raikes, G.A., *The History of the Honourable Artillery Company* Vol II (London: Richard Bentley & Son, 1879); Goold Walker, G., et al, *The Honourable Artillery Company 1537-1987* (London:

strong, comprising light horse, artillery and infantry, with headquarters at Armoury House in the City Road, Finsbury. Its members paid a five-pound admission fee, an annual two guineas subscription, and expenses, including '£20 to £25 on joining'. These costs were significantly higher than those of London Volunteer corps. Its role was largely ceremonial – guards of honour and firing royal salutes – and social. Chartered in 1537 by Henry VIII, it was ancient, privileged, enjoying 'ample funds', idiosyncratic and sometimes obstreperous, a select City club which excluded "…persons whose occupations or habits render them improper to be admitted."

Although its infantry uniforms resembled those of the Grenadier Guards, it was of questionable military value. It made its own rules. Its captain-general and colonel, appointed by the monarch, was traditionally royal: from 1843 to 1861 Prince Albert and from 1863 Albert Edward, Prince of Wales. He enjoyed his role and took a keen interest in the Company. He led it at reviews and frequently visited Armoury House, attending parades, balls and smoking concerts. Nevertheless the Company governing body, the Court of Assistants, still went its own way. Although the HAC attended Volunteer reviews, it was legally separate from the Volunteer Force. Clause 52 of the 1863 Volunteer Act stated that, "…nothing in this Act shall apply to the Honourable Artillery Company of London." Moreover it repeatedly refused to allow London Volunteers to use its Finsbury drill ground, despite parliamentary pressure by Sir John Lubbock, of bank holiday fame, and others. Invited by the Prince of Wales, his former equerry Loyd-Lindsay was from November 1866 to August 1881 its lieutenant colonel commanding. He and his wife donated cash prizes for rifle-shooting. He disagreed with the Court of Assistants over control of the unit, asserting his authority. For example, in November 1868 he indignantly rejected proposals which would "…restore to the Court of Assistants the control of the military affairs of the Regiment." In passing the resolutions the Court "… placed itself in antagonism to the Military Authorities" and it was his duty as commanding officer to "…disregard these resolutions, even if carried, and to treat them as illegal and therefore nugatory."

In December 1868 he accused the Court of "… an unwarrantable interference with the Authority of the Commanding Officer" over transfers, and in March 1871 he insisted that he 'sanction' the appointment of the new bandmaster.[68] In August 1874 he wrote to the Court of Assistants that the Prince of Wales, with the agreement of the Duke of Cambridge, the commander-in-chief, desired that the uniform be changed from red to blue. The Court replied that this would be expensive for its members, probably cause many to resign, and "…in a serious degree reduce the strength of the Regiment"; the colour was not changed. Loyd-Lindsay reported on the Company to the secretary of state for war that, "… as a military body it fails to comply with what is required of it." He tried to make it less a social club and more a military unit but had limited success; "… the feeling of the regiment in favour of the old order of things proved too strong to be efficiently broken through."[69]

Without his leadership, after his retirement, the Company apparently deteriorated and in December 1888 was in crisis: corruption revealed, and internal conflict. Loyd-Lindsay's successor, the Duke of Portland, who had taken little interest in the Company, alleged that it was, "…in a most unsatisfactory state as regards discipline." The Prince and Portland resigned.

Honourable Artillery Company, 1986); *The Cardew-Rendle Roll of Members of the Honourable Artillery Company* (London: Honourable Artillery Company, 2014).
68   Court Minutes (1869-1874), pp. 49, 189.
69   Wantage, *Lord Wantage*, p. 157.

The Conservative Secretary of State for War, Edward Stanhope, ordered that the Company be disarmed, and its artillery, rifles and ammunition were summarily removed to Tower of London and Woolwich.[70] The press reported and commented, and Volunteers were "...rejoicing with an unholy joy at the downfall of the haughty." Later however, under increased War Office control, the Company returned to normal and in 1893 the Prince resumed his post. Wantage resigned from the Company in 1896.

In the 1850s rifles were, to most Britons, unfamiliar new modern weapons, of impressive range and accuracy. Rifle-shooting was crucial to the Volunteer movement, which was closely connected to the new National Rifle Association.[71] The NRA was founded in November 1859 by Earl Spencer, Lord Elcho, Earl Grosvenor and other keen supporters of the Volunteer movement, with the declared purpose of "... encouraging Volunteer Rifle Corps and promoting rifle-shooting throughout the kingdom." They intended to strengthen and perpetuate the Volunteer movement by providing a "...central object of distinct and universal interest" and to "render the use of the rifle as familiar to our population generally as was the use of the long bow in the days of the Plantagenets, and thereby to secure our country from the possibility of invasion". They were influenced by the example of Switzerland and its *Tir Federal* and *Tirs Cantonneaux*. The NRA soon gained royal and official approval. The Prince Consort became patron and Sidney Herbert, the secretary of state for war, became president. The NRA established their rifle ranges at Wimbledon Common, with a maximum distance of 1,000 yards without danger to the locals. In July 1860 Queen Victoria opened their first annual meeting, before thousands of spectators. In the following years the summer meetings continued successful and popular, with Volunteers, regulars, colonials and foreigners competing. They were part of the London social season, with 'luxury and display' and many champagne cups drunk. However, there was also among the sightseers, "...a rowdy element, odious to residents in the neighbourhood."[72]

Loyd-Lindsay, a good shot, was an early member of the NRA, joined its council, and was its president from 1887 to 1891. At the annual Wimbledon events he and his wife had reception tents "...picturesque with Eastern hangings collected abroad", where they provided luncheons, afternoon parties, dinners and camp entertainments to, among others, the Prince and Princess of Wales and the King of Greece. During his presidency the NRA had the contentious problem of finding a new location.[73] Under pressure from Putney and Wandsworth vestries and the Duke of Cambridge, and with the increased range of rifles, they had to leave Wimbledon. Wantage and his colleagues visited several possible sites. Richmond Park, attractive and convenient, was first suggested, but this was opposed by the ranger, the Duke of Cambridge, and vetoed by the first commissioner of works. Northerners favoured Cannock Chase, Staffordshire, and others Brighton or the War Office site at Bisley, Surrey, convenient for Aldershot. Wantage offered a site of approximately one square mile on Compton Downs in Berkshire and was determined to make the site a success if it were selected. At the council meeting in February 1889 the

---

70 *Annual Register 1888* Part II, p. 62; Walker, *Honourable Artillery Company*, pp. 250-4.
71 *Annual Register 1860* part II, p. 114; Beckett, *Riflemen Form*, pp. 33-4; Cunningham, Hugh, *The Volunteer Force: A social and political history 1859-1908* (Hamden: Connecticut, Archon Books, 1975), pp. 113-6.
72 *The Times* 14 July 1890, p. 9.
73 Wantage, *Lord Wantage*, p. 327; Humphry A.P & Fremantle, T.F., *History of the National Rifle Association during its first fifty years 1859-1909* (Cambridge: Bowes & Bowes, 1914), pp. 305-11.

majority voted for Bisley. Wantage was disappointed, but accepted the decision and supervised the removal, including of the clock tower and other buildings, to Bisley. In July 1890 he presided at the first Bisley meeting, opened by the Prince of Wales who spoke of "...making the rifle of today what the bow was in the days of the Plantagenets".[74] After the meeting Wantage resigned from the NRA presidency.

Red Cross

Frank Prochaska has written, "No nation on earth can lay claim to a richer philanthropic past than Britain"[75], and its golden age was the Victorian era. In 1885, according to *The Times*, the income of London charities exceeded that of the government of Sweden, Denmark, Portugal or Persia, and was double that of the Swiss Confederation.[76] The numerous British charities ranged from the parochial to those which, like Mrs Jellyby's, were 'telescopic', and included some for servicemen and their families, though the most important, James Gildea's Soldiers' and Sailors' Families Association, came later, in 1885.[77] Loyd-Lindsay, impelled to charity by his Christianity and sense of duty and responsibility, had a wide choice of organizations. His Crimean experience made him choose the Red Cross, and for he last thirty years of his life he had a leading role in it.[78]

The international Red Cross had begun in Switzerland in 1863, following the publication of Jean Henri Dunant's *Un Souvenir de Solferino,* and in the 1860s national societies were founded in France, Germany, Spain, and elsewhere. In Britain there were suggestions by Loyd-Lindsay and others for a British Red Cross organization. Loyd-Lindsay's Crimean memories shaped his attitudes: his widow wrote that, "... what he saw and experienced during that campaign impressed itself deeply on his mind."[79] He believed that a Red Cross society in the Crimean War could have saved many lives and prevented much suffering. However, the most famous survivor of that war, Florence Nightingale, believed the underlying Red Cross principle of voluntary rather than governmental medical provision, was wrong.[80] In 1868 John Furley, Harrovian, humanitarian and member of the Order of St John of Jerusalem, and others established a provisional committee.

Following the outbreak of the Franco-Prussian War Furley, also a Volunteer, contacted Loyd-Lindsay, and in London in August 1870 they and others founded the National Society for Aid to the Sick and Wounded in War (NAS), the British branch of the Red Cross and often informally

---

74 *The Times* 14 July 1890, p. 7; Wantage, *Lord Wantage*, p. 327.
75 Prochaska, Frank, *The Voluntary Impulse: Philanthropy in Modern Britain* (London: Faber & Faber, 1998), p. 86.
76 *The Times*, 9 January 1885, p. 9.
77 Roger T.Stearn, 'A Great Philanthropist: Sir James Gildea and the Soldiers' and Sailors' Families Association', *Soldiers of the Queen: Journal of the Victorian Military Society* 142, September 2010.
78 On Loyd-Lindsay and the Red Cross largely from the Wantage Papers, British Red Cross Museum and Archives, Moorfields, London; Wantage, *Lord Wantage*, chapters VIII –X; Best, S.H, *The Story of the British Red Cross* (London: Cassell & Co., 1938), chapters I-IV; Oliver, Beryl, *The British Red Cross in Action* (London: Faber & Faber, 1966), chapters I-XI.
79 Wantage, *Lord Wantage*, p. 173.
80 Bostridge, *Florence Nightingale*, p. 614. Nevertheless, she joined the Ladies' Committee of the new National Society.

called the English Red Cross Society. Loyd-Lindsay, who donated £1,000 to launch it, was chosen chairman, and its committee included Lord Shaftesbury, the most admired philanthropist of the age, and Lord Overstone. A ladies' committee was appointed, in which Princess Christian and Mrs Loyd-Lindsay had leading roles. The public gave generously, subscribing over £200,000, and medical assistance was sent to both sides. NAS organisation in France was largely by Furley and Captain Henry Brackenbury; by appealing directly to Cardwell Loyd-Lindsay secured the latter's leave from the Royal Military Academy, Woolwich.[81] Loyd-Lindsay worked hard at the British headquarters. In October 1870, on behalf of the Society, he briefly visited the war zone. At Versailles he met Bismarck and the King and Crown Prince of Prussia. He then, by special arrangement, visited the besieged French force in Paris. Disregarding warning not to walk in the street, he was arrested as a spy by *gardes mobiles*, 'ruffians', but rescued by a 'real officer', and returned home. He reported to the Society that he was 'entirely satisfied with the result and usefulness' of his mission. He also condemned the misuse of the red cross emblem, including by bogus hospitals, and the 'Irish so-called ambulance' whose members were so drunk and violent they had to be escorted aboard ship by armed *gardes mobiles*. Loyd-Lindsay and his wife gave a large banquet at Greenwich for those who had served the NAS during the war. The work of the new Society had been improvised and experimental. It succeeded, and the Society, later renamed the British Red Cross, became part of British life, and led by Loyd-Lindsay continued, though with some criticism and controversy. For the next few years it was inactive, its reserve fund of £70,000 untouched in Coutts Bank.

In 1876 the Balkans, part of the 'Eastern Question', were an emotive and divisive issue in Britain, with the massive Bulgarian atrocities agitation, fanned by Gladstone's *The Bulgarian Horrors and the Question of the East*.[82] Liberals condemned, but Disraeli and other Conservatives favoured the Turks. In July the Turco-Serbian War began, and in Britain Sir Edmund Letchmere, of the Order of St John, and other pro-Serbians demanded that the NAS send assistance. Loyd-Lindsay and the council initially refused, arguing the conflict was outside the NAS remit as Serbia was not an independent country. Under pressure from public opinion and the formation by Letchmere and others of the Eastern War Sick and Wounded Fund, the NAS decided to send medical assistance to the armies of both sides. Loyd-Lindsay chose to go himself, as the Society's chief commissioner in the war zone, to superintend the relief, observe the campaign and study the politics of the area. With a party including surgeons from St Thomas's and, according to the *Daily News*, "… two gentlemen whose functions were not apparent", in August he went to Belgrade.[83] As a Conservative, Loyd-Lindsay may have been biased in favour of the Turks. He was unfavourably impressed by the Serbs, and notably Serb politicians, 'cunning rascals'. He alleged the prime minister was a rogue who "…will very soon be off with the money which he has stolen" and that the leading Serbs were men who in other countries "… would think themselves fortunate if they obtained the posts of managers and markers in billiard saloons".

---

81 On Brackenbury and the NAS from Brice, *Thinking Man's Soldier*, chapter 9.
82 Seton-Watson, R.W., *Disraeli, Gladstone and the Eastern Question: a study in diplomacy and party politics* (London: Macmillan, 1935), chapters III, VIII; Shannon, R.T., *Gladstone and the Bulgarian Agitation 1876* (London: Thomas Nelson, 1963), *passim*.
83 On Loyd-Lindsay and Serbia from the Wantage Papers, British Red Cross Museum and Archives; and from Wantage, *Lord Wantage*, chapter X and Anderson, Dorothy, *The Balkan Volunteers* (London: Hutchinson, 1968), pp. 11-12, 29-34. The latter book is less favourable to him than the former.

He also alleged the war resulted from a Russian conspiracy 'to humiliate England by doing what we forbade them to do in 1853-6'. After completing arrangements in Serbia, including a British Red Cross hospital, the Katharine Hospital, in Belgrade, he went through Bulgaria to Constantinople and subsequently observed the Turkish army. He returned to England in October, and at Wantage was welcomed by Yeomanry, Volunteers, Oddfellows in regalia, the volunteer fire brigade, bands, flags, and a large and enthusiastic crowd cheering and singing 'See the Conquering Hero Comes'. He reported to the NAS that 'the work of the Society in Servia has been a complete success'.

However, his views of the Serbs and the war, reported in the British press, offended both British Liberals and Serbs. The Liberal *Daily News* criticised him. Its Belgrade correspondent alleged that, as in the Franco-Prussian war, "...English incapacity for the management of Red Cross work", emphasising that the NAS's "...eleventh hour interposition" was after both the Russian Red Cross and the British St John party, achieved very little, and left in Serbia "... the worst impression". The *Daily News* published a letter from a Belgrade professor castigating Loyd-Lindsay, "... so small a politician", for his 'astonishing bad taste' and for openly expressing "... unfriendly sentiments" towards Serbians. Archibald Forbes, the celebrated war correspondent, wrote in the *Daily News* that Loyd-Lindsay had confused his position as a Conservative MP with that as chairman of a neutral voluntary aid society, and used opportunities granted to the Red Cross for "... party and political purposes."[84] Loyd-Lindsay apparently saw no contradiction in his two roles. He was "...blunt, straightforward and sympathetic to Turkey." Stratford de Redcliffe wrote to Gladstone on Loyd-Lindsay, "... although his sincerity cannot be doubted, he may *possibly* have drawn his conclusions rather from biased reporters than from his own limited experience of the country".[85]

Loyd-Lindsay's cautious, inactive peacetime policy was controversial within the NAS. John Furley and others claimed its best preparation for major war was to maintain in peacetime a full, active organisation which would assist at civilian accidents. Loyd-Lindsay argued that major war was improbable and that the public would not support any elaborate organisation of personnel and supplies in peacetime. In 1877 the NAS split, and Furley and others helped found the St John Ambulance Association. Furley believed the NAS should be under military direction, and in late 1885 he criticised it in a scathing article in the *Nineteenth Century*. He contrasted the NAS with foreign Red Cross organisations which were government-subsidised, military-directed, and in constant readiness for mobilisation or emergency. The NAS depended on private initiative, was virtually asleep, and by its inaction encouraged the formation of rival funds. Others, in various publications, joined the criticism, alleging apathy, asserting the necessity of an active organisation in peacetime, and calling for a new council. Loyd-Lindsay replied in *The Times*, defending the NAS and his leadership, and continued in office.

Although he never again went to a war zone, under Loyd-Lindsay's leadership the NAS provided medical aid in successive British imperial and foreign wars, culminating in its greatest effort hitherto, in the Boer War. By then Loyd-Lindsay, while active in appealing to the public and in organisation, was limited by his age and deteriorated health. In 1885 Wolseley had written to him, advising that "...the gentlemen who represent the Society in the field should, if possible

---

84 Anderson, *Balkan Volunteers*, p. 41.
85 Anderson, *Balkan Volunteers*, p. 41.

have served themselves in the Army."[86] This had been Loyd-Lindsay's policy from the start, and the Society largely, though not exclusively, used officers as its war zone organizers; these included two major generals, one in France and one in Serbia. Other charities Loyd-Lindsay supported included in the 1890s the Duke of Westminster's Grosvenor House Committee, to aid Armenians, and the Cretan Distress Fund, of which Loyd-Lindsay was a founder. He was friendly with King George I of the Hellenes, and at the time of the 1897 Graeco-Turkish War Wantage and Lady Wantage sent out 10,000 blankets for the Thessalian refugees.

Landowner

"What between the duties expected of one during one's lifetime and the duties exacted from one after one's death, land has ceased to be either a profit or a pleasure", declared Lady Bracknell. This was not true of Loyd-Lindsay. He inherited land before Goschen's and Harcourt's death duties, accepted the social and other duties expected, and gained both profit and pleasure. After his 1859 retirement from the regular army he largely devoted himself to the Lockinge estate, near Wantage, Berkshire, settled on him and his wife by Overstone.

The Loyd-Lindsays had a London house, 2 Carlton Gardens, St James's, but their principal residence was Lockinge House. It was an eighteenth-century, red brick and grey stone, three-storey house, incorporating a superb seventeenth-century oak screen from a London livery-company hall, and had an orangery. The Loyd-Lindsays altered and enlarged the house, adding wings and a picture gallery, and 'beautified' it: part of, "…the great Victorian efflorescence of new and enlarged country houses."[87] The drawing room was red silk-walled and oak and gold pilastered, and the tapestry room was panelled in old Italian carved woodwork. They demolished nearby old cottages and farm buildings, and so gained more privacy and larger gardens, with lawns, flowery terraces, and a picturesque rockery constructed by the medal-winning James Pulham and Son. At their 'great mansion' they entertained lavishly royalty, politicians, 'the county', generals and others.[88] Art had long been a status symbol favoured by the *nouveaux riches*; one such was Lord Armstrong, the armament manufacturer. The Loyd-Lindsays collected paintings, and inherited Overstone's collection.[89] They owned both old and recent works, but almost no military paintings, and no works by Victorian military artists. To Loyd-Lindsay his pictures gave "…unfailing delight in his latter years." He and his wife attended fashionable art exhibitions: they are in Henry Brooks' group portrait, 'Private View of

---

86 Wantage, *Lord Wantage*, p. 299. Of course not only military but also non-military and anti-military persons were active in relief work: notably the Quakers, including in the Franco-Prussian War, see Greenwood, J.O., *Quaker Encounters I. Friends and Relief* (York: William Sessions, 1975) *passim*.
87 Girouard, *Victorian Country House*, p. 86.
88 After Lady Wantage's death, childless, on 9 August 1920, Lockinge House was inherited by a Loyd cousin, whose son demolished it in 1947: part of the wave of post-war destruction of country houses, which included Frederick Burnaby's Somerby Hall, Leicestershire, in 1949. In the same period some houses were given to the National Trust.
89 On the Wantage's collection from (A.G. Temple), *Catalogue of pictures forming the collection of Lord and Lady Wantage at 2, Carlton Gardens, London, Lockinge House, Berks, and Overstone Park and Ardington House* (London: F. Wetherman & Co., 1902) and Wantage, *Lord Wantage*, pp. 347, 428.

the Old Masters Exhibition, Royal Academy, 1888'.[90] Loyd-Lindsay also enjoyed shooting and hunting with the Pytchley and Old Berkshire Hounds. His wife, a 'fearless' horsewoman, also hunted, and in 1870 broke her leg while hunting, partly causing her later lameness.

Their Lockinge estate was no ancient feudal inheritance, but a Victorian *nouveau riche* capitalist construct. Its nucleus, the East Lockinge estate, had been bought in 1854 as an investment by Overstone's banker father Lewis Loyd (1768-1858).[91] Loyd-Lindsay by continued purchases gradually extended and consolidated the estate. Crucially, following the death of its owner in 1861, he purchased the adjoining village and estate of Ardington. He also purchased, piecemeal, cottages and other small properties. Initiated by Lord Derby in 1872, the 'New Domesday' was an official survey of United Kingdom landowners and their estates, excluding London, published in 1874 as a parliamentary paper *Return of Owners of Land 1872-3*. John Bateman, a Conservative Essex squire, apparently assumed it supported the existing system of landholding against its radical critics. He rearranged and corrected the *Return* data and published it in book form, *The Great Landowners of Great Britain and Ireland* (final edition 1883). This stated that Loyd-Lindsay's estate comprised 20,528 acres, with a gross annual value of £26,492.[92] It was the largest in Berkshire, nearly one-twentieth of the county. Loyd-Lindsay continued to enlarge it, reaching completion in the 1890s at about 26,000 acres.

Through the 1850s and 1860s and into the 1870s agriculture was prosperous and profitable, and 'high farming', involving substantial investment by landlords and farmers, continued popular. Loyd-Lindsay was an enthusiastic, innovative 'high' farmer and an optimistic improving landlord.[93] His farms included arable, cattle and sheep. He bought a Fowler steam plough and other modern machinery, built roads, experimented with crops, irrigation, fertilizers and ranching, and planted woods, copses and shelter belts. He was a leading shire-horse breeder, and from 1889 president of the Shire Horse Society.[94] His stallion Prince William, bought in 1885 for £1,500 was a notably successful stud and in 1891 won the champion gold medal of the Royal Agricultural Society. Loyd-Lindsay, accepting a lower return than he might have gained from investment in shares, invested much in his estate. Local farmers said "…the Colonel will soon get tired of losing money on his farms", but he persisted.[95]

Designing and building model cottages was a favoured hobby of benevolent paternalists, from Prince Albert to Miss Brooke, although in narrowly economic terms they were a bad investment.[96] When the Loyd-Lindsays took control of their estate its cottages were, Lady Wantage later wrote, "…fast decaying hovels through whose "wattle and dab" a walking stick

---

90 Now in the National Portrait Gallery. After Wantage's death his widow generously supported the National Art Collections Fund.
91 Havinden, M.A., *Estate Villages: A Study of the Berkshire villages of Ardington and Lockinge* (London: Lund Humphries, 1966), p. 31.
92 Bateman, John, *The Great Landowners of Great Britain and Ireland* (Leicester: Leicester University Press, 1971), p. 271.
93 On Loyd-Lindsay as landlord and farmer from, Wantage, *Lord Wantage*; Havinden, *Estate Villages*; Stearn, 'Lindsay, Robert'.
94 Agriculture, like the army, depended on horses: in 1881 about two million, Winton, Graham, *'Theirs Not To Reason Why': Horsing the British Army 1875-1925* (Solihull: Helion, 2013), p. 42.
95 Cornish, James George, *Reminiscences of Country Life* (London: Country Life, 1939), p. 90.
96 Havinden, Michael, 'The Model Village' in Mingay, G.E. (ed), *The Victorian Countryside* II (London: Routledge & Kegan Paul, 1981), p. 417.

could easily be thrust", and some were "surrounded by muck-yards."[97] The Loyd-Lindsays designed cottages and other buildings – "an architect has rarely been employed" – and largely rebuilt East Lockinge and other villages. Their new three-bedroom cottages, set in gardens, were picturesque, mixing traditional Berkshire and Victorian gothic, with steeply-pitched roofs, elaborate porches, dormers, and leaded windows, the timber painted chocolate brown and the plaster yellow. A visiting journalist wrote that an artist would be enraptured by the sight. The Loyd-Lindsays also built schools and reading rooms. They provided allotments, co-operative stores on 'the Rochdale system', and a savings bank paying five percent interest though, Lady Wantage regretted, some villagers did not use it because they did not want their savings known. Loyd-Lindsay was a generous benefactor of the Established Church. He restored churches and purchased advowsons of local livings, ending neglect by absentee Oxford-fellow incumbents. There were no dissenting chapels. Church attendance twice on Sunday was required, and absence had to be explained. Mrs Loyd-Lindsay supervised the villagers' lives: "...she knew the inside of every cottage well."[98]

Lord Overstone died in November 1883 leaving most of his property to the Loyd-Lindsay, massively enriching them by investments and land. "Three addresses always inspire confidence, even in tradesmen", declared Lady Bracknell. The Loyd-Lindsays had four main residences: Lockinge, Carlton Gardens, Ardington House, and Overstone Park. They owned over 30,000 acres in Northamptonshire, Buckinghamshire, Warwickshire, Cambridgeshire, Huntingdonshire, Leicestershire, Oxfordshire, Berkshire, Bedfordshire, Middlesex and Camarthenshire. However, even before Overstone's death landowning was becoming problematic. From 1875 the country suffered the agricultural depression, started by bad weather and bad harvests, and continued by imports of cheap foreign produce. Although its impact varied, prices, rents and arable acerage all fell, and many farmers left. Cushioned by his non-agricultural income, Loyd-Lindsay attempted when possible to, "...keep tenants on their legs" by rent remission. Unable to obtain suitable tenants for some farms, he farmed them himself, finally farming about 13,000 acres – probably the largest farmer in Britain – using economies of scale: on his big farm he had sixty horses, whereas his predecessors on the same area had ninety. He claimed that "... the first and foremost requirement for successful farming is adequate capital to carry on the business", and he continued to invest despite poor returns. He advocated smallholdings, partly for Conservative political advantages from increasing "... the body of men interested in maintaining the rights of property." In 1893 he was invited to be chairman of the royal commission on agricultural depression but declined, and in 1894 he gave evidence to it. His widow claimed that, "... over the great area of land which he owned, his presence and influence became a powerful force for the economic, social, and moral uplifting of the inhabitants."[99] He warned them against betting, 'the curse of many a rural village', agitators, agricultural trade unionism, and the propaganda 'red vans' of the Land Restoration League. His widow claimed that because of his opposition "...in the Lockinge district this movement was dead in a week or two."[100]

---

97 Wantage, *Lord Wantage*, pp. 343-4.
98 Cornish, *Reminiscences*, p. 124. Cornish, an Oxonian, was rector of East Lockinge, 1893-1903. His attitude to Lady Wantage apparently resembled that of Mr Collins to his noble patroness.
99 Wantage, *Lord Wantage*, p. 376.
100 Wantage, *Lord Wantage*, p. 395.

Victorian and Edwardian middle and upper classes enjoyed wearing historic garb, especially armour, from the Eglinton tournament through costume balls to the Edwardian 'pageantitis': picturesque manifestations of a romanticised past, including an imagined 'Merrie England'. Such were the two-day 'Lockinge Revels' in August 1885.[101] Begun as an attempt to replace the monotony of the annual garden party, it became "...a revival of the pageants of the Elizabethan era." Selected guests from the leading county families were invited to Lockinge to "... the festival of the Summer Queen, and a joust and divers ancient pastymes and merry disportes." Several hundred came "... attired in the richest old English costumes" and the estate cottagers wore 'mediaeval garb' with coifs and hoods. Wantage and his wife led a long procession of lords of manors and other guests, with pages, heralds, jesters, yeomen, halberdiers, foresters, forest maidens, falconers, bands and choristers. The Summer Queen, Lady Wantage's beautiful young cousin Madeleine Ryan, was enthroned on car drawn by four white oxen with gilded horns and attended by flower-maidens. The procession moved through the park, then watched a play, 'Robin Hood and his Merrie Men', followed by a tournament and 'old English sports'. It was, Lady Wantage wrote, "... a dream of gorgeous colour ... a thing of beauty to be ever remembered in the annals of Berkshire".

Wantage's benevolent paternalism was much praised, and he was lauded as generous landlord and a model employer. Others, however, disagreed. The 'Norman yoke', land-ownership, 'landlordism' and agricultural workers had long been bitter and contentious political issues, emphasised by radical politicians and press. The Liberal *Daily News*, Loyd-Lindsay's critic during the 1876 Turco-Serbian War, sent investigative journalists to the countryside,[102] including in 1872 Archibald Forbes, the war correspondent, who wrote privately that he had been 'inventing Joseph Arch, and describing the situation of the clods'[103]. In 1891 it sent George F. Millin as its 'Special Commissioner' and his reports were subsequently published as a shilling book, *Life in Our Villages*, dedicated to Gladstone.[104] Millin reported on, among others, Wantage's Berkshire estate. He wrote that it seemed, "... a little rural paradise ... delightful." He praised the cottages, allotments, co-operative store, reading room and school. However, he criticised the low wages and the "... control and management of the people", the fear, cringing to agents, and concealing of opinions. He quoted a labourer: "they daren't blow their noses over at Ard'n'ton without the bailiff's leave." Politics and pigs were banned; the villages were spoken of as a 'political Dead Sea, in which no public opinion ever was known to manifest itself'. Millin condemned the model-village paternalism as "... rotten and bad ... social and political death." He alleged that "Lord Wantage has done for the people, in the true spirit of benevolent Toryism, what the people ought to be able to do for themselves ... the people control nothing" and contrasted this with the Liberal ideal of "...free, individual, manly life and sturdy citizenship."

---

101 On the 'Revels' from *The Times* 27 August 1885, p. 5; Wantage, *Lord Wantage*, pp. 351-2; Readman, Paul, *Land and Nation in England: Patriotism, National Identity and the Politics of Land, 1880-1914* (Woodridge: Boydell Press, 2008), p. 163. See also Girouard, *Return to Camelot*, chapter 7.
102 Freeman, Mark, *Social investigation and rural England 1870-1914* (Woodridge: Boydell Press, 2003), chapters 2 &3.
103 Quoted, Roger T.Stearn, 'Forbes, Archibald', *ODNB*.
104 Millin, G.F., *Life in Our Villages*. 'Letter XVI. Arcadia realised' is about Wantage's estate.

Oxford Military College

Loyd-Lindsay and his father-in-law Lord Overstone had a Victorian belief in education. In 1861 they built new lofty stone gothic-style schools at Lockinge and Ardington, and they improved other schools on their estates. Loyd-Lindsay was a benefactor of the Wantage and Abingdon grammar schools. He was also involved in an ultimately unsuccessful educational venture, the Oxford Military College.[105]

"Examinations, sir, are pure humbug from beginning to end. If a man is a gentleman he knows quite enough", declared Lord Fermor. In the Victorian era the old system of patronage, influence and purchase, which Loyd-Lindsay had enjoyed, was largely replaced by one based on competitive examinations. These were held for entrance to the Indian and home civil service, Woolwich, Sandhurst, Staff College, and the Militia. For a would-be officer the usual sequence was first a public school – using the term loosely, as often did Victorians – followed by specialised examination training at a private tutorial establishment known as a crammer's. Crammers were a response to competitive examinations, and they varied much. Among the best-known were Captain Lendy's at Sutton and Captain James' at Kensington. Crammers were expensive – a letter to *The Times* complained that "…entrance into the service is again becoming a matter of purchase" – and for their proprietors profitable. In 1883 the governors of the Royal Military College reported that of 198 candidates who had passed into the RMC from various public schools, 75 percent had been aided by crammers. Among the many who used crammers were Charles Gordon, Redvers Buller – who described his crammer's at Tunbridge as a 'sink of iniquity' – Horatio Herbert Kitchener, Ian Hamilton, Winston Churchill – whose crammer, Captain James, "… held the Blue Ribbon among the Crammers" – Charles à Court (later Repington), John French, Douglas Haig, Henry Wilson, Edmund Allenby, and J.F.C. Fuller. Various alternatives to crammers were attempted. Some schools – notably Wellington, Haileybury, Cheltenham, Bedford Grammar, Clifton, and the United Services College – specialised in army entrance, and others also provided army classes. The United Services College, Westward Ho, less impressive than its name might suggest, was started in 1874 by a group of army officers and was largely an army school; Kipling wrote, "… it was our pride that we passed direct from the School to the Army." The USC, like various other new schools of the period, was established through a company. Also established through a company was another alternative to crammers, the Oxford Military College at Cowley. It was a private venture, a boys' school run on military lines to prepare for the Woolwich and Sandhurst entrance and for the Militia examinations.

The Oxford Military College, known to contemporaries as the OMC or Cowley College, had a short life, from 1876 to 1896. It was initiated by Major John Graham of the Pembrokeshire Artillery Militia, and founded by officers and others, including Loyd-Lindsay. In January 1876 the Oxford Military College Ltd was registered. Its capital was £50,000 in £10 shares. The intention was to enable shareholders to support a worthy cause while gaining a modest return on their capital, not a lucrative speculation. Loyd-Lindsay had 125 shares. In 1876 he joined

---

105 On Oxford Military College from Roger T.Stearn, 'Oxford Military College 1876-1896', *Soldiers of the Queen: Journal of the Victorian Military Society* 83, December 1995, and works there cited, especially John Tecklenborough (Henry Naidley), *Seven Years' Cadet-Life, containing the records of the Oxford Military College, anecdotes of cadet-life and essays on education* (Oxford: Slatter & Rose, 1885).

the OMC executive committee and, the college secretary Henry Naidley wrote, "...his name inspired with confidence many who had hitherto held aloof and induced them to join." He played an active part in the management of the OMC. It opened in September 1876. Its pupils, called students not cadets, came from approximately the same background as Sandhurst gentlemen cadets. They wore a dark blue uniform with a 'pill-box' forage cap. They had lessons, chapel, military and technical instruction – riding, carbine drill, sword and lance exercises, and infantry drill – gymnastics, swimming and games. OMC teams played those of Oxford colleges and schools. The OMC cadet corps was attached to the local Light Infantry and sometimes trained with 'the Varsity Corps'. Student numbers reached a peak of 141 in 1881. Thereafter numbers fluctuated, and with them the college finances. Of the 450 cadets and Militia officers trained by the OMC in its first seven years most went to Sandhurst and the Militia, and only a minority to Woolwich; possibly indicative of relatively low standards at the OMC, since Woolwich had the highest entrance standards.

The OMC had started with ambitious optimism; the original committee intended a college of some four hundred students. Yet from the start it was dogged by troubles. Many of the students were unsuitable, previously rejected elsewhere: according to Naidley, "...the O.M.C. had become a place of refuge for all the hopeless." There were financial difficulties, disagreement between the civil and military staff, student disorder, and unfavourable rumours and press reports on the college discipline, morality and standard of tuition. Naidley stated the OMC's problems in a letter written in October 1882 to Loyd-Lindsay before a board meeting, emphasising, "... the very critical state of money matters ... the whole property is mortgaged up to the hilt ... our sole resource is therefore the revenue & that has fallen off term after term." He linked this to the OMC's disciplinary problems, "Bad discipline means bad reputation, bad reputation fewer students, fewer students loss of revenue." The OMC continued, through vicissitudes and problems – of staffing, finance and reputation – into the 1890s. It had a reputation for bad management and bad discipline. Latterly it was failing to pass sufficient students into the cadet colleges. In 1891, for example, there were at Sandhurst only eight from the OMC. Its financial condition became serious, but it was subsidised by Wantage: "... placed in a solvent condition by means of a large sum practically given to it by Lord Wantage." Nevertheless, in late 1896 the headmaster, George Grundy, resigned and the debenture holders closed the OMC. Lady Wantage later wrote that "... gradually, as special Army Classes were started in our public schools and universities, the *raison d'être* of Cowley College ceased to exist, and it was finally closed." This was only partially true. The OMC's greatest disadvantages were its staff, intake, and reputation. Overall, apparently, too many of its headmasters and assistants were unsuitable and their turnover was high. Its results failed to attract a sufficient number of students, let alone a sufficient number of capable students. The OMC was apparently caught in a downward spiral. Exacerbating this was its reputation: Grundy wrote that he "...had to fight the past reputation of the college at every turn." Yet Wantage could not be blamed for the OMC's failure. His role had been altruistic and entirely creditable.

Wantage was also involved in a more successful educational venture, the new university college at Reading, later Reading University, part of the succession of Victorian civic institutions of higher education, largely financed by local philanthropists. The Reading college was originally an extension of Christ Church, Oxford, and was founded in 1892 and headed by the geographer Halford Mackinder, later famous for his 'heartland' hypothesis. Wantage was elected president of the new college council. He and Mackinder pressed for degrees in agricultural science, but in

1898 but this was rejected by Oxford Convocation, by 47 votes to 45.[106] Wantage and his wife were generous benefactors – in 1897 he gave £1,000 to its building fund - and after his death his widow gave a hall of residence, Wantage Hall, in his memory. It was built in 1908 the style of a Tudor Oxford or Cambridge college, with a crenelated clocktower. Including the building and endowment of Wantage Hall, Lady Wantage donated nearly £150,000 to the University College.

Loyd-Lindsay was a notable benefactor of the neighbouring market town of Wantage. He commissioned for it a marble statue of Alfred the Great by Count Gleichen. Alfred, reputedly born in Wantage, was a Victorian hero; 'the father of the British people', the patriot king who defeated foreign invasion, and the legendary founder of the Royal Navy, University College, Oxford, and Oxford University, and burner of cakes. In July 1877 the Prince and Princess of Wales visited Wantage, welcomed by Loyd-Lindsay and guarded by local Yeomanry and Volunteers.[107] The Prince unveiled the statue. After speeches and anthems the royal party went to Lockinge, where Loyd-Lindsay entertained them at a large garden party – with Indian jugglers – and at dinner. Loyd-Lindsay's later donation to Wantage, of a gallery of paintings by Desanges, also affirmed the military virtues of patriotism and heroism.

Louis William Desanges (1822-1887), Chevalier Desanges, was an English painter, the great-grandson of an immigrant French nobleman.[108] He painted historical subjects and fashionable portraits and exhibited at the Royal Academy from 1846 to 1874. Following the establishment of the Victoria Cross, and apparently influenced by Vernet and other French military artists, he painted a series of scenes of recipients, including Lindsay, in their Cross-winning combat. He wrote that he painted "…from the description given to me by my gallant sitters themselves, assisted by their friends and companions-in-arms." He sold some of the paintings, but most he exhibited to the paying public, from 1859 at the Egyptian Hall, Piccadilly and from 1862 to 1897 at the Crystal Palace. In 1864 he sold them to Harry Wood of Leeds, but they continued in the Crystal Palace. At the end of the century Lord Wantage bought the collection for about £1,000 and offered it to Wantage town. The urban district council accepted, and Lord Wantage paid for the conversion of the former corn market to the Victoria Cross Gallery. In November 1900 was held the formal presentation, attended by some 500 people, and "…the proceedings closed with cheers for Lord and Lady Wantage and their friends."[109] The public were admitted to the gallery on payment of 3d each. The forty-six paintings, some very large, portrayed mostly scenes from the Crimea and the Mutiny, and were disproportionately of 'distinguished young officers'[110]. They portrayed the Victorian ideal of military heroism, of which Loyd-Lindsay was a leading exemplar.

---

106 Wantage, *Lord Wantage*, p. 370; Brock, M.G and Curthoys, M.C, *The History of the University of Oxford* VII. *Nineteenth Century Oxford*, Part II (Oxford: Clarendon Press, 2000) p. 474.
107 *The Times* 14 July 1877, p. 12.
108 On Desanges and his VC paintings largely from Colin Robins, 'Louis William Desanges and the missing Victoria Cross paintings', *Journal of the Society for Army Historical Research* XC, Autumn 2012. In the 1950s nadir of anti-Victorian prejudice, despite pleas from John Betjeman and others, the UDC dispersed the collection; the building now contains offices and shops.
109 *Jackson's Oxford Journal* 17 November 1900.
110 Hichberger, J.W.M., *Images of the Army: the military in British art, 1815-1914* (Manchester: Manchester University Press, 1988), p66. See also Harrington, Peter, *British Artists and War: the face of battle in paintings and prints, 1700-1914* (London: Greenhill Books, 1993), pp. 153-4.

Final Years

From the autumn of 1897 Wantage's health began to show signs of failing and 'the shadows of eventide gradually gathered round him'. Despite his fluctuating illness he continued involved in his varied interests. During the Boer War he was again active in the Red Cross, and also in sending Berkshire auxiliary units. He presided at farewell events for Berkshire Yeomanry and Volunteers leaving for South Africa. In February 1901 he attended Queen Victoria's funeral at Windsor. He died, aged sixty-nine, at Lockinge on 10 June 1901, and his peerage became extinct. His funeral at Holy Trinity parish church, Ardington, was impressive.[111] Like the earlier funeral of a greater philanthropist, Lord Shaftesbury, it assembled representatives of the varied aspects of his life and the organisations he had served: family, tenantry, Volunteers, freemasons, and charitable and educational institutions. The mourners included Prince Christian, the warden of Merton College, Halford Mackinder representing the Reading College, and about a hundred Berkshire Volunteers. The Volunteers fired three volleys over the grave and sounded the last post. Simultaneously with the funeral a memorial service was held at the Chapel Royal, St James's in London, attended by, among others, Lord Chelmsford and Sir Evelyn Wood. Lady Wantage erected a stone memorial cross, a replica of the fifteenth-century San Zenobio cross in Florence, high on the Ridgeway near Lockinge. Florence Nightingale wrote of Wantage, *"All are better than if he had not lived, and this betterment is for always – it does not die with him. That is the true estimate of a great life."*[112]

---

111 *The Times* 14 June 1901, p. 10; Wantage, *Lord Wantage*, p. 423.
112 Wantage, *Lord Wantage*, p. 430.

Bibliography

Chapter 1

Archives
British Library
India Office Library, Mss European F108 White papers.
India Office L/MIL/17/5/1617, Record of Lord Kitchener's Administration of the Army in India 1902-1909. Simla, 1909.
India Office L/MIL/17/5/1616, Summary of the Measures during the Viceroyalty of the Earl of Elgin and Kincardine 1894-1898 by Major -General Sir E.H.H. Collen M.M.
Kandahar correspondence: Sirdar Ayub Khan's Invasion of Southern Afghanistan, Defeat of General Burrows' Brigade, and Military Operations in consequence. India Office Library, Miscellaneous Public Documents, 2 vols, 1880-81.
Correspondence with Members of the Viceroy's Staff attached to the Forces for the Relief of Kandahar. Commencing from 10 August, 1880. India Office Library, Miscellaneous Public Documents.

Liddell Hart Archives, King's College London
Hamilton papers.

The National Archives (Kew)
WO108/399 Confidential telegrams,

National Army Museum
Rawlinson Papers
Roberts Papers

Books & Articles
Amery, Leo, (ed.), *The Times History of the War in South Africa*. 7 vols. (London: Sampson, Lowe & Marston, 1900-09).
Anglesey, The Marquess of, *A History of the British Cavalry*, vol. 4: 1899-1913 (London: Leo Cooper, 1986).
Atwood, R.A.S., 'How the Royal Artillery Saved Sir Redvers Buller', *New Perspectives on the Anglo-Boer War, 1899-1902* (Bloemfontein: War Museum of the Boer Republics, 2013).

Barrow, General Sir George de S, *The Fire of Life* (London: Hutchinson, 1942).
Birdwood, Field-Marshal Lord, *Khaki and Gown* (London & Melbourne: Ward Lock, 1941).
Bremner Smith, R. J. *Sir George Stewart White*, Vol. 3 (London: Soldiers of the Queen Library, 1900).
Brett, M.V (ed.), *Journal and Letters of Reginald Viscount Esher*, 4 vols. (London: Ivor Nicholson & Watson, 1934-38).
Brice, Christopher, *The Thinking Man's Soldier: The Life and Career of General Sir Henry Brackenbury 1837-1914* (Solihull: Helion & Co., 2012).
Buck, J., *Simla Past and Present*, 2nd ed. (Bombay: Thacker, Spink & Co., 1925).
Churchill, Winston, *From London to Ladysmith via Pretoria* (London: Longmans, Green & Co., 1900).
Churchill, Winston, *Frontiers and Wars* (London: Penguin Books, 1972).
Coates, Thomas F.G., *Sir George White V.C. The Hero of Ladysmith.* (London: Grant Richards, 1900).
Crosthwaite, Sir Charles, *The Pacification of Burma* (London: Edward Arnold, 1912).
Curtin, Philip, *Disease and Empire: the Health of European Troops in the Conquest of Africa* (Cambridge: CUP, 1998).
David, Saul, *The Indian Mutiny, 1857* (London: Viking Penguin, 2002).
Durand, Mortimer, *The Life of Field-Marshal Sir George White.* 2 vols. (Edinburgh & London: Blackwood & Sons, 1915).
Farwell, Byron, *The Great Boer War* (London: Allen Lane, 1977).
Fuller, W.C., *Strategy and Power in Russia 1600-1914* (New York: Free Press, 1992).
Gardyne, Lt-Cols C.G. & A.G., *The Life of a Regiment: the History of the Gordon Highlanders from 1816-1898* (London: The Medici Society, 1929).
Gerard, Lt-Gen. Sir M.G., *Leaves from the Diary of a Soldier and Sportsman 1865-1885* (London: John Murray, 1903).
Grenville, J.A.S., *Lord Salisbury and Foreign Policy: The Close of the Nineteenth Century* (London: Athlone Press, 1970).
Haldane, General Sir Aylmer, *A Soldier's Saga* (Edinburgh & London: William Blackwood & Sons, 1948).
Hamilton, Lord George, *Parliamentary Reminiscences and Reflections*, 2 vols. (London: Murray, 1922).
Hamilton, Ian, *The Happy Warrior: A Life of General Sir Ian Hamilton by his Nephew* (London: Cassell, 1966).
Hanna, Henry, *The Second Afghan War 1878-1879-1880: Its Causes, Its Conduct and Its Consequences.* 3 vols. (London: Constable & Co., 1899-1910).
Harrison, Frederic, *Martial Law in Kabul.* Reprinted from the *Fortnightly Review* (London: Chapman & Hall, 1880).
Heathcote, T.A., *Balochistan. The British and the Great Game: The Struggle for the Bolan Pass, Gateway to India* (London: Hurst & Co., 2015).
Heathcote, T.A., *The Military in British India: The development of British Land Forces in South Asia, 1600-1947* (Manchester & New York: Manchester University Press, 1995).
Hensman,,Howard, *The Afghan War* (London: W.H. Allen & Co., 1881).
Hopkirk, Peter, *The Great Game* (Oxford: OUP, 1991).

Hunter, Archie, *Kitchener's Sword Arm: the Life and Career of General Sir Archibald Hunter* (Staplehurst: Spellmount, 1986).
Johnson, Rob, *The Afghan Way of War: Culture and Pragmatism: A Critical History* (London: Hurst & Co., 2011).
Jones, Martin, 'The War of Lost Footsteps: A Re-assessment of the Third Burmese War,' *Bulletin of the Military Historical Society*, vol. xxxx, no. 157 (August, 1989),
Kruger, Rayne, *Good-bye Dolly Gray* (London: Foursquare Books, 1959).
Lowry, Donal, 'The Play of Forces world-Wide in their Scope and Revolutionary in their Operation: the South African War as an International Event', *South African Historical Journal*, vol. 41, issue 1 (1999),
Lyons, F.S.L., *Ireland Since the Famine* (London: Fontana, 1973).
Macdonald, Donald, *How We Kept the Flag Flying: The Story of the Siege of Ladysmith* (London: Ward, Lock & Co., 1900).
Macgregor, Major-Gen. Sir C.M., *The Second Afghan War*, 6 vols. (Simla & Calcutta: The Government of India, 1885-86).
Maurice, Frederick, *History of the War in South Africa*, 3 vols. (London: Hurst & Blackett, 1906-08).
Maurice, Frederick, Revised by James Lunt, 'George Stuart White' *ODNB* (Oxford: OUP, 2004).
Menezes, Lt-Gen. S.L., *Fidelity and Honour: The Indian Army from the Seventeenth to the Twenty-First Century* (New Delhi: OUP, 1993).
Nasson, Bill, *The South African War, 1899-1902* (London: Hodder Education, 1999).
Nevill, Captain H. L., *Campaigns on the North-West Frontier* (Uckfield: The Naval & Military Press, 2005).
Nevinson, Henry, *The Diary of a Siege* (London: Methuen, 1900).
Nevinson, Henry, *The Fire of Life* (London: James Nisbet & Co., 1935).
Pakenham, Thomas, *The Boer War* (London: Weidenfeld & Nicolson, 1979).
Roberts, P.E., *History of British India* (Delhi: OUP, 1977).
Roberts, Field Marshal Lord, *Forty-One Years in India* (New York: Longmans, Green & Co.,, 1897).
Robson, Brian, *The Road to Kabul: The Second Afghan War 1878-1881* (Staplehurst: Spellmount, 1986).
Smith, Iain, *The Origins of the South African War 1899-1902* (London & New York: Longman, 1996).
Soboleff, Major-Gen L.N., *The Anglo-Afghan Struggle*, Transl. by Major Gowan (Calcutta: The Government of India, 1885).
Spiers, E.M., *The Late Victorian Army 1868-1902* (Manchester & New York: Manchester University Press, 1992).
Stewart, A.T.Q., *The Pagoda War: Lord Dufferin and the Fall of the Kingdom of Ava 1885-86* (London: Faber, 1972).
Sykes, Percy, *Sir Mortimer Durand* (London: Cassell & Co., 1926).
Symons, Julian, *Buller's Campaign* (London: Cresset Press, 1963).
Thomas, Hugh, *The Story of Sandhurst* (London: Hutchinson, 1961).
Vibart, Colonel Henry M., *The Life of Sir Harry N.D. Prendergast* (London: Eveleigh Nash, 1914).

Warwick, Peter, *The South African War: The Anglo-Boer War 1899-1902* (Harlow: Essex: Longmans, 1980).
Younghusband, Sir George, *A Soldier's Memories in Peace and War* (London: Herbert Jenkins, Ltd, 1917).

Chapter 2

Archives
British Library
Barrow Mss,
Browne Mss,
Campbell-Bannerman Mss,
Elgin Mss,
Hutton Mss,
India Office Records,
Lansdowne Mss,
White Mss

Cambridge University Library, Cambridge
Cambridge Mss

Cornwall Record Office, Truro
Pole-Carew Mss

Devon Record Office, Exeter
Buller Mss

Liddell Hart Centre for Military Archives, King's College
Hamilton Mss

National Army Museum
Kempster Mss,
Roberts Mss,
Spenser Wilkinson Mss

National Library of Scotland
Aylmer Haldane Mss

National Library of Wales, Aberystwyth
Hills-Johnes Mss

Royal Artillery Museum, Woolwich
Brackenbury Mss

Wiltshire and Swindon History Centre, Chippenham
Methuen Mss

Books, Articles & Theses

Barthorp, Michael, *The Frontier Ablaze: The North West Frontier Rising, 1897-98* (London: Windrow & Greene, 1996).

Bates, Darrell, *The Abyssinian Difficulty: The Emperor Theodorus and the Magdala Campaign, 1867-68* (Oxford: Oxford University Press, 1979).

Beattie, Hugh, *Imperial Frontier: Tribe and State in Waziristan* (Richmond: Curzon, 2002).

Beattie, Hugh, 'Negotiations with the Tribes of Waziristan, 1849-1947: The British Experience', *Journal of Imperial and Commonwealth History* 39 (2011), pp. 571-87.

Beckett, Ian F. W, 'The Stanhope Memorandum of 1888: A Re-interpretation', *Bulletin of the Institute of Historical Research* 57 (1984), pp. 240-47.

Beckett, Ian F. W., 'Command in the Late Victorian Army', in Gary Sheffield (ed.), *Leadership and Command: The Anglo-American Military Experience since 1861* (London: Brasseys, 1997), pp. 37-56.

Beckett, Ian F. W., 'Selection by Disparagement: Lord Esher, the General Staff and the Politics of Command, 1904-14', in David French and Brian Holden Reid (eds.), *The British General Staff: Reform and Innovation, 1890-1939* (London: Frank Cass, 2002), pp. 41-56.

Beckett, Ian F. W., 'Soldiers, the Frontier and the Politics of Command in British India', *Small Wars and Insurgencies* 16 (2005), pp. 280-92.

Birdwood, Field Marshal Lord, *Khaki and Gown: An Autobiography* (London: Ward, Lock & Co., 1941).

Callwell, Charles, 'Notes on the Strategy of Our Small Wars', *Minutes of the Proceedings of the Royal Artillery Institution* 12 (1884), pp. 531-52.

Callwell, Charles, *Small Wars: Their Principles and Practice* 3rd edn. (London: HMSO, 1906).

Callwell, Charles, *Tirah, 1897* (London: Constable & Co., 1911).

Chandler, David G., 'The Expedition to Abyssinia, 1867-68', in Brian Bond (ed), *Victorian Military Campaigns* (London: Hutchinson, 1967).

Churchill, Winston S., *The Story of the Malakand Field Force: An Episode of Frontier War* (London: Longmans & Co., 1898).

Churchill, Randolph S., *Winston S Churchill Vol. I Companion Part 2, 1896-1900* (London: Heinemann, 1967).

Creagh, Sir O'Moore, *The Autobiography of General Sir O'Moore Creagh* (London: Hutchinson, 1924).

Durand, Sir Mortimer, *The Life of Field Marshal Sir George White* 2 vols. (Edinburgh and London: William Blackwood & Sons, 1915).

Ewans, Martin, *Securing the Indian Frontier in Central Asia: Confrontation and Negotiation, 1865-95* (Abingdon: Routledge, 2010).

Fincastle, Viscount, and Eliott-Lockhart, P. C., *A Frontier Campaign: A Narrative of the Operations of the Malakand and Buner Field Forces, 1897-98* (London: Methuen & Co., 1898).

Forrest, George W., *Sepoy Generals: Wellington to Roberts* (Edinburgh and London: William Blackwood and Sons, 1901).

Haldane, Sir Aylmer, *A Soldier's Saga: The Autobiography* (Edinburgh & London: William Blackwood & Sons, 1948).

Hamilton, General Sir Ian, *Listening for the Drums* (London: Faber & Faber, 1944).

Heathcote, T. A., *The Military in British India: The Development of British Land Forces in South Asia, 1600-1947* (Manchester: Manchester University Press, 1995).

Hogben, W. Murray, 'British Civil-Military Relations on the North West Frontier of India', in Adrian Preston and Peter Dennis (eds.), *Swords and Covenants* (London: Croom Helm, 1976), pp. 123-46.

Hutchinson, Colonel H. D., *The Campaign in Tirah, 1897-98: An Account of the Expedition against the Orakzais and Afridis under General Sir William Lockhart based on Letters Contributed to The Times* (London: Macmillan & Co., 1898).

Intelligence Branch, *Frontier and Overseas Expeditions from India*, 6 vols. (Calcutta: Superintendent of Government Printing, 1907-13).

James, Lionel, *The Indian Frontier War: Being an Account of the Mohmund and Tirah Expeditions, 1897* (London: William Heinemann, 1898).

Johnson, Robert, 'The Penjdeh Crisis and Its Impact on the Great Game and the Defence of India, 1885-97', Unpublished PhD, University of Exeter, 1999.

Johnson, Robert 'Russians at the Gates of India? Planning the Defence of India, 1885-1900', *Journal of Military History* 67 (2003), pp. 697-744.

Johnson, Rob, *The Afghan Way of War: Culture and Pragmatism - A Critical History* (London: Hurst & Co., 2011).

Keay, John, *The Gilgit Mission: The Explorers of the Western Himalayas* (London: John Murray, 1977).

Lockhart, William, and Woodthorpe, Robert, *The Gilgit Mission, 1885-86* (London: Eyre & Spottiswode, 1889).

MacGregor, Lady, *The Life and Opinions of Major General Sir Charles Metcalfe MacGregor* 2 vols. (Edinburgh & London: William Blackwood & Sons, 1888).

MacMunn, Sir George, *The Romance of the Indian Frontiers* (London: Jonathan Cape, 1931).

MacMunn, Sir George, *Vignettes from Indian Wars* (London: Sampson Low, Marston & Co., 1932).

Miller, Stephen M., *Lord Methuen and the British Army: Failure and Redemption in South Africa* (London: Frank Cass, 1999).

Moreman, Tim, 'The British and Indian Armies and North-West Frontier Warfare, 1849-1914', *Journal of Imperial and Commonwealth History* 20 (1992), pp. 35-64.

Moreman, Tim, 'The Arms Trade and the North West Frontier Pathan Tribes, 1890-1914', *Journal of Imperial and Commonwealth History* 22 (1994), pp. 187-216.

Moreman, Tim, *The Army in India and the Development of Frontier Warfare, 1849-1947* (Basingstoke; Palgrave, 1996).

Nevill, H. L., *Campaigns on the North West Frontier* (London: John Murray, 1912).

Preston, Adrian, 'Sir Charles MacGregor and the Defence of India, 1857-77', *Historical Journal* 12 (1969), pp. 58-77.

Preston, Adrian, 'Frustrated Great Gamesmanship: Sir Garnet Wolseley's Plans for War against Russia, 1873-80', *International History Review* 2 (1980), pp. 239-65.

Robinson, Charles N., *Celebrities of the Army* (London: George Newness Ltd, 1900).

Robson, Brian, *The Road to Kabul: The Second Afghan War, 1878-81* (London: Arms and Armour Press, 1986).

Shadwell, Leonard, *Lockhart's Advance Through Tirah* (London: W. Thacker & Co., 1898).

Smith, Martin, *General Sir William Stephen Alexander Lockhart: Soldier of the Queen Empress* (Hunstanton: Privately published, 2011).

Smith-Dorrien, General Sir Horace, *Memories of Forty-Eight Years' Service* (London: John Murray, 1925).

Surridge, Keith, 'More than a Great Poster: Lord Kitchener and the Image of the Military Hero', *Historical Research* 74 (2001), pp. 298-31.
Surridge, Keith, 'The Ambiguous Amir: Britain, Afghanistan and the 1897 Northwest Frontier Uprising', *Journal of Imperial and Commonwealth Hi*story 36 (2008), pp. 417-34.
Temple, Arthur, *Our Living Generals* (London: Andrew Melrose, 1900).
Thomsett, Richard, *With the Peshawar Column, Tirah Expeditionary Force* (London: Digby, Long & Co., 1899).
Tripodi, Christian, *Edge of Empire: The British Political Officer and Tribal Administration on the North West Frontier, 1877-1947* (Farnham: Ashgate, 2011).
Trousdale, William (ed.), *War in Afghanistan, 1879-80: The Personal Diary of Major General Sir Charles Metcalfe MacGregor* (Detroit, Michigan: Wayne State University Press, 1985).
Vetch, R. H., 'Lockhart, Sir William Stephen Alexander', Rev. T. R. Moreman, *Oxford Dictionary of National Biography* (Oxford: Oxford University Press, 2004).
Yapp, Malcolm, 'British Perceptions of the Russian Threat to India', *Modern Asian Studies* 21 (1987), pp. 647-65.
Yate, A. C., *Lieutenant Colonel John Haughton: A Hero of Tirah – A Memoir* (London: John Murray, 1900).

Chapter 3

Archives
British Library
Napier of Magdala, corresp. and papers, MS Eur. F 114
Letters to Sir Stafford Northcote, Add. MS 50029
Letters to H. M. Durand and J. Rivett-Carnac, MS Eur. C 265
Letters to Lord Elgin, MS Eur. F 83
Correspondence with George Hutchinson, MS Eur. E 241
Letters to Sir Richard Temple, MS Eur. F 86

Bodleian Library
Letters to Benjamin Disraeli
Letters to Lord Kimberley

Cambridge University Library
Correspondence with Lord Mayo

Hove Central Library
Wolseley Papers, letters to Viscount Wolseley

National Army Museum
Roberts Papers, letters to Lord Roberts

The National Archives (Kew)
WO 107/8 Abyssinia Expedition
FO 401/60 Abyssinia: 1867

Books

Anon., *Lord Napier of Magdala (reprinted from the Times of India)* (Bombay: The Times of India, 1876).
Atwood, Rodney, *The Life of Field Marshal Lord Roberts* (London: Bloomsbury, 2015).
Bates, Darrell, *The Abyssinian Difficulty* (Oxford: Oxford University Press, 1979).
Bond, Brian (ed.), *Victorian Military Campaigns* (London: Hutchinson & Co., 1967).
Brice, Christopher 'The Expedition to Abyssinia, 1867-68', in Stephen. M. Miller (ed), Queen Victoria's Campaigns: British Military Campaigns, 1857-1902 (Cambridge: Cambridge University Press, 2021).
Brice, Christopher, *Brave As a Lion: The Life and Times of Field Marshal Hugh Gough, 1st Viscount Gough* (Solihull: Helion & Co. Ltd, 2017) .
Buckland, C. E., *Dictionary of Indian Biography* (London: Swan Sonnenschein & Co., 1906).
Chandler, David. G., The Expedition to Abyssinia, 1867-68, in Brian Bond (ed.), *Victorian Military Campaigns* (London: Hutchinson & Co., 1967).
Curtin, Phillip, *Disease and the Empire* (Cambridge: Cambridge University Press, 1998).
Haythornthwaite, Phillip, *The Colonial Wars Source Book* (London: Caxton Publishing Group, 2000).
Heathcote, T. A., *The military in British India: the development of British land forces in South Asia, 1600–1947* (Manchester: Manchester University Press, 1995).
Holland, Trevenen and Hozier, Henry, *Record of the Expedition to Abyssinia*, 2 vols. (London: HMSO, 1870).
Hozier, Henry, *The British Expedition to Abyssinia* (London: Macmillan & Co., 1869).
Myatt, Frederick, *The March to Magdala* (London: Leo Cooper, 1970).
Napier, H.D, *Field-Marshal Lord Napier of Magdala: A memoir by his son* (London: Arnold & Co., 1927).
Napier, H.D., *Letters of Field-Marshal Lord Napier of Magdala concerning Abyssinia, Egypt, India, South Africa, etc*, ed. H. D. Napier (London: Jarrold & Sons, 1936)
Napier, R. C., *Despatches of Major-General Sir R. Napier reporting the operations of the second division of the China force in the expedition of 1860* (Hertford: Privately Printed, 1873) .
Napier, R. C., *Personal narrative written shortly after the actions of Moodkee and Feroze-Shuhur* (Hertford: Privately Printed, 1873).
Napier, R. C., *Report on the engineering operations at the siege of Lucknow in March 1858: by the chief engineer (now Brigadier General Sir R. Napier)* (Calcutta: Surveyor General's Office, 1859).
Porter, W., *History of the corps of royal engineers*, vol. II (London: Longmans, Green, 1889).
Roberts, F.S., *Forty-one years in India*, 2 vols. (London: Bentley & Son, 1897).
Thackeray, E.T., *Biographical notes of officers of the royal (Bengal) engineers* (London: Smith Elder, 1900).
Vibart, H. M., *Addiscombe: Its heroes and men of note* (Westminster: Archibald Constable, 1894).

Journals

Knollys, W. W., 'Field Marshal Lord Napier of Magdala', *Fortnightly Review*, 53 (1890), 397–403.
Royal Engineers Journal, 20 (Chatham: Royal Engineers Institute, 1890).

Chapter 4

Archives

British Library
C. W., 'Our Army Chiefs: Major-General Sir John Ardagh, K.C.I.E., C.B.', in *Lloyd's Weekly Newspaper* (London), 26th April 1896, issue 2788. [Gale Group Cengage Learning: 19th Century British Newspapers Online, accessed 31 Jan 2015]

House of Commons Parliamentary Papers
Report of His Majesty's Commissioners Appointed to Inquire into the Military Preparations and other Matters Connected with the War in South Africa, 1904, [Cd. 1789], Vol. 1
Royal Commission on the South African War: Minutes of Evidence Taken before the Royal Commission on the South African War, 1904, [Cd. 1790], Vol. 1
Royal Commission on the South African War: Minutes of Evidence Taken before the Royal Commission on the South African War, 1904, [Cd. 1791], Vol. 2

The National Archives (Kew)
PRO 30/40: Major General Sir John Ardagh Papers
WO 106: Directorate of Military Operations and Military Intelligence, and predecessors: Correspondence and Papers
FO 32/537: Frontier Rectification Boundary Commission, Major Ardagh, Captain de Wolste (1881)

Books
Beaver, William, *Under Every Leaf: How Britain Played the Greater Game from Afghanistan to Africa* (London: Biteback Publishing, 2012).
Black, Jeremey, *A History of Diplomacy* (London: Reattion, 2010).
Brice, Christopher, *The Thinking Man's Soldier: The Life and Career of General Sir Henry Brackenbury 1837-1914* (Solihull: Helion & Co., 2012).
Fergusson, Thomas, G., *British Military Intelligence 1870-1914: The Development of a Modern Intelligence Organisation* (Frederick, Maryland: University Publications of America, 1984).
Ferris, John, Robert, 'Lord Salisbury, British Intelligence and British Policy toward Russia and Central Asia 1874-1878' in Ferris, J. R., *Intelligence and Strategy: Selected Essays* (London and New York: Routledge, 2005).
Hamer, W. S., *The British Army: Civil-Military Relations 1885 – 1905*, (Oxford: Clarendon Press, 1970).
Medlicott, W. N., *The Congress of Berlin and After: A Diplomatic History of the Near Eastern Settlement 1878-1880*, (London: Frank Cass & Co. Ltd., 1963).
Nicholl, Fergus, *Gladstone, Gordon and the Sudan Wars* (Barnsley: Pen & Sword Military, 2013).
Preston, Adrian, 'Wolseley, the Khartoum Relief Expedition and the Defence of India, 1885-1900, *Journal of Imperial and Commonwealth History*, Vol. 6 (1978), pp. 254-280.
Shibeika, Mekki, *British Policy in the Sudan 1882-1902* (London, New York, Toronto: Oxford University Press, 1952).
Spiers, Edward M., 'Ardagh, Sir John Charles (1840–1907)', *Oxford Dictionary of National Biography* (Oxford: Oxford University Press, 2004) <http://www.oxforddnb.com/view/article/30437> (accessed 31 Jan 2015).

Spiers, Edward M., *Late Victorian Army 1868-1902* (Manchester: Manchester University Press, 1992).
Spiers, Edward M., 'The Use of the Dum Dum Bullet in Colonial Warfare', *Journal of Imperial and Commonwealth History*, Vol. 4 (1875), pp. 3-14.
Surridge, Keith Terrance, *Managing the South African War, 1899-1902: Politicians v. Generals* (Woodbridge: Boydell Press & RHS, 1998).
Susan, Countess of Malmesbury (Lady Ardagh), *Life of Sir John Ardagh* (London: John Murray, 1909).
Tucker, Albert V., 'Army and Society in England 1870-1900: A Reassessment of the Cardwell Reforms, *Journal of British Studies*, Vol. 2 (1963), pp. 110-141.
Wade, Stephen, *Spies in the Empire: Victorian Military Intelligence* (London: Anthem Press 2007).
Wirthwein, Walter, G., Britain and the Balkan Crisis 1875-1878, (New York: Columbia University Press, 1935).

Chapter 5

Archives
The National Archives (Kew)
Colonial Office Papers 48/485;
War Office Papers 32/7678, 32/7680, 32/7681, 32/7683, 32/7684

National Army Museum
Cunynghame Papers 7805-42

Books & Periodicals
Adye, Colonel John, *Sitana: A Mountain Campaign on the Borders of Afghanistan* (London: Richard Bentley, 1867).
Baden, Candan, The *Ottoman Crimean War (1853–1856)* (Leiden and Boston: Brill, 2010).
Benyon, John, 'Frere, Sir (Henry) Bartle Edward, first baronet (1815–1884)', *Oxford Dictionary of National Biography (*Oxford: Oxford University Press, 2004, online edition, January 2008) <http://www.oxfroddnb.com/view/article/10171> (accessed 14 August 2014).
British Parliamentary Papers, 1875, LII (C. 1342–1). Cape, Correspondence, Griqualand West, 1874–5; 1876, LII (C. 1401). Cape, Correspondence, Griqualand West, 1875; 1878, LV (C. 1961), (C. 2000). South Africa, Correspondence, 1877–78; 1877, LX (C. 1748). Transvaal, Native Affairs, 1875–6; 1877, LX (C. 1776). Paper re. Annexation of Transvaal, 1876–77; 1878, LVI (C. 2079), (C. 2100), (C. 2144). South Africa, Further Correspondence, 1877–78.
Chichester, H.M. & Rev. James Lunt, 'Cunynghame, Sir Arthur Augustus Thurlow (1812–1884)', *Oxford Dictionary of National Biography* (Oxford: Oxford University Press, 2004, online edition, January 2008) <http://www.oxfroddnb.com/view/article/6940> (accessed 19 March 2012).
Cunynghame, Captain Arthur, *An Aide-de-Camp's Recollections of Service in China, a Residence in Hong- Kong, and Visits to Other Islands in the Chinese Seas* (London: Saunders & Otley, 1844).

Cunynghame, Lieut.-Col. Arthur, *A Glimpse of the Great Western Republic* (London: R. Bentley 1851).

Cunynghame, A.A.T., *Travels in the Eastern Caucasus, on the Caspian and Black Seas, especially in Daghestan, and on the Frontiers of Persia and Turkey, during the Summer of 1871* (London: John Murray, 1872).

Cunynghame, General Sir Arthur Thurlow, *My Command in South Africa 1874-1878: Comprising Experiences of Travel in the Colonies of South Africa and the Independent States* (London, Macmillan, 2nd ed., 1880).

Gon, Philip, *The Road to Isandlwana. The Years of an Imperial Battalion* (Johannesburg & London: Ad. Donker, 1979).

Great Britain, War Office, *Field Exercise and Evolution of Infantry* (London: Her Majesty's Stationary Office, pocket edition, 1877).

H.S. 'The Kaffir War. By an English Officer in South Africa', *Fraser's Magazine*, February 1878, pp. 250–58.

Illustrated London News, 22 March 1884, Sir Arthur Cunynghame obituary.

Kinglake, A.W., The *Invasion of the Crimea: Its Origin, and an Account of its Progress down to the Death of Lord Raglan* (Edinburgh & London: William Blackwood & Sons, 1888), vol. VI.

Knight, Ian and Adrian Greaves, *The Who's Who of the Anglo-Zulu War, Part I: The British* (Barnsley, England, Pen & Sword Military, 2006).

Laband, John, *The Transvaal Rebellion: The First Boer War 1880–1881* (Harlow, United Kingdom: Pearson Longman, 2005).

Laband, John, *Historical Dictionary of the Zulu Wars* (Lanham, Maryland, Toronto, Oxford: The Scarecrow Press, 2009).

Laband, John, *Zulu Warriors: The Battle for the South African Frontier* (New Haven and London: Yale University Press, 2014).

Laband, John (ed), *Lord Chelmsford's Zululand Campaign 1878–1879* (United Kingdom: Alan Sutton Publishing for the Army Records Society, 1994).

Laband, John, '"The Direction of the Whole of the Forces Available": The Disputed Spheres of Military and Civil Authority in the Eastern Cape (1877 –1878), Natal (1879) and Zululand (1888)', *Scientia Militaria, South African Journal of Military Studies*, 41 (2) (2013), pp. 60–77.

Lewsen, Phyllis, *The First Crisis in Responsible Government in the Cape Colony* (Pretoria: Archives Year Book, V, ii, 1943).

Lewsen, Phyllis (ed), *Selections from the Correspondence of J. X. Merriman 1870–1890* (Cape Town: Van Riebeeck Society, 1960).

Lewsen, Phyllis. *John X. Merriman: Paradoxical South African Statesman*, (New Haven and London: Yale University Press, 1982).

Mason, Philip, *A Matter of Honour* (New York, Chicago and San Francisco: Holt, Rinehart and Winston, 1974).

Mercer, Patrick & Graham Turner, *Inkerman 1854: The Soldiers' Battle* (London: Osprey Military, 1998).

Milton, John, *The Edges of War: A History of the Frontier Wars, 1702–1878* (Cape Town: Juta, 1983).

Ouchterlony, Lieutenant John, *The Chinese War: An Account of All the Operations of the British Forces from the Commencement to the Treaty of Nanking* (reprint: New York, Washington and London: Praeger, 1970).

Pine, L.G. (ed.), *Burke's Peerage, Baronetage & Knightage* (London: Burke's Peerage, 102nd edition, 1959).
St Aubyn, Giles, *The Royal George 1819–1904. The Life of H.R.H. Prince George Duke of Cambridge* (New York: Alfred A. Knopf, 1964).
Slade, Rear-Admiral Sir Adolphus, *Turkey and the Crimean War: A Narrative of Historical Events* (London: Smith, Elder, 1867).
Smith, Keith, *The Wedding Feast War: The Final Tragedy of the Xhosa People* (London: Frontline Books, 2012).
Smithers, A.J. *The Kaffir Wars 1779–1877* (London, Leo Cooper, 1973).
Spiers, Edward M., *The Army and Society 1815-1914* (London and New York: Longman, 1980).
Spiers, Edward M., *The Late Victorian Army 1868-1902* (Manchester: Manchester University Press, 1992).
Spiers, Edward M., 'The British Army in South Africa: Military Government and Occupation, 1877–1914', in Peter B. Boyden, Alan J. Guy and Marion Harding (eds) *'Ashes and Blood': The British Army in South Africa 1795–1914* (London: National Army Museum, 1999).
Spiers, Edward M., 'George, Prince, second duke of Cambridge (1819–1904)', *Oxford Dictionary of National Biography* (Oxford: Oxford University Press, 2004) <http://oxforddnb.com/view/article/33372> (accessed 6 October 2004).
Stapleton, Timothy J., *A Military History of South Africa from the Dutch-Khoi Wars to the End of Apartheid* (Santa Barbara, California: Praeger, 2010).
The Times, 10 July 1894, Frances Lady Cunynghame obituary.
Likenesses wood engraving, *Illustrated London News*, 23 March 1878
Streatfeild, Frank N., *Kaffirland: A Ten Month's Campaign* (London: Sampson, Marston, Searle and Rivington, 1879).

Chapter 6

Archives
Bodleian Library
Spenser Wilkinson Mss
Cambridge University Library
Hardinge Mss
Churchill College Archive Centre, Cambridge
Churchill Mss
National Army Museum
Roberts Mss,
Spenser Wilkinson Mss
National Records of Scotland, Edinburgh
Ewart Mss

Books & Articles
Amery, Leo S., *The Times History of the War in South Africa, 1899-1902* (London: Sampson Low, Marston & Co., 1900).
Atwood, Rodney, *The Life of Field Marshal Lord Roberts* (London: Bloomsbury, 2015).

Beckett, Ian, '"Selection by Disparagement": Lord Esher, the General Staff and the Politics of Command, 1904-1914', in French, David & Holden-Reid, Brain (eds) *The British General Staff: Reform and Innovation c. 1890-1939* (London: Frank Cass, 2002).
Beckett, Ian F.W., *The Victorians at War* (London: Hambledon & London, 2003).
Beckett, Ian F.W., 'Soldiers, the Frontier and the Politics of Command in British India', *Small Wars and Insurgencies*, 16:3 (December 2005), pp. 280-292.
Biddulph, Michael, *The March from the Idus to the Helmund and Back, 1878, 1879* (London: R.U.S.I., 1880).
Bond, Brian, *The Victorian Army and the Staff College, 1854-1914* (London: Eyre Methuen, 1972).
Brett, Maurice V. (ed) *Journals and Letters of Reginald Viscount Esher, Vol. II., 1903-1910* (London: Ivor Nicholson & Watson, 1934).
Callwell, Charles, *Small Wars: Their Principles and Practice*, 3rd ed. (London: HMSO, 1906).
Callwell, Charles, *Tirah, 1897* (London: Constable & Co., 1911).
Charteris, John, *Field-Marshal Earl Haig* (New York: C. Scribner's Sons, 1929).
Churchill, Winston S., *The Story of the Malakand Field Force: An Episode of Frontier War* (London: Longmans & Co., 1898).
d'Ombrain, Nicholas, *War Machinery and High Policy: Defence Administration in Peacetime Britain, 1902-1914* (London: Oxford University Press, 1973).
Ehrman, John, *Cabinet Government and War, 1890-1940* (Cambridge: Cambridge University Press, 1958).
Gooch, John, *The Plans of War: The General Staff and British Military Strategy c. 1900-1916* (London: Routledge & Kegan Paul, 1974).
Gooch, John, *The Prospect of War: Studies in British Defence Policy, 1847-1942* (London: Frank Cass, 1981).
Gooch, John, '"A Particularly Anglo-Saxon Institution": The British General Staff in the Era of Two World Wars', in French, David & Holden-Reid, Brain (eds) *The British General Staff: Reform and Innovation c. 1890-1939* (London: Frank Cass, 2002).
Haldane, Richard B., *Before the War* (London: Cassell & Co., 1920).
Haldane, Richard B., *Richard Burdon Haldane: An Autobiography* (Garden City, N.Y.: Doubleday, Doran, 1929).
Hamer, W. S., The British Army: Civil-Military Relations, 1885-1905 (Oxford: Oxford University Press, 1970).
Hanna, Henry B., *The Second Afghan War, 1878-79-80: its causes, its conduct and its consequences*, three vols. (Westminster: Constable & Co., 1899-1910).
Heathcote, T.A., *The Military in British India: The Development of British Land Forces in South Asia, 1600-1947* (Manchester: Manchester University Press, 1995).
Heathcote, T.A., *The British Field Marshals, 1763-1997: A Biographical Dictionary* (South Yorkshire: Leo Cooper, 1999).
Hensman, Howard, *The Afghan War of 1879-80* (London: W. H. Allen & Co., 1882).
Holmes, Richard, *The Little Field-Marshal: Sir John French* (London: Jonathan Cape, 1981)
Hutchinson, Colonel H. D., *The Campaign in Tirah, 1897-98* (London: Macmillan, 1898).
Jeffrey, Keith, *Field Marshal Sir Henry Wilson: A Political Soldier* (New York: Oxford University Press, 2008).
Johnson, Robert, 'Russians at the Gates of India'? Planning the Defense of India, 1885-1900', *The Journal of Military History*, 67:3 (July 2003), pp. 697-744.

Johnson, Robert, *The Afghan Way of War: How and Why They Fight* (Oxford: Oxford University Press, 2012).
Lambert, Nicholas A., *Sir John Fisher's Naval Revolution* (Columbia, SA: University of South Carolina Press, 1999).
Lee, John, *A Soldier's Life: General Sir Ian Hamilton, 1853-1947* (London: Macmillan, 2000).
Macleod, Jenny, *Reconsidering Gallipoli* (Manchester: Manchester University Press, 2004).
MacGregor, Charles Metcalfe, *The Second Afghan War: Office Account* (London: J. Murray, 1908).
Mackay, Ruddock F., *Fisher of Kilverstone* (Oxford: Oxford University Press, 1973).
Marder, Arthur J. (ed.) *Fear God and Dread Nought, The Correspondence of Admiral of the Fleet Lord Fisher of Kilverstone*, three vol. s (Cambridge, MA: Harvard University Press, 1952-59).
Maurice, John Frederick, *Military History of the Campaign of 1882 in Egypt* (London: HMSO., 1887).
Metcalfe, Charles, *The Defence of India: A Strategical Study* (Simla: 1884).
Moreman, T.R., 'The arms trade and the North-West frontier Pathan tribes, 1890-1914', *The Journal of Imperial and Commonwealth History*, 22:2 (1994), pp. 187-216.
Moreman, T.R., 'Nicholson, William Gustavus, Baron Nicholson (1845-1918)', *Oxford Dictionary of National Biography*, Oxford University Press (2004).
Morley, John, *Recollections*, 2 vols. (New York: The Macmillan Co., 1917)
Preston, Adrian, 'Sir Charles MacGrefor and the Defence of India, 1857-1887', *The Historical Journal*, 12:1 (1969), pp. 58-77.
Pakenham, Thomas, *The Boer War* (London: Abacus, 2009).
Roberts, F.S., *Forty-One Years in India: From Subaltern to Commander-in-Chief* (London: Macmillan, 1898).
Robson, Brian, *The Road to Kabul: the Second Afghan War 1878-1881* (London: Arms & Armour, 1986).
Scott-Moncrieff, G.K., 'Memoir: Field Marshal Lord Nicholson, G.C.B., Colonel Commandant, R.E.', *The Royal Engineers Journal*, 28:6 (December 1918), pp. 237-249.
Smith-Dorien, H. L., *Memories of Forty-Eight Years' Service* (New York, N.Y.: Dutton, 1925).
Spiers, Edward M., *The Army and Society, 1815-1914* (London: Longmans, 1980).
Spiers, Edward M., *Haldane: An Army Reformer* (Edinburgh: Edinburgh University Press, 1980).
Spiers, Edward M., *The Late Victorian Army, 1868-1902* (Manchester: Manchester University Press, 1992).
Strachan, Hew, 'The Continental Commitment', in French, David & Holden-Reid, Brain (eds.) *The British General Staff: Reform and Innovation c. 1890-1939* (London: Frank Cass, 2002).
Wessels, Andre, *Lord Roberts and the War in South Africa, 1899-1902* (London: Sutton Publishing for the Army Records Society, 2000).
Wilkinson, H. Spenser, *Thirty-Five Years, 1874-1909* (London: Constable, 1933).
Williamson, Samuel R., *The Politics of Grand Strategy: Britain and France Prepare for War, 1904-1914* (Cambridge: Harvard University Press, 1969).
Wyatt, Christopher M., *Afghanistan and the Defence of Empire: Diplomacy and Strategy during the Great Game* (London: I.B. Tauris, 2011).

Chapter 7

Archives
British Red Cross Archives, Moorfields, London
Honourable Artillery Company Archives, Armoury House, London

Books
Anderson, Dorothy, *The Balkan Volunteers* (London: Hutchinson, 1968).
Bateman, John, *The Great Landowners of Great Britain and Ireland* (Leicester: Leicester University Press, 1971).
Ian F.W. Beckett, *Riflemen Form: A Study of the Rifle Volunteer Movement 1859-1908* (Aldershot: Ogilvy Trusts, 1982).
Bostridge, Mark, *Florence Nightingale: The Woman and Her Legend* (London: Penguin, 2009).
Bruce, Anthony, *The Purchase System in the British Army, 1660-1871* (London: Royal Historical Society, 1980).
Cook, Edward, *The Life of Florence Nightingale Vol. II* (London: Macmillan, 1913).
Curtin, Philip D., *Disease and Empire: The Health of European Troops in the Conquest of Africa* (Cambridge: Cambridge University Press, 1998)
G.E.C. et al, *The Complete Peerage XII* (London: St Catherine Press, 1959).
Hansard's Parliamentary Debates, Third Series CCIV, CCVIII (1871).
Havinden, M.A., *Estate Villages: A Study of the Berkshire Villages of Ardington and Lockinge* (London: Lund Humpphries, 1966).
Havinden, M.A., 'The Model Village' in G.E.Mingay (ed.) *The Victorian Countryside Vol. II* (London: Routledge & Kegan Paul, 1981).
Humphry A.P. & Fremantle, T.F., *History of the National Rifle Association during its first Fifty Years 1859-1909* (Cambridge: Bowes & Bowes, 1914).
Loyd-Lindsay, Harriet, *Lord Wantage, V.C., K.C.B.: A Memoir* (London: Smith Elder & Co., 1907).
Millin, G.F., *Life in Our Villages* (London: Cassell, 1891).
Oxford Dictionary of National Biography (Oxford: Oxford University Press, 2004).
Pelling, Henry, *Social Geography of British Elections 1885-1910* (London: Macmillan, 1967).
Prochaska, Frank, *The Voluntary Impulse: Philanthropy in Modern Britain* (London: Faber & Faber, 1998).
Rubinstein, W.D., *Men of Property: The Very Wealthy in Britain Since the Industrial Revolution* (London: Social Affairs Unit, 2006).
Skelley, Alan R., *The Victorian Army at Home: The Recruitment and Terms and Conditions of the British Regular, 1859-1899* (London: Croom Helm,1977)
Spiers, Edward M., *The Late Victorian Army 1868-1902* (Manchester: Manchester University Press, 1992)
Walker G.G., et al, *The Honourable Artillery Company 1537- 1987* (London: Honourable Artillery Company, 1986).

Periodicals
Flatow, A.F., Volunteers in Brussels, 1866', *Journal of the Society for Army Historical Research*, 44, 1966.

Loyd-Lindsay, Robert, 'The Coming of Age of the Volunteers', *Nineteenth Century*, X, August 1881.
Loyd-Lindsay, Robert, 'A Visit to the Boers', *Nineteenth Century*, XIV, December 1883.
Mitchie, Ranald C., 'Income, Expenditure and investment of a Victorian Millionaire; Lord Overstone , 1823-83', *Bulletin of the Institute of Historical Research*, LVIII, 1985.
Robins, Colin, 'Louis William Desanges and the Missing Victoria Cross Paintings', *Journal of the Society for Army Historical Research*, XC, Autumn 2012.
Stearn, Roger T., 'Oxford Military College', *Soldiers of the Queen*, 83, December 1995.
Stearn, Roger T., 'A Great Philanthropist: Sir James Gldea and the Soldiers' and Sailors' Families Association', *Soldiers of the Queen*, 142, September 2010.

Index

A
Afghanistan, 10-11, 13, 19, 23-24, 31-32, 45-46, 48, 52, 64, 107, 118, 166, 209-212, 215-217
Anglo-Egyptian War (1882), 67, 109, 128-130, 152, 213-215, 245-246.
Ardagh, Major-General Sir John, 111-153, 246

B
Birdwood, Captain (later Field Marshal Sir) William, 60. 62, 67-68
Blood, General Sir Bindon, 29, 54, 56, 58, 63, 69
Brackenbury, General Sir Henry, 26-28, 41, 48-49, 52-54, 111, 134-137, 139, 152, 157, 243-244, 246, 255
Buller, General Sir Redvers, 26, 28, 31-32, 35-42, 111, 131, 147, 187, 220, 225, 246-247, 261
Burma, 11, 21-23, 26-27, 29, 31-32, 40, 47, 57-58, 213-214

C
Callwell, Major-General Sir, 59, 65, 167, 223, 224, 226-227, 229
Cardwell, Lord Edward, 121, 152, 157, 165, 167, 242-245, 248, 251, 255
Carnarvon, Earl of, 174-177, 187, 189-191, 194, 245
China, 60, 93-95, 98, 138, 142, 154, 157-159, 168
Commander-in-Chief India, 11, 18, 26-28, 31, 35, 40, 42, 44, 52, 57, 67, 69, 82, 84, 92, 94, 101, 106-108, 216-217, 227
Crimean War (1853-56), 63, 67, 116, 118, 135, 146, 158, 161, 163-164, 187, 237-239, 242, 246, 248, 254
Cunynghame, General Sir Robert, 154-198
Curzon, Lord George, 30, 41, 66, 69-70

D
Dargai (1897), 30, 59-61, 63, 65-68, 223
Defence Committee, 140, 216-218
Duke of Cambridge, 21, 23, 26-27, 47-49, 51-52, 56, 71, 99, 100, 103, 107-110, 114, 137, 140-141, 161-165, 170, 195, 197, 219-220, 243, 247, 252-253

E
East India Company, 10, 13, 73-74, 76, 93, 110, 163, 165, 173, 238
Egyptian Army, 57, 128, 141, 213

F
Formations/Units
Divisions
1st, 57-59, 61-62, 95, 161-162, 164
1st (Multan), 206-7
2nd (Quetta), 206
2nd, 57-59, 62, 94-95, 97-98
4th, 162
Gwalior, 92

Regiments of Foot
3rd (East Kent/Buffs), 94, 157
4th (King's Own), 104, 105
13th (First Somersetshire), 160, 175, 225
20th (East Devonshire), 161-162
24th (South Warwickshire), 175-177, 179-180, 183, 187, 191, 193-194
27th (Inniskilling), 12, 161
33rd (Duke of Wellington's), 104, 106, 126
36th (Herefordshire), 128, 167, 197
51st (2nd Yorkshire West Riding), 161
60th (King's Royal Rifle Corps), 129, 157
80th (Staffordshire Volunteers), 179-180
88th (Connaught Rangers), 179, 187, 191
90th (Perthshire Light Infantry), 189, 194

92nd (Gordon Highlanders), 10-11, 13, 15-19, 30, 60-62, 67
Frere, Sir Bartle, 94, 100, 179-180, 182-184, 186-187, 189-195

G
Gordon, General Sir Charles, 130, 133-134, 152, 203, 261

H
Haldane, Captain (later General Sir) Aylmer, 44, 53, 59, 69-69
Haldane, Richard Burdon, 199-200, 203, 231, 233-234
Hamilton, Lord George, 29, 57, 68-69
Hamilton, Colonel (later General Sir) Ian, 11, 26, 32, 34, 39, 56-59, 63, 69, 201-202, 218-219, 235, 261

I
India
  Commander-in-Chief, 11, 26-27, 31, 40, 42, 44, 52, 69, 81-82, 84, 92, 98, 106-108, 211, 216-218, 227
Indian Army, 15, 17, 26-27, 41, 43, 49, 52, 54, 63, 65-66, 69-71, 99, 107-108, 166, 215, 227, 232, 234, 243
India Office, 26, 29, 47, 57, 107, 119

K
KCB (Knight Commander of the Bath) 47, 160, 167, 227, 249
Kitchener, Lord Horatio Herbert, 27, 37, 41-42, 68, 70, 141-142, 201-202, 234, 261

L
Ladysmith, 10-11, 16, 32, 34-41, 146-147
Lansdowne, Lord, 26, 28, 36-37, 41, 65, 68-69, 137-141, 145, 147-148, 248
Lockhart, General Sir William, 23, 28-30, 32, 42-70, 200, 220-221, 223-225, 227, 235

M
Malakand Expedition (1897, 28-29, 54, 56-58, 63, 66
Merriman, John X., 182-183, 189-190, 192-193

N
Napier, Field Marshal Lord, 44, 71-110, 245
Natal, 32, 34-36, 40-41, 146-147, 149, 168-169, 172-174, 176-177, 179-180, 189, 195
Nicholson, Field Marshal Sir William, 34-35, 40, 44, 53-54, 56-57, 59-60, 62, 64, 66-70, 146, 199-236

Ninth Cape Frontier War (1877), 154, 185, 197
North-West Frontier, 28, 30, 32, 42, 47, 64, 76, 166, 197, 205, 215-219, 221, 227, 234

O
Oxford Military College, 261

P
Penn Symons, Major-General Sir William, 23, 32, 34, 36-37, 40, 56-58, 61, 67
Punjab Command, 23, 32, 56, 61, 149

R
Roberts, Field Marshal Lord Frederick, 11, 26, 26, 41-42, 47, 109-111, 150, 152, 202, 215, 219-220

S
Second Afghan War (1878-80), 45, 205-206, 212, 215, 251
South African War (1899-1902), 31, 67, 140, 146, 153, 200, 207
Staff work, 66, 91, 198, 200, 212, 236
Sudan, 21, 42, 68, 70, 111, 128, 131-135, 141-142, 152, 246

T
Times of India, 26, 29-30, 108
Tirah Campaign (1897-98), 32, 42-43, 52-58, 63, 67, 70, 221-227, 232

V
Volunteer Force, 186, 241, 248, 250, 252

W
Wantage, Lord, 237-264
White, Field Marshal Sir George, 10-41, 44, 47, 49, 53-54, 56-63, 67, 70, 146-147
Wolseley, Field Marshal Sir Garnet, 6, 21, 31-32, 35, 42, 48, 56, 62, 68, 71, 108-109, 129-130, 133-134, 136-142, 149, 152, 155, 168, 176, 203, 213, 215, 220, 225, 243-248, 251, 256
Wood, Field Marshal Sir Henry Evelyn, 31, 60, 68, 121, 138-139, 243, 245, 247, 251, 264

Z
Zulu, 32, 36, 40, 68, 172, 180-181, 196, 245

The period 1815-1914 is sometimes called the long century of peace. It was in reality very far from that. It was a century of civil wars, popular uprisings, and struggles for Independence. An era of colonial expansion, wars of Empire, and colonial campaigning, much of which was unconventional in nature. It was also an age of major conventional wars, in Europe that would see the Crimea campaign and the wars of German unification. Such conflicts, along with the American Civil War, foreshadowed the total war of the 20th century.

It was also a period of great technological advancement, which in time impacted the military and warfare in general. Steam power, electricity, the telegraph, the radio, the railway, all became tools of war. The century was one of dramatic change. Tactics altered, sometimes slowly, to meet the challenges of the new technology. The dramatic change in the technology of war in this period is reflected in the new title of this series: From Musket to Maxim.

The new title better reflects the fact that the series covers all nations and all conflict of the period between 1815-1914. Already the series has commissioned books that deal with matters outside the British experience. This is something that the series will endeavour to do more of in the future. At the same time there still remains an important place for the study of the British military during this period. It is one of fascination, with campaigns that capture the imagination, in which Britain although the world's predominant power, continues to field a relatively small army.

The aim of the series is to throw the spotlight on the conflicts of that century, which can often get overlooked, sandwiched as they are between two major conflicts, the French/Revolutionary/Napoleonic Wars and the First World War. The series will produced a variety of books and styles. Some will look simply at campaigns or battles. Others will concentrate on particular aspects of a war or campaign. There will also be books that look at wider concepts of warfare during this era. It is the intention that this series will present a platform for historians to present their work on an important but often overlooked century of warfare.

Submissions

The publishers would be pleased to receive submissions for this series. Please contact series editor Dr Christopher Brice via email (christopherbrice@helion.co.uk), or in writing to Helion & Company Limited, Unit 8, Amherst Business Centre, Budbrooke Road, Warwick, Warwickshire, CV34 5WE.

Books in this series:
1. *The Battle of Majuba Hill: The Transvaal Campaign 1880-1881* John Laband (ISBN 978-1-911512-38-7)*
2. *For Queen and Company: Vignettes of the Irish Soldier in the Indian Mutiny* David Truesdale (ISBN 978-1-911512-79-0)*
3. *The Furthest Garrison: Imperial Regiments in New Zealand 1840-1870* Adam Davis (ISBN 978-1-911628-29-3)*
4. *Victory over Disease: Resolving The Medical Crisis In The Crimean War, 1854-1856* Michael Hinton (ISBN 978-1-911628-31-6)*
5. *Journey Through the Wilderness: Garnet Wolseley's Canadian Red River Expedition of 1870* Paul McNicholls (ISBN 978-1-911628-30-9)*
6. *Kitchener: The Man Not the Myth* Anne Samson (ISBN 978-1-912866-45-8)
7. *The British and the Sikhs: Discovery, Warfare and Friendship (c.1700–1900)* Gurinder Singh Mann (ISBN 978-1-911628-24-8)*
8. *Bazaine 1870: Scapegoat for a Nation* Quintin Barry (ISBN 978-1-913336-08-0)
9. *Redcoats in the Classroom: The British Army's School for Soldiers and Their Children During the 19th Century* Howard R. Clarke (ISBN 978-1-912866-47-2)
10. *The Rescue They Called A Raid: The Jameson Raid 1895-96* David Snape (ISBN 978-1-913118-77-8)*
11. *Hungary 1848: The Winter Campaign* Johann Nobili (ISBN 978-1-913118-78-5)
12 *The War of the Two Brothers: The Portuguese Civil War 1828-1834* Sérgio Veludo Coelho (ISBN 978-1-914059-26-1)
14 *Forgotten Victorian Generals* Christopher Brice (ISBN 978-1-910777 20-6)

* Denotes books are paperback 248mm × 180mm.